W9-AEW-149

EDUCATION LIBRARY
UNIVERSITY OF KENTUCKY

A CALL FOR CHARACTER EDUCATION AND PRAYER IN THE SCHOOLS

A CALL FOR CHARACTER EDUCATION AND PRAYER IN THE SCHOOLS

WILLIAM H. JEYNES

Foreword by William J. Murray

PRAEGER

An Imprint of ABC-CLIO, LLC

A B C CLIO

Santa Barbara, California • Denver, Colorado • Oxford, England

Educ.

LC
311
.J48
2010

Copyright 2010 by William H. Jeynes

All rights reserved. No part of this publication may be reproduced, stored in a retrieval system, or transmitted, in any form or by any means, electronic, mechanical, photocopying, recording, or otherwise, except for the inclusion of brief quotations in a review, without prior permission in writing from the publisher.

Library of Congress Cataloging-in-Publication Data

Jeynes, William.
    A call for character education and prayer in the schools / William H. Jeynes ; foreword by William J. Murray.
      p. cm.
    Includes bibliographical references and index.
    ISBN 978–0–313–35103–7 (hard copy : alk. paper) — ISBN 978–0–313–35104–4 (ebook)
1. Moral education—United States. 2. Prayer in the public schools—United States. I. Title.
LC311.J48   2010
370.11′4—dc22   2009038231

14 13 12 11 10   1 2 3 4 5

This book is also available on the World Wide Web as an eBook.
Visit www.abc-clio.com for details.

ABC-CLIO, LLC
130 Cremona Drive, P.O. Box 1911
Santa Barbara, California 93116-1911

This book is printed on acid-free paper ∞

Manufactured in the United States of America

Copyright Acknowledgment

The author and publisher gratefully acknowledge permission for use of the following material:
Jeynes, William (2007). "Do Americans Need Prayer and Moral Education Returned to the Public Schools?" In W. Jeynes & E. Martinez (Eds.), *Christianity, Education & Modern Society* (pp. 3–36). Charlotte, NC: Information Age Publishing.

CONTENTS

FOREWORD

In this time of moral decadence and social decline, unprecedented in our American history, William Jeynes has thrown out a challenge to our nation. His very well documented book, *A Call for Character Education and Prayer in the Schools*, urges parents and educators to turn the public schools away from the godless and amoral path they have been following for the past 30 plus years, a path that has so clearly failed and wrecked the lives of countless young people. His alternative is a commonsense and proven way to help youngsters develop sound moral values, the inclusion of character education and prayer.

Jeynes first presents the whole sad epic of how a few atheist extremists, including my own mother, Madalyn Murray O'Hair, were aided by an unwise and complicit Supreme Court in removing prayer, Bible reading, and, by default, character education from the public schools. When reverence for God and the teaching of God's moral laws were banned in the schools, our society slowly became unmoored from its Christian heritage and adrift in a hedonistic world where the main values of life are personal pleasure, status, and material possessions.

Perhaps the prescriptions in this book, if implemented in the schools, cannot undo all the damage, but new generations of young people could be taught that there is a better and a higher way.

William J. Murray

Chairman

Religious Freedom Coalition

Washington, D.C.

ACKNOWLEDGMENTS

I am very thankful to many individuals who played a large role in making this work possible. I want to thank numerous people in the academic world at Harvard University and the University of Chicago for helping me give birth to this project and in guiding me through the early stages of planning this book. I especially want to thank the late Bob Jewell for his encouragement. I want to thank several academics for their input into this project. These individuals include Wendy Naylor, Chris Ullman, and Byron Johnson. I also want to thank several dear friends whose encouragement with respect to this project touched me deeply. Among these friends are Wayne Ruhland, Jean Donohue, Rick Smith, Larry and Vada DeWerd, Joyce Decker, Jessica Choi, and Sylvia Lee.

I count myself fortunate to have been married for 24 years to my wife, Hyelee, whose support has been exemplary. We have three wonderful boys, whom I thank for their love and inspiration. May this book open many eyes and hearts.

1

DO AMERICANS NEED MORAL EDUCATION AND RELIGIOUS FREEDOM RETURNED TO THE PUBLIC SCHOOLS?

Schools have undergone a substantial transformation in the last 40 or 45 years. There are challenges and problems that schools face today that would have been unfathomable four or five decades ago. In the 1940s and 1950s, public school teachers ranked the top seven major student discipline problems as talking, chewing gum, making noise, running in the halls, getting out of turn in line, dress code infractions, and not putting paper in the waste basket. Using the same survey, contemporary teachers rank drug abuse, alcohol abuse, pregnancy, suicide, rape, robbery, and assault as the top seven prominent problems. Moreover, contemporary American youth are 32 times more likely to be arrested of a crime than in 1950. American schools in the past several decades have encountered baleful quandaries such as barrage of school shootings, violence against teachers and students, a plethora of illegal drug and alcohol abuse, and teenage pregnancies. A seemingly interminable number of statistics testify to the fact that the American school children are in trouble. Even at the academic level, illiteracy is higher than 40 or 45 years ago (Bennett, 1983; Coleman, 2004; Jeynes, 2002c, 2007; Toch, Gest, & Guttman, 1993; U.S. Census Bureau, 2001).

Clearly, something has changed among America's youth and in its schools that is unquestionably very disturbing. There are clearly several reasons why these trends have materialized. Beyond question, the United States underwent drastic change during the 1960s and a host of issues contributed to these transformations. Nevertheless, there is abundant evidence that the removal of prayer and moral teaching out of the public schools is likely one reason for the increase in delinquent behavior among America's school age youth. The purpose of this chapter is to investigate this claim that is gaining support among a growing number of social scientists that in order to resolve many of the behavioral problems among juveniles in the country moral education and religious freedom need to be reinstituted in the public schools. In examining this problem, we will first address facts associated with juvenile behavioral problems, then we will examine the events leading up to the removal of prayer and moral education in the schools, and finally we will focus on the evidence suggesting that religious commitment and religious schools improve student behavior and achievement (Carlston, 2004; Fowler, 1999; Jeynes, 2007; Matera, 2001; Matusow, 1984; Michaelsen, 1970; Miles, 2004; O'Neill, 1971; Sikorski, 1993).

ADDRESSING THE FACTS

Widespread Deterioration in Social Behavior among American Youth

To be sure, over the last 45 years behavioral trends have emerged among America's youth that are very disconcerting. Virtually every major measure of adolescent delinquent behavior has soared over this period of time. Not only has this behavior surged, but students are assaulting teachers at a disconcerting rate, causing 1,000 teachers a month to either be hospitalized or seek medical attention (Casserly, Herbert, Raymond, Etzoni, & Shanker, 1985; U.S. Department of Health and Human Services, 1998; U.S. Department of Justice, 1999).

As disconcerting as the rise is in school violence, there are other trends that have emerged since prayer and moral education were removed out of the schools in 1962 and 1963. First, preadolescents and adolescents have significantly increased their consumption of illegal drugs since the 1960s. From about 1965 to 1980, youth consumption of illegal drugs soared to unprecedented heights. Since then the number of youth taking illegal drugs has stabilized. Nevertheless, the overall level of illegal drug consumption remains high, particularly compared to its pre-1965 levels (U.S. Department of Justice, 1999).

Second, youth are much more likely to engage in sexually promiscuous behavior than before prayer and moral education were removed from the public schools. Sexually promiscuous behavior was relatively stable during the 1940s and 1950s, but after prayer and moral education were removed from the schools, premarital pregnancy rates multiplied by seven times. Rates of adolescent and preadolescent rape surged by over three times for the first generation (1963–1980) of youth to complete their schoolings without prayer in the schools. The transformation of the adolescent landscape in terms of sexual behavior is evident not only in the changes in frequency of specific behaviors but in the age of the incipiency of sexual behavior. Surveys indicate that over half of single youth and adolescents had their first sexual experience at the age of 10 (Irvine, 2002; Melody & Peterson, 1999; U.S. Department of Health and Human Services, 1998; U.S. Department of Justice, 1999).

Third, following the removal of prayer from the public schools in 1962 and 1963, academic achievement in the United States plummeted. Scores on the nation's most prestigious measure of academic outcomes, the Scholastic Achievement Aptitude Test (SAT), plummeted for 17 consecutive years from 1963 to 1980. Concurrently virtually every major standardized assessment of educational outcomes showed similar declines, including the American College Test (ACT), the Graduate Record Examination (GRE), the Iowa Test of Basic Skills (ITBS), the Iowa Test of Educational Development (ITED), and the Stanford Achievement Test (Clearly & McCandless, 1976; U.S. Department of Education, 2001; Wirtz, 1977).

The decline in scholastic outcome measures beginning in 1963 ushered in an era of academic and literary decline unprecedented in American history. SAT scores, which had never undergone as much as even a two consecutive year decline, dropped for 17 consecutive years. During this period, SAT scores ostensibly dropped 90 points from about 1,000 to 910. Of even greater concern, however, is that the College Board concluded in its reports entitled *On Further Examination* that the actual decline was 110 points because via administration of earlier and later versions of the SAT, the Board determined that tests in the 1970s were about 20 points easier than those administered in the 1960s (Armbruster, 1977; Wirtz, 1977).

Although the College Board concluded that demographic changes in the United States contributed significantly to the decline in SAT scores, statistical analysis of the College Board report indicates that about 62 percent of the decline resulted from academic deterioration. The analysis also indicates that on other state and nationwide assessments, demographic factors can only explicate a minute amount of the educational decline. The Stanford Achievement Test, for example, showed declines of about 1 and 1/2 years in mathematical outcomes for middle school students, even when analysis is confined to the 1964–1973 period (Armbruster, 1977; Cooperman, 1985; Jeynes, 2003a).

Other developments during the post-1963 period also point to a real academic decline. For example, many academics point out that rates of illiteracy have risen in the country and now stand at unacceptable levels. The American literacy rate which at its best point stood at 1/2 of 1 percent, the lowest in the world, has now increased by six times and stands at 3 percent. This rate is now one of the highest in the industrialized world and as a result the American literacy rate now only ranks tied for 62nd in the world. In fact, some Third World nations, such as Tonga, Mongolia, Trinidad and Tobago, Guyana, Turkmenistan, and Tajikistan, have higher literacy rates than does the United States. Reading research confirms that the literacy levels of Americans may lag those of past generations. Research comparing the reading levels of contemporary textbooks with those of the 1930s and 1880s indicates that textbooks from this period were at a reading level of least two years higher than most contemporary books (Barton, 2004; Central Intelligence Agency, 2006; Gatto, 2001; Harman, 1987; Kozol, 1985; Sykes, 1995; U.S. Census Bureau, 2001).

School Shootings

Naturally, the recent barrage of school shootings are the most ostensible sign of the moral deterioration that is apparent among the youth. Nevertheless, it is simply the most pronounced sign of moral decay amidst a cacophony of other indicators that over the years have painted an ominous picture of the moral fabric of this country. Having stated this, one should note that contrary to popular belief, school shootings did not begin in 1996. They only became associated with the suburbs in 1996. Beginning in the 1960s, urban areas would often report school shootings. However, they did not receive the press coverage that suburban shootings of the late 1990s and early 2000s received. One reason for this is that a myriad of Americans possess a belief that violence is an unfortunate but expected part of the fabric of the urban lifestyle. In contrast, people are flabbergasted and agape when a shooting occurs in the so-called tranquil suburbs. The reality is, however, that the school shootings of the last 40 or 45 years are a sign of the moral deterioration of American society (Brown & Merritt, 2002; Carlston, 2004; Kopka, 1997; Matera, 2001; Scott & Nimmo, 2000; Zoba, 2000).

One of the indications that American society has paid a costly price for the removal of prayer and moral education from the schools is that school shootings have regularly emerged on the American scene. These violent episodes arose in the mid-1960s in urban areas. However, they really did not gain national attention until 1996 when on February 2 these shootings began their penetration of rural and suburban vicinities (Kopka, 1997). On this date Barry Loukaitis, a 14-year-old from Moses Lake, Washington, killed two students and a math teacher (Coleman, 2004). Loukaitis said that he was influenced by two movies (*Natural Born Killers* by Oliver Stone and *The Basketball Diaries*), a video (Pearl Jam's *Jeremy*), and especially by Stephen King's novel, *Rage*. At the time of the killing, Loukaitis quoted the book by stating, "It sure beats algebra, doesn't it?"

In 1996 and 1997 additional shootings continued, with a principal and various students falling victim. Some of the killings were clearly expressions of anti-Christian hatred. On December 1, 1997 Michael Carneal ambushed a prayer gathering before school and killed three and wounded five. In October 1997 the instigator was a boy who was a Satan worshipper who hated his ex-girlfriend as well as Christians. In 1997–1998, school shootings took the lives of parents, ex-girlfriends, and many youth. The events in Jonesboro, Arkansas, Fayetteville, Tennessee, and Springfield, Oregon received some of the most publicity. However, other shootings occurred in El Cajon and Santee, California, Deming, New Mexico, Stamps, Arkansas, Conyers, Georgia, Fort Gibson, Oklahoma, Mount Morris Township, Michigan, and in numerous other locales (Coleman, 2004; Matera, 2001).

In April 1999 the most infamous of the school shootings occurred at Columbine High School in Littleton, Colorado. At this time, Eric Harris and Dylan Kliebold exploded 30 bombs and sprayed the school with 188 shots resulting in the death of 15 students and wounding 14 others.

As dastardly as these outcomes make the plot appear, the plan was to blow up the entire school. Fortunately, two huge 20-pound propane bombs planted in the cafeteria failed to detonate. Scores of handmade pipe bombs also did not explode (Brown & Merritt, 2002; Carlston, 2004; Matera, 2001; Scott & Nimmo, 2000; Zoba, 2000).

Contrary to the assertions of some, Harris and Kliebold were hardly two innocent boys who simply did not like being bullied. Eric Harris stated on his Web site, "My belief is that if I say something, it goes. I am the law, if you don't like it you die. If I don't like you or I don't like what you want me to do, you die" (Brown & Merritt, 2002, p. 84). In addition, Harris warned of the impending attack, "I will rig up explosives all over a town and detonate each of them at will after I mow down the whole [expletive] area" (Scott & Nimmo, 2000, p. 15). Harris wrote in Dylan's handbook, "God I can't wait until they die. I can taste the blood now . . . You know what I hate? MANKIND! Kill everything . . . Kill everything" (Brown & Merrit, 2002, p. 94). Eric Harris was also hurt by a former girlfriend and sought vengeance against her (Brown & Merritt, 2002).

After the Columbine attack, various youth collaborated to plot similar attacks, but by this time the FBI and police had become much more adept at intercepting their communications prior to the assault. On a few occasions, the plots were so prodigious in scope that they dwarfed the Columbine strategy. One episode in 2001 in New Bedford, Massachusetts witnessed law officials intercept an e-mail that revealed the placement of bombs far more lethal than Columbine in an attempt to blow up at least an entire school (Coleman, 2004; Matera, 2001; Newman, 2004).

Just what factors caused the adolescent conspirators to act so maliciously vary from one shooting to the next. A majority of students had a penchant for the music of Marilyn Manson. Most also loved violent video games and many were obsessed with guns. Quite a number recently had their girlfriends break up with them. However, one wonders if far fewer shootings would have occurred if students from these schools, especially the assailants, had been given training in forgiveness, anger management, loving others, showing respect, defending those children who are bullied, and dealing with others tenderly (in breaking up with boyfriends, girlfriends, and so forth). The abundance of shootings raises serious questions about the moral health of America's young (Brown and Merritt, 2002; Coleman, 2004; Matera, 2001).

Concluding Thoughts about the Changes in Youth Behavior

To be sure, several factors contributed to deterioration in adolescent violent and sexual behavior, as well as in their academic prowess. Moreover, several of the factors that contributed to this decline were inextricably connected. For example, the College Board cites an increase in divorce rates and substance abuse as two factors that contributed to declining school outcomes. Moreover, the Board notes a decline in morality and in the work ethic as salient contributing factors. One can certainly make a viable argument that the removal of prayer and moral education influences adolescent moral behavior. Furthermore, one can make an argument that reinstituting prayer and moral education in the schools could help student behavior and achievement. However, to make this assertion, most efficaciously one must address the issue of whether there is evidence that moral instruction and allowing religious freedom in the schools can improve student behavior and achievement. In order to do this, one needs to: (1) investigate the research literature regarding the extent to which religious commitment or expression improves student behavior and achievement; and (2) investigate the research literature regarding the extent to which religious schools, which allow prayer and moral education, influence student behavior and achievement. We will now examine the events surrounding the removal of prayer and moral education out of the schools and then address the two issues just mentioned to help determine whether providing moral instruction and allowing religious freedom in the schools can improve student behavior and achievement (Jeynes, 2007; Wirtz, 1977).

THE REMOVAL OF PRAYER AND MORAL EDUCATION FROM THE PUBLIC SCHOOLS

Prior to 1962, for many generations liberty and religion were inseparable to most Americans. Tocqueville believed the two were closely related and that this was largely what made America strong. He sincerely doubted whether a man could "support complete religious independence and entire political liberty at the same time" (Tocqueville, 1966, p. 409). This belief pervaded not only American public and educators but the legal profession as well. Justice William Douglas asserted in the 1952 Supreme Court decision in *Zorach v. Clauson*, "We are a religious people" and that our "institutions presuppose a Supreme Being" (*Zorach v. Clauson*, 1952).

The Supreme Court Decisions

Nevertheless, in a series of Supreme Court decisions, prayer and Bible reading were removed from the public schools in 1962 and 1963. The first of these Supreme Court decisions was *Engel v. Vitale* (1962), which prohibited corporate school prayer. *Abington School District v. Schempp* (1963) disallowed Bible devotional reading. *Murray v. Curlett* (1963) prohibited not only school prayer but also Bible reading. The parent in that case, Madalyn Murray O'Hare, became the most outspoken atheistic leader in the United States. Her son Bill, who was the child directly involved in the case, later greatly regretted his role in the case. He authored a letter of apology to the American people in a Baltimore newspaper, where the family had lived. He later converted to Christianity, became a minister, and dedicated his life to reinstituting the freedom to pray in the public schools (Murray, 1982).

The Engel case was quite an unusual Supreme Court decision. Michaelsen states, "In a most unusual fashion, Justice Black, in writing the opinion of the Court in Engel, did not appeal to a single court case as precedent setting. The opinion consists largely of historical references to such things as actions involving the Book of Common Prayer" (Michaelsen, 1970, p. 199). Justice Douglas went on to repudiate almost every position he had taken accommodating religion in his previous judicial decisions. He mentioned that he opposed the word "God" in the pledge of allegiance and the benefits of the school lunch act being extended to students from private schools. As David Louisell in the *Yale Law Journal* asserted, it seemed that Black was determined to "root out . . . every vestige, direct and indirect, of religion in public affairs" (Louisell, 1964, p. 991).

The prayer in the Engel case was used as part of New York State's program of moral education that was entitled "Statement on Moral and Spiritual Training in the Schools" (Kliebard, 1969, p. 198). In the court proceeding itself, the justices acknowledged that no student was compelled to say the prayer. Any child, who so chose, did not have to take part (*Engel v. Vitale*, 1962). In fact, Paul Blanshard (1963) observes that the prayer was doubly voluntary. Not only could parents opt out of the prayer, but local school boards could also opt out. The justices also acknowledged that this practice in New York schools was essentially the same as the practice of the U.S. Supreme Court beginning each day, that is, it was asking for God's blessing (*Engel v. Vitale*, 1962). Justice Douglas also specifically noted that this prayer certainly did not establish a religion (*Engel v. Vitale*, 1962). In spite of this, the Supreme Court disallowed the prayer.

In *Abington v. Schempp* (1963), the Supreme Court heard a case regarding the reading of the Bible in the classroom. Pennsylvania possessed a law that stated, "At least ten verses from the Holy Bible shall be read, without comment, at the opening of each public school on each school day. Any child shall be excused from such Bible reading, or attending such Bible reading, upon the written request of a parent or guardian" (Pennsylvania Statute). *Murray v. Curlett* (1963) involved a similar situation.

In the Engel decision and in the 1963 case of *Abington v. Schempp*, Black and the other Supreme Court justices who sided with him relied on the "separation principle" to argue the case, although the phrase of "separation of church and state" never appears in the Constitution. Justice Stewart disagreed with this interpretation of neutrality. He believed that prohibiting religious expression was showing bias against people of faith and that the only way to maintain neutrality was to allow religious expressions by those who desired them (Kliebard, 1969). Stewart stated that prohibiting religious expression produced not "the realization of state neutrality, but rather . . . the establishment of a religion of secularism" (*Abington v. Schempp*, 1963).

The Public Reaction

Paul Blanshard (1963, p. 21) observes that when the U.S. Supreme Court handed down the decision on the New York Regent's prayer on June 25, 1962, it "was the greatest publicity explosion that ever greeted an American decision about religion." He continues by stating:

> The *New York Times* devoted almost eighteen columns to the prayer story on the day after the decision. The next day there was an editorial and at least three more columns of news and review. Lesser newspapers, with fewer columns available, gave the decision commensurate coverage. For many weeks the public discussion of the decision produced headlines, editorials and a flood of letters to the editor. (Blanshard, 1963, p. 21)

The reaction by the American public and its leadership was not positive. Dwight Eisenhower responded by saying:

> I always thought that this nation was essentially a religious one. I realize, of course, that the Declaration of Independence antedates the Constitution, but the fact remains that the Declaration was our certificate of national birth. It specifically asserts that we as individuals possess certain rights as an endowment from our Creator—a religious concept. (*New York Times*, p. 1)

Former President Hoover said the Supreme Court decision constituted "a disintegration of a sacred American heritage." He added, "The Congress should at once submit an amendment to the Constitution which establishes the right to religious devotion in all government agencies—national, state, or local" (*National Catholic Almanac*, p. 69). On June 26, just one day following the Court's decision, Francis Cardinal Spellman, the foremost leader of the American Catholic Church, "made a blistering attack on the prayer decision" (Blanshard, 1963, p. 51). Bishop Pike also strongly criticized the Court (Blanshard, 1963, p. 57). Of all the strong criticisms launched at the Court by religious leaders such as Spellman, Pike, Billy Graham, and Reinhold Niebuhr, it was Spellman who attacked the Court the most severely. He said:

> I am shocked and frightened that the Supreme Court has declared unconstitutional a simple and voluntary declaration of belief in God by public school children. The decision strikes at the very heart of the Godly tradition in which American children have for so long been raised. (*New York Times*, p. 1)

There were many strong opinions voiced by both religious and political leaders in the days immediately following the Supreme Court's Engel decision in June of 1962. Congressman Frank Becker called the Engel decision "the most tragic in the history of the United States" (House Committee on the Judiciary, 1962). In many American religious publications, people voiced their outrage. For example, the *Brooklyn Tablet* called the decision "preposterous" (Sikorski, 1993, p. 418). In the weekly publication *America*, the decision was said to be "asinine," "stupid," and "doctrinaire" (Sikorski, 1993, p. 418). John Bennett, dean of Union Theological Seminary, opposed the Engel decision and accurately predicted that in response many Protestant schools would be started (Alley, 1994).

Congressional representatives were firm in their disapproval of the Court's decision. In the *Congressional Record* for the following day, there was not one individual in Congress who defended the Court's edict (Blanshard, p. 52). An unsuccessful movement was started to impeach the Supreme Court Chief Justice Earl Warren (Blanshard, p. 53). Senator Eugene Talmadege claimed, "the Supreme Court has set up atheism as a new religion" (Hearings before the Committee on the Judiciary, 1962, p. 140).

An August 30, 1963 Gallup Poll indicated that Americans were opposed to the Engel, Murray, and Schempp decisions by a 3-1 margin. Even the newspaper media, often criticized for being left of center politically, was about twice as likely to express opposition to the Engel decision. Many states, especially in the East and South, initially asserted that the injunction did not apply to them. Some of the states taking this position included Delaware, New Jersey, Ohio, New Hampshire, Massachusetts, Pennsylvania, Arkansas, North Carolina, Iowa, and Oklahoma. Nevertheless, a study indicated that in four eastern states (New Jersey, Pennsylvania, Maine, and Massachusetts), 96 percent of the schools *did* have Bible reading before 1962 and 97 percent *did not* have Bible reading after 1962 (Sikorski, 1993).

Taken together, the Engel, Schempp, and Murray court decisions eliminated public school prayer, religious released-time taking place on school premises, and school-sponsored group prayer. Although these three court decisions curtailed the expressions of people of faith in the classroom, there were certain activities involving religion that were still allowed. First, there could be religious released-time off school premises. Second, ceremonies that were patriotic or civic in purpose with religious references were also acceptable. Third, the objective study of teaching about religion was also permitted (Michaelsen, 1970).

There have been other cases that have further specified what activities are permissible on school grounds. In *Reed v. Van Hoven* (1965), a Michigan Supreme Court case, the court asserted that saying grace over your lunch at school was allowed only if you did not move your lips. And indeed there had been many children suspended from school for saying grace aloud at school. One recent case involved a six-year-old child who was placed on in-school suspension because he prayed before he ate at school (Barton, 1990; Rock of God, 2002).

A copious number of people objected to the Supreme Court's decisions not merely because of the decisions themselves but also on the basis of the unusual lack of judicial experience that the Supreme Court justices had. In almost every case, the justices were appointed to the

Supreme Court following a long history of political rather than judicial experience.

- Chief Justice Earl Warren had served as Governor of California for 10 years before his appointment;
- Justice Hugo Black had been a U.S. Senator for 10 years;
- Justice William Douglas was chairman of the Security and Exchange Commission;
- Justice Arthur Goldberg served as Secretary of Labor; and
- Justice Felix Frankfurter was an assistant to the Secretary of Labor and served as a founding member of the ACLU.

Ironically, the only justice with extended federal Constitutional experience before he began his service on the U.S. Supreme Court, Justice Potter Stewart, was also the only justice to object to the removal of prayer and Bible reading (*McCollum v. Board of Education*, 1948).

The Frequent Erroneous Application of the Decisions

Although the Supreme Court decisions are themselves controversial, the prayer and moral education in school has become even more divisive because of the means by which school officials either properly or improperly apply these decisions. There have been many educational administrators who, acting either out of ignorance or out of more prejudicial motives, have suspended many children for taking their Bibles to school. This problem became sufficiently pervasive so that in late June of 1995 the Committee on the Judiciary of the House of Representatives held hearings on this issue. One of the cases that emerged during these hearings was that of April Fiore. Ms. Fiore's daughter, Rebecca, and two of her friends sometimes carried Bibles in the school. The school admonished them to immediately refrain from carrying their Bibles in school, or they would be suspended from school for 10 days (the same punishment as for possession of illegal drugs). The girls maintained that their rights of freedom of religion were being stifled. When they were caught carrying their Bibles on another occasion, school authorities suspended them from school for 10 days and strongly urged the parents to send their children to another school (House Committee on the Judiciary, 1995).

The hearings before the House Committee on the Judiciary created a large degree of consternation. Consequently, shortly after the completion of the hearings, on July 12, 1995, Bill Clinton was compelled to speak to the issue of religious freedom in the public schools. In a speech at James Madison High School in Vienna, Virginia, Clinton stated, "nothing in the First Amendment converts our public schools to religion-free zones or requires all religious expression to be left at the schoolhouse door." Although Clinton probably meant well, a voluminous number of reports continue to emerge of students who believe that they have had their rights to religious freedom of speech violated. On May 19, 2000 a teacher at Lynn Lucas Middle School in Texas threw the Bibles of Angela and Amber Harbison in the trash asserting, "This is garbage!" The school justified the action by stating the Bible includes "hate speech." In 1999, a number of schoolboys were suspended for praying in front of their classmates. Praying in school and Bible reading are probably the most common types of religious expressions that are punished by suspension. A first grader at Haines Elementary School was sent to the principal's office for reading a Bible passage, even though the teacher had asked the students to read aloud any literature passage of their choice. On April 1, 2002, Palm Desert California school officials declared that a student was forbidden to give a religious gift (a video) to another student (Blessings for Life, 2002; Dominion School, 2002; Libertocracy, 2002; Religious Tolerance, 1995, 2002; Spin-Tech, 1999).

The ostensible religious restrictions have extended to a number of different areas. In 1997, a high school student in Florida was suspended for handing out religious literature, before and after school hours, even though he did not engage in this activity during school hours. Another student was suspended for saying "Jesus Christ is Lord" in the classroom. One student was told not to bring any more Christian material to school or suspension would likely follow. In February 2000 a principal forbade a Bible Club from using the cross as a club symbol. Religious clothing has also been an area of concern. An Alabama school blocked students from wearing crosses (Christianity.com, 2002; Jeremiah Project, 2002; *Maranatha Christian Journal*, 1999; Religious Tolerance, 2002; Spin-Tech, 1999).

Although most Americans do not want teacher-led prayer, Gallup and Harris polls indicate that about 75 percent of Americans do want voluntary prayer in the schools. They do not favor a school environment that is hostile to religion. Most Americans believe that there should be a period of silence given to children, whatever their religious or personal beliefs, during which they can pray or just simply collect their thoughts (Barton, 1990).

The Removal of Prayer's Influence on Moral Education

The Supreme Court's expunging of vocal prayer and Bible reading from the public schools had a dramatic impact on the teaching of moral education in the public schools. Prior to 1962, moral education was founded on the Bible. Once Bible reading was forbidden, schools no longer emphasized moral teachings such as "turning the other cheek," "you should not covet," and "honoring your mother and father" for fear that many would interpret these as religious and moral teachings. A great deal of this change was not a product of the desires of school officials, but their fear of parental lawsuits. Many administrators were convinced that if they persisted in teaching these moral principles, of which a majority had Christian roots, an atheist parent would bring the school officials to court. Indeed, it may well be that the sudden decline in school-sponsored moral instruction had even a greater negative impact on student behavior than the thwarting of religious freedom by banning vocal prayers in the school.

The removal of moral teaching from the public schools quickly became associated with a religious and moral decline in the nation as a whole. It is difficult to determine how much of this decline resulted from the removal of vocal prayer and Bible reading from the school and how much the moral decline influenced the Supreme Court decisions on this matter. The direction of causality is likely in both directions. Nevertheless, the removal of Bible reading and verbal prayer had a dramatic impact on the extent to which teachers dared address moral education (Sikorski, 1993). Paul Vitz (1994) also notes that following 1962 public school textbook manufacturers substantially reduced the number of moral lessons that had previously been a recurring thread in many American textbooks.

IS THERE EVIDENCE THAT MORAL INSTRUCTION AND ALLOWING RELIGIOUS FREEDOM IN THE SCHOOLS COULD IMPROVE STUDENT BEHAVIOR AND ACHIEVEMENT?

Although there is a considerable amount of evidence to suggest that the removal of prayer and moral instruction in the schools had a deleterious effect on human behavior, if one is to strengthen this argument it is vital to demonstrate that religiosity as expressed by both individual students and by schools has an ameliorative effect on student behavior and academic achievement. Two of the primary sets of studies about the possible effects of reintroducing moral education and religious freedom in the classroom are studies on the influence of religious commitment and religious schools.

Religious Commitment Studies

In reviewing research of religious commitment, it is important to define what is meant by religious commitment or religiosity. For the purposes of this chapter, religious commitment was defined as the extent to which an individual considered himself or herself religious and the consistency with which an individual attended a church, Bible study, youth group meeting, or other place of worship. Although some studies include all kinds of religions in their research, the overwhelming number of religious people that were examined were Christians. Nicholas and Durrheim (1996) undertook research to confirm the concept of religiosity. They examined 1,817 college students and found that religiosity increased "as a function of the fundamentalism of religious beliefs" (p. 89).

The Effects of Religious Commitment on Academic Achievement

The oldest component of the debate on the effects of religion has to do with the American education system. Over the last 35 or 40 years, there has been a considerable amount of debate on the effects of religion on education. The larger portion of this debate has focused on the effects of religious schools on the educational achievement of children. Nevertheless, a growing number of social scientists are studying Christian and religious commitment. For example, Dijkstra and Peschar (1996) examined the influence of religious commitment on the academic achievement of Dutch children. Dembo, Levin, and Siegler (1997) found that Israeli children attending "ultraorthodox" schools performed better in reasoning problems than their counterparts in mainstream schools. Richard Koubek (1984) found that among Christian Evangelical high school students, there was a positive correlation between the extent of a student's religious commitment and academic achievement. Jeynes (1999, 2002a, 2003b) examined the National Educational Longitudinal Study (NELS) and found that not only do religiously committed African American and Hispanic students do better academically than their less religious counterparts, but that when one examines these religious minority students who are in intact families, the academic gap versus white students disappears (Dembo, Levin, & Siegler, 1997; Gaziel, 1997; Lee & Bryk, 1993).

Recent meta-analyses have statistically combined all of those studies that have been done on the effects of religious commitment on the academic outcomes of children. These meta-analyses found that individual religious commitment has a consistently positive association with strong academic outcomes (Jeynes, 2002a, 2003a, 2004a, 2004b).

There are a number of reasons that social scientists frequently give for the positive relationship between religiosity and school outcomes. The first of these reasons, and historically probably the most acknowledged, deals with a religious work ethic. Although a work ethic is commonly referred to as the "Protestant work ethic," recent research indicates that such a work ethic may extent beyond the Protestant sphere to other religious groups as well. Second, a relationship between religiosity and educational outcomes emerges from the tendency for religious people to abstain from behaviors that are regarded as undisciplined and harmful to academic achievement. A number of studies indicate that religiously committed teens are less likely to become involved in drug and alcohol abuse. Other studies indicate that religiously committed teens are less likely to engage in sexual behavior or become pregnant while they are still teenagers. The third reason emerging from research suggests that religiosity is likely to cause people to have an internal locus of control. Educational psychologists have found a rather consistent relationship between possessing an internal locus of control and performing well in school (Bahr, Hawks, & Wang, 1993; Beck, Cole, & Hammond, 1991; Brownfield & Sorenson, 1991; Jackson & Coursey, 1988; Johnson, 1992; Mentzer, 1988; Miller & Olson, 1988).

Religious Commitment and Juvenile Delinquency

Over the last few decades, researchers have presented a substantial amount of empirical evidence indicating that religiosity has a substantial degree of impact on a wide range of physical, social, and behavioral outcomes. Perhaps the most comprehensive analysis done along these lines was undertaken by Harold Koenig, Michael McCullough, and David Larson in their book, *Handbook of Religion and Health*, published by Oxford University Press. In this thorough review of the literature, the authors examined over 1,000 studies on religiosity's relationship with physical and mental health, substance abuse, and delinquency (Koenig, 1993,

1999; Koenig, McCullough, & Larson, 2001). Social scientists have initiated other similar reviews as well. Johnson, Le, Larson, & McCullough (2000) specifically addressed the relationship between religiosity and delinquency in a systematic review. In each of these studies, the researchers found that religious commitment was usually associated with positive physical, emotional, and social outcomes. For the purposes of this chapter, we are most concerned with the effects of religious commitment on behavior outcomes, particularly of adolescents.

General Delinquent Behavior

During the 1990s and early 2000s, a growing amount of research addressed the relationship between religiosity and juvenile delinquency. Previous to this time, several studies examined this relationship, but they were not particularly great in number. The earlier studies stirred a debate about whether the influence of religiosity was dependent on it being exercised in a "moral community" as opposed to a secular one. Indeed, whether religiosity has a greater impact in an environment that esteems morality more than in a setting which does not is an intriguing question that is patently related to the school prayer debate, and we will address this issue shortly (Albrecht, Chadwick, & Alcorn, 1977; Burkett & White, 1974; Cochran, 1992, 1993; Hirschi & Stark, 1969; Johnson, Jang, & Li, 2000; Stark, Kent, & Doyle, 1982).

Research from the 1990s and early 2000s has demonstrated a pretty consistent pattern, indicating that religious commitment is associated with lower levels of juvenile delinquency. Even if one focuses on the entire body of research on this topic, about five out of six studies examining the association between religious commitment and juvenile delinquency show an inverse relationship. In a systematic review of the relationship between religiosity and delinquency, Johnson, Li, Larson, and McCullough (2000) found that of the 40 studies included in their analysis only one found that religiosity was associated with higher levels of delinquency. Several ostensible patterns emerge from most of the studies examining religiosity and juvenile delinquency. First, adolescent religious commitment influences both the behaviors and attitudes of youth. Second, the religious commitment of teens appears to reduce both major and minor manifestations of delinquent behavior. Third, adolescents of faith appear to engage in less antisocial and destructive behavior even in secularized and socially deleterious environments. Fourth, there is a considerable degree of evidence that religious, usually Christian, delinquency prevention programs do positively impact adolescent behavior so that deviance declines. Fifth, there is evidence that suggests that the longer and/or the deeper the experience of religious commitment, the greater the influence of the religious orientation on delinquent behavior (Baier & Wright, 2001; Cochran, 1992, 1993; Evans et al., 1996; Jang & Johnson, 2001; Johnson, Jang, & Li, 2000; Jeynes, 2002c, 2003d; Johnson, Larson, Jang, & Li, 1999, 2000).

To the extent that the above findings are true, one should not be surprised that juvenile crime skyrocketed after the Supreme Court removed the expression of prayer and Bible reading from the public schools. Instead, as President Bill Clinton asserted in 1995, the United States now possesses a public school system that communicates to students that they must leave their faith at the front door of the school. And the public school educators often maintain that Christianity and Judaism, in particular, have little or no value in today's secularized society (Decter, 1995; Olasky, 1988; Religious Tolerance, 1995).

That is a substantial amount of evidence indicating that American public schools at best de-emphasize and frequently omit the contribution of church, synagogues, and faith in American historical and contemporary life. In addition, the presentation of religion by many public school textbooks and educators is often negative. Paul Vitz (1994), a professor at New York University (NYU), undertook a study of textbooks used in American public schools and determined that the overwhelming number of American textbooks leave out substantial sections of religious references that add essential information and context to speeches and events and appeared consistently in earlier versions of the textbooks (Jeynes, 2003a; Vitz, 1994). Vitz (1994) also noted that public school textbooks often make negative references to Christianity much more than positive ones.

When integrating research findings to assess the influence that the removal of prayer and moral education from the public schools may have had on public school students, two questions are especially important to address. First, to what degree does religiosity have a more trenchant impact in a moral community rather than a secular one? Second, to what degree do religious solutions to the presence of juvenile delinquency work better than secular solutions? Addressing these questions is essential if one is to comprehend the impact that the reintroduction of moral education in the public schools is likely to have. To see why this is the case, let us now examine each of these questions.

To What Extent Does Religiosity Have More of a Viable Impact in Moral Communities Rather Than Secular Ones?

There is no question that juvenile crime is at a much higher rate than was the case prior to the decision to remove prayer from the public schools. Although, the removal of prayer and moral education from the schools is clearly not the only factor contributing to this development, the removal of moral education from any institution is likely to have a negative impact. However, the question emerges, if a moment of silence is permitted in the public schools, along with the implementation of moral education, will the positive effects be similar to those yielded before the Supreme Court decisions of 1962 and 1963? According to Stark, Kent, & Doyle (1982), the answer to this question is "no" in many places in the United States, because the nation is less of a moral community than it was before 1963 (Jeynes, 2010, in press; U.S. Department of Justice, 2001).

It is true many will acknowledge that the reintroduction of moral education and the allowance of a moment of silence in the classroom will not reduce juvenile delinquency to pre-1963 levels, because American society is less religious than was the case then. Nevertheless, it may well be the case that reintroducing moral education and allowing a moment of silence will have a greater impact than one imagines. For example, evidence suggests that the influence of religious schooling on student behavior and school outcomes is greater for less religious students than for religious ones. One hypothesis for this result is that because students of faith are more likely to already be grounded in faith and the self-disciplined life that often accompanies this, they receive less additive benefit than people who are not of faith. If this hypothesis is correct, then the behavioral and academic advantage to adding moral education and a moment of silence in the schools is more akin to the advantages derived from less religious people attending Evangelical, Catholic, or other religious private schools than it is for people of faith attending these schools (Jeynes, 2003c; Johnson, Larson, Jang, & Li, 1999, 2000; Sander, 1996; Stark, Kent, & Doyle, 1982).

To What Degree Do Religious Solutions to the Presence of Juvenile Delinquency Work Better than Secular Solutions?

This question is important to address for two reasons. First, there are secularists who would espouse a moral education component to the curriculum but would like to avoid what they consider Christianity-based components such as treating others as you would want to be treated and the central nature of forgiveness. Some people would also like to exclude the idea of a moment of silence. Second, some contend that although restoring public schools will succor the development of more pro-social behavior among adolescents, it will not have the influence of faith-based initiatives because the religious component is vital to maximize the pervasive nature of its impact (Barton, 1990, 2004; Meier, 2002; Sandin, 1992).

There is evidence that faith-based programs such as Teen Challenge, the Salvation Army, and Catholic Charities are generally more efficacious in treating manifestations of juvenile delinquency than their non-faith-based counterparts. Although the findings favoring faith-based initiatives are consistent, one should keep in mind that they are also limited in number. Therefore, social scientists need to know more about how widespread the faith-based initiative advantage is versus their non-faith-based counterparts (Bicknese, 1999; Florida Department of Corrections, 2000; Johnson, 2002; O'Conner, 2001; Young et al., 1995).

Nevertheless, to the extent that faith-based initiatives are more effective than secular ones, this suggests that totally decoupling moral education from any semblance of religious principle would be unwise. This is especially true because the Christian concept of treating others as one would like to be treated is probably a prerequisite for common decency to prevail in society. Furthermore, certain Judeo-Christian principles have become so interwoven in society that these ideas are inextricably connected with American culture. Consequently, to fail to teach such notions would be to refuse to teach American culture in the classroom. Second, it seems plausible that religious-based morality will have the greatest impact if the religious beliefs that form the basis of that morality are allowed to remain. With this in mind, one can argue that the positive effects of attending a Catholic, Evangelical, or other religious school will outweigh the benefits of attending a public school, even with the addition of moral education (Barton, 1990, 2004; Meier, 2002; Nord, 1995).

The Effects of Religious Commitment on the Use of Illegal Drugs and Alcohol

Cochran (1992, 1993), Cochran, Beeghley, and Bock (1992), and Jeynes (2006) determined that adolescent religious commitment was associated with lower drug and alcohol use. Cochran asserts, however, that religiosity leads to a reduced incidence of drug use more than a reduced incidence of alcohol use. Cochran did, however, find a relationship between the religious commitment of secondary school students and decreased alcohol use, particularly among evangelical Christians. Research also indicates that religious commitment may help some people deal with their stress. A large degree of and/or the frequent consumption of alcohol is sometimes, although certainly not always, associated with a high level of stress. To the extent that people seek to become "high" on drugs or alcohol to relieve stress, religious commitment might be a meaningful alternative (Curtin, Lang, Patrick, & Stritzke, 1998; McFarlane, 1998).

Social scientists may have established some sense of causality in terms of religious commitment affecting attitudes and behaviors toward drugs. One question that has emerged, as a result of particular studies, is whether the religious commitment of individuals affects their use of certain drugs more than others. Free (1994) found that religious commitment affects the use of less serious drugs more than it does the use of more serious drugs. Corwyn, Benda, and Ballard (1997) found that the religious commitment of individuals affected their use of some drugs, but not others. Why does religiosity affect the use of less serious illegal drugs, such as marijuana, more than it does the use of more serious illegal drugs, such as cocaine? Possibly there exist more societal forces that reduce the consumption of more serious drugs like cocaine. To the extent that religious commitment is one of the societal forces that discourages the use of all drugs, one would think that religious commitment would have a greater impact on lowering the usage of a particular drug, in cases where there are fewer other societal forces working to reduce drug usage (Francis, 1997).

Premarital Sex

There is also evidence that religious commitment is associated with a decreased incidence in premarital intercourse. For example, Sharon Lock and Murray Vincent (1995) found that among 564 predominantly black adolescent girls, religious commitment played a strong role in predicting low levels of premarital sex. Velma Murry-McBride (1996) addressed this same issue, focusing on 109 middle-income African American females and found similar results. Some researchers have attempted to examine the effects of religiosity on both attitudes and behaviors regarding premarital intercourse. Brent Miller and Terrence Olson (1988) examined 2,423 adolescents and found that there was not only a strong relationship between attitudes and behaviors about premarital sex but that religious commitment predicted both. Jeynes (2003d) found the same relationship using the NELS data set. Peterson and Donnenwerth (1997) obtained data from the cumulative social surveys and found that conservative Protestants maintained the most consistent beliefs over time about premarital sex being morally wrong. Scott Beck (1991) and his colleagues examined the National Longitudinal Survey of Youth and concluded that Evangelical and Pentecostal Christians were the least likely to engage in premarital sex (Bryan & Freed, 1993; Sheeran, Abrams, Abraham, & Spears, 1993).

Part of the research literature addresses very specific issues regarding the relationship between religious commitment and premarital intercourse. Social scientists have examined the effects of religiosity on sexual satisfaction, the use of contraceptives, and the relationship between religiosity and biological factors. The effects of religious commitment on the tendency for adolescents to have less permissive attitudes and behaviors regarding premarital intercourse and premarital childbirth has been the subject of international research as well (Davidson, Darling, & Norton, 1995; Halpern et al., 1994).

Limitations of Studies on Religious Commitment

Although the research literature is clear that religiosity reduces the propensity for delinquent behavior, what is not evident is what components of religious commitment have the greatest impact. Johnson, Li, Larson, & McCullough (2000) identified six components of religious commitment: attendance at a church or other place of worship, salience (i.e., the degree to which a person regards religious commitment as an integral part of one's life), denominational affiliation, the extent to which one prays, whether one attends a Bible study, and the extent to which one participates in other religious activities. Johnson, Li, Larson, and McCullough found that 50 percent of the studies they examined used only one or two of these six components. Generally, social scientists chose to use salience of religiosity or attendance at a church or other place of worship or both of these variables. Johnson and his colleagues aver that the research community would know more about the specific nature of religious commitment if more social scientists would examine the influence of these other variables.

How many components of religiosity are included in a study apparently has a considerable impact on the findings that emerge in a study. Johnson and his colleagues (2000) found that for the 38 percent (15 of 40) of the studies that included four or more religious commitment variables, 100 percent of them found that religious commitment reduces delinquency. This finding, in conjunction with other results already mentioned, suggests the following. First, various components of religious commitment collectively apparently have a greater impact on delinquency than one or two aspects of religious commitment examined separately. Second, different components of religious commitment likely have a differing effect on various individuals. For some people, just examining the influence of attendance and salience is sufficient to yield a statistically significant effect for religious commitment. For other people, however, only the combination of a few components of religiosity will yield statistically significant effects.

It is apparent that including several components of religious commitment is preferable for at least two reasons. First, incorporating several measures of religious commitment will give a more complete perspective on the influence of religiosity. Second, including more measures will also give one a sense of what aspects of religious commitment have a greater impact than others. For example, does one's prayer life have a greater influence on delinquent behavior than attending church or another type of worship service?

Religious School Studies

In addition to the primacy of studies on the influence of religious commitment on student behavioral and academic outcomes, if one is to argue that moral education and the practice of religious freedom will enhance student's lives, studies examining the influence of religious schools are also instructive. Most of the research on the effect of religious schools, primarily Christian (Evangelical and Catholic), has focused on academic achievement more than it has on school behavior. The vast majority of studies examining the impact of attending religious schools on student achievement indicate that students attending religious schools outperform their counterparts in public schools. Researchers differ about the reasons why students from religious schools may outperform students from public schools. Gaziel (1997) claims that the achievement gap can specifically be attributed to differences in school culture. Some social scientists argue that to the extent to which this is true, religious schools do a better job of helping disadvantaged students. An alternative or supplemental view, given by some, is that religious schools promote parental involvement more than public schools do (Bryk, Lee, & Holland, 1993; Coleman, 1988; Coleman, Hoffer, & Kilgore, 1982; Gaziel, 1997; Jeynes, 2002b; Marsch, 1991; Morris, 1994; Riley, 1996).

There are some educators who doubt the extent to which this advantage is due to certain positive qualities in the way the schools are run. Some researchers believe that students from religious schools outperform public school students because public schools have a high percentage of low-socioeconomic-status (SES) and racial minority children. They assert that religious schools have an advantage in that they are able to choose which students they want to attend their schools and this fact causes the average private school family to have a higher level of SES. Moynihan (1989), however, propounds evidence that suggests that the racial distribution of students in religious schools is similar to that found in public schools. In addition, some research suggests that religious schools may especially benefit students of color. In addition, in research that examines family income, parents sending their children to public school made, on average, only about 18 percent less than parents sending their children to Catholic school. These researchers also point out that the religious school advantage is not due to increased expenditures per student because religious schools spend about two-thirds of what public schools do on a per student basis (American Association of University Women Educational Foundation, 1992; Baker, 1998, 1999; Bryk, Lee, & Holland, 1993; Coleman, Hoffer, & Kilgore, 1982; Gewirtz, Ball, & Bowe, 1995; Hall, 1986; Hardy & Vieler-Porter, 1995; Lee, 1987; Murphy, 1990; Neal, 1997).

Religious Schools and Student Achievement

Jeynes conducted meta-analyses that indicate that even when studies controlled for SES, children who attended Evangelical and Catholic schools academically outperformed their counterparts who attended public schools. Moreover, over time an increasing number of public school educators are acknowledging that they have a great deal to learn from the private school. For example, the Chicago public school system is attempting to model several aspects of the Catholic school system. Although some factors that contribute to the success of religious schools may be difficult to imitate, many social scientists believe that religious schools serve as a useful model for the public schools (Bryk, Lee, & Holland, 1993; Hudolin, 1994; Jeynes, 2003a, 2003c; LePore & Warren, 1997; McEwen, Knipe, & Gallagher, 1997).

Bryk, Lee, and Holland (1993, p. ix) state:

> For anyone who is concerned about the renewal of America's educational institutions, the organization and operation of Catholic schools offer important lessons to ponder.

Religious Schools and Student Behavior

Based on the assertions of these two sets of researchers, one can argue that it may be that the values present in religious schools may benefit disadvantaged children the most. Coleman, Bryk, and others believe that an emphasis on values also affects student behavior. Chubb and Moe (1990) contend that this is especially important because in their view, "Drugs and violence have poisoned the learning environment" (p. 1). Bryk, Lee, and Holland (1993) note that disciplinary problems are far less likely in Catholic schools than they are in public schools. They note that while one-half of public school students report that cutting class is a problem in their schools, only one-tenth of Catholic students report cutting problems in their schools. Public school students are also at least twice as likely as Catholic school students to report problems at their schools with students obeying teachers and talking back to teachers (Bryk, Lee, & Holland, 1993).

Meta-analyses and the examination of nationwide data sets have shown that students attending Evangelical and Catholic schools were less likely to engage in violent behavior, be disobedient to parents, and engage in theft. These studies also indicate that Evangelical and Catholic schools are much more likely than their public school counterparts to be racially harmonious, have few gangs, and have few verbal and physical threats against students. It is clear from the research that social scientists have undertaken that the moral and learning atmosphere in Evangelical and Catholic schools tends to be considerably different from that one would find in public schools (Jeynes, 2002d, 2003a).

RAMIFICATIONS OF THE EVIDENCE EXAMINED

Unquestionably, there is a plethora of evidence indicating that the presence or absence of a religious orientation, a religious or moral teaching, and a religious culture has a considerable impact on student behavioral and academic outcomes. Given the findings of this review, it becomes extremely hard to dismiss the correlation that exists between removal of prayer and moral education from the schools and the sudden surge in delinquent behavior. Meta-analyses, studies based on nationwide data sets, and individual analyses all indicate that there is a relationship between a personal and/or school religious orientation and favorable student behavioral and academic outcomes. Given this overwhelming evidence, the question arises as to why American schools insist on a secularist agenda that often exhibits disdain for Christian commitment and values, such as abstinence. The reason clearly is not the preference of the American people. Once again, one should recall that Gallup and Harris polls indicate that about 75 percent of Americans want voluntary prayer in the schools, in the form of a moment of silence (rather than teacher-led prayers). They do not support a school environment that is hostile to religion. Instead, the reasons are more likely to reside in the liberal bent of several Supreme Court justices and in many of the nation's educators, as well as the fact in the last few decades the United States often does not function as a democracy or a republic but a form of government catering to the litigious and the iconoclastic (Barton, 1990; Bryk, Lee, & Holland, 1993; Cochran, 1992, 1993; Coleman & Hoffer, 1987; Jeynes, 1999, 2003c).

Unfortunately, the United States is paying a huge price for its insistence on turning its back on God. This is not to say that the removal of prayer and moral teaching from the public schools was solely or even overwhelmingly responsible for the sudden surge in delinquent behavior beginning in 1963. Clearly, there was a concurrent decline in the moral climate in the nation as a whole during this period. Given this fact, one can argue that the Supreme Court's decision to remove prayer out of the school also likely reflected the moral decay that had occurred at least among members of the American judiciary. Nevertheless, it is interesting that the soaring crime rate beginning in 1963 was largely a juvenile phenomenon and that would certainly lead one to believe that the removal of prayer and moral education had an impact (Barton, 1990; Jeynes, 2010, in press; Wirtz, 1977).

Religious faith, which in the United States is in overwhelming numbers primarily the Christian faith, clearly has an ameliorative impact on student behavioral and academic outcomes. That being the case, one would think that political leaders, social scientists, and educators would do all that they can to encourage religious faith. However, one can argue that many of these individuals do just the reverse. Academics, public educators, and other leaders often frown on the Christian faith and other beliefs and often make it more difficult for people of faith to practice their faith freely in the public sphere. Once again, there is likely a cause and effect relationship present, and consequently one can argue that the United States is currently in a vicious circle. That is, once prayer and moral education were removed by the schools, moral behavior declined. Then, over time, as moral behavior declined, people developed more of an aversion to religious people. After all, among those who engage in promiscuous and delinquent behavior, religion is seen as an obstacle that discourages people from doing what they truly want to do (Decter, 1995; Jeynes, 1998; Olasky, 1988).

The evidence that is ostensible regarding the influence of religious faith and a moral orientation on student behavior and achievement indicates that Americans should encourage and not discourage the practice of religious faith. Moral education and religious faith appear to influence a wide spectrum of behaviors and practices. The nation can only benefit from this influence. The evidence appears undeniable that the United States would benefit from moral education and greater religious freedom in the schools.

REFERENCES

Abington Township v. Schempp, 374 U.S. 203 (1963).

Albrecht, S. L., Chadwick, B. A., & Alcorn, D. (1977). Religiosity and deviance: Application of an attitude-behavior contingent consistency model. *Journal for the Scientific Study of Religion, 16*, 263–274.

Alley, R. S. (1994). *School prayer: The Court, the Congress, and the First Amendment*. Buffalo: Prometheus.

American Association of University Women Educational Foundation. (1992). *The AAUW report: How schools shortchange girls*. Washington, D.C.: The AAUW Educational Foundation and National Educational Association.

Armbruster, F. E. (1977). *Our children's crippled future*. New York: New York Times.

Bahr, S. J., Hawks, R. D., & Wang, G. (1993). Family and religious influences on adolescent substance abuse. *Youth and Society, 24* (4), 443–465.

Baier, C. J., & Wright, B. R. (2001). If you love me, keep my commandments. *Journal of Research in Crime & Delinquency, 38* (1), 3–21.

Baker, D. P. (1998). The "eliting" of the common American Catholic school and the national education crisis. *Phi Delta Kappan, 80* (1), 16–23.

———. (1999). It's not about the failure of Catholic schools: It's about demographic transformations. *Phi Delta Kappan, 79* (8), 6–12.

Barton, D. (1990). *Our godly heritage (video).* Aledo, TX: Wallbuilders.

———. (2004). *Four centuries of American education.* Aledo, TX: Wallbuilders.

Beck, S. H., Cole, B. S., & Hammond, J. A. (1991). Religious heritage and premarital sex: Evidence from a national sample of adults. *Journal for the Scientific Study of Religion, 30,* 173–180.

Bennett, W. J. (1983). Authority, discipline, excellence. In R. Reagan, W. Bennett, & E. W. Lefever (Eds.), *Reinvigorating our schools.* Washington, D.C.: Ethics & Public Policy Center.

Bicknese, A. (1999). The Teen Challenge drug treatment program in comparative perspective (Doctoral Dissertation: Northwestern University). DAI-A 60/06-2203.

Blanshard, P. (1963). *Religion and the schools.* Boston, MA: Beacon Press.

Blessing for Life. (2002). *Prayer in the schools.* Retrieved June 11, 2002 from www.blessingsforlife.com.

Brown, B., & Merritt, R. (2002). *No easy answers: The truth behind death at Columbine.* New York: Lantern Books.

Brownfield, D., & Sorenson, A. (1991). Religion and drug use among adolescents: A social support conceptualization and interpretation. *Deviant Behavior, 12* (3), 259–276.

Bryan, J. W., & Freed, F. W. (1993). Abortion research: Attitudes, sexual behavior, and problems in a community college population. *Journal of Youth & Adolescence, 22* (1), 1–22.

Bryk, A., Lee, V., & Holland, P. (1993). *Catholic schools and the common good.* Cambridge, MA: Harvard University Press.

Burkett, S., & White, M. (1974). Hellfire and delinquency: Another look. *Journal for the Scientific Study of Religion, 13* (4), 455–462.

Carlston, L. (2004). *Surviving Columbine.* Salt Lake City, UT: Deseret.

Casserly, M., Herbert, V., Raymond, J., Etzoni, A., & Shanker, A. (1985). Discipline: The political football. In Beatrice & Ronald Gross (Eds.), *The great school debate.* New York: Simon & Schuster.

Central Intelligence Agency. (2006). *World fact book.* Washington, D.C.: Central Intelligence Agency.

Christianity.com. (2002).

Chubb, J. E., & Moe, T. M. (1990). *Politics, markets, and America's schools.* Washington, D.C.: Brookings Institute.

Clearly, T. A., & McCandless, S. A. (1976). *Summary of score changes (in other tests).* Princeton, NJ: Educational Testing Service.

Cochran, J. K. (1992). The effect of religiosity on adolescent self-reported frequency of drug and alcohol use. *Journal of Drug Issues, 22* (1), 91–104.

———. (1993). The variable effects of religiosity and denomination on adolescent self-reported alcohol use by beverage type. *Journal of Drug Issues, 23* (3), 479–491.

Cochran, J. K., Beeghley, L., & Bock, W. E. (1992). The influence of religious stability and homogamy on the relationship between religiosity and alcohol use among Protestants. *Journal for the Scientific Study of Religion*, 31 (4), 441–456.

Coleman, J., Hoffer, T., & Kilgore, S. (1982). *High school achievement: Public, Catholic, and private schools compared.* New York: Basic Books.

Coleman, J. S. (1988). "Social capital" and schools: One reason for higher private school achievement. *Education Digest, 53,* 6–9.

Coleman, L. (2004). *The copycat effect.* New York: Paraview.

Cooperman, P., in National Committee on Excellence in Education. (1985). A nation at risk. In B. Gross & R. Gross (Eds.), *The great school debate.* New York: Simon & Schuster.

Corwyn, R. F., Benda, B. B., & Ballard, K. (1997). Do the same theoretical factors explain alcohol and other drug use among adolescents? *Alcoholism Treatment Quarterly, 15* (4), 47–62.

Curtin, J., Lang, A. R., Patrick, C. J., & Stritzke, W. G. K. (1998). Alcohol and fear-potential competing cognitive demands in the stress-reducing effects of intoxication. *Journal of Abnormal Psychology, 107,* 547–557.

Davidson, J. K., Darling, C. A., & Norton, L. (1995). Religiosity and the sexuality of women: Sexual behavior and sexual satisfaction revisited. *Journal of Sex Research, 32* (3), 235–243.

Decter, M. (1995). A Jew in Anti-Christian America. *First Things, 56* (10), 25–31.

Dembo, Y., Levin, I., & Siegler, R. S. (1997). A comparison of the geometric reasoning of students attending Israeli ultraorthodox and mainstream schools. *Developmental Psychology, 33,* 92–103.

Dijkstra, A., & Peschar, J. L. (1996). Religious determinants of academic achievement in the Netherlands. *Comparative Education Review, 40,* 47–65.

Dominion School. (2002). n.t. Retrieved June 11, 2002 fromwww.dominionschool .com/mewstud.pdf.

Engel v. Vitale, 370 U.S. 421 (1962).

Evans, D. T., Cullen, F. T., & Burton, V. S., Jr. (1996). Religion, social bonds, and delinquency. *Deviant Behavior, 17* (1), 43–70.

Florida Department of Corrections (2000). *Comparing Tomoka Correctional Institution's faith-based dorm (Kairos Horizons) with non-participants.* Tallahassee, FL: Bureau of Research and Data analysis.

Fowler, R. B. (1999). *Enduring liberalism: American political thought since the 1960s.* Lawrence, KS: University of Kansas Press.

Francis, L. J. (1997). The impact of personality and religion on attitude towards substance use among 13–15 year olds. *Drug and Alcohol Dependence, 44* (2/3), 95–103.

Free, M. D. (1994). Religiosity, religious conservatism, bonds to school, and juvenile delinquency among three categories of drug users. *Deviant Behavior, 15* (2), 151–170.

Gatto, J. T. (2001). *The underground history of American education.* New York: Oxford Village Press.

Gaziel, H. H. (1997). Impact of school culture on effectiveness of secondary schools with disadvantaged students. *Journal of Educational Research, 90* (5), 310–318.

Gewirtz, S., Ball, S., & Bowe, R. (1995). *Markets, choice, and equity in education.* Buckingham: Open University.

Hall, S. (1986). Hispanics and Catholic schools. *Education Digest, 51,* 48–50.

Halpern, C. T., Udry, J. R., Campbell, B., Suchindran, C., et al. (1994). Testosterone and religiosity as predictors of sexual attitudes and activity among adolescent males: A biological model. *Journal of Biosocial Science, 26* (2), 217–234.

Hardy, J., & Vieler-Porter, C. (1995). Race, schooling, and the 1988 Education Reform Act. In M. Flude & M. Hammer (Eds.), *The Education Reform Act, 1988: Its origins and implications* (pp. 173–185). London: Falmer Press.

Harman, D. (1987). *Illiteracy: A national dilemma.* New York: Cambridge Book Company.

Hirschi, T., & Stark, R. (1969). Hellfire and delinquency. *Social Problems, 17* (2), 202–213.

House Committee on the Judiciary. (1962). Hearings before the Committee on the Judiciary, 1962, p. 140.

———. (1995). Hearings on religious freedom in the schools. Washington, D.C.: U.S. House of Representatives.

Hudolin, G. J. (1994). Lessons from Catholic schools: Promoting quality in Chicago's public schools. *Educational Forum, 58* (3), 282–288.

Irvine, J. M. (2002). *Talk about sex.* Berkeley, CA: University of California Press.

Jackson, L. E., & Coursey, R. D. (1988). The relationship between God control and internal locus of control to intrinsic religious motivation, coping, and purpose in life. *Journal for the Scientific Study of Religion, 27*, 399–410.

Jang, S. J., & Johnson, B. R. (2001). Neighborhood disorder, individual religiosity, and adolescent use of illicit drugs: A test of multilevel hypotheses. *Criminology, 39* (1), 109–143.

Jeremiah Project. (2002). n.t. (www.jeremiahproject.com).

Jeynes, W. (1998). Are America's public educational institutions anti-religious? *Education, 119* (1), 172–175.

———. (1999). The effects of religious commitment on the academic achievement of black and Hispanic children. *Urban Education, 34* (4), 458–479.

———. (2002a). A meta-analysis of the effects of attending religious schools and religiosity on black and Hispanic academic achievement. *Education & Urban Society, 35* (1), 27–49.

———. (2002b). Educational policy and the effects of attending a religious school on the academic achievement of children. *Educational Policy, 16* (3), 406–424.

———. (2002c). The relationship between the consumption of various drugs by adolescents and their academic achievement. *The American Journal of Drug and Alcohol Abuse, 28* (1), 1–21.

———. (2002d). Why religious schools positively impact the academic achievement of children. *International Journal of Education and Religion, 3* (1), 16–32.

———. (2003a). *Religion, education, and academic success.* Greenwich, CT: Information Age Press.

———. (2003b). The effects of black and Hispanic twelfth graders living in intact families and being religious on their academic achievement. *Urban Education, 38* (1), 35–57.

———. (2003c). The effects of religious commitment on the academic achievement of urban and other children. *Education & Urban Society, 36* (1), 44–62.

———. (2003d). The effects of religious commitment on the attitudes and behavior of teens regarding premarital childbirth. *Journal of Health and Social Policy, 17* (1), 1–17.

———. (2004a). A meta-analysis: Has the academic impact of religious schools changed over the last twenty years? *Journal of Empirical Theology, 17* (2), 197–216.

————. (2004b). Comparing the influence of religion on education in the United States and overseas: A meta-analysis. *Religion & Education, 31* (2), 1–15.

————. (2006). Adolescent religious commitment and their consumption of marijuana, cocaine, and alcohol. *Journal of Health and Social Policy, 21* (4), 1–20.

————. (2007). *American educational history: School, society and the common good.* Thousand Oaks, CA: Sage Press.

————. (2010, in press). The relationship between Bible literacy and behavioral and academic outcomes in urban areas: A meta-analysis. *Education & Urban Society.*

Johnson, B. R. (2002). Assessing the effectiveness of religion and faith-based organizations: A systematic review. Center for Research on Religion and Urban Civil Society (CRRUCS Report 2002-1). University of Pennsylvania, and the Center for Civil Innovation, Manhattan Institute: Manhattan, New York.

Johnson, B. R., Li, S. D., Larson, D. B., & McCullough, M. (2000). A systematic review of religiosity & delinquency literature: A research note. *Journal of Contemporary Criminal Justice, 16* (1), 32–52.

Johnson, B. R., Jang, S. J., & Li, L. S. (2000). The invisible institution and black youth crime: The church as an agency of local social control. *Journal of Youth & Adolescence, 29* (4), 479–496.

Johnson, S. (1992). Extra-school factors in achievement, attainment, and aspiration among junior and senior high school-age African American youth. *Journal of Negro Education, 61* (1), 99–119.

Kliebard, H. M. (1969). *Religion and education in America.* Scranton, PA: International Textbook Company.

Koenig, H. G. (1993). Religion and aging. *Reviews in Clinical Gerontology, 3* (2), 195–203.

————. (1999). *The healing power of faith.* New York: Simon & Schuster.

Koenig, H. G., McCullough, M. E., & Larson, D. B. (2001). *Handbook of Religion and Health.* New York: Oxford University Press.

Kopka, D. L. (1997). *School violence: A reference handbook.* Santa Barbara: ABC-CLIO.

Koubek, R. J. (1984). Correlation between religious commitment and students' achievement. *Psychological Reports, 54,* 262.

Kozol, J. (1985). *Illiterate America.* Garden City, NY: Anchor.

Lee, V., & Bryk, A. (1993). *Catholic schools and the common good.* Cambridge, MA: Harvard University Press.

Lee, V. E. (1987). Minorities in Catholic schools: Why do they read better? *Education Digest, 52,* 20–23.

LePore, P. C., & Warren, J. R. (1997). A comparison of single-sex and coeducational Catholic secondary schooling: Evidence from the National Educational Longitudinal Study of 1988. *American Educational Research Journal, 34* (3), 485–511.

Libertocracy. (2002). *Web essays.* Retrieved June 11, 2002 fromwww.libertocracy.com/webessays/religion/persecution.

Lock, S. E., & Vincent, M. (1995). Sexual decision-making among rural adolescent females. *Health and Values, 19* (1), 47–58.

Louisell, D. (1964). The Supreme Court and the first amendment. *Yale Law Journal, 73,* 990–994.

Marantha Christian Journal. (1999). Alabama school stops student from wearing cross (www.mcjonline.com).

Marsch, H. W. (1991). Public, Catholic single-sex, and Catholic coeducational high schools: Their effects on achievement, affect, and behaviors. *American Journal of Education, 99* (3), 320–356.

Matera, D. (2001). *A cry for character.* Paramus, NJ: Prentice Hall.

Matusow, A. J. (1984). *The unraveling of America.* New York: Harper & Row.

McCollum v. Board of Education, Dist. 71, 333 U.S. 203 (1947).

McEwen, A., Knipe, D., & Gallagher, T. (1997). The impact of single-sex and coeducational schooling on participation and achievement in science: A 10-year perspective. *Research in Science and Technological Education, 15* (2), 223–233.

McFarlane, A. C. (1998). Epidemiological evidence about the relationship between PTSD and alcohol abuse: The nature of the association. *Addictive Behaviors, 23* (6), 813–825.

Meier, M. M. (2002). *Understanding the school prayer issue and the related character education and charter school movements.* Pittsburgh, PA: Dorrance Publishing.

Melody, M. E., & Peterson, L. M. (1999). *Teaching America about sex.* New York: New York University Press.

Mentzer, M. S. (1988). Religion and achievement motivation in the United States: A structural analysis. *Sociological Focus, 21,* 307–316.

Michaelsen, R. (1970). *Piety in the public school.* London: Macmillan.

Miles, B. (2004) *Hippie.* New York: Sterling Press.

Miller, B. C., & Olson, T. D. (1988). Sexual attitudes and behavior of high school students relation to background and contextual factors. *Journal of Sex Research, 24* (1), 194–200.

Morris, A. (1994). The academic performance of Catholic schools. *School Organization, 14* (1), 81–89.

Moynihan, D. P. (1989). What the Congress can do when the Court is wrong. In E. M. Gaffney (Ed.), *Private schools and the public good* (pp. 79–84). Notre Dame: Notre Dame Press.

Murphy, J. (1990). Class inequality in education. In I. McNay & J. Ozga (Eds.), *Policy-making in education: The breakdown of consensus* (pp. 315–333). Oxford, England: Pergamon Press.

Murray v. Curlett, 374 U.S. 203 (1963).

Murray, W. (1982). *My life without God.* Nashville: Thomas Nelson Publishers.

Murry-McBride, V. (1996). An ecological analysis of coital timing among middle-class African American adolescent females. *Journal of Adolescent Research, 11* (2), 261–279.

National Catholic Almanac, 59 (3), 69.

Neal, D. A. (1997). The effects of Catholic secondary schooling on educational achievement. *Journal of Labor Economics, 15,* 98–123.

Newman, K. S. (2004). *Rampage: The social roots of school shootings.* New York: Basic Books.

Nicholas, L. J., & Durrheim, K. (1996). Validity of Rohrbaugh and Jessor religiosity scale. *Discourse Processes, 13,* 89–90.

Nord, W. A. (1995). *Religion and American education.* Chapel Hill, NC: University of North Carolina Press.

O'Conner, T. (2001). From prison to the free world: An evaluation of an aftercare program in Detroit, Michigan. Maryland: Center for Social Research.

Olasky, M. N. (1988). *Prodigal press: The anti-Christian bias of the American news media.* Westchester, IL: Crossway Books.

O'Neill, W. L. (1971). *Coming apart: An informal history of America in the 1960s.* Chicago, IL: Quadrangle.

Reed v. Van Hoven, 237 F. Supp. 48 (W.D. Mich. 1965).

Religious Tolerance. (2002). *News* (www.religioustolerance.org).

Riley, R. W. (1996). Promoting involvement in learning. *Professional Psychology: Research and Practice, 27* (1), 3–4.

Rock of God. (2002). *Pressroom.* Retrieved from www.rockofgod.org/pressroom.html.

Sander, W. (1996). Catholic grade schools and academic achievement. *Journal of Human Resources, 31,* 540–548.

Sandin, R. T. (1992). *The rehabilitation of virtue: Foundations of moral education.* New York: Praeger.

Scott, D., & Nimmo, B. (2000). *Rachel's tears.* Nashville, TN: Thomas Nelson.

Sikorski, R. (1993). *Controversies in constitutional law.* New York: Garland.

Spin-Tech. (1999). *Spin-Tech letters to the editor.* Retrieved June 11, 2002 from www.spintech.mag.com.

Sykes, C. (1995). *Dumbing down our kids*. New York: St. Martin's Press.

Toch, T., Gest, T., & Guttman, M. (November 8, 1993). Violence in schools. *U.S. News & World Report, 115* (18).

Tocqueville, A. (1966). *Democracy in America*. New York: Harper & Row.

U.S. Census Bureau. (2001). *Census 2000*. Washington, D.C.: U.S. Census Bureau.

U.S. Department of Education. (2001). *Digest of education statistics*. Washington, D.C.: U.S. Department of Education.

U.S. Department of Health and Human Services. (1998). *Statistical abstracts of the United States*. Washington, D.C.: Department of Health and Human Services.

U.S. Department of Justice. (1999). *Age-specific arrest rate and race-specific arrest rates for selected offenses, 1965–1992*. Washington, D.C.: U.S. Department of Justice.

Vitz, P. (1994). In J. Kennedy (Ed.), *The hidden agenda (video)*. Ft. Lauderdale, FL: Coral Ridge Presbyterian Church.

Wirtz, W. (1977). *On further examination*. New York: College Entrance Examination Board.

Young, M. C., Gartner, J., O'Conner, T., Larson, D. B., & Wright, K. (1995). Long-term recidivism among federal inmates trained as volunteer prison ministers. *Journal of Offender Rehabilitation, 22*, 97–118.

Zoba, W. M. (2000). *Day of reckoning: Columbine & the search for the American soul*. Grand Rapids, MI: Brazos Press.

Zorach v. Clauson, 343 U.S. 306 (1952).

2

THE SCHOOLS OF EDUCATIONAL PHILOSOPHY

THE HISTORY OF CHARACTER EDUCATION AS MANIFESTED IN THE PHILOSOPHY OF EDUCATION

An overwhelming number of educational historians credit Plato with being the first to advocate a system of schools to educate the populace. It is both insightful and profoundly important that Plato declared that moral education was the most essential aspect of the school curriculum. For about 2,000 years following the life of Plato, virtually every educational philosopher affirmed Plato's views about the primacy of character instruction and in many cases asserted that it needed to be in even a more eminent place than Plato proposed. One indispensable way of procuring a superior understanding of the place of moral education in the curriculum is to inquire into the place it held in schools historically (Dupuis, 1966; Marrou, 1956).

Most commonly, the history of philosophy of education is divided into six schools of thought: (1) the Greeks, (2) the Romans, (3) the Early Christians, (4) the Renaissance Humanists, (5) the Early Liberals, and (6) the Later Liberals. Educational philosophers generally classify the first four schools as conservative and the later two as being liberal. Each of the six schools of thought contributed to educational change in one way or another. The significance of each of these schools of thought is best comprehended if one is first cognizant of the four most recognized schools of thought in the philosophy of education.

The Four Primary Schools of Thought in the Philosophy of Education

Philosophers generally recognize four primary schools of thought within educational philosophy, two of them conservative and two of them liberal. They are as follows:

Perennialism: Of the four philosophies of education, this is the most conservative school of thought as well as the oldest. This perspective burgeoned during the era of Plato and Aristotle. Perennialists maintain that there are various permanent values and goals that exist throughout time and place. They frequently point to mathematical and scientific axioms to attempt to prove their point. Perennialists aver that the teaching and application of these principles is a prerequisite to success in education (Walker, 1963).

Essentialism: Supporters of this perspective affirm that a more limited number of educational values and goals exist that are permanent and established as absolute truths (Walker, 1963). Essentialists assert that "progressive education has failed to follow established patterns but should try to get back on the right track by teaching those things that are necessary" (Walker, p. 10).

Progressivism is a moderately liberal perspective that emerged during the late nineteenth and twentieth centuries. Progressives opine that schools should transform as society changes, in order to address the needs of modern day society. Progressives assert that the world is in a state of constant flux and therefore teachers need to adjust their educational practices accordingly, including their values (Dupuis, 1966).

Reconstructionism is the most liberal approach of the four schools of thought. Advocates of this perspective believe that education should be used to "reconstruct the social order" (Walker, p. 7). Moreover, many theorists of this viewpoint believe that schools are the ideal vehicle to seek to change the views of people, because they have not yet established convictions about how they should live.

PLATO

Plato (427–347 BC) was the philosopher who first propounded the idea of an education system. The concept was first spawned in his mind through being a blessed recipient of the tutelage of Socrates. Plato was awakened by Socrates's beatific knowledge and wisdom. Plato concluded that it would be a wonderful development indeed if people throughout Greece could benefit from the sagacity of prominent teachers such as Socrates. In Plato's eyes, as vital as it was for students to gain from Socrates's scholastic learning, it was even more important for them to learn from his wisdom. Plato believed that Socrates's listeners would not only learn from his perceptive acumen but also from his life (Dupuis, 1966).

Under the Greek school of thought, Plato developed the idea of widespread schools. As a student of Socrates, he believed that society would benefit if students were exposed to wise and brilliant instructors such as Socrates. Plato developed a classical curriculum that included math, the reading of the classics, civics, science, music, art, and physical education (what Plato termed gymnastic). The fact that Aristotle supported Plato's rubric enhanced its support among the Greek. Moreover, Isocrates's efforts to spread Plato's schools across Greece increased the popularity of Plato's model (Dupuis, 1966; Marrou, 1956).

With this framework in mind, Plato founded a school, the Academy, to serve as a place where these kinds of learning could take place. Plato asserted that there were three particular reasons why education was so vital. First, he believed that Greek lacked leaders who could guide the people both at a practical and at a moral level. Schools, he believed, could instruct leaders and enable them to become people of character. He also averred that schools could equip future national representatives with many of the qualities they needed to flourish as leaders (Klein, 1965; Plato, 2000, 2004).

Second, Plato believed that schools should serve as a source of character education. Plato claimed a nation was only as strong as the character of its people. He claimed that it was even more important for a nation to have a people of character than it was for the citizenry to be intelligent. His reasoning was that character gave proper guidance to intelligence. Wise citizenries generally possessed wise leaders and this produced a strong country (Plato, 2000, 2004).

A third reason Plato envisioned for schools is that they helped prevent division among various factors of society. Plato asserted that it was vital for schools to teach individuals how to put themselves in the shoes of others so that factionalism would decrease. In Plato's view, people of character were not unnecessarily divisive (Plato, 2000, 2004).

Plato believed that character instruction was the centerpiece of education. As John Elias (1995, p. 41) notes, "Since antiquity the development of the moral or virtuous person has been the primary aim of education."

The central nature of virtue and the declaration that it can be taught are examined by Socrates in Plato's classic book *Meno*. The book focuses on the question of whether virtue can be taught.

In *Meno*, Socrates systematically urges his listeners to continuously examine and seek to purify their souls. Socrates further argues that there were myriad absolute rights and wrongs that instructors needed to teach and students needed to internalize. To the Greeks, as Elias (1995, p. 46) states, "Moral truth like all truth is absolute. There are unchanging moral values, and moral absolutes." The Greeks were well known for divulging and proving various and sundry mathematical truths through the likes of Pythagoras and Euclid (Plato, 2004).

The essence of the Greek argument regarding absolutes was as follows: There are a plethora of mathematical and scientific truths that are immutable. The prime numbers, for example, do not change. The square root of 2 is always the same (more than 1.4) and the square root of 3 is also always the same. Although it may vary a little with altitude, the overall boiling point of water is consistently the same. The speed of light and sound are also quite consistent. The Greeks did not believe that everything was "black" and "white." They asserted that there was room for gray as well. Nevertheless, the Greek averred that it was a complete fallacy to claim that everything was gray or relative. Moreover, Plato argued that although he had met many individuals who claimed to be relativists, he had never actually met one. According to Plato, the reason why is because every person has absolute values somewhere. For example, in modern society one might claim that he or she has no absolutes. One can then respond by asking, "Do you believe that racism is wrong?" The other person then replies, "Oh yes, absolutely." This person's belief about racism is therefore an absolute value.

Plato conceptualized moral education in such a way that he not only viewed it as a subject in its own right but also viewed it as inextricably connected with any number of subjects. Elias (1995) observes that Plato believed that it was a mistake to view moral instruction as in a totally separate sphere from the remainder of the curriculum. He even assayed that participation in sports had moral value particularly when it did not involve competitive sports (Elias, 1995). Plato also contended that one's intellectual and occupational potential could rise only so far as that person's character (May, 1988; Plato, 2000). Plato viewed wisdom and truth as inextricably connected. In his classic work, *Republic*, Plato stated,

"And is there anything more closely connected than wisdom and truth?" (Plato, 2000, p. 62). Plato believed that one's ability to think, speak, communicate, and succeed were all dependent on the condition of the human heart (Klein, 1965; May, 1988). He states, "Entire ignorance is not so terrible or extreme in evil, and is far from being the greatest of all; too much cleverness and too much learning, accompanied with ill bringing-up, are far more fatal" (Plato, 2004, p. 34) and "to do injustice is the greatest of all evils" (Plato, 1979).

In Plato's eyes, it was vital that a healthy society value virtue and morality above everything else. In Plato's *Republic* he declared, "All the gold which is under or upon the earth is not enough to give in exchange for virtue" (Plato, 2004, p. 24). He also asserted, "Good actions give strength to ourselves and inspire good actions in others" (Plato, 2009, p. 3). From Plato's perspective, one could be the most knowledgeable citizen in Greece, but unless one's intellect was guided by wisdom trouble would result. Plato (2009, p. 6) observed, "knowledge becomes evil if the aim be not virtuous." In Plato's eyes, wisdom made one humble, serving, and discerning. He stated, "He who is not a good servant will not be a good master" (Plato, 2009, p. 1). The idea was that there were many people who were knowledgeable but they did not possess the wisdom to best utilize that knowledge. Moreover, although the possession of a great deal of information often makes one proud, wisdom sobers one and enables him to be humble even though he has obtained an impressive degree of knowledge. Without wisdom, knowledge was useless and could produce much evil. With wisdom, knowledge could yield a great deal of good. Plato (2009, p. 1) stated, "The wisest have the most authority." Unfortunately, according to Plato, most people did not value wisdom as highly as they should. He declared, "There are three classes of men; lovers of wisdom, lovers of honor, and lovers of gain" (Plato, 2009, p. 7).

Plato believed that it was important for all people to have wisdom, but it was particularly key for leaders. Leaders set the tone for entire nation and served as examples for others to follow. Plato averred that knowledge might enable a person to obtain power, but wisdom guided the leader to best know how to implement that power. Plato (2009, p. 5) states, "The measure of man is what he does with power." In Plato's eyes, power often caused people to act abruptly and insensitively with little regard to how one's actions affected surrounding people. Plato believed that part of the wisdom was acting kindly toward other people. Plato (2009, p. 3) asserted, "Be kind, for everyone you meet is fighting a battle." As much as Plato argued for the presence of wise leaders, he was nevertheless quick to acknowledge that there were very few wise people. Plato (2009, p. 4) stated, "A hero is born among a hundred, a wise man is found among a thousand."

Plato's ideas about a nationwide system of schools were noteworthy enough so that another Greek philosopher, Isocrates, started schools based on Plato's model across much of Greece. Throughout the course of educational history, there have usually been those who generate schooling ideas and then others who develop the rubric propounded by the originator. Isocrates applied Plato's ideas in this way (Jeynes, 2007).

Aristotle (384–322 BC), a student of Plato, became one of Greece's two most respected philosophers. Aristotle and Plato generally agreed on most matters. However, the degree to which they agreed on the centrality of character education was monumental and helped the Greek people to embrace its importance. Elias (1995, p. 45) asserts, "For Aristotle, virtue is not inborn but rather a consequence of training." When the Greek people observed that their two esteemed philosophers agreed on the primacy of moral education, it served to secure the place of character education in the classical school curriculum (Jeynes, 2007).

In Aristotle's mind "prudence is the keystone of all virtues" (Elias, 1995, p. 45). In positing this belief, Aristotle made a salient distinction between wisdom and knowledge. This was an important declaration because the Greeks often idolized knowledge and did not sufficiently honor wisdom. Aristotle (1985) believed that wisdom was even more important than knowledge. Nevertheless, Aristotle maintained that wisdom found the most fertile ground in the intelligent and knowledgeable individual. Consequently, wisdom could reach its pinnacle of expression in knowledgeable individuals. Therefore, Aristotle stated that one should seek both wisdom and knowledge (Aristotle, 1985).

Aristotle maintained that in order for good character to thrive in individuals, teachers needed to ensure that godly habits emerge in the hearts and lives of children. To Aristotle, for good character to truly thrive it needed to be consistent in each individual's life, and this was possible only to the extent that good habits were established (Aristotle, 1941, 1985; Elias, 1995).

Because Aristotle, like Socrates and Plato before him, averred that virtue could be taught, he maintained that good habits abetted all types of learning, including both intellectual and moral training. Many centuries later,

William James would propound a theory similar to this, with a particular emphasis on academic training (Aristotle, 1941, 1985).

ROMAN SCHOOL OF THOUGHT AND CICERO

Cicero (106–43 BC) and Quintilian (AD 35–100) led the Roman school of thought. Cicero, one of the greatest orators in history, was a resolute supporter of Plato's model of education. Cicero differed from Plato's approach in only two ways. First, he asserted that students should be taught to speak well. Second, he emphasized the primacy of virtue even more than Plato did. Quintilian, although lesser known than Cicero, contributed a great deal to defining many of the specific practices used in the schools today. Quintilian developed the practices of assigning term papers, recitation, and dividing up into small groups to discuss the lectures (Dupuis, 1966; Marrou, 1956).

Cicero adhered to the primacy of character instruction even more than Plato did. Cicero maintained that the most dangerous person in the world was one who was intelligent, but not virtuous. Cicero (2001) declared, "Virtue, we all admit, occupies the loftiest and most distinguished position in human life." Cicero believed that living a righteous life made one more efficacious in other aspects of his or her life, including the way he or she expressed oneself in the oral and written word. In other words, Cicero contended that the moral state of the heart ultimately impacted one's mental prowess and acumen. This declaration is particularly interesting because even to this day myriad experts regard Cicero as one of the greatest orators who ever lived. On this basis, one can make an argument that part of Cicero's success can be attributed to his purity of heart (Cicero, 2001; Cicero & Grose, 1966; Cicero & Higginbotham, 1967; Jeynes, 2007; May, 1988; Quintilian, 1922).

Cicero contended that one's character, that is, the moral condition of a person's heart, ultimately affected his or her actions. Moreover, Cicero emphasized virtue so much that he believed that only a person who had established a reputation of character was worthy of being elected to public office. Perhaps the most vital aspect of virtue, in Cicero's eyes, was to be on the side of right. Cicero saw a vivid distinction between the forces of good and evil. Strong character was ultimately determined by the extent to which one was on the side of good (Cicero, 2001; Cicero & Grose, 1966; May, 1988). Cicero (in May, 1988, p. 55) asserts:

On our side fights modesty, on their side shamelessness; on our side morality, on theirs debauchery; on our good faith, on theirs deceit; on ours
respect for right, on theirs crime; on ours steadfastness, on theirs madness;
on ours honor, on theirs disgrace; on ours self-control, on theirs a surrender
to passion; in short justice, temperance, fortitude, prudence, all the virtues,
contend with injustice, extravagance, cowardice, folly, all the vices. In a
word abundance fights against poverty, incorrupt principles against corrupt, sanity against insanity, well founded hope against general desperation.

Rolfe (1963, p. 65) states, "Oratory was, in fact, the mainstream of his
[Cicero] career, and his efforts to perfect himself as a speaker were
thorough and unremitting. He made a careful study of rhetoric, a subject
on which he made a number of epoch-making works." Regarding public
speaking, Cicero (2009, p. 2) insisted that in order to be an efficacious
orator, an individual must "have a firm foundation of general knowledge."
In order words, it is insufficient to practice eloquence and formidable
techniques of homiletics without cognizance and agile use of knowledge.
Concurrently, Cicero nevertheless believed that it was imperative for a
speaker to maximize the intensity and influence of one's message. Consequently, an orator needed to master both the content and the delivery of
any given speech in order to realize one's potential (Rolfe, 1963).

To accomplish the feat of being a strong orator took character because
progress in society was contingent on the articulate expression of the best ideas
and persuasive and accurate ideology being saturated in the presentation.
Because of the confluence of character, perspicacious ideas, and eloquent
expression, Cicero placed a great deal of emphasis on oratory. Rolfe (1963,
pp. 69–70) states, "Cicero was the first to give the proper finish to oratorical
style. He was the first to adopt a method of selection in the use of words to cultivate an artistic arrangement. He had learned by experiences and practice, the
qualities of the best type of oratory." Because of his adept study and elucidation
of profound concepts, Cicero soon emerged as such an accomplished speaker
that his name became equated with ethereal and dynamic oratory. Rolfe notes
that Cicero even surpassed the greatest of his predecessors "in careful arrangement of his material and by his great attention of elegance of diction, as well as
in variety of sentiments and vivacity of wit, Cicero is regarded as having
excelled Demosthenes" (Rolfe, 1963, pp. 69–70). One of the reasons why Cicero
was so successful is that he utilized a wide array of methods in his speeches.
He used wit, humor, and illustrations to enliven his talks (Cicero, 1991).

One of the reasons why Cicero's talks were so puissant is because he maintained that there were absolute truths that he convincingly needed to communicate. From Cicero's perspective the existence of God was self-evident. According to Rolfe (1963, p. 152), he believed "that the existence of God is to be inferred from the orderly arrangement of the universe." Cicero believed that one's conviction regarding the existence of virtue inspired one to deliver the best speeches. Hence, one should address character issues often when one speaks and personal virtue will also make a person a better speaker.

Cicero's declaration had a profound influence throughout the Roman Empire. No contemporary of Cicero's words had the impact of Cicero's. As Quintilian observes, "Cicero has come to be regarded not as the name of a man, but the name of eloquence itself" (Quintilian, 1922, pp. 111–112). In the Roman mind, the fact that Cicero was an eloquent spokesman had ramifications far beyond the sphere of oratory specifically. First, what proceeded from one's mouth reflected the moral state of one's heart. Consequently, the Romans believed that those individuals whose lives epitomized great character manifested this fact through eloquent speech. As May notes, "Oratory, by its very nature, involves character" (May, 1988, p. 162). Second, in order to be an efficacious orator one must be intelligent. From the Roman perspective, one could be intelligent only insofar as he was a person of virtue. Third, an eloquent individual was a person who had learned to be disciplined in his speech. To the Romans, if one could exercise impressive control over one's speech, this was one element of character. Fourth, in the minds of some Romans, fluent oratory indicated divine favor; and this ethereal blessing alighted on people of character. As Cicero (2009, p. 1) himself declared, "No one was ever so great without some portion of divine inspiration." From Cicero's perspective, God was willing to inspire because of His love for His creation. Cicero (2009, p. 1) averred, "Next to God we are nothing. To God we are everything."

EARLY CHRISTIAN THOUGHTS ON MORAL EDUCATION

The greatest contributions of the Christian school of thought, in terms of moral education, were related not only to the content of character education but also to the number of people reached by the instruction. Although the Greeks and the Romans before them viewed character education as extremely important, they conceptualized it as limited to leaders in a nation. In contrast, the Christians asserted that God's truths, which they contended were the basis of education, should be available to all people. The early Christians defined character education broadly. It encompassed not only biblical truths that facilitated salvation but all of God's truths that applied to everyday upright living (Cubberley, 1920, 1934; Jeynes, 2007; Marrou, 1956; Plato, 2000, 2004).

The early Christians maintained that it was imperative that the truths of the Bible be made available to all (Marrou, 1956). No longer was the emphasis simply to be on reaching the Jews, as it had been in the Old Testament period. Although Christians trace their roots to Judaism and consider Abraham (b. 1991 BC?) to be their spiritual earthly father, they believe the teachings of the Old Testament are best apprehended in light of the New Testament. Like the Jewish people, Christians follow the teachings of Abraham, Moses (b. 1526 BC?), David (1040–970 BC), and others, but given that they see Christ as God incarnate, it is Jesus Christ's teachings that are preeminent. Christ made it clear that God's truths were to be explicated to the ends of the earth (Holy Bible, Matthew 28:16–20). In Acts 1:8 of the Bible, Christ declares: "But you will receive power when the Holy Spirit comes on you; and you will be my witnesses in Jerusalem, and in all Judea and Samaria, and to the ends of the earth." Christ believed that everyone needed to be a beneficiary of moral tutelage. It was not to be limited merely to the elite, nor was it to be limited by gender, race, demographics, or religion. Palmer (2001, p. 21) states:

> Jesus' teaching style was egalitarian. This, in itself, would have attracted attention within a highly structured and class-conscious society. As bees to honey, the lower classes of Jews couldn't get enough of this Rabbi from Galilee. His message of hope for a new day of mercy and justice attracted the poor and the marginalized. Perhaps more influential than even these words was that Jesus treated everyone he encountered as having worth. His actions were congruent with his words.

The Apostle Paul echoed this belief that Christians needed to proclaim God's moral truths to all individuals. The belief that character education was to be taught to all human beings finds its roots in the early Christian belief that all human beings were equal. In Galatians 3:28 the Bible states: "There is neither Jew nor Greek, slave nor free, male nor female." As a result of this belief, 80 percent of the early Christians were either slaves or women (Dupuis, 1966). In contemporary America, such a declaration is merely consistent with the assertion in the Declaration of Independence that God created all humans equal. Nevertheless, at the time the assertion that all people were equal was considered revolutionary. Every culture in the world assumed that those who ruled were superior to their subjects, servants, and slaves. Whether one was an emperor, shogun, queen, king, or other type of leader, the belief that monarchs and dictators were superior to those in the general population was regarded as an undeniable axiom. Within this context, the Christian declaration that all humans were equal was considered a massive threat designed to instigate revolution. It is largely for this reason that there was widespread persecution of the church in the early centuries AD. Although Jesus in no way intended Christianity to be a political movement, but rather a spiritually renewing experience, myriad political leaders interpreted Christianity's assertion that all were equal as a viable and direct political threat. If there was a movement that could organize the masses against the political leadership, Christianity appeared to be the prime candidate (Dupuis, 1966; Gangel & Benson, 1983; Marrou, 1956).

It is from the Christian edict that all people are equal that proceeds the notion that teachers should instruct the entire populace. Moreover, the early Christians maintained that character training represented the most vital part of the curriculum They posited that although it was important for people to possess high levels of intelligence, whether a person was an individual of love and integrity was more important. Saint Augustine declared this was possible only if a person experienced a spiritual transformation. Augustine asserted that once a person had God in his or her heart, the love of God would flow out (Augustine & Howe, 1966; Dupuis, 1966; Holy Bible, Luke 10:27; I Corinthians 13:13; Marrou, 1956; Oates, 1948).

The early Christian school was founded on the biblical principles expounded by Jesus Christ, the Apostle Paul, and Augustine. Augustine taught that the teacher needed to reach out to the student in his or her condition and, as Palmer (2001, p. 28) notes, "offer encouragement." The early Christians supported the classical curriculum espoused by Plato. To the early Christians, however, the Bible was to be the central focus of the curriculum. This emphasis was because the Christians maintained that the Bible had the most spiritual and moral value of any aspect of the curriculum (Dupuis, 1966; Hunt & Maxson, 1981; Marrou, 1956).

THE RENAISSANCE HUMANISTS

The Renaissance Humanists, guided by Martin Luther (1483–1546), John Calvin (1509–1564), and Desiderius Erasmus (1466–1536), were strong advocates of character instruction. In contemporary society when one thinks of humanists, unbelievers come to one's mind. Centuries ago, however, humanists were often Christians. Luther and Calvin were concerned about how the reality of God related to the human experience (Dupuis, 1966; Harbison, 1964; Hitchcock, 1982).

Just as the early Christians emphasized a personal faith in Christ, the Renaissance Humanists maintained this focus well. They believed that in order for a person to experience a personal relationship with Christ, teachers needed to instruct their students in the Bible. As Dillenberger (1961, p. xxvii) notes, "The transition from unfaith to faith occurs through the Word." The Renaissance Humanists supported the same general curriculum model as the early Christians. The foremost contribution of the Renaissance Humanists is that they broadened the curriculum. In other words, before the Renaissance Humanists emerged, educators almost unanimously claimed that issues such as rape and incest were taboo and not appropriate for classroom instruction. The Renaissance Humanists averred that even the Bible examines these issues, instructing readers to avoid these behaviors. Therefore, as long as the instructors emphasized that these behaviors were wrong, they should engage in sharing about these realities (Dillenberger, 1961; Dupuis, 1966; Harbison, 1964).

The Views of Martin Luther

Luther believed that teachers should emphasize grace and faith in the curriculum. In Luther's eyes, grace and faith were the most salient qualities that children were to be taught. As Dillenberger observes, "In faith, man stands before God in the light of grace." In addition, Dillenberger (p. xxviii) states, "The life of faith is the mode of existence which finds its vital source and center in God's forgiving and renewing grace." In his *Preface to the New Testament*, Martin Luther (1999/1546, p. 1) stated the following, "Understand this, that a man is given righteousness, life, and salvation by faith." Luther received a doctor of theology from the University of Wittenberg and became both a preacher and a professor. For centuries, this was a common occupational combination (Jeynes, 2007).

In order to edify students in the truths of grace, faith, and other spiritual truths, Luther urges educators to place the Bible at the center of the curriculum. He felt particularly comfortable in making this assertion because most schools were run by churches. He declared, "The first duty of a preacher of the gospel is to declare God's law and the nature of sin. Everything is sinful that does not proceed from the spirit" (Luther, 1956, p. 271).

To Luther, the Bible was the chief means of fostering student righteousness and helping them eschew wrongs often associated with youth. Luther believed in dualism, asserting that humans had a "two fold nature, a spiritual and bodily one" (Dillenberger, 1961, p. 53). Luther believed that a student's study of the Bible helped ensure that one's spiritual nature would predominate over bodily one. In Luther's mind, whichever was "fed" the most, the spirit or the flesh (the typical Christian spiritual expression for the body), would eventually prevail. Luther hoped that children would internalize what they learned from the Bible to such a degree that it would influence not only the most overt actions but also their most secret sins. From Luther's perspective, the overt expressions of sin were much more easily dealt with than one's secret actions. To adequately deal with this level of behavior, youth needed to be intimately familiar with the "Word of God" (Dillenberger, 1961; Luther, 1956).

Martin Luther, like the early Christians before him, believed that moral education should not only be an important component of the school curriculum but it should be spiritually enlightening. In other words, Luther envisioned morality as inextricably connected with drawing closer to God. Luther like so many of his Christian and Roman predecessors believed that morality was a spiritual issue. Therefore, he claimed that the essence of character instruction must be spiritual (Dillenberger, 1961; Luther, 1956).

Luther's belief was that teachers must repeatedly incorporate a God-centered orientation. This would teach students to rely on God for character. In Luther's view, this reliance on God was rooted in a dependence on the grace of God. The Protestant Reformation, led by Luther, was founded in the notion that people were not saved by their own individual efforts, but rather salvation was a direct result of the workings of the grace of God. In spite of Luther's emphasis on grace, he also affirmed that God gave each person free will. It was of paramount importance, therefore, to submit one's will to God's truths and commands. Luther therefore concluded that it was critical for instructors to teach their students how to walk in God's will (Luther, 1956; Rupp & Watson, 1969).

Luther asserted that teachers needed to be very clear about what it meant to abide in God's will. According to Luther, it was imperative that students comprehend that they either served God or were in bondage to Satan. In order for students to understand what it meant to serve God and be in bondage to Satan, the key was for schools to teach students the Bible. Luther asserted that it was vital that instructors teach students the Bible at two levels: first, the intellectual or mind level; and second, at the level of their heart. Luther believed that as important as it was to know the Bible intellectually, it was even more vital to know it in their hearts and demonstrate this by godly behavior (Rupp & Watson, 1969).

There is no question that in Luther's mind student spiritual development took precedence over his or her intellectual growth. Luther's main goal was for individuals to emerge from schooling who were people of faith and lived righteous lives filled with the love of God (Dillenberger, 1961). Luther believed that all that was virtuous emanated from God's grace and faith. Luther (1999/1546, p. 1) stated, "Understand this, that a man is given righteousness, life, and salvation by faith."

One of the reasons why Luther vigorously believed in the primacy of the Bible in the classroom and elsewhere is because he affirmed that it had been robbed of that position by the Catholic Church. According to Luther, the Catholic Church had replaced the Bible with its own doctrines and papal edicts. Via the printing press, the Bible was now more available than ever before and therefore people should enthusiastically read and study its contents.

Luther believed that character education needed to be present in the student curriculum at a very young age. He averred that by establishing a strong moral foundation early in a child's life, it makes him or her more inclined to excel academically in the future. It was Luther's belief that beginning at an early age, teachers could instruct youth in the qualities that they needed to excel intellectually. Intellectual development, then, had a spiritual base (Rupp & Watson, 1969).

Luther's Priorities

Consistent with his background, Luther placed mental disciplines on a higher plain than physical disciplines (Luther, 1956). Among the academic subjects, Luther believed that the Bible was the most important. He averred that the Bible should be placed on a higher level than theology.

In other words, Luther contended that schools should emphasize a close relationship with God more than simply a scholarly knowledge of God. In Luther's view the theological teachings that should be emphasized the most in school are those that have the greatest practical value. Luther properly distinguished between instruction geared toward the mind and the heart (Brooks & Rupp, 1965; Dillenberger, 1961; Luther, 1956; Luther & Rupp, 1969; Todd, 1965).

Luther averred that school instruction needed to help the student in his or her daily life. According to Luther's worldview, instructors needed to guide youth into a comprehension that God had bestowed them with free will. Nevertheless, it was up to them how they utilized that free will. Luther maintained that it was absolutely imperative that students comprehend that their choice was either to serve God or to be in bondage to Satan. Ultimately, students needed to possess wisdom in order to make the right decisions in life (Luther & Rupp, 1969).

Luther insisted that educators needed to challenge students along a number of lines. First, he believed that teachers should encourage students to work diligently, but to know that their success depended on the grace of God. Second, teachers needed to train students to accurately exegete some of the most obscure portions of Scripture. Third, teaching should exhort the students to seek God more and seek a more intimate relationship with Him. Two of the keys to that intimacy were seeking to love God and submission to God's molding process of our lives. Luther would often refer to Jeremiah 18:16, "Like the clay in the potter's hand, so you are in my hand." By acknowledging God's role as potter, students will learn to take sin seriously and avoid it, as well, and also better appreciate the extent to which they need to look to God consistently in order to better experience His will and His anointing throughout the day (Luther, 1999/1546; Luther & Rupp, 1969; Rupp & Watson, 1969).

In most ways, the Renaissance Humanist leaders confirmed the views of key philosophers who preceded them. For example, Luther maintained an elevated view of Cicero and asserted that he was history's greatest orator. This was a particularly grand compliment because Luther was "one of the greater preachers in history" (McGiffert, 1911, p. 50). However, he also averred that teachers should go beyond what the three precious schools of thought have taught and objectively address some of the key issues of the time (McGiffert, 1911; Quintilian, 1922).

The Views of Erasmus and Calvin

Erasmus was another prominent Renaissance Humanist and was ordained a priest in 1492 (Palmer, 2001). John Todd (1965, p. 248) notes, "Erasmus and Luther never met, although they are the most notable figures of the ecclesiastical scene in the first half of the sixteenth century." Erasmus (1941, 1964, 1974) was concerned about the immoral and profligate tendencies in the church of the era. He therefore believed that churches and schools should place a great deal of emphasis on character education. Erasmus was particularly concerned about the "degenerate" behaviors in the Catholic Church (Todd, 1965, p. 250). Erasmus provided "energy for education reform" particularly in its moral teachings "and the simplification of Christian teachings" (Cooper, 2003, p. 111). He believed that it was vital that the church emphasize virtue and the state of "the heart" more than pure intellect and the state of "the head" (Palmer, pp. 37–38).

Like Luther, Erasmus asserted that the Bible needed to be the centerpiece of moral and spiritual training. Consistent with this belief, Erasmus made it a major priority to provide a new translation of the Bible. Todd (1965, p. 248) observes, "The most notable work of Erasmus . . . was to provide a new text of the New Testament, much more accurate than that of the Vulgate, St. Jerome's Latin translation from the Greek. Erasmus' text was used by Luther to great benefit. It was made from the original Greek and had notes and commentaries, or rather, more frequently, pastoral applications." The section that included commentary by Erasmus was helpful to both ministers and schoolteachers in terms of guiding students spiritually and morally. Like his contemporaries, Erasmus maintained that as much as intellectual tutelage possessed value, spiritual and moral training had greater inherent value (Erasmus, 1941, 1964, 1974).

John Calvin (1509–1564) believed in making the Bible and its teachings available to as many people as possible. He declared that studying the Bible enabled one to develop strong character and that an intimate knowledge of the Bible enabled one to communicate broadly about the important moral issues of the time.

Commonalities in the Four Schools of Thought

These schools of philosophical thought had far more central agreements than they did divergences. Two of the central commonalities were as follows.

First, they believed in dualism. Dualism is the belief that human beings have a virtuous part of their being and a selfish aspect. The primary function of education, according to the four conservative schools of thought, is to teach the good part to prevail over the selfish aspect. For the Greeks and Romans, this meant that reason must be taught to triumph over the drives of the body. For the Christians and Renaissance Humanists, this meant that one needed to be born-again into a personal relationship with Christ. The Christians asserted that only God could help one overcome his or her selfish tendencies. Second, all four schools of thought averred that character education was the primary goal and theme of education. They believed that although intellectual training was valuable, it could not replace moral instruction (Dupuis, 1966; Marrou, 1956; Strauss, 1968).

OTHER PHILOSOPHIES OF EDUCATION OUTSIDE THE WESTERN SPHERE

Chinese and Other East Asian Traditions

Confucianism and Taoism

Confucius (551–479 BC) played a major role in the development of education in China and other Far Eastern nations, such as Korea and Japan. As John Renard (2002, p. 7) notes, "He spent many years teaching privately." At the age of 50, he became an official in the Kingdom of Lu and about a year later he became the Minister of Justice. Confucius conceived a plan to weaken the aristocracy, which had dominated China for so long and had often governed selfishly and unwisely. His initiative failed and he went into exile, during which time he tutored countless students in social etiquette, morality, and academics. The "establishment" (Cooper, 2003, p. 58) of Confucianism as an official ideology did not occur until 100 BC during the Han Dynasty (this dynasty continued until AD 220). This was significant not only because of the elevation of Confucianism itself but because this event set in motion the practice of written examinations that would eventually be used for the selection of government officials. The use of these examinations took place to a limited degree in the Han Dynasty, but it did not play a major role in the selection of government officials until the Tang Dynasty (AD 618–907). Although education was limited to the very elite, in the eighth century Emperor Wu incorporated the use of the exam in a more competitive way than had existed previously (Cooper, 2003; Durant, 1931; Palmer, 2001; Reagan, 2005).

Confucius was convinced that China was not living up to its potential and this message was attractive, particularly since China was in decline. As one of his most outstanding students, Mencius (in Durant, 1931, p. 7), stated, "That whereby man differs from the lower animals is little. Most people throw it away." As Durant (p. 6) observes regarding Confucius, "He far more resembles Socrates than Jesus." Confucius did not believe that people were born equal; instead he asserted that a society should provide tutelage to their most gifted individuals so that they could become leaders. Confucius believed that it was wise for a nation to "keep ignorant persons from public office, and secure their wisest men to rule" (Durant, 1931, p. 7). According to Confucius, one of the indications that one had wisdom was the willingness to learn from a wide range of people. Consistent with this orientation, many Chinese in the mainland and those who came to the West lauded George Washington as either the finest or one of the finest people in the Western world (Durant, 1931; Jiyu, 1989).

Although Confucius clearly emphasized the academic aspect of instruction, he believed in moral education, particularly those aspects that were related to social development and proper etiquette (Palmer, 2001). Confucius averred that learning and morality should be inseparable (Cooney, Cross, & Trunk, 1993). Jing-pan Chen (1994, p. 353) declares, "Confucius was not a teacher of religion, but a religious teacher." Confucius instructed his students in myriad moral truths, although they focused on social development, proper etiquette, and daily adages. Although Confucius did not write his works, his students passed on his aphorisms. Confucius believed that drawing from the lives of the wisdom of forefathers was a practice that yielded much utility. In *Antiquity* 7:19 Confucius (n.d.) states, "I am not one who was born in the possession of knowledge; I am one who is fond of antiquity and earnest in seeking it there." He also believed that it was character education that elevated some people above others. In *Antiquity* 17:2 Confucius (n.d.) declares, "By nature, men are nearly alike, by practice, they get wide apart." He stood by various and sundry strong principles, including the belief that "suffering ... prepares men for great services" (Chen, 1994, p. 214) and that people should work "for the good of the public" rather than to benefit oneself (Chen, 1994, p. 191).

At first, Confucianism competed with Taoism for the hearts and minds of the Chinese people, but as Renard (2002) points out, Taoism was more of a set of traditions rather than a philosophy of education. In addition, Taoists saw no need for an educational network. Eventually, Confucianism would compete with Buddhism and subsequently decline in popularity in China, although it did experience some resurgence during the Song Dynasty (AD 960–1279). Confucianism fared better in Korea where it was the nation's official religion from 1392 to 1910. Confucianism further declined in influence during the mid-twentieth century in China and other spheres. Due to its suppression by Communists and the fact that many people found Confucian adages to be too intuitive compared to those found in other religions and philosophies, Confucianism was not practiced as often as it had been previously. As Cooper (2003, p. 67) describes, "Unlike Socrates—or Jesus and the Buddha—Confucius has not retained his awesome reputation." Nevertheless, Confucius contributed to the high esteem that many East Asians maintain for etiquette and socially appropriate behavior (DeBary, 1996; Liu, 1996; Renard, 2002).

Buddhism

Buddhism was birthed in India before 500 BC at an opportune time when the nation was immersed in a period of moral corruption. Buddhism emphasized "the universal norms that are constant" and "apply to everyone" (Sharma, 1994, p. ix). Buddhists believed in a "moral code" that was of "a universal nature." Buddhists did not develop a program of moral instruction at a level commensurate to that of Confucianists, but they nevertheless viewed it as essential. Because education was not their strength, historically they have relied on the schooling procedures practiced by other religions. Buddhist education was limited largely to monasteries. Buddhist moral instruction had more of a psychological orientation than most religions in that it emphasized wisdom, ethics, meditation, and the ultimate goal of nirvana, which is supposedly a state of bliss based on emptying oneself of desires. As Hinduism entered India, Buddhism generally became a religion associated with the Far East (Reagan, 2005; Sharma, 1994).

Japan: Combining Shintoism, Buddhism, and Confucianism

Until Meiji was proclaimed emperor in 1868 and called on Japan to imitate the West, particularly the United States, Shintoism, Buddhism, and Confucianism were the principal perspectives influencing Japanese society and attempts at education. As Yamashita (1996, p. 132) opines, "Few would deny the importance of Confucianism for modern Japan." Nevertheless, in terms of moral education and its influence on society, Confucianism never enjoyed the influence in Japan that it had in China and Korea. Moreover, its effects decreased noticeably in Japan well before it declined in China. Fukuzawa Yukichi (1835–1901) urged people to "leave Asia" and search for truth in the West (Yukichi in Shils, 1996, pp. 113–114). Yukichi argued that according to Darwin's teachings, non-white culture was inferior to that of whites and therefore the only hope for Asian races to survive was to learn from the West. Darwin's racist predictions that those whose skin was darkest in hue would go extinct first appeared to affect the Japanese philosophical beliefs more than their religious beliefs. Therefore, early moral education was primarily a Buddhist initiative with a strong Shinto influence (Bunge, 1983; Eagan, 2002; Gould, 1981; Renard, 2002; Shils, 1996; Tu, 1996).

In ancient Japan, education was highly esteemed but rarely practiced in a formalized sense. During the AD 710–1185 period, elite Buddhist priests and monks received character training consistent with Buddhist tenets. For the following four centuries, however, even for these elites schooling of any type declined substantially. Efforts to train leaders and some commoners, particularly in moral instruction, resurfaced during the Tokugawa (1603–1868) period (Bunge, 1983; Khan, 1997).

Shintoism provided a rich tradition of respect for the forefathers and foremothers of the Japanese nation. Shintoism developed in the AD 500s and gave the Japanese their own religious system and their own developmental origins. Shintoism promoted high ethical standards and ancestor veneration. This ancestor veneration has traditionally caused Japanese to view life in a way distinct from many nations. They respect the contributions of their ancestors to their personal and national well-being to a degree that surpasses virtually all of the more populated countries. In addition, Shintoism teaches that people possess an individual spirit when they die that is either "content or disgruntled" (Renard, 2002, p. 52). If the person's spirit is disgruntled, Shintoism teaches that it is one's moral obligation to appease it by showing veneration to that spirit. If one has wronged that person and is personally responsible for that person's suffering, Shintoism teaches that one should petition that person's spirit to show mercy and not seek revenge upon the living person. Therefore, for centuries, out of moral conscience Japanese have shown veneration to the spirit of their relatives for acts of selfishness, betrayal, abortion, insensitivity, and so forth. Perhaps even more than Confucianism, Shintoism has had major effects on the teaching of character education in Japan. With the emergence of Emperor Meiji in 1868, moral education took on a more prominent role in Japanese schooling than ever before and Meiji put in place the modern system of character instruction. This will be examined in Chapter 9 (Renard, 2002; Schmidt, 2007).

India and Hinduism

Although Buddhism found its origins in India, eventually Hinduism prevailed as the nation's foremost religion. Traditionally, India has been open to religious and philosophical influence. Nevertheless, as Cooper (2003, p. 50) points out, historically the schools of thought that have thrived in India have been more focused on "reality and knowledge" rather than having a traditionally moral focus. It is conceivable that this may explain why some philosophers, for example, Hegel (1956) and Krishna (1991), found India enigmatic in that the nation possessed high levels of spiritual emphasis and immorality simultaneously. The moral education that exists in India is often focused on the spiritual example of certain individuals whose advancement is such that they have reached high levels of discovery and can serve as a teacher for others. Beyond the presence and teaching of a recognized spiritual leader, the devotee is encouraged to engage in self-discovery within the context of the larger universe (Cooper, 2003).

African Traditions

Moral education in most African nations was heavily dependent on useful adages. Educational instruction in Africa also usually included seven cardinal goals that included character education, but also placed physical discipline at a higher level of priority than in any other area of the globe, including even the Greeks. Fafunwa (1974) notes that honesty, respectability, skill, conformity, and physical ability were generally the most highly esteemed qualities in African culture (Ray, 1976; Reagan, 2005).

Islam

Muhammad (AD 570–632) transformed the religious and moral orientation of the Middle East in only a quarter of a century. Islamic leaders traditionally emphasize the teaching of doctrine, spirituality, and common sense (Reagan, 2005). Moral education is highly structured and dependent on the doctrine taught by religious leaders and the teaching of the Koran, with special emphasis on the five pillars of Islam. These pillars include a profession of faith, praying five times a day, almsgiving, fasting especially during Ramadan, and taking a pilgrimage to Mecca. The growth of Islam grew more as a result of being a religious community and a set of national movements than it did as an educational effort. Consequently, Islam probably did more to shape the cultural and nationalistic inclinations of people than any other religion. Concurrently, although its emphasis on doctrine and moral instruction is undeniable, its formal development came at a later stage than was the case with Christianity, Confucianism, and some other religions (Reagan, 2005; Schmidt, 2007).

Judaism

The first moral teachings of Judaism find their roots in Abraham, the father of the Jewish people. The Jewish people especially follow the teachings of Abraham, Moses, David, and the major prophets. They particularly honor the teachings of the Torah, which give specific directions about the attitudes one should have in training one's children and the importance of passing on the laws, the holidays, and the festivals that their children might remember the God of their parents. Although the number of people in contemporary society following Judaism is small, one must remember that Judaism gave birth to Christianity, the largest religion in the world. Christians consider their roots to be the same as those of Jewish people. In addition, those of the Islamic faith regard both the Old and the New Testaments to be holy books (Palmer, 2001).

CONCLUSION

The teaching of character education has widespread and deep roots in virtually every major section of the globe. Moral instruction in the West has existed consistently for centuries and has remained quite stable in its content for over 2,000 years. Character education in other parts of the globe has also been present for centuries, although it varied in the degree to which it was systematized in a school system and whether the primary source was the home, a house of worship, or a school. Nevertheless, the presence of character education is a worldwide phenomenon, which is a testimony to its acknowledged importance and value.

REFERENCES

Aristotle. (1985). *Nicomachean ethics*. Indianapolis: Hackett.

Aristotle. (1941). *The basic works of Aristotle*. New York: Random House.

Augustine & Howe, Q., Jr. (1966). *Selected sermons of Saint Augustine*. New York: Holt, Rinehart & Winston.

Brooks, P. N., & Rupp, E. G. (1965). *Christian spirituality*. London: S. C. M. Press.

Bunge, F. M. (1983). *Japan: A country study*. Washington, D.C.: U.S. Government Printing Office.

Chen, J. (1994). *Confucius as a teacher*. Beijing: Foreign Language Press.

Cicero, M. T. (1991). *On duties*. Cambridge, MA: Cambridge University Press.

Cicero. (2009). Brainyquote. Retrieved January 14, 2009 fromwww.brainyquote .com/quotes/quotes/m/marcustull163183.html.

Cicero, M. T., & Grose, H. H. (1966). *The speeches: Pro lege Manila, Pro Caecina, Pro Rabiro perduellionis*. Cambridge: Harvard University.

———. (2001). *On moral ends*. Cambridge, MA: Cambridge University Press.

Cicero, M. T., & Higginbotham, J. (1967). *On moral obligation. A new translation of Cicero's De Officis with introduction and notes*. Berkeley, CA: University of California Press.

Confucius. (n.d.). *Antiquity* 7:19.

———. *Antiquity* 17:2.

Cooney, W., Cross, C., & Trunk, B. (1993). *From Plato to Piaget*. Lanham, MD: University Press of America.

Cooper, D. E. (2003). *World philosophies: An historical introduction*. Malden, MA: Blackwell.

Cubberley, E. (1920). *The history of education*. Boston: Houghton Mifflin.

———, ed. (1934). *Readings in public education in the United States: A collection of sources and readings to illustrate the history of educational practice and progress in the United States*. Cambridge, MA: Riverside Press.

DeBary, W. T. (1996). Confucian ideals and the real world. In W. Tu (Ed.), *Confucian traditions in East Asian modernity* (pp. 2–37). Cambridge, MA: Harvard University Press.

Dillenberger, J. (1961). *Martin Luther: Selections from his writing*. New York: Doubleday, Doran, & Company.

Dupuis, A. M. (1966). *Philosophy of education in historical perspective*. Chicago, IL: Rand McNally.

Durant, W. (1931). *Great men of literature.* Garden City, NY: Garden City Publishers.

Eagan, K. (2002). *Getting it wrong from the beginning.* New Haven: Yale University Press.

Elias, J. L. (1995). *Philosophy of education: Classical and contemporary.* Malabar, FL: Krieger.

Erasmus, D. (1941). *The praise of folly.* Princeton, NJ: Princeton University Press.

———. (1964). *The essential Erasmus.* New York: New American Library.

———. (1974). *The correspondence of Erasmus.* Toronto: University of Toronto.

Fafunwa, A. B. (1974). *History of Nigeria.* London: Allen & Unwin.

Gangel, K. O., & Benson, W. S. (1983). *Christian education: Its history and philosophy.* Chicago, IL: Moody.

Gould, S. J. (1981). *The mismeasure of man.* New York: Norton.

Harbison, E. E. (1964). *Christianity and history, essays.* Princeton, NJ: Princeton University Press.

Hitchcock, J. (1982). *What is secular humanism? Why humanism became secular and how it is changing our world.* Ann Arbor, MI: Servant.

Hunt, T. C., & Maxson, M. M. (1981). *Religion and morality in American schooling.* Washington, D.C.: University Press of America.

Jeynes, W. (2007). *American educational history: School, society & the common good.* Thousand Oaks: Sage Publications.

Jiyu, X. (1989). George Washington and the American political system. In R. D. Arkush & L. O. Lee (Eds.), *Land without ghosts.* Berkeley, CA: University of California Press.

Khan, Y. (1997). *Japanese moral education: Past and present.* Madison, NJ: Fairleigh Dickinson University Press.

Klein, J. (1965). *Commentary on Plato's Meno.* Chapel Hill, NC: University of North Carolina Press.

Liu, S. (1996). Confucian ideals and the real world. In W. Tu (Ed.), *Confucian traditions in East Asian modernity* (pp. 92–111). Cambridge, MA: Harvard University Press.

Luther, M. (1956). *Sermons on the passion of Christ.* Rock Island, IL: Augustana Press.

———. (1999/1546). *Preface to the New Testament: Luther's Works, Volume 36.* (J. J. Pelikan, H. C. Oswald, & H. T. Lehman). Philadelphia, PA: Fortress Press.

Luther, M., & Rupp, E. G. (1969). *Luther and Erasmus: Free will and salvation.* Philadelphia: Westminster Press.

Marrou, H. I. (1956). *A history of education in antiquity.* New York: Sheed & Ward.

May, J. M. (1988). *Trials of character: The eloquence of Ciceronian ethos.* Chapel Hill, NC: University of North Carolina Press.

McGiffert, A. C. (1911). *Martin Luther: The man and his work.* New York: Century.

Oates, W. J. (1948). *Basic writings of Saint Augustine.* New York: Random House.

Palmer, J. A. (2001). *Fifty major thinkers.* London: Routledge.

Plato. (1979). *Gorgias.* New York: Oxford University Press.

———. (2000). *The republic.* Cambridge, MA: Cambridge University Press.

———. (2004). *Protagoras and Meno.* Ithaca, NY: Cornell University Press.

———. (2009). From *Quotes by author.* Work cited February 17, 2009 (www.quotesandpoem.com/quotes/listquotes/author/plato).

Quintilian. (1922). *Institiones Oratoriae.* London: Heinemann.

Ray, B. (1976). *African religions.* Englewood Cliffs, NJ: Prentice Hall.

Reagan, T. (2005). *Non-western educational traditions.* Mahwah, NJ: Erlbaum.

Renard, J. (2002). 101 questions and answers on Confucianism, Daoism, and Shinto. New York: Paulist Press.

Rolfe, J. C. (1963). *Cicero and his influence.* New York: Cooper Square.

Rupp, E. G., & Watson, S. (1969). *Luther and Erasmus: Free will and salvation.* Philadelphia, PA: Westminster Press.

Schmidt, A. (2007). *The world religions cookbook.* Westport, CT: Greenwood.

Sharma, S. N. (1994). *Buddhist social and moral education.* Delhi: Parimal.

Shils, E. (1996). Reflections on civil society and Chinese intellectual tradition. In W. Tu (Ed.), *Confucian traditions in East Asian modernity* (pp. 38–71). Cambridge, MA: Harvard University Press.

Strauss, L. (1968). *Liberalism, ancient & modern.* New York: Basic Books.

Todd, J. M. (1965). *Martin Luther.* Westminster, MD: Newman Press.

Tu, W. (1996). Japan. In W. Tu (Ed.), *Confucian traditions in East Asian modernity* (pp. 113–118). Cambridge, MA: Harvard University Press.

Walker, W. (1963). *A philosophy of education.* New York: Philosophical Library.

Yamashita, S. H. (1996). Confucianism and the Japanese state. In W. Tu (Ed.), *Confucian traditions in East Asian modernity* (pp. 132–154). Cambridge, MA: Harvard University Press.

3

PRAYER IN THE SCHOOL AND MORAL EDUCATION IN AMERICA PRIOR TO THE REVOLUTIONARY WAR

The European settlers who came to the United States prior to the Revolutionary War generally placed a great deal of emphasis on moral education. This was particularly true of the Pilgrims and Puritans who arrived in the New World in 1620 and 1630, respectively. The focus on character education that the early European settlers had was especially important because it established a foundation from which all other Americans built (Bailyn, 1960; Cubberley, 1920, 1934). Some of the most salient accomplishments in American educational history were made in the first few decades after the arrival of the Pilgrims and Puritans in particular (Bailyn, 1960; Cubberley, 1920, 1934; Willison, 1945, 1966). Their educational success in establishing Harvard College, the nation's first secondary school (Boston Latin School), and compulsory education helped launch the nation's schooling system that would one day become the envy of the world (Jeynes, 2004). Douglas McKnight (2003, p. 2) accurately summarized this emphasis when he states, "In general educational historians . . . asserted that before the American Revolution education in America was primarily concerned with the development of a godly life."

THE INFLUENCE OF THE PILGRIMS AND PURITANS ON CHARACTER EDUCATION

Although there were many groups of settlers coming to the United States during the 1600s, the Puritans and Pilgrims indubitably were the people that had the greatest impact on American education. There are two primary reasons for this fact. One of the reasons is that the Puritans and Pilgrims emphasized education to a considerable degree. The second reason is that for many years they had a positive relationship with Native Americans that served as a model for other settlers for over half a century (Bailyn, 1960; Cubberley, 1920, 1934; Willison, 1945, 1966).

The Puritan Emphasis on Character Education

The Puritans maintained that moral instruction was the most salient component of education. Puritan practices in character training established a foundation for continued practices in character education for decades to come (Middleton, 2004). The Puritans were very religious people and their dissemination throughout New England helped establish this area as the "Bible Belt" of the colonies throughout the 1700s and 1800s. Throughout this era, the people abiding in the Northeastern states were more religious than those living in the South (Jeynes, 2007; Middleton, 2004).

The Puritan reliance on moral education radiated from their belief in a variation in the philosophical belief termed dualism, referred to in Chapter 2. Dualism is the perspective that human beings have both a selfish part and a good part to their nature. Like the classical Greeks and Romans, the Puritans believed that human selfishness went very deep. They asserted that the selfishness of humans went so deep that people in and of themselves were incapable of overcoming it without God's help (Dupuis, 1966; Jeynes, 2007).

Douglas McKnight (2003, p. 2) notes, "The ultimate purpose of schooling for the colonial Puritans possessed a decisively religious tone." McKnight (p. 2) calls this emphasis one of "godly learning." To the Puritans, this emphasis was even more important than academic prowess. In fact, John Elias (1995) notes that the emphasis on character both in antiquity and in the colonial period actually predated the focus on intellectual development. This orientation was patent not only at the elementary and secondary school level but in colleges as well (Friedman, 2001). For example, Harvard, Yale, and Princeton were founded "as a training ground for future generations of ministers" (Friedman, p. 50). The primary concern of university leaders was for Harvard graduates to be godly, upright, and loving individuals even more than it was to produce individuals with intellectual perspicacity. As Moroney (2001, p. 54) observes, "The minister of a community served as its moral and sometimes political head." Therefore, it was imperative that ministers be people of integrity and conduct themselves in an exemplary way (Hiner, 1988; Jeynes, 2007).

The Puritans averred that ministers were primary catalysts in enabling the general populace to know life's truths and so be set free. It was particularly essential that ministers serve as moral leaders because they functioned not only as the spiritual leaders of the community but as the intellectual leaders as well. This was the deep conviction not only of the Puritans but also of virtually all the settlers who lived at this time. At the time, settlers from Europe assumed that those who sought God, and therefore wisdom as well, must diligently seek knowledge more intensively. The prevailing thought at the time was that society was most secure when the wisest individuals were also the most knowledgeable. This perspective was not unique to the colonists. Rather, one can trace the origins of this genre of thinking all the way back to Cicero. Cicero posited that the most dangerous person in the world was someone who was knowledgeable, but was not virtuous. Martin Luther King echoed virtually the same words many years later (Beard & Beard, 1944; Cicero in Freeman Institute, 2009; Dupuis, 1966; Jeynes, 2007; King in Freeman Institute, 2009).

It was with Cicero's assertions in mind that the United States maintained that ministers stand as a community of the most erudite people. Knowledge in the hands of those who were not wise, according to the settlers, was a baleful combination. In contrast, they believed that information possessed by the wise helped secure the stability and well-being of a society. The settlers, particularly the Puritans, maintained this view because they believed that people of perspicacity were wise enough to utilize learning for the promotion of human welfare (Beard & Beard, 1944; Eavey, 1964; Jeynes, 2007; Urban & Wagoner, 2000).

As much as the colonies valued virtue in their ministers, they also highly esteemed this goal in the lives of all their inhabitants (Eavey, 1964). The Puritans averred that an intelligent person who had a dearth of virtue was dangerous at any level, as Cicero had declared (Jeynes, 2007). On this basis, they practiced an educational rubric that emphasized virtue and character, as a means of glorifying God, as its most ethereal goals (Marshall & Manuel, 1977). McClellan (1999, p. 1) observes, "The vast array of European peoples who settled in the American colonies brought with them an extraordinary commitment to moral education." Some groups emphasized character instruction more than others. McClellan (p. 1) notes, "It was Protestants from northern Europe, especially from Great Britain, who did the most to give moral education its character in the thirteen colonies."

The Puritans were at the forefront of these efforts in moral instruction. They were convinced that in order to fabricate a thriving society that not only did ministers need to be virtuous, but also the general populace did as well. The Puritans averred that character education "could encourage good behavior and create a society that would both glorify God and win divine blessings in the form of stable, harmonious, and prosperous communities" (McClellan, 1999, p. 2). Although the Puritans averred that parents emerged as the primary educators, they also realized that schools provided an efficacious and supportive role in this regard (Beard & Beard, 1944; Eavey, 1964; Jeynes, 2006, 2008).

The Puritan Emphasis on the Pursuit of Truth and on Education Generally

In contemporary society, individuals frequently make a considerable distinction between academic and moral education. The Puritans and the other settlers of the seventeenth and eighteenth centuries did not make such a vivid distinction between the two. First, they defined education as the pursuit of God's truth, all truth both moral and intellectual. Therefore, they viewed education holistically. Consistent with this view and their religious fervor, they passionately sought truth through education (Bartlett, 1978; Edwards (2004); Ryan & Bohlin, 1999).

The Puritans emphasized education principally because they believed that the Bible commanded people to be educated. This conviction was founded on the biblical declaration, "You shall know the truth and the truth will set you free" (Holy Bible, John 8:32). It cannot be gainsaid that when Christ made this statement, He especially referred to spiritual truth. Nevertheless, the Puritans believed that moral and intellectual truths both radiated from God and were inextricably connected. They affirmed that since all of God's creation represented His truth, education in a more general sense was worth pursuing. The college leaders of the pre–Revolutionary War era resolutely believed that the quest for additional knowledge was doing the work of God. Although they recognized that this verse was principally a spiritual adage designed to apply to one's daily walk with God, they also interpreted the verse more broadly to apply to the search for scholarly knowledge. From their perspective, God created the physical and the spiritual world and the natural order that exists in each. Therefore, it was both natural and glorifying to God to aspire to comprehend more of God's truth not only in the spiritual world but in the physical and academic one as well (Bartlett, 1978; Jeynes, 2007; Reuben, 1996).

Because the college leaders adhered to the belief that God created the physical world, they believed in what is commonly called a "unity of truth." That is, they opined that the truth that they would find in the physical world would only confirm the truth that was evident in the spiritual world. On this basis, the college leaders of the day encouraged intensive academic study. The founders of Harvard "believed that all knowledge ultimately illuminated the Divine and also that they had a religious obligation to increase their knowledge" (Reuben, 1996, p. 17). Reuben describes the common consensus of the time by stating that "the colonists believed that all knowledge was knowledge about God" and "they assumed that ultimately all truths agreed and could be unified." This worldview held for the eighteenth and nineteenth centuries. In his 1874 article "The Nobility of Knowledge," Harvard chemistry professor Josiah Cooke pronounced that "all truth is one and inseparable" (in Reuben, p. 17). At the time Cooke did not even have to explicate his views because of the prevalence of this worldview (Reuben, 1996).

Within a few months after their arrival in Massachusetts, the Pilgrims elected William Bradford as their second governor, after their first governor Deacon John Carver died prematurely. Bradford was a fervent advocate of proclaiming an intelligent gospel. Consistent with this orientation, the Puritans and Pilgrims kept records of the number of volumes of books that they owned. Although the Pilgrims were economically poorer than the Puritans, Bartlett (1978, p. 17) observes, "Like the Puritans, the Pilgrims honored education." The Puritans and Pilgrims viewed the Bible as the most important book that one could own and virtually every home possessed at least one copy. The Puritan passion for books reflected their emphasis on literacy but also their focus on moral education. The overwhelming majority of the Puritan ministers who first came over to America graduated from Oxford and Cambridge. During this period,

Oxford and Cambridge were considered the foremost colleges in England and perhaps in the world. Therefore, Puritan leaders adhered to the highest educational standards and sought to implement those standards in New England (Bartlett, 1978; Brooke, Highfield, & Swaan, 1988; Marshall & Manuel, 1977; Pulliam & Van Patten, 1991).

Charles Chauncy (1655, p. 3), an early leader in Massachusetts, averred that education was necessary in order to prevent children from becoming intellectually "naked." To the Puritans spiritual and intellectual nakedness were related. The Puritans placed a great deal of emphasis on literacy, because although literacy was not essential to experiencing salvation, it surely facilitated salvation. With this full appreciation of the relationship between literacy and salvation, the Puritans in Massachusetts became the core of the printing industry in the New World (the first printing press in the colonies was established in Cambridge in 1638 [Cremin, 1976; Smith, 1973]).

The Puritan pursuit of truth and education generally was also reflected in several educational firsts. In 1635 these settlers founded America's first secondary school, Boston Latin School, and in 1636 they founded the continent's first college, Harvard. In 1642 the Massachusetts legislature passed the Massachusetts Compulsory Education Law requiring that the head of every household teach all the children in one's home, both male and female. There was a special focus on helping youth to read and understand the principles of religion and the capital laws of the country. Cubberley (1920, p. 354) elucidated on the salience of the 1642 law when he stated that "for the first time in the English-speaking world, a legislative body representing the State ordered that all children should be taught to read." The salience of religious and character instruction was even more ostensible in legislation that was passed in 1647 that is commonly referred to as the "Old Deluder Satan Act." At the heart of the legislation was a declaration that Satan desired people to be ignorant, especially of the Bible. The legislation necessitated that each community of 50 or more householders assign at least one person to teach all the children in that community. This teacher was to instruct the children to read and write and would receive pay from the townspeople (Cubberley, 1934; Fraser, 2001; Hiner, 1988; Johnson, 1997; Rippa, 1997).

Second, they believed that the discovery of truth would set them free. The Puritans believed that much of life was to encompass the goals of seeking the truth and then living out the reality of that truth. Books used in schools were vital to character education. Most books used in Puritan schools and in their society overall "were either very theological or really concerned with hard facts" (Bark & Lefler, 2004, p. 103). The orientation of these books reflected the worldview of the Puritan people. They demonstrated the love the Puritans possessed for objective truth. They believed that truth found in God and truths revealed in unassailable mathematical formulas and scientific facts were simply different ways in which God revealed Himself. Therefore, whether one sought God in the Bible or in addressing the truths of science or math, the devotee still has the same goal in mind: to seek after God. It was this perspective that caused the Puritans to have such an academic orientation. The Puritans were so scholastically oriented that any given New England town had about as many graduates of Cambridge and Oxford as any similar-sized town in England (Bark & Lefler, 2004; Fay, 1966; Tyler, 1878).

The Puritans believed that there was a clear interrelationship between character education, the Bible, and literacy. In their minds, the Bible was the central piece of literature necessary for character education to take place. Out of the desire to promote character education and salvation the Puritans placed a great deal of emphasis on literacy. Hence, in the practices of the Puritans literacy and character education were intimately connected. As Jensen and Knight (1981, p. 73) state, "These Puritans believed that it was important for everyone to be able to read in order so that they could read the Scriptures. As a result, schools were established relatively soon after settlement, especially in the New England colonies where settlement patterns in towns made common schools relatively easy to establish . . . Early schools were exclusively religious in nature because the motivation for literacy came from the need to study the Bible." Gilpin (1982, p. 5) states that the "Bible played a major role in establishing the methods and goals of colonial education." The Puritans contended that leaders needed to possess a balanced approach to education so that the ultimate goals of instruction were "piety, civility, and learning" (Gilpin, p. 8). To the extent to which instructors incorporated these goals into the curriculum, one's academic studies could lead to the discovery of truth and this would set one free (Cubberley, 1920, 1934; Jensen & Knight, 1981).

Third, the Puritans believed in balance and diligence in fulfilling the school's role in both character education and scholastics. The early curriculum of the New England settlers focused on reading, writing, arithmetic, and religious instruction. Both boys and girls usually started attending school at the age of six or seven. School was in session six days each week, except during the summer. School days were generally longer than one sees practiced in America today. There was a considerable degree of variation in how many years boys and girls remained in school. This was largely dependent on how badly they were needed at home to tend to more mature duties, such as planting and harvesting the crops. Prayer, Bible reading, and moral instruction were essential parts of the school day, especially at the beginning and the end of each school day (Pulliam & Van Patten, 1991). Ray Hiner (1988, p. 6) notes, "Beyond the creation of a regenerate man, the Puritans had other educational goals, equally explicit. Most of these were encompassed by the characteristics of the civil man . . . He respected authority, obeyed the laws of the community, and accepted his responsibilities as parent, provider, husband."

Max Weber (1864–1920), the renowned sociologist, in his book, *The Protestant Ethic and the Spirit of Capitalism,* traces the American Protestant work ethic to the Pilgrims and the Puritans. Weber posited that Calvinism, as epitomized in the Puritans and Pilgrims, had a profound effect on the American work ethic. It is apparent that this orientation manifested itself in schooling and was rooted in the pursuit of God. Weber pointed out that Protestants were highly affected by the Apostle Paul who emphasized diligence and was a highly educated individual. Other philosophies, most notably Confucianism, also emphasized hard work. Moreover, recent research suggests that there is a broader Christian ethic, rather than merely a Protestant work ethic, that encompasses the other Christian groups as well (Chen, 1994; Mentzer, 1988; Weber, 1930).

THE PURITAN PHILOSOPHY OF EDUCATION

The Puritans asserted that the family, the church, and the school all had special responsibilities when it came to moral education. These three participants in moral education might be called the "holy triad" (Jeynes, 2007).

The Home: The Puritans asserted that the home was the central place of character education (Jeynes, 2005; McClellan & Reese, 1988). They surmised that if the home environment was not morally right, even if the child attended the best church and the best school, the child would not grow up to be an adult of integrity. The colonists asserted that the home was where the spiritual training given at church and the academic training given at school were applied to everyday living (McClellan & Reese, 1988). In colonial days, particularly among the Puritans, the father was much more involved in the raising of the children than we commonly see today (McClellan & Reese, 1988). McClellan (1999, p. 5) adds, "Before 1750 fathers were heavily involved and probably even the primary providers of moral education." Part of this paternal involvement resulted from the Christian concept of the Trinity: the Heavenly Father, the Son, and the Holy Spirit. They opined that children formed an image of who the Heavenly Father was based on their relationship with their father. Consequently, they surmised that the father had a very special role in raising the children. The Puritans inferred a child could only gain a sense of the love and righteousness of their Heavenly Father by examining the life of his or her earthly father. McClellan (p. 5) notes that "Puritans did not differentiate between the values to be taught to boys and girls."

Most colonial families would hold family devotionals in which they would study the Bible and pray together as a family. This family time would serve the purposes of fostering spiritual growth, family unity, increasing the children's reading skills, and implanting within the children seeds of spiritual wisdom (Hiner, 1988).

The Puritans maintained high expectations of what their children could achieve in terms of moral development. Some individuals believe that Puritans viewed children as little adults. Actually, Puritans really did not possess this belief. The Puritans did possess higher expectations of children than is present in contemporary American society. This was largely due to necessity. The life spans of people were shorter than today, and the agriculturally based society meant that work participation depended on one's physical size more than on one's age. Older children would also help care for their younger siblings (Smith, 1973).

The Church: In terms of moral development, the Puritans regarded the church as the most important member of the triad. However, they believed that the family had more of a salient role than the church in educating children. The church's purpose in instruction was to educate the colonists regarding the teachings of the Bible and how to be caring and righteous individuals. The church was where people came to procure wisdom. The church also functioned as the administration center for an abundance of educational endeavors at the level of elementary, secondary, and collegiate education. They also trained their church's members to edify their families at home (Hiner, 1988). McClellan (1999, p. 6) states that the Puritans "used materials that were suffused with religious and moral imagery. Primers contained simple verses, songs, and stories designed to teach at once the skills of literacy and virtues of Christian living."

The School: The Puritans asserted that the most vital function of the school was to help produce virtuous individuals. John Clarke, a leading educator, maintained a perspective that epitomized those of New England educators at the time. He averred that a school master must "in the first place be a man of virtue. For ... it be the main end of education to make virtuous men" (Clarke, 1730, p. 93). Because reading the Bible was a paramount goal of education, teachers placed a special emphasis on reading. The Puritans desired schools to have a stabilizing influence on society via drawing children closer to God (Clarke, 1730; Pulliam & Van Patten, 1991).

THOUGHTS ON THE PURITAN CONTRIBUTION TO CHARACTER EDUCATION

As Cayton and Williams (2001, p. 50) note, "The Puritan's imprint on American ideology and culture is inestimable." One of the ways that the Puritans affected American culture as a whole, and college culture specifically, was through their degree of optimism. The Puritans particularly had an optimism regarding the pursuit of truth. They believed that if one genuinely pursued truth, then he or she would find truth. The Puritans believed that theology was the most reliable means of seeking truth, but they also emphasized ethics and logic as two of their primary means of seeking truth. Puritan educational practices eventually permeated much of the country, and it is clear that in the colonial period their influence on schooling may have surpassed all other groups combined (Bailyn, 1960; Cubberley, 1920, 1934; Kennedy, 2001).

CHARACTER EDUCATION THROUGHOUT THE COLONIES

Quakers

The Quakers in Pennsylvania and New Jersey probably emphasized character education more than any group outside of New England. As part of their emphasis on character education, the Quakers emphasized the salience of pacifism as a significant part of what it meant to be a virtuous human being. The Quakers emphasized that not only was the act of pacifism a righteous behavior generally, but it also served as a means of keeping under control the motivations that lead to war. That is, the Quakers adhered to the belief that covetousness was usually the motive that was at the heart of war (Weddle, 2001). As Meredith Weddle (p. 162) notes, "Inappropriate and excessive desires—lusts—of all kinds created the opportunity for war." He further asserts, "Taking away the occasion of war, then, was being obedient to God."

In addition to emphasizing the salience of pacifism in the classroom and the home, Quaker adults did as much as they could to set an example for their children. In terms of proximity, the people they could best apply this orientation with were the Native Americans. The Quakers did their best to not only apply pacifistic principles with the Native Americans but remove even the opportunity for war. For example, the Quakers allowed Native Americans to serve on juries and the Quakers refused to serve in armies. In fact, in the one case in which Quakers dominated a state's population, Rhode Island, the colony refused to raise an army. Even when the Native Americans attacked the Quaker settlement of Providence and these settlers lost 84 percent of their houses due to fire and all but two of its homes overall, the Quakers, in accordance with their beliefs, refused to defend their city and fled. Quakers in other Rhode Island cities were also attacked and despite the pleading of Roger Williams to at least defend their homes, the Quakers simply left the areas under assault as the Native Americans approached and ransacked their towns. The Quakers taught pacifism in the schools as one of the most important parts of their character education curriculum (Ammerman, 1995; Schultz & Tougias, 1999; Weddle, 2001).

Dutch and Other Settlers in the Mid-Atlantic Colonies

The Dutch treasured the presence of character education, although they did not develop as elaborate an education system as the Puritans. Nevertheless, the Mid-Atlantic settlements in Pennsylvania, New York, New Jersey, Delaware, and Maryland were second only to New England in terms of possessing the most developed elementary education system. For example, the Dutch in New York, the Catholics in Maryland, and the Moravians, Lutherans, Friends, Quakers, and Mennonites in Pennsylvania and New Jersey attempted to establish a school at every church that was founded. These schools, like the ones in New England, used the Bible as their primary textbook for character education. In 1683, Pennsylvania passed a law that required parents to school their youth to read at a level sufficient to be able to read the Bible. In nearly all of these schools, tuition was free to those who could not afford it and for others it was on a sliding scale. The generosity of philanthropists made these sliding tuition schools possible. Residents of New Jersey also showed a commitment to character instruction and the availability of these schools (Cubberley, 1920; Eavey, 1964). The idea that all children should have access to schooling whether they could afford it or not was a deeply held conviction of the early churches. The ministers of the time asserted that greatest contribution to education of the early Christians of biblical times and the early centuries that followed is that they esteemed all people worthy of receiving an education (Dupuis, 1966; Marrou, 1956). This belief was largely built on the verse from the Bible that asserts, "There is neither Jew nor Greek, slave nor free, male nor female, for you are all one in Christ Jesus" (Holy Bible, Galatians 3:28).

Other groups focused on character education as well. The first Jewish settlers to arrive in the United States came from Brazil in 1654 and settled in New Amsterdam (present-day New York City). In 1760 the Spanish and Portuguese Congregation Shearith Israel started the first Jewish American school within their synagogue, which focused particularly on moral instruction, relying on the Torah as well as the historical and prophetic components of the Old Testament for their instruction (Gartner, 1969).

The Settlers in the South

In the South, people perceived moral schooling and education as more of a family matter than in other parts of the country. As a result of maintaining this view, the majority of families either taught their children themselves or hired tutors to do the schooling. Instruction in the South also was more home based because the distances between farms and plantations made community schools impossible. Some church people did found some free private schools in Virginia, including Syms in 1647 and Eaton in 1659. In addition to this form of homeschooling, missionary societies were also involved in training children both morally and intellectually. They were especially helpful to families who could not afford tutors, because they made their services available on a freewill donation basis. The most renowned of these missionary groups was the Society for the Propagation of the Gospel. This Society established 170 missionary stations for education, one in nearly every major East Coast town, between 1701 and 1776 (Cremin, 1970; Urban & Wagoner, 2000; Welling, 2005; Wright, 1957).

HOW SCHOOLS IN THE EARLY SETTLEMENTS PROMOTED CHARACTER EDUCATION

There were salient ways in which the schools of colonial period promoted character education that were evident in virtually all the European settlements from Puritan New England and down the North Atlantic coast in particular. First, schools provided explicit character instruction in which educators taught from the Bible and other religious books that quoted and relied on the Bible. The Christian mind-set of the times was that character was a direct reflection of the intimacy of the relationship that one had with God. Therefore, instructors provided spiritual and moral tutelage by incorporating a great deal of biblical teaching. When teachers drew from the Bible in this way, they emphasized that youth needed to comprehend and apply the moral principles that were inherent in each lesson. Consequently, a student understood that such character instruction was to influence him or her as a person.

A second way in which character education was encouraged was through the example of the teacher. In nearly all schools of the period, teachers were expected to abide by a code of conduct. Most schools were either church-run schools or were strongly influenced by the churches in the community. Because of this, teachers were very cognizant of what behaviors positively and negatively affected children. School leaders emphasized the salience of one's behavior being consistent with one's teaching. Colonists were keenly aware that the kind of lifestyle they led ultimately influenced the children that they had instructed. Teachers during this time effused with a sense of responsibility that they not only teach what was right but live what is right. Instructors maintained a belief that they would be abashed if they trained students to be intelligent people devoid of godly virtue. These educators insisted that godliness in children provided the fertile ground in which instructors could plant seeds of knowledge that would flourish interminably. Without this fertile ground, added learning could actually become a hindrance to developing an improved society, because the leaders of tomorrow would not possess the virtue and maturity to know how to most compassionately and wisely implement their learning (Beard & Beard, 1944; Eavey, 1964; Michaelsen, 1970; Pulliam & Van Patten, 1991; Spring, 2005).

A third way that colonial schools emphasized character education was in its integration into the general curriculum. The teachers and school headmasters of the era believed that a good deal of the curriculum in virtually every discipline lent itself to the incorporation of moral education. To them, good character was vital 24 hours a day and was inextricably connected with almost every activity people undertake. Therefore, it was only plausible for teachers to integrate character education into the curriculum as much as possible. For example, one might find a subtraction problem that indicated that Susie had three cookies and Ken ate six and got sick. The subtraction problem would then read, "How many more cookies did Ken have than Susie?" It is patent that authors of a math problem such as this were attempting to convey two messages. First, there is, of course, the more overt lesson that six minus three equals three. However, it is ostensible that the math book is alluding to the fact that while eating three cookies is reasonable, eating six cookies is excessive. To the textbook writers of the period, if moral lessons could be provided within the text, the instruction was doubly efficacious (Martin, 1894; Michaelsen, 1970).

To the colonists, especially the Puritans, if the character curriculum was strong, this provided the ideal atmosphere in which knowledge could expand. And indeed, as long as people sought knowledge within this edifying context, the quest for knowledge would indubitably be encouraged (Cubberley, 1920, 1934; Lippy, 2001; Stephens, 1872). Lippy (2001, pp. 78–79) notes that to the Puritans "knowledge itself is a gift from God to be used to praise God even if it benefits humanity. Hence Puritanism gave a tremendous boost to scientific inquiry in the colonial period." In the eyes of myriad pious settlers to pursue knowledge was one of the foremost ways that one could glorify God. The religious settlers of the era did not compartmentalize divine pursuit and intellectual study in the same fashion that many people do today. For example, the settlers thought of philosophy as "the love of wisdom" or "the desire to find one's place in the symphony of the cosmos" (Kennedy, 2001, p. 87). Largely because the early settlers believed God was the Creator of the world, they tended to be optimistic people. This was particularly true of the Puritans. Rick Kennedy (p. 89) observes, "They believed the pursuer of truth would find it. Logic and ethics were the two great concerns of Puritan philosophy."

To the Puritans and many of the colonists, scholarship was intellectual but also indubitably practical. The Puritans emphasized the concept of "covenant" in their relationship with God. Therefore, drawing closer to

God and seeking to keep His commandments and one's personal promises to Him was of utmost importance in education and in every other facet of life. This is largely why the most beloved aspects of philosophy in the eyes of the Puritans and other colonists were ethics and logic, which were the most practical and morally based aspects of philosophy. Ethics is patently a form of moral education, which instructors usually teach in college or high school. In the eyes of the Puritans it was imperative that students at these levels learn how to engage in righteous decision-making and evaluation so that they could make appropriate moral decisions in life. The settlers believed that ethics should be taught to as many students as possible, because again, in their view, character education should be inculcated to all students not merely a small percentage. A society of civility and compassion emerged when all its people were instilled with character rather than a select few. This perspective influenced virtually all colonial undertakings. For example, the Puritans brought something new to the continent in that they allowed church parishioners to vote on church matters, including the approval of pastoral appointments. This is the principal reason that they would later be known as the Congregationalist denomination (Jeynes, 2007; Kennedy, 2001).

One of the emphases in the pre–Revolutionary War schools was that students could make a difference in the world. The essence of this truth was founded on the notion that people of character are those who make a difference in the world. The conviction of the time was that virtuous people do make a difference because they are people of character. Because character education involves influencing children's thoughts, intentions, and behavior in real life, colonial teachers sought to guide children through real and play-acting situations that helped them apply their moral lessons to real life. For example, students often studied conflict resolution and were actually trained to become playground mediators in early elementary school. One of the keys to preparing children to be effective in this regard was training them to listen carefully to what other people were saying (Bailyn, 1960; Cubberley, 1920, 1934; Dowling & Scarlett, 2006).

Teachers of the era tended to be very specific about how people were to treat one another, how they were to react to one another, and how they were to deal with hurts, disagreements, and tensions. They were also taught what constituted responsible behavior and how they were to hold themselves accountable. Teachers often provided moral tutelage in how to treat others who were above and below them on the academic and socioeconomic totem pole, as well as those who were different from them (Dowling & Scarlett, 2006). One Quaker motto was representative of the moral orientation that many religious groups possessed at the time: "Let your life speak" (p. 370).

One stereotype that many people hold of people during this period is that they were intolerant. However, there is actually a considerable amount of the curriculum dedicated to providing tutelage in tolerance. Instructors taught children to cherish the variety of individuals in the world, understanding that each person was an important part of God's spiritual puzzle and that each person revealed (among a couple of other things) a part of God's character. It is true that communities in that era had more definitive convictions about right and wrong, but once one goes beyond this framework, the colonists were generally much more tolerant than modern day stereotypes would indicate (Dowling & Scarlett, 2006).

The pedagogy employed by teachers during the colonial period was similar to that employed since the time of Quintilian during the days of the Roman Empire. Quintilian recommended that classroom instruction first involve a teacher lecturing and then he believed that children should break up into small groups and discuss the lecture. It was, in fact, Quintilian who established the idea of small groups in the classroom. Often teachers elucidated a character concept and this was followed by time of prayer, and then a time of class discussion either in small groups or as an entire class (Dowling & Scarlett, 2006; Dupuis, 1966; Jeynes, 2007).

It is important to understand that character education, whether it was studied at the elementary or secondary school level or whether it was studied in the form of ethics or theology at the collegiate level, was a vital aspect of the curriculum. In fact, character education often involved the reading and studying of some of the most profound pieces of literature that the students read. At the college level, Harvard, the nation's first college founded in 1636, started the college day at dawn and it continued until the night. Most of the curriculum during this period involved the teaching of religion, morality, and ethics (Bark & Lefler, 2004).

THE PHILOSOPHY OF EDUCATION OF THE COLONIES IN GENERAL

The early settlers were strong believers that the early days of a child's schooling presented a wonderful opportunity to constitute a moral foundation on which the remainder of a child's development could burgeon. Ratcliff and May (2004, p. 7) eloquently express the colonial belief of the day as well as the perspective that most evangelical Christians have today: "There is a spiritual essence that all human beings share. It is a craving deep within for transcendence and meaning." The earlier settlers sought to construct a type of moral instruction that would appeal to that "craving" after spiritual reality so that the child's longing after God would be satisfied. This notion of creating a character curriculum that would be appealing to children's yearnings was based on the assumption that, as Ratcliff & May (2004, p. 7) describe, "children are just as much spiritual beings as are the adults in their lives."

There were certain assumptions that colonists had about the maturity and qualities of children that help one understand why the former insisted that moral instruction was so vital and what the nature of that edification should be. First, they believed that children were fully human, made in the image of God. They believed that human life started at conception. Second, children were gifts from God and were to be regarded as sources of great joy. This made them worthy of love and respect. Third, children could relate to God and be blessed by God. Fourth, children were developing beings that were in need of nurturing and guidance. Fifth, children represented a special class of human beings before God. On the one hand, this meant that the settlers maintained that children should be treated with the utmost tenderness. For example, they believed that children's brains required periodic relief, silence, and rest from the demands of studying. On the other hand, they viewed children as more complex and sophisticated than is commonly the case in modern society. They believed that youth were capable of more responsibility and adult-like behavior than contemporary psychologists recognize. In fact, leaders of the colonial era would likely view adolescence as at least partially a spurious modern psychological construct that seeks to delay adulthood by downplaying the factuality of biological changes into adulthood. Myriad settlers would likely state that by artificially delaying adulthood rather than acknowledging patent biological realities, it is not surprising that the teenage years are often associated with so much parental and adolescent frustration. Settlers of the era would interpret changes that contemporary psychologists call the transition into adolescence as the birth pangs of adulthood. They would argue that unless one acknowledges these changes as such by giving these young people increased responsibilities and flexibility, as well as having higher expectations of them, one is simply postponing the process of maturing (Bailyn, 1960; Bartlett, 1978; Berryman, 2004; Bunge, 2004; Issler, 2004; Jeynes, 2007).

There is no question that from 1607 until as late as 1900, the European inhabitants of the New World had considerably higher expectations of those youth aged 13–21 than Americans possess today. The reading levels of textbooks are two to five years higher for a given grade than what one witnesses today. By the 1840s, political and educational leaders expected that algebra would be taught in the fourth grade. Older girls were expected to help mothers with child rearing and older boys were required to help harvest the family crops. Of course, all of these statements must be taken in the context that the average life span of individuals during this period was considerably shorter than it is now. Consequently, partially as a result of necessity, children needed to mature faster than is the case in contemporary society. Nevertheless, the fact that 13- to 21-year-olds were able to complete many of these tasks indicates the degree to which members of this age group are able to engage in adult-like functions a good deal earlier than is commonly acknowledged today (Barton, 2004; Jeynes, 2007; Troen, 1988).

THE ROLE OF EXAMPLE AND COMMUNITY IN CHARACTER EDUCATION

The settlers throughout the east coast were also aware of the impact of being a living example of the principles shared in the schools. The Puritans and Quakers were particularly cognizant of the power of example and sought to do great acts of kindness toward strangers, Native Americans, and other groups. Their acts of compassion far exceeded those of the other colonists in that time period. The colonists of the period also emphasized community. Character education was a community affair. Usually, particularly in highly religious colonies such as the Puritans and the Quakers, the church worked to unify the community. The church was aware that the community's activities needed to be right not only because of issues of right and wrong but because these actions would have a lasting impact on the youth (McClellan & Reese, 1988).

The Puritans, Pilgrims, and Quakers were generally the best colonial groups in terms of their treatment of Native Americans. Each of these groups believed that it was vital to live lives of integrity when dealing with the Native Americans and also to offer character training to them. Part of the reason for this is that the Quakers were totally pacifistic and did not believe in war under any circumstances. The Puritans and Pilgrims were relatively pacifistic and averred that one could defend himself, but one could not start a military conflict (Jeynes, 2007; Marshall & Manuel, 1977).

Each of these groups made a profound attempt to reach out to Native Americans and establish peaceful relationships with them. The Pilgrims are well known for inviting the Native Americans over for the first Thanksgiving Feast in 1621. The Pilgrims even conveyed to the Native Americans that the Pilgrims did not expect them to bring any food to the feast but consistent with their overall generous attitude the Wampanoag brought a great deal of food to the feast. Another example for the Pilgrims reaching out to the Native Americans is when Massasoit, the chief of the Wampanoag, sent word to the Pilgrims that he was about to die from a deadly disease that had blinded him (Willison, 1945). Numerous other Native Americans were also dying from the same disease. The Pilgrims dispatched Edward Winslow and two other settlers in order to apply their medical abilities to bring Massasoit back to health. Just a few days after taking the medicine Massasoit recovered and the other tribes-people had regained their health as well (Willison, 1945). Massasoit was overjoyed over his dramatic recovery and declared, "Now I see the English are my friends and love me and whilst I live, I will never forget this kindness they have showed me" (Willison, 1945, p. 222). The Puritans were committed to fostering a good relationship with Native Americans in much the same way. In fact, Harvard College's charter states that one of the original purposes of the college was to educate not only white children but Native Americans as well. The education of Native Americans was especially important because to the surprise of the settlers, Native Americans "put out their children to the English, to be brought up by them" (Connecticut Record, 1736, pp. 102–103).

In addition, from early in Harvard's history, in the 1640s or before, the Puritans made it a priority to educate Native Americans. In response, some Native Americans began to attend Harvard along with the other students. Harvard's charter of 1650 patently states that the college was committed to "the education of the English and Indian youth of the country" (Wilson, 2004, p. 3). The Puritans arranged to make it possible for Native Americans to attend Harvard free of charge. Ultimately, the Puritans concluded that to make this invitation to Harvard more appealing there needed to be a building within Harvard College to educate Native

Americans. The building of the Native American facet of Harvard College was initiated in 1653 and completed in 1655. At first, Native Americans went to Harvard side by side with whites, but due to practical, often language-based, reasons and Native American preference, they later often attended separate classes. At the elementary school level, the Puritans often taught Native Americans together with whites (Adams, 2005; Cremin, 1970; Lin, 2005; Marshall & Manuel, 1977).

The relationship between the Puritans and the Native Americans was generally a positive one as long as Massasoit lived. While he lived, Native Americans and the settlers would offer each other their practical and cultural strengths. The Native Americans offered their knowledge of agriculture and survival and the settlers offered their medicine and education. The early successes between the Pilgrims and the Native Americans were largely due to a high degree of tolerance by both sides. The tolerance of the Pilgrims emerged primarily from their suffering from persecution in England and their experiences after fleeing to the Netherlands. The tolerance of the Pilgrims/Puritans and the Native Americans was manifested to other groups as well, contrary to some of the stereotypes held by some individuals. It is true that the Pilgrims/Puritans did not allow all groups to abide with them, but they often helped many different groups of people. They were very hospitable to all kinds of people, including the homeless, strangers, shipwreck victims, and even some of their enemies who had committed deleterious acts against them (Bartlett, 1978; Marshall & Manuel, 1977; Robinson, 1851).

CHARACTER EDUCATION IN HIGHER EDUCATION BEFORE THE REVOLUTIONARY WAR

The Role of Character

The colleges of the era recognized that it was an act of trust for parents to send their children to college. They also realized that via college living, leaders possessed an opportunity to have an explicit effect on the character development of youth. As a means toward reaching this end, colleges generally required certain levels of church and chapel attendance, as well as formal dress throughout nearly all of a school day. College leaders also emphasized civility in the treatment of others, tolerance, and respect toward the professors (Middleton, 2004).

Colleges had a distinct advantage over elementary and secondary schools when it came to moral instruction. That is, unlike the situation in most precollege institutions, the students usually lived on campus. This enabled colleges to enjoy a much greater moral influence in student lives outside the classroom. This influence not only manifested itself in the chapel services and dress requirements but also in moral codes and rules of etiquette that were common knowledge among the students (Middleton, 2004; Reuben, 1996).

Within this context, colleges regarded the moral example of the professors as extremely important. In the eyes of college leaders, the personal example of the professors stood as at least equal in stature to their proficiency to teach. A faculty member who fell due to moral failure was released from the college much more readily than one who was an inefficacious instructor. The college leaders of the time opined that the damage done by one semester's worth of deficient lectures was not as deleterious as the effects of an immoral lifestyle (Gaustad & Schmidt, 2002; Reuben, 1996).

Because the state of an individual's lifestyle was so vital, the college president was regarded not only as the school's best scholar but as one of the foremost examples of righteous living in the college. With this in mind, it should come as no surprise that nearly all colleges of the era required a senior course in moral and mental philosophy, which was the capstone of the school's curriculum (Middleton, 2004; Reuben, 1996). As Reuben (pp. 22–23) notes, "It drew together the knowledge learned in the previous three years and placed it in a Christian framework."

It is only logical that moral instruction should play a large role in college training, because originally all the early colleges were founded with the primary purpose of preparing preachers for the work of the ministry. Harvard College was the first institution of higher education founded in the United States. Like its other Ivy League counterparts, Harvard was founded primarily as a college for training "learned and godly ministers" (Beard & Beard, 1944, p. 65). At the time, ministers were generally the most educated people in the New World. The colleges naturally thought that character instruction was imperative for training ministers. As Harvard became a nucleus for inculcating people from other professions as well, they too would benefit from this emphasis on moral instruction. The Puritans founded Harvard as a highly religious college. Crimson was chosen as the official color of the college, representing the blood of Christ (Beard & Beard, 1944).

William & Mary, the nation's second college, was established in 1693. It was founded in Virginia, where support for education was substantially less than in the Bible Belt of New England and the Mid-Atlantic states. Nevertheless, the purpose of William & Mary, much like Harvard, was "to provide a seminary for the training of ministers and to make possible the right training of the young that the cause of the Gospel might be advanced" (Eavey, 1964). Yale was founded in 1701 and was established by Puritans, who were concerned that Harvard was less conservative than it had originally been and a more conservative alternative that was also close to New York was needed. Princeton was founded by the Presbyterians in 1746 for essentially the same two reasons that Yale was founded. Princeton was the first of a series of colleges established as a direct result of the Great Awakening, which emphasized spiritual revival but also highlighted the salience of character instruction in the colleges as a means of preparing tomorrow's leadership (Stewart, 1969).

The colleges were desirous of shaping a moral instruction curriculum that was intellectually and spiritually challenging. Most of the college presidents were cognizant of the fact that in order to discern the appropriate moral response, one first needed to properly decipher the relevant moral problem. Although there was an understanding that character training was aimed primarily at the spiritual aspect of human beings, school leaders also fathomed the fact that decisions regarding virtue and faith involved ethics and therefore directly involved the mind (Gilligan, 1981; Hester, 2003).

The Great Awakening

The First and Second Great Awakening, 1730–1760 and 1790–1840, were great religious revivals that would affect the U.S. education system both before and after the Revolutionary War. Several of the Great Awakening's most prominent leaders had a dramatic influence on America's education system and specifically on the nation's character education curriculum. Jonathan Edwards was one of the great preachers of the First Great Awakening. He believed in the importance of speaking to college audiences and other elite groups. He not only held religious services in these venues but spoke in other forums such as at Yale's commencement in 1741. He wrote a number of books that were used in college, including *Distinguishing Marks of a Work of the Spirit of God* (1741). He eventually became president of Princeton (then called the College of New Jersey; Cowing, 1971; Holmes, 2001; Middleton, 2004; Piper, 2004).

Jonathan Edwards believed that the greatest heights of the experience of spiritual truth and intellectual insight are totally consistent and that it is completely logical for the two to occur simultaneously. Edwards believed in an intelligent Christianity. Those people who followed Edwards were called New Light Calvinists. Edwards viewed the Great Awakening revival as an intercolonial event, which he trusted would sweep all through the colonies (Cowing, 1971; Kidd, 2007; Piper, 2004).

George Whitefield was another gifted preacher. He was born in Gloucester, England in 1714. Like most ministers of his day, Whitefield was highly educated. He had attended Oxford University. Although Whitefield was born in England, he possessed a special desire to have a powerful influence in the United States. Whitefield believed that the United States would have a prominent role in future world affairs. He was extremely eloquent and earned a great deal of respect among America's leaders and in the media. Although the New England area was probably the most affected by the Great Awakening, virtually every colony was influenced. In addition, although prominent ministers such as Edwards, Whitefield, and Wesley had a major influence, there were other preachers too, who although their ministries tended to be more localized, nevertheless carried a great deal of influence. Two of these men were James Davenport and Andrew Croswell, who were especially prominent in New England (Kidd, 2007; Middleton, 2004).

The Great Awakening had a considerable impact on the practice of character education in America's schools. The sermons of the era especially had an influence on the moral education curriculum. For example, Jonathan Ashley of Deerfield, Massachusetts wrote a character education book entitled *The Great Duty of Charity*.

The Great Awakening also influenced educators, who in turn founded colleges and schools. For example, this revival had a tremendous effect on Eleazar Wheelock, who may have been the Great Awakening's most dedicated supporter in the state of Connecticut. Wheelock later founded Dartmouth, one of the eight Ivy League universities and originally founded as a college for Native Americans. The *Boston Gazette* kept records of church and school growth, as a result of the Great Awakening, and indicated major increase in each. In fact, the Great Awakening was instrumental in changing the lives of the attendees, that George Whitefield shared that so many people were coming to him in his preaching and counseling that he was having trouble finding time to eat (Gaustad, 1957).

Those individuals touched by either the First (1730–1760) or the Second Great Awakening (1790–1840) had many of the same values as the Puritans, particularly regarding character education. Consistent with the Puritan focus on moral instruction, the Great Awakening strengthened the orientation that American education already had toward character instruction (Beecher, 1835; Cowing, 1971).

The Great Awakening particularly influenced American education at the college level, especially at Princeton and Yale. Princeton was founded as a result of the Great Awakening in 1746 so that it quickly became a center of intellectual spirituality. In the case of Yale, the college was able to retain its vision largely because of the influence of the Great Awakening (Hall, 1982; Middleton, 2004).

Another minister who affected education, who was prominent during the Great Awakening, was John Wesley. John Wesley (1703–1791) was a very bright individual who studied at Oxford University but decided to leave Oxford in order to minister in the New World. Wesley, like nearly all of his contemporary minister colleagues, believed that education and spiritual freedom were closely aligned. This was no more clearly apparent than in Wesley's perspective regarding schooling African American slaves in the South (Dowling & Scarlett, 2006).

Before the time of the Revolutionary War, there was one period of time when there was a golden age for starting colleges. It was during the 1740s and 1750s, immediately following the Great Awakening. During the Great Awakening, many preachers rallied the people into an awareness of educating the religious leadership. During this period, some of America's greatest colleges were founded, including Princeton, Columbia, and Penn. The founding of Brown, some years later, was also said to be a result of the effects of the Great Awakening. As a result of the establishing of these colleges, the percentage of Americans that attended college slowly edged upward, although it was some time before any significant percentage of Americans attended college (Michaelsen, 1970).

Devout religious people, however, founded all the Ivy League schools, with religious purposes in mind. It was understood that these schools would serve as a conduit for spreading the gospel. The Dutch Reformed Church also founded Rutgers during the same period. In many respects, the colonists faced greater challenges in establishing elementary and secondary schools than they did colleges. Much of this was due to the threat of Native American attacks upon the schools. College age individuals could defend themselves, but primary and secondary school children were far more helpless (Tewksbury, 1932).

During the mid-to-late 1700s, influential evangelical clergy, called "New Light" clergy, influenced by the Great Awakening were at the forefront of the college education movement and were determined to establish colleges that maintained deep religious and moral roots. Several Ivy League colleges were founded by these "New Light" clergy, including Princeton in 1746, Brown in 1764, and Dartmouth in 1769. "New Light" clergy also founded Rutgers (originally named Queen's) in 1766. These men of the cloth also established Rutgers in 1766. "New Light" clergy came from a variety of denominational affiliations, including Baptist, Presbyterian, Congregationalist, and Dutch Reformed (Marsden, 1994). In fact, the founding of Princeton in 1746 was a direct result of the nonacceptance of "New Light" clergy at Yale. Two other Ivy League universities, Columbia (originally called King's College) and Penn, founded in 1754 and 1755, respectively, were founded by a broader coalition of non–New Light clergy. Although all of these universities were religious in nature and placed great value on daily and curricular expressions of character, the New Light colleges demonstrated particular rigor in this regard (Marsden, 1994).

CONCLUSION

Perhaps at no time in American history was there such an emphasis on character education. The settlers realized the necessity of moral instruction at all levels of schooling—elementary school, secondary school, and college. Through charity schools they also made moral instruction available to all children, whether they could afford it or not. Generous individuals paid for the tuition of 50, 100, and 200 students. Many settlers also did what they could to make character education available to students of color. The valiant efforts of these individuals serve as a reminder of the importance of character education to all ages and to all groups of children.

REFERENCES

Adams, J. (2005). Harvard excavates past in Indian College anniversary. *Indian Country Today*, December 7, p. 3.

Ammerman, M. (1995). *Roger Williams.* Uhrichsville, OH: Barbour.

Bailyn, B. (1960). *Education in the forming of American society.* Chapel Hill, NC: University of North Carolina Press.

Bark, O. T., & Lefler, H. T. (2004). Educating the youth throughout the New World. In M. C. Ryan (Ed.), *Living in colonial America* (pp. 93–110). San Diego, CA: Greenhaven Press.

Bartlett, R. M. (1978). *The faith of the Pilgrims.* New York: United Church Press.

Barton, D. (2004). *Four centuries of American education.* Aledo, TX: Wallbuilders.

Beard, C. A., & Beard, M. R. (1944). *A basic history of the United States.* New York: Doubleday, Doran, & Company.

Beecher, L. (1835). *A plea for the West.* n.p.

Berryman, J. W. (2004). Children and mature spirituality. In D. Ratcliff & M. G. McQuitty (Eds.), *Children's spirituality* (pp. 22–42). Eugene, OR: Cascade Press.

Brooke, C. N., Highfield, J. R., & Swaan, W. (1988). *Oxford and Cambridge.* New York: Cambridge University Press.

Bunge, M. J. (2004). Historical perspectives on children in the church: Resources for spiritual formation and a theology of children today. In D. Ratcliff & M. G. McQuitty (Eds.), *Children's spirituality* (pp. 42–53). Eugene, OR: Cascade Press.

Cayton, M. K., & Williams, P. W. (2001). *Encyclopedia of American cultural & intellectual history.* New York: Scribner.

Chauncy, C. (1655). Charles Chauncy on liberal learning. In W. Smith (Ed.) (1973), *Theories of education in early America* (pp. 15–23). Indianapolis, IN: Bobbs-Merrill Company.

Chen, J. (1994). *Confucius as a teacher.* Beijing: Foreign Language Press.

Cicero in Freeman Institute (2009). Quotable quotes (www.freemaninstitute.com/quotes.htm, retrieved March 12, 2009).

Clarke, J. (1730). John Clarke's classical program of studies. In W. Smith (Ed.) (1973), *Theories of education in early America* (pp. 38–45). Indianapolis, IN: Bobbs-Merrill Company.

Connecticut Record, Volume VII, 1726–1735. (1736).

Cowing, C. B. (1971). *The Great Awakening and the American Revolution.* Chicago, IL: Rand McNally.

Cremin, L. A. (1970). *American education: The colonial experience, 1607–1783.* New York: Harper & Row.

———. (1976). *Traditions of American education.* New York: Basic Books.

Cubberley, E. (1920). *The history of education.* Boston, MA: Houghton Mifflin.

————, ed. (1934). *Readings in public education in the United States: A collection of sources and readings to illustrate the history of educational practice and progress in the United States.* Cambridge, MA: Riverside Press.

Dowling, E. M., & Scarlett, W. G. (2006). *Encyclopedia of religious and spiritual development.* Thousand Oaks, CA: Sage Publications.

Dupuis, A. M. (1966) *Philosophy of education in historical perspective.* Chicago, IL: Rand McNally.

Eavey, C. B. (1964). *History of Christian education.* Chicago, IL: Moody Press.

Edwards, J. (2004). Puritan society: A moral role model. In M. C. Ryan (Ed.), *Living in colonial America* (pp. 87–92). San Diego, CA: Greenhaven Press.

Elias, J. L. (1995). *Philosophy of education: Classical and contemporary.* Malabar, FL: Krieger.

Fay, J. W. (1966). *American psychology before William James.* New York: Octagon.

Fraser, J. W. (2001). *The school in the United States.* Boston, MA: McGraw-Hill.

Friedman, R. E. (2001). Puritanism as a cultural and intellectual force. In M. K. Cayton & W. Williams (Eds.), *The Encyclopedia of American cultural and intellectual history* (pp. 43–51). New York: Scribner.

Gartner, L. P. (1969). *Jewish education in the United States.* New York: Teachers College Press.

Gaustad, E. S. (1957). *The Great Awakening in New England.* New York: Harper.

Gaustad, E. S., & Schmidt, L. E. (2002). *The religious history of America.* New York: Harper San Francisco.

Gilligan, C. (1981). Moral development. In A. W. Chickering (Ed.), *The modern American college.* San Francisco, CA: Jossey-Bass.

Gilpin, W. C. (1982). The creation of a new order: Colonial education and the Bible. In D. L. Barr & N. Piediscalzi (Eds.), *The Bible in American education* (pp. 5–23). Philadelphia, PA: Fortress Press.

Hall, P. D. (1982). *The organization of American culture, 1700–1900.* New York: New York University Press.

Hester, J. P. (2003). *The ten commandments.* Jefferson, NC: McFarland.

Hiner, N. R. (1988). The cry of Sodom enquired into: Educational analysis in seventeenth century New England. In *The social history of American education.* Urbana, IL: University of Illinois Press.

Holmes, S. (2001). *God of grace and God of glory: An account of the theology of Jonathan Edwards.* Grand Rapids, MI: Eerdmans.

Holy Bible. (1973). Grand Rapids, MI: Zondervan.

Issler, K. (2004). Biblical perspectives on developmental grace for nurturing children's spirituality. In D. Ratcliff & M. G. McQuitty (Eds.), *Children's spirituality* (pp. 54–73). Eugene, OR: Cascade Press.

Jensen, L. C., & Knight, R. S. (1981). *Moral education: Historical perspectives.* Washington, D.C.: University Press of America.

Jeynes, W. (2004). Immigration in the United States and the golden years of education: Was Ravitch right? *Educational Studies, 35* (3), 248–270.

———. (2005). A meta-analysis of the relation of parental involvement to urban elementary school student academic achievement. *Urban Education, 40,* (3), 237–269.

———. (2006). Standardized tests and Froebel's original kindergarten model. *Froebel Teachers College Record, 108* (10), 1937–1959.

———. (2007). *American educational history: School, society, and the common good.* Thousand Oaks, CA: Sage Publications.

———. (2008). What we should and should not learn from the Japanese and other east Asian education systems. *Educational Policy, 22* (6), 900–927.

Johnson, P. (1997). *A history of the American people.* New York: Harper Collins.

Kennedy, R. (2001). Philosophy from Puritanism to the enlightenment. In M. K. Cayton & W. Williams (Eds.), *The Encyclopedia of American cultural and intellectual history* (pp. 87–95). New York: Scribner.

Kidd, T. S. (2007). *The Great Awakening: The root of evangelical Christianity in colonial America.* New Haven, CT: Yale University Press.

King, M. L., in Freeman Institute (2009). Quotable quotes (www.freemaninstitute .com/quotes.htm, retrieved March 12, 2009).

Lin, J. C. (2005). Indian tribe back in yard. *Harvard Crimson,* April 11, p. 6.

Lippy, C. H. (2001). Anglo-American religious traditions. In M. K. Cayton & W. Williams (Eds.), *The encyclopedia of American cultural and intellectual history* (pp. 77–85). New York: Scribner.

Marrou, H. I. (1956). *A history of education in antiquity.* New York: Sheed & Ward.

Marsden, G. M. (1994). *The soul of the American university.* New York: Oxford University Press.

Marshall, P., & Manuel, D. (1977). *The light and the glory.* Grand Rapids, MI: Fleming Revell.

Martin, G. (1894). *The evolution of the Massachusetts public school system.* New York: Appleton.

McClellan, B. E. (1999). *Moral education in America.* New York: Teachers College Press.

McClellan, B. E., & Reese, W. J. (1988). *The social history of American education.* Urbana, IL: University of Illinois Press.

McKnight, D. (2003). *Schooling, the Puritan imperative, and the molding of an American national identity.* Mahwah, NJ: Erlbaum.

Mentzer, M. S. (1988). Religion and achievement motivation in the United States: A structural analysis. *Sociological Focus, 21*, 307–316.

Michaelsen, R. (1970). *Piety in the public school*. London: Macmillan.

Middleton, R. (2004). Religion and education. In M. C. Ryan (Ed.), *Living in colonial America* (pp. 65–74). San Diego, CA: Greenhaven Press.

Moroney, S. (2001). Education in early America. In M. K. Cayton & W. Williams (Eds.), *The encyclopedia of American cultural and intellectual history* (pp. 53–61). New York: Scribner.

Piper, J. (2004). *A God entranced vision of all things: The legacy of Jonathan Edwards*. Wheaton, IL: Crossway.

Pulliam, J. D., & Van Patten, J. J. (1991). *History of education in America*. Upper Saddle River, NJ: Merrill/Prentice Hall.

Ratcliff, P., & May, S. (2004). Identifying children's spirituality. In D. Ratcliff & M. G. McQuitty (Eds.), *Children's spirituality* (pp. 7–21). Eugene, OR: Cascade Press.

Reuben, J. A. (1996). *The making of the modern university*. Chicago, IL: University of Chicago Press.

Rippa, S. A. (1997). *Education in a free society*. White Plains, NY: Longman.

Robinson, J. (1851). *Works*. London: John Snow.

Ryan, K., & Bohlin, K. E. (1999). *Building character in schools*. San Francisco, CA: Jossey-Bass.

Schultz, E. B., & Tougias, M. J. (1999) *King Philip's war*. Woodstock, VT: Countryman Press.

Smith, W. (1973). *Theories of education in early America*. Indianapolis, IN: Bobbs-Merrill Company.

Spring, J. (2005). *The American school 1642–2004*. White Plains, NY: Longman.

Stephens, A. H. (1872). *History of the United States*. New York: Hale & Son.

Stewart, G., Jr. (1969). *A history of religious education in Connecticut*. New York: Arno Press & the New York Times.

Tewksbury, S. (1932). *Founding of American colleges and universities before the Civil War*. New York: Teachers College Press.

Troen, S. K. (1988). Popular education in nineteenth century St. Louis. In E. McClellan & W. J. Reese (Eds.), *The social history of American education* (pp. 119–136). Urbana, IL: University of Illinois Press.

Tyler, M. C. (1878). *A history of American literature*. New York: Putnam.

Urban, W., & Wagoner, J. (2000). *American education: A history*. Boston, MA: McGraw-Hill.

Weber, M. (1930). *The Protestant ethic and the spirit of capitalism*. Translated by T. Parsons. New York: Scribner.

Weddle, M. B. (2001). *Walking in the way of peace: Quaker pacifism in the seventeenth century.* Oxford: Oxford University Press.

Welling, G. (2005). *From revolution to reconstruction.* Groningen, the Netherlands: University of Groningen.

Willison, G. F. (1945). *Saints and strangers.* New York: Reynal & Hitchcock.

———. (1966). *Saints and strangers.* London: Longman.

Wilson, R. (2004). 350th anniversary of Indian college commemorated. *Harvard University Gazette*, April 13, p. 3. Retrieved May 15, 2005 from www.news.harvard.edu/
gazette/2005/04.14/03-indian.html.

Wright, L. B. (1957). *The cultural life of the American colonies, 1607–1763.* New York: Harper.

4

CHARACTER EDUCATION DURING THE POST–REVOLUTIONARY WAR PERIOD

THE FOUNDERS' PERSPECTIVES ON THE PLACE OF CHARACTER EDUCATION

The founders of the United States possessed a deep appreciation for the value of character instruction. Often these founders approached the issue from different vantage points, utilizing different types of logic to reach similar conclusions regarding the necessity of this moral instruction.

George Washington

Although the founding fathers were naturally all in favor of democracy, some of the founders warned of the potential excesses of democracy (Washington, 1796). In his farewell address, George Washington warned of what he termed an "unbridled democracy." That is, George Washington believed that as people exercised their newfound freedom, they could become self-centered and do whatever they pleased. Washington was nevertheless optimistic that through the presence of religious and moral education, the United States could avoid becoming an "unbridled democracy." McClellan describes well the attitude of many Americans toward freedom and the need for character education, especially by the 1800s. To many of the nation's citizens this newfound liberty "required the development of strong internal controls. In the minds of nineteenth century

Americans, the price of liberty was rigorous self-discipline and upright personal conduct" (McClellan, 1999, p. 35).

George Washington believed, as many of the people of the era did, that religion and morality were inextricably connected; that is, he maintained that human morality was rooted in being religious. He asserted that religion and morality were two of the pillars of society. In his Farewell Address of September 19, 1796, Washington declared, "of all the dispositions and habits which lead to political prosperity, religion and morality are indispensable supports. In vain would that man claim the tribute of patriotism, who should labor to subvert these great pillars of human happiness" (Washington, 1796). In a 1779 speech Washington declared to his listeners that they would "do well to learn . . . above all the religion of Jesus Christ" (Washington, 1779).

Washington and many of his colleagues in his two presidential administrations believed that in addition to the teaching of morality in the home and the schools, Sunday schools provided an important source of moral instruction. Sunday schools were church-sponsored schools designed to provide religious and character instruction, as well as academic instruction, particularly in reading, mathematics, and social studies, throughout the day each Sunday. In the minds of myriad Americans, as a result of the liberty that emerged after the Revolutionary War, schools need to emphasize character education even more than they did before. The founding of the Sunday school appeared to be the ideal way to ameliorate the problem of an increased need for character education. Many Americans believed that the combination of proper child rearing by the family and moral education in both the regular schools and the Sunday schools would enable youth to develop appropriately. Raikes (1735–1811) of England originally founded the Sunday school in 1780 and educators in the United States quickly adopted the same model beginning in 1785. In its incipiency the Sunday school was used "to instruct poor children in eastern cities, teaching them reading and writing, as well as moral values" (McClellan, 1999, p. 22). Over time, as it developed, however, the Sunday school became an educational extension and integral part of most major denominations in America (Eavey, 1964). The Sunday school became a wonderful combination of a supplemental school tutoring center and church. The Sunday school served to abet the educational and character training efforts of parents and schools (Cremin, 1970; Davis, 1997; Eavey, 1964; Fraser, 2001; Jeynes, 2003, 2007; McClellan, 1999).

Federalists, such as George Washington and Alexander Hamilton, certainly embraced and valued democracy but also maintained that democracy presented certain dangers. To the Federalists, the best hope for America's future was to have the teaching of piety and character closely tied in America's schools. The Federalists insisted the nation's freedoms and laws were intended for upright people (Adams, 1854; Kirk, 1953). Consequently, character instruction was necessary to ensure that the nation's future generations would be virtuous and therefore able to live by the nation's freedoms (Hall, 1982). The mode of behavior that Federalists especially wanted to encourage was "self-control" (Hall, 1982, p. 90). John Adams, like George Washington, dreamed of a nation that should take the Bible for its only law book (Adams, 1756, p. 5).

Benjamin Rush

Benjamin Rush, a signer of the Declaration of Independence, was regarded as the nation's foremost physician and one of its leader educators. Rush probably influenced post–Revolutionary War schooling perhaps more than any other individual except Noah Webster. Benjamin Rush strongly believed in the place of moral education in the schools. He firmly maintained the youth in school should be trained to be people of integrity, who are rooted in the Bible and can be valuable citizens who make important contributions to the United States. He also believed that teachers should guide children lovingly and with gentleness. Rush advocated a position called "Republicanism" in which young Americans are encouraged to embrace the qualities necessary to be people of faith and loyal citizens. Republicanism, as Cathy Matson (2001, p. 170) asserts, involved "frugality, temperance, industry, simplicity, and self-restraint." The republicanism that Rush advocated was thoroughly grounded in Christianity. In 1798 Rush stated, "The only foundation for a useful education in a republic is to be laid in religion" (Rush, 1798, p. 5). He claimed that religious moral training was necessary in the schools in order for people to learn a self-disciplined and self-restrained lifestyle. Rush asserted that this type of lifestyle was vital in order for freedom to survive. He believed that if this moral restraint was absent, America's freedoms could become abused and harm people, causing America's freedoms to eventually be reduced in response. Rush argued that this self-disciplined, moral, and patriotic way of life was formed in the first 20 years of one's life. Therefore, it was imperative that parents train their children accordingly and that teachers initiate efforts to instill these qualities in children during their school years (Blinderman, 1976; Gutek, 1997; Hunt & Maxson, 1981; Hunt & Mullins, 2005; Lewy, 1996; Matson, 2001; Moss, 1984; Rollins, 1980; Rush, 1786, 1951; Unger, 1998; Urban & Wagoner, 2000).

Rush believed that in order for character instruction to be successful, the Bible needed to be at the center of the curriculum. He declared, "Every precept of the Gospel inculcates those degrees of humility, self-denial, and brotherly kindness" (Rush, 1786, p. 5). Benjamin Rush believed that teachers needed to not only instruct students in love and kindness but also exhibit this behavior. Blinderman (1976, p. 20) states, "Rush's ideal teacher is a temperate who treats children gently and with familiarity." Benjamin Rush, as the president of the University of Pennsylvania, maintained certain views about college education as well. He opposed the presence of college dormitories because he believed that it spawned various expressions of immorality (Blinderman, 1976; Jensen & Knight, 1981).

Noah Webster

If Benjamin Rush's primary influence was through recommending school policy, Noah Webster's primary impact was through the influence of his books. Noah Webster (1758–1843) was recognized as the most influential educator of his era and earned the nickname "America's schoolmaster." He wrote dozens of educational books and to this day the cumulative sales of his books ranks as the second or third all-time among American authors. Webster studied law at Yale University, wrote some of the nation's most popular first schoolbooks, and gave the nation its first dictionary and Bible, written in American English (Bark & Lefler, 2004; Gilpin, 1982; Jeynes, 2007; Kennedy, 2001).

Webster's speller, first released in 1783, contained many encouragements which exhorted school children to righteous behavior both at school and home. As Blinderman (1976, p. 28) notes, "Like Rush, Webster was a pious man." Not surprisingly therefore, Webster averred that it was absolutely essential that students be taught character education. Consistent with this belief, Webster asserted that ministers ought to be involved in all levels of education. He was particularly interested in clergy providing tutelage in moral instruction and in literacy. Preachers were generally the most educated individuals in the country and therefore it seemed logical that they also engage in teaching reading to students (Blinderman, 1976; Hunt & Mullins, 2005; Jeynes, 2007).

Webster's idea that ministers should be involved in training students in moral education and reading was not a new idea. For centuries many Europeans, as well as those in the New World, thought that it was only natural that those who were recognized as being the wisest and most knowledgeable in their communities guide youth into obtaining these qualities.

The character education of the Revolutionary War era emphasized restraint and moral purity. Noah Webster and Benjamin Rush were the two educational leaders of the era. Both argued for the need to emphasize moral education in both public and private schooling. One of the reasons why the school leaders of the time placed such an emphasis on self-restraint and purity is because they recognized that with the new orientation toward freedom that accompanied the land's new status as a liberated nation, all types of personal excesses could develop unless these teachers, parents, and ministers instructed students in the value of self-discipline (Jeynes, 2007; Lewy, 1996; McClellan, 1999; Urban & Wagoner, 2000; Webster, 1834).

Thomas Jefferson

Thomas Jefferson also highly esteemed character education and believed that it was an equally valuable pursuit as was the education of the mind (Cousins, 1958). Jefferson stated, "Give up money, give up fame, give up science, give up the earth itself and all it contains rather than do an immoral act. And never suppose that in any possible situation or under any circumstances, it is best for you to do a dishonorable thing, however slightly so it may appear to you" (Jefferson in Thompson, 1991).

In spite of Jefferson's support for character instruction, he believed that state governments rather than the church denominations should determine its content. Consequently, at one point Jefferson tried to do what he could to change William & Mary from a private college to a state institution. After New Hampshire stepped in and took over Dartmouth, New York took over Columbia (then known as King's College), and Pennsylvania assumed control over Penn, Jefferson took the seemingly indefensible position of favoring the state takeover of these private colleges. Dartmouth eventually took the case to the U.S. Supreme Court. In what is generally regarded as the U.S. Supreme Court's most important decision for education in the nineteenth century, the court voted the states could not unilaterally move in and take over a private college. The 1819 *Dartmouth v. Woodward* decision was a landmark albeit obvious decision that enabled private colleges the right to exist. The decision also allowed private colleges to develop their own character education curriculum (Current, 1964; Jeynes, 2007; Marshall, 1967).

Benjamin Franklin

Benjamin Franklin (1706–1794) emphasized education in a more subtle way. That is, Franklin did not vocalize his views on education to the extent that Rush and Webster did. Nevertheless, because of his prominence, his words and beliefs influenced many people. As Blinderman (1976, p. 11) notes, "Like Luther, he believed that it is easier to educate youth than to cure adults." He was heavily involved in giving money to support African American schools. Franklin believed strongly in the place of American education because he claimed that it was easier to educate youth than to cure adults of their psychological and moral ailments (Cousins, 1958; Spring, 2005; Washington, 1969).

John Jay

John Jay, along with Alexander Hamilton, jointly founded the Federalist Party. He was one of the authors of the Federalist papers. Jay served as the nation's first Chief Justice of the Supreme Court. President George Washington had such confidence in Jay that he allowed Jay to choose the cabinet position that he preferred. John Jay was a strong advocate of teaching character education in the schools and using the Bible as the principal textbook for that instruction. As president of the American Bible Society and, like Washington and Hamilton, a pious individual, Jay believed that the Bible should be the central focus of moral instruction in the school and the home as well (Cousins, 1958; Johnson, 1997).

Samuel Adams

Samuel Adams was the governor of Massachusetts and a strong advocate for "virtuous education" in the schools (Adams in Cousins, 1958). Like John Jay, Samuel Adams was a devout Christian and was clearly not restrained in his insistence that instruction in the Bible and morality had ameliorative effects. He also asserted that education, as a whole, had a valuable and puissant influence (Adams, 1794; Cousins, 1958). Adams (1794, p. 1) averred, "Education has a greater influence on manners than human laws can have." He further asserted, "But a virtuous education is calculated to reach and influence the heart, and to prevent crimes," and declared that the Bible "will impress their minds with a profound reverence for the Deity" (Adams, p. 1). Adams believed that if the Bible is used as the central textbook for instruction in virtue, "It will excite in them a just regard to Divine Revelation . . . and it will inspire them with a sense of true honor" (p. 1). Moral education, in Adams's mind, will encourage youth to "search for truth" (p. 1).

An Overview of the Views of the Founders

The post–Revolutionary War period was an important one for the development of character education. America's political and school leaders valued the religious base of moral instruction, but they did so in the context of acknowledging that the United States was a fledgling democracy. Character instruction now served a purpose not only of strengthening a student's faith but of molding them into faithful and productive American citizens. The educational philosophies of Benjamin Rush and Noah Webster typified the coupling of religious moral education and a "republican" education. Both Rush and Webster maintained that a successful spiritual-based moral education would ultimately yield a loyal and plenteous American citizenry. George Washington (1796) echoed the assertions of Rush and Webster by asserting that religious faith was a prerequisite for true patriotism. Washington and other Americans believed that character education was a means to this end (Cousins, 1958; Hunt & Maxson, 1981; Kliebard, 1969; Lewy, 1996; Moss, 1984; Rollins, 1980; Unger, 1998; Urban & Wagoner, 2000; Webster, 1807; Yulish, 1980).

The moral instruction that political and educational leaders had in mind was a demanding one both in terms of the expectations of the development of virtue and the intellectual capacity needed to comprehend moral truths. This, however, must be understood in the context of the fact that those who lived in the 1600s, 1700s, and 1800s possessed higher expectations of youth than most people have today. There are a number of reasons that will facilitate an understanding as to why this was so. First, people's life spans were shorter than they are today. This fact necessitated that schooling become more concentrated in time. Second, boys and girls often helped their parents with harvesting the crops and domestic responsibilities, especially beginning in their adolescent and preadolescent years. That is, people expected teenagers to assume adult responsibilities at a younger age than is currently the case. This reality translated into fewer years of schooling and meant that teachers needed to teach more information in a shorter period of time than is done today. Consequently, by the 1840s, myriad schools required algebra in the fourth grade (Fogel, 2004; Holmes, 2001; Howard, 1943; Riley, 2001; Robson, 1985; Somerville, 2002; Waller, 1950).

Third, because the United States was a fledging nation, an educated populace was considered key to the nation's survival. In the post–Revolutionary War era, the United States was surrounded by a host of great powers, which could pose a threat to national security. Britain and Spain remained adversaries and desired to expand their territory in the Western Hemisphere. A number of Native American tribes were hostile to the new country and the French, although they were allies during the Revolutionary War, soon had their own revolution and would ultimately be led by Napoleon, who had expansionist aspirations consistent with his autocratic rule. The hazardous situation intensified the nation's desire to have a strong nation based on an educated populace (Gerson, 1966; Holmes, 2001; Howard, 1943; Johnson, 1997; Kamen, 2003; McKay & Scott, 1983; Robson, 1985; Waller, 1950).

The declaration of the Northwest Ordinance (1787) was representative of the prime place that educators gave to moral education in their schooling of students. This ordinance stated: "Religion, morality, and knowledge, being necessary to good government and the happiness of mankind, schools and the means of education shall forever be encouraged." Moral education was therefore a prominent component of the elementary and secondary school education of the post–Revolutionary War era (Beard & Beard, 1944; Eisner, 1994; Hunt & Maxson, 1981).

The Revolutionary War also had some effect in determining the denominations that would have the greatest impact on the development of character education in America. Those denominations that strongly resisted the British—Presbyterians, Lutherans, Congregationalists, and Catholics—were those that had the greatest influence in shaping moral instruction (Stoll, 2001).

THE INFLUENCE OF THE TWO GREAT AWAKENINGS ON CHARACTER EDUCATION

The First Great Awakening

Aside from the fact that the United States was now a liberated and independent country, there was another factor, the First Great Awakening of the mid-1700s, that convinced Americans of the primacy of possessing a strong spiritual foundation. Various historians have commented that the Great Awakening had a tremendous influence on the nation's desire and quest for independence. The preachers of the Great Awakening envisioned America as a nation that would serve as a city set upon a hill that could serve as an example for many nations around the world to follow. Ministers such as George Whitefield, Jonathan Edwards, and John Wesley exhorted the nation to rise up and live up to her mission and call and become more distinct (Holmes, 2001; Kidd, 2007; Middleton, 2004; Orr, 1989).

Jonathan Edwards was an unusually prolific writer, penning volumes of biblically and theologically significant works. Edwards's writings had a dramatic influence on the Great Awakening and also helped shape character education through the mid-1700s to the early 1800s (Conforti, 2001).

During Edwards's early days and continuing for many years, his approach was called New England Theology. Over a period of time, his approach and that of his followers was called Divinity Theology. Those who espoused a New Divinity Theology played an active role in shaping both the development of character education and the political architecture of the Federalist Party (Conforti, 2001). The moral education that was espoused by New Divinity theologians was based on the notion that "All nations were rewarded or punished based on whether they adhered to God's moral law" (Conforti, p. 210).

As New Divinity ministers became the dominant scholarly thinkers in the North, their influence became evident in schooling and in the multi-faceted dimensions of character education. Under the leadership of these clergy, character emerged at the forefront of the school curriculum as well as general issues in society as a whole. The New Divinity concept of character not only included a full gamut of personal behaviors but also consisted of appropriate perspectives that although they were moral in nature, were also political. Because Federalists were more likely to emphasize "character issues" as part of their political platform, these New Divinity thinkers possessed a penchant to support the Federalist Party. On no issue was this more evident than the issue of slavery, because Federalists were generally opposed to this opprobrious institution (Conforti, 2001).

John Wesley was one of the preachers of the era who believed that Christians should dedicate themselves to the task of providing daily structured spiritual and moral guidance to the youth. In other words, the influence of the gospel should not be limited to church gatherings, but instead schools should represent a salient part of Christian mission (Dowling & Scarlett, 2006). As much as any preacher of his time, Wesley emphasized holiness, based on the biblical exhortation of Matthew 5:48, "Be perfect, therefore, as your heavenly Father is perfect" (Holy Bible, NIV).

The learning of the Word of God among America's youth in particular was of great concern among America's founders. The nation's leaders were aware of the shortage of Bibles in the country. Consequently, Congress passed a resolution ordering the importation of 20,000 Bibles (Boles, 1965).

The Second Great Awakening and the Continuation of Spiritual Lineage of Jonathan Edwards

The spiritual lineage of Jonathan Edwards through Timothy Dwight continued through other ministers who had an effect on the spiritual atmosphere of the nation as well as the inculcation of character truths through moral training in the classroom. One of the ways that Timothy Dwight's influence expanded was through the ministry of Lyman Beecher, a preacher from the Second Great Awakening (1790–1840). Lyman Beecher entered Yale in 1793, graduated in 1797, and then continued by studying theology with Timothy Dwight (Fraser, 2001).

Early in his career, Lyman Beecher wanted to return to the nation to "the golden days of Puritan New England" (Fraser, 2001, p. 4). Timothy Dwight captured the imagination of Lyman Beecher. After studying with Timothy Dwight, Lyman Beecher became a truly devout Christian (Fraser, 2001). Beecher contended that a complete education could not be obtained without there education taking place at the church school level. One of Beecher's most cited statements was "A Bible for every family, a school for every district" (Beecher, 1820, p. 5). Beecher believed that pulpit preaching and school instruction needed to be sufficiently stimulating that it would promote the moral and intellectual well-being of the country, as well as its overall prosperity. Like the preachers of the First Great Awakening, Lyman Beecher often spoke at the nation's leading institutions, including Yale College (Beecher, 1828; Fraser, 2001).

Beecher advocated a Christianity that was generally a few steps ahead of the progress of society. He demonstrated this orientation in a number of distinct ways. First, it was Beecher's belief that modern tools could be used to reach more people. Second, Beecher asserted that universal education was one of the best ways to civilize the West. Third, he made the contribution to the creative development of new modes of character education (Fraser, 2001). Fourth, Beecher was heavily involved in addressing many of the primary social ills of the day and raised his children to honor these same goals (Beecher, 1828, 1835; Fraser, 2001).

Lyman Beecher was quite forward looking. He was a committed advocate for utilizing the tools available to further the cause of Christianity and character education. In addition, he was keenly aware of the new frontiers that were available to serve as fertile ground for this cause. Beecher believed that magazines were some of the most splendid tools to accomplish these goals and that the West not only represented fertile ground but also critical ground for this cause (Beecher, 1835). Beecher believed that universal education through public schools based on moral instruction was the key to civilizing the West. Furthermore, his admonitions took place at that time when the "West" represented most of what would become the modern day United States, which was vital for the nation's future welfare (Beecher, 1835; Fraser, 2001). In Beecher's view, the growth of the common school, particularly in the West, would play a salient role in the expansion of faith and morality. Fraser (2001, p. 97) avers, "The public school movement fit well with the needs of Beecher's style of evangelical Christianity and the public schools became a part of the broader movement for a century."

Creative Development of New Modes of Character Education

In colonial days the primary function of the colleges was theological training. Over time, as colleges began to prepare students for several different occupations, religious individuals saw the need for specialized institutions to prepare individuals for the ministry. Consequently, beginning in 1808, there was the founding of the first theological seminary and from that point onward the founding of these seminaries became more common in the United States. Lyman Beecher played a prominent role in the development of the vision for these seminaries. As hard as it was for Lyman Beecher to leave Boston where he had ministered for so many years, Beecher believed in the importance of the seminary and moved to take a position at Lane Seminary in Cincinnati (Cubberley, 1920, 1934; Fraser, 2001; Jeynes, 2007).

Beecher asserted that character instruction needed to saturate every level of the curriculum, from one's first day in school until one's college experience (Beecher, 1835). Beecher (1835) stated, "I have said that the acquisition of knowledge is not the chief end of collegiate education, but to secure vigor and discipline of mind."

Addressing Many of the Primary Social Ills

Lyman Beecher believed that the two most ostensible social ills of the time were slavery and alcoholism. Therefore, as much as any person in his era, Beecher led the charge against slavery and alcohol abuse. In addition, he exhorted his children to also address the key debates of the era. Beecher invested a great deal of time in his children and was convinced that if he did so, they too could have a major impact on society (Jeynes, 2007; Snyder, 1991).

Beecher's children did, in fact, have a major influence on society, including having a major effect on character education (Beecher, 1874; Snyder, 1991). One of his daughters, Harriet Beecher Stowe, wrote the classic book *Uncle Tom's Cabin*. This book changed the nature of character instruction in the public schools. Not only did many leaders and Americans, as a whole, peruse the book and were influenced by it, but teachers utilized it in high schools and colleges. Within this context, *Uncle Tom's Cabin* served as an important form of character education, which strongly influenced attitudes toward slavery in the North. Catherine Beecher, another daughter, was perhaps the most influential woman in education during her era. She founded schools and female seminaries with the foremost goal of producing women of character (Beecher, 1874; Schreiner, 2003; Snyder, 1991).

All in all, Lyman Beecher not only continued the tradition of Jonathan Edwards but also set the foundation, particularly through his children, for future generations.

EFFORTS BY RELIGIOUS PEOPLE AND FEDERALISTS TO EXPAND MORAL EDUCATION

A substantial part of the character instruction movement was birthed in New England and the North Atlantic states such as New York, Pennsylvania, and New Jersey. There was a concerted strategy to see this movement expand. Before the Revolutionary War the efforts to expand the geographic scope of moral tutelage were largely a religious effort, but after the war the Federalists were also becoming involved in the strategy. The Federalists maintained that it was absolutely essential to the nation's survival for Americans to share certain central values. One of these moral convictions was to possess an antislavery orientation. Many Federalists believed that the best chance to extirpate the nation from slavery was to train the youth to maintain this conviction. With religious and Federalist political forces combined, character education emphasis spread throughout the entire country, including the South. The southern curricula almost never included an antislavery component, but character education programs spread nevertheless. The success of these Northeast-sponsored programs had interesting ramifications, including significantly increasing the number of southerners who attended Northeastern colleges (Hall, 1982; Jeynes, 2007; Mather, 1708).

It should be emphasized, however, that the desire for character instruction certainly was not limited to those of the Federalist political persuasion. Rather, it was simply that character education movement of the post–Revolutionary War period had religious and Federalist roots (Hall, 1982; Jeynes, 2007). Democratic-Republicans also were quick to point out the need for training in virtue. For example, Thomas Jefferson (in Thompson, 1991) stated:

> Give up money, give up fame, give up science, give up the earth itself and all it contains rather than do an immoral act. And never suppose that in any possible situation, or under any circumstances, it is best for you to do a dishonorable thing, however slightly so it may appear to you.

Even as certain religious groups maintained a more substantial influence over moral instruction during the 1607–1776 period, particular denominations also exerted the most influence in the post–Revolutionary War period. Which denominations thrived depended largely on how anti-British they were during the war of independence. The denominations that benefited most from being anti-British were the Congregationalists (the Puritans), the Presbyterians, the Catholics, and the Lutherans. Being supportive of the Revolution in this respect facilitated the influence of these denominations in two ways. First, as has just been suggested, Americans were enamored by groups opposed to the war. Second, religious denominations that supported the Revolution most avidly were also those most likely to espouse educational independence from Britain. These advocates opined that in order for the United States to develop an independent-thinking and sophisticated citizenry and electorate, the United States needed to train its young using American teachers and professors. Prior to the Revolutionary War, the elite usually sent their offspring to European schools to receive what was then the best preparation at the time. In addition, a large proportion of the elementary and secondary school teachers were Hessians, who were loyal to the Crown. Those denominations that most fervidly supported the Revolution were cognizant of the fact that if the fledgling nation was to thrive and prosper, a strongly independent education system was indispensable (Brown, 1890; Jeynes, 2007; Stoll, 2001; Tewksbury, 1932).

THE CHARITY SCHOOL MOVEMENT

The Essence of the Charity School Movement

One of the dominant themes in education during the post–Revolutionary War period and continuing into the mid-1800s was the rise of the charity school movement. This movement was a private school initiative that was based on the notion that all children should receive an education, even those who could not afford to pay. Ultimately, families paid what they could afford which meant that most children paid little or nothing. Instead, wealthy and middle-class individuals paid for the students who otherwise would have been unable to go. In the 1600s and 1700s, there was an understanding that those with wealth were responsible for helping those who were poor. Jones (1964, p. 3) called this period "the age of benevolence." After the Revolutionary War, however, the charity school movement evolved into a nationwide effort encompassing many sponsors. In addition, the movement matured into the defining school movement of the post–Revolutionary War era (Cremin, 1976, 1980; Jones, 1964; Rothstein, 1994).

The Puritans initiated the formation of charity schools in the mid-1600s in both the New World and Europe (Cremin, 1980). Although these schools expanded impressively during the 1600s, charity schools remained primarily a Puritan effort (Jones, 1964). Charity schools grew at a rapid pace in the 1600s largely due to the fact it was generally an organized effort and because the Puritans firmly believed that because all people were equal before God, if at all possible, all youth should be educated. This principle was based on various Bible verses, including "There is neither Jew nor Greek, slave nor free, male nor female" (Holy Bible, Galatians 3:28).

The Puritans were not the first to propose the idea of charity schools. Many church leaders, including Martin Luther, had propounded this perspective for centuries. However, the Puritans were clearly the first group to successfully initiate a system that would make charity or free schools a widespread practice (Eavey, 1964; Jones, 1964; Raitt & McGinn, 1987; Randell, 1988).

One of the central goals of the charity school was to reduce poverty and crime. Juvenile reformatories were also started with this goal in mind. If these schools could help youth become virtuous and empower children to stay away from a criminal element, the schools could perform a vital service for the community. In order to accomplish these goals, teachers expounded on the truths contained in the Bible. Teachers also taught students how to act civilly toward one another, what true friendship really entailed, loyalty, love, kindness, compassion, and how to demonstrate patience. The character curriculum also included sensitive issues such as resolving conflicts with other people, how to forgive one who has done you harm, and how to act as a peacemaker in a conflict. The pastors and teachers who ran the schools often provided after-school jobs for older children. Through performing these tasks, the older children developed habits of responsibility, diligence, and community that contributed to their growth. Through all these teachings, it was important that the youth learn character not only through the training of the mind and the heart but through their actual actions (Connecticut Record, 1736; Eavey, 1964; Hiner, 1988; Hunt & Maxson, 1981; Jeynes, 2007; Jones, 1964; Prison Discipline Society, 1855; Spring, 2005).

At the heart of charity schools was an emphasis on moral education grounded in Christianity. Teachers focused on this both in terms of a morally based curriculum and the example established by teachers. The Christian emphasis of American charity schools of the 1600s, 1700s, and 1800s may seem foreign to people living now. However, to individuals living in the eighteenth and nineteenth centuries, schooling without religion was inconceivable. Moreover, the vast majority of teachers at the time viewed moral education as the most important aspect of education. Foundational to morality, this meant that religious instruction needed to be present in the schools. And to the extent that religion was taught, the schools also encouraged their teachers to live lives of integrity and demonstrate the character traits that they taught in everyday living. This desire was facilitated by the fact that teachers and students were often neighbors and attended the same church. Educators considered the practice of teachers sitting next to their children in church especially salutary, because it constituted a close and personal form of moral example (Hunt & Maxson, 1981; Jones, 1964; Michaelsen, 1970; Yulish, 1980).

In the early days of the charity school initiative, the movement was specifically a church-sponsored movement with several goals in mind: (1) to reduce some of the social and moral ills often associated with lower socioeconomic status; (2) to spread the gospel; and (3) to educate children in the reading, writing, and mathematical skills they required to succeed in society (Hunt & Maxson, 1981; Jones, 1964).

The American and English charity school systems did not educate every single child, which was the ultimate goal of the system. Nevertheless, the charity schools in these nations reached hundreds of thousands of students (Cremin, 1980; Jones, 1964). The British charity school movement was so successful that literacy among poor youth soared during the 1700s (Jones, 1964). The American and British charity schools were an impressive success not only along educational fronts but in terms of religious commitment as well (Eavey, 1964; Jones, 1964). In fact, Jones (1964, p. 59) notes, "The schools were of greater consequence to religion than any other design which had been on foot since the Reformation."

The largest organization sponsoring charity schools was the Society for the Propagation of the Gospel. This Society originated in England and soon expanded to the United States. By 1729, in England and the United States combined, the Society had 1,658 schools. The New England populace was willing to support charity schools because the Puritans maintained deeply held convictions about the importance of citizens doing what they could to relieve social ills, eliminate slavery, spread the gospel, and promote the work ethic. The Puritans highlighted and inculcated these values in the charity schools. Charity schools gladly accepted attendees from outside their own churches, including both religious and less religious people. Nevertheless, religious people consistently expressed greater interest in attending charity schools than their less religious counterparts. As a consequence of this fact, over time the church community tended to be considerably more educated than less religious individuals (Bailyn, 1960; Carter, 1969; Cubberley, 1920; Jones, 1964; Stewart, 1969).

Initially, nearly all the sponsors were religious groups. Nevertheless, as the success of the charity schools became manifest, a vast array of organizations became involved. Consequently, as Jones (1964, pp. 3–4) observes, "The charity school was their favorite form of benevolence" and educators established thousands of charity schools. The charity schools were established out of a real sense of compassion for children who normally would not be able to attend school. The compassion that people felt for these children was broad. It encompassed not only a concern for literacy and numerical skills but also a focus on character. These concerned individuals were convinced that charity schools would produce a God-fearing population and, at the same time, would inoculate the children against the habits of sloth, debauchery, and beggary (Jones, 1964; Rothstein, 1994).

The charity school movement was largely a clergy-initiated movement. This was patently clear among religious charity schools and was also ostensible among the community-based schools. Most children attended the church-based charity schools, but pastors and priests strongly encouraged the formation of community-based charity schools as well. They opined that community-based charity schools could reach some people who normally did not attend church or did so only sporadically. The clergy argued that to fail to reach these less churched or unchurched would be to do a disservice to humanity and exacerbate the educational gap that already existed between religious and less religious people (Bobbe, 1933; Cornog, 1998; Fitzpatrick, 1969; Jeynes, 2007; Jones, 1964; Michaelsen, 1970; Rothstein, 1994).

Those involved in the charity school movement were very sensitive to monetary and educational differences. Moreover, they believed that inadequacies in each were highly related. That is, those who were poor tended to be less educated and those who were wealthy tended to be more educated. The Puritans had in the 1600s developed these attitudes that emerged as foundational to the charity school movement. They believed that instruction, particularly in character, would help one to be successful in life. Consistent with their attitude of helping the poor generally, the Puritans placed a great deal of emphasis on philanthropy. This attitude remained with charity school authorities for innumerable years and enabled these schools to thrive for many years. The emphasis on caring for the poor by charity school educators had another benefit as well. The act of philanthropy was an act of compassion and in itself a manifestation of strong character and served as an inspiring example to the students who were aware of this compassion and generosity. This example of character reinforced its teaching in the charity schools (Carter, 1969; Connecticut Record, 1736; Jones, 1964).

The charity schools were designed to fight poverty and vice. The attempts to fight poverty were not merely limited to giving these children an opportunity to attend school but by providing them the tools to make certain that poverty would not be passed on to from previous generations. As a result, the schools often provided after-school sessions and apprenticeship programs. At the heart of these programs were efforts to encourage self-discipline and virtue. The idea was to make these students productive and moral citizens. The belief was that instruction in virtue was to be accomplished to a great degree as early as possible and then myriad other desirable qualities would follow (Carter, 1969; Connecticut Record, 1736; Jones, 1964).

There was wide support for these charity schools. The populace appreciated the great contributions that the private religious charity schools were making. The churches were also supportive of the community-based, nonchurch-based charity schools. In fact, research indicates that the best predictor of the success of these schools was the extent to which local ministers were actively supportive of these schools. One of the reasons why charity schools of a variety of types operated in such supportive environment is because there was such unanimity among the American people about the salience of character education. In addition, there was a general consensus among Americans that the character instruction needed to be religious in nature. However, this is not the situation that materialized because public school regulations required that they teach good morals. In both church-based and community-based charity schools, the teachers placed a great deal of emphasis on student participation in signing hymns and in prayer. Instructors taught the Bible every day. Schools emphasized a great deal of Bible memorization, including putting to memory many entire chapters of the Bible. In the Book of Psalms alone, students were usually required to memorize many of the most popular psalms, including first, eighth, fifteenth, twenty-third, and countless others. Students were also taught the Lord's Prayer and the Apostles' Creed (Jones, 1964).

One of the reasons that charity schools experienced the favor they did in American culture is because many of the most prominent revivalists in the country not only advocated the expansion of charity schools but aiding the poor. John Wesley believed the people needed to give sacrificially to the poor. The Methodists and Evangelicals at the time believed that churches needed to spend the money necessary to help and educate the underprivileged (Jones, 1964; Stewart, 1969).

In the minds of the Puritans, it was extremely important to preserve the welfare of their settlements. They believed that in order to accomplish this, students at the college, elementary, and secondary school level needed to be instructed in character education based on theological orthodoxy. They asserted that this was necessary in order to ensure the survival of the settlement, which was of the highest priority (Marsden, 1994).

The Charity School Movement Becomes Nationwide

The Massachusetts model for charity schools was highly regarded and emulated in many areas across the land. However, the charity schools that the Puritans had developed were intimate in nature and geared toward small communities and areas where there were not a disproportionate number of poor people. In this context, there arose an innovative Englishman named Joseph Lancaster, who had a powerful impact on American schools. Joseph Lancaster was born in England in 1778. Lancaster possessed considerable respect for the Puritan charity schools. As a Quaker, Lancaster highly esteemed the dual emphasis that the Puritans placed on moral and academic education. Nevertheless, Lancaster believed that if charity schools were to reach the poor masses, they needed to be large and efficient. Consequently, he proposed a new system that was designed to significantly increase class size and draw in a larger degree of help from older students (Kaestle, 1973, 1983; Spring, 2005).

A key factor in Lancaster's success, from a financial standpoint, was the alacrity of myriad Quaker philanthropists to sustain Lancaster's charity schools. Quakers were enthusiastic about Lancaster's schools because one of Lancaster's emphases was that children be given a "Scriptural education" (Kaestle, 1973, p. 36). Therefore, Quakers were some of the first to apply the Lancaster model in their charity schools. Both churches and nonecclesiastical organizations concurred that the Lancaster system provided a practical way of educating children who were not currently attending religious charity schools. The Lancaster method especially gained great repute when the New York Free School Society, under the leadership of DeWitt Clinton, adopted the Lancaster system (Cornog, 1998; Kaestle, 1973; Spring, 2005).

The main focus of the Lancaster charity schools, like the Puritan charity schools, was a spiritual and moral one. The two primary architects of the charity school movement, Joseph Lancaster and Andrew Bell, elucidated on the primary purposes of the charity schools. Joseph Lancaster declared, "To train children in the practice of such moral habits as are conducive to their future welfare as virtuous men and useful members of society" (Lancaster, 1805, p. 25). Bell directed charity schools to develop "good scholars, good men, good subjects, and good Christians" (Bell, 1807). Lancaster maintained that instructors needed to do their utmost to inspire children to learn, practice, and internalize godly attitudes and specific virtuous practices. They needed to grow in their ability to discern the difference between righteous and loving behavior on the one hand, and selfish and hurtful behavior on the other. Lancaster believed in using merit tickets as one of the primary tools that teachers should use to encourage meritorious behavior (Kaestle, 1973).

DeWitt Clinton, president of the New York Free School Society founded in 1805, facilitated the growth of the Lancaster model. Clinton was approbatory of the fact that many churches were actively engaged in teaching character instruction. He lionized the presence of church charity schools and their emphasis on love and compassion. Clinton opined that if the nation wanted to school the mass of incoming immigrants effectively, the cost effective and morally based Lancaster system was the best means of accomplishing this goal. Clinton said, "I consider his system as creating a new era in education, as a blessing sent down from heaven to redeem the poor" (Bourne, 1870, p. 128). "In 1809 Clinton launched a major push to apply the Lancaster system in New York City's charity schools" (Fitzpatrick, 1969, p. 150). Furthermore, Clinton argued, "It (the Lancaster system) comprehends reading, writing, arithmetic, and the knowledge of the Holy Scriptures. It arrives at its object with the least possible trouble and expense" (Fitzpatrick, p. 150). Initially, these New York free schools and similar organizations across the country were private schools, but toward the middle of the nineteenth century, these groups encouraged an increasing percentage of government support so that these charity schools eventually presaged the public school system (Bobbe, 1933; Cubberley, 1920;

Fitzpatrick, 1969; Pulliam & Van Patten, 1991; Spring, 2005; Ulich, 1968; Urban & Wagoner, 2000).

Clinton and Lancaster were determined to remain true to the charity schools' Puritan roots and believed that character education was the key to the success of these schools. The religious influence was especially conspicuous in the Society's moral education program. Clinton and Lancaster believed in the teaching of the Bible in the classroom in a nonsectarian fashion. They averred that this teaching should serve as the foundation for a school's moral education program. Some of the major aims of these schools were to make children more loving, more civil, and more cooperative. Over time, the charity schools, including the New York Free School Society, became well known for the efficacy of their moral education program (Clinton, 1829). Clinton stated:

> Of the many thousands who have been instructed in our free schools in the City of New York, there is not a single instance known of anyone being convicted of a crime. (Fitzpatrick, 1969, p. 54)

It would be unfathomable to believe that a big city American mayor would make such a statement today (Fitzpatrick, 1969; Kaestle, 1973; Spring, 2005; Ulich, 1968; Yulish, 1980).

Both Clinton and Lancaster were strong believers in reaching the maximum number of children with the charity school experience. Fitzpatrick (1969, p. 49) notes that "Just as Clinton drew no sex line in education, so he drew no color line." African Americans made up 7–8 percent of the student body (Fitzpatrick, 1969).

African Americans in the North Benefit from the Character Education in Charity Schools

African Americans in the North were some of the main beneficiaries of free schools. Most African Americans in the North were freed slaves and did not have much money with which to pay for education. Free schools, therefore, arose as the ideal means through which many African Americans could capitalize on the availability of free education. In most cases, African Americans attended the same schools as whites. The Puritans, the first group to educate African Americans in North America, focused on establishing integrated schools. In some cases, educators founded free schools that specifically focused on educating African Americans. Some Christian groups, such as the Quakers, put in vigorous efforts to open up schools for freed slaves. In just one year, 1797, the Quakers opened up seven schools for African Americans. Pennsylvania, Rhode Island, Maryland, New Jersey, and other Northeastern states were also diligent in opening up schools for freed slaves during the 1780s and 1790s (Andrews, 1969; Curran, 1954; Klinker & Smith, 1999; McClellan & Reese, 1988; Spring, 2005; Wilson, 1977; Woodson, 1968; Woodson & Wesley, 1962).

Many Christian groups also sent teachers to instruct slaves in the South in both academic and moral instruction. The Baptists and Methodists had an especially noteworthy influence in their character instruction for African Americans living in both the North and the South. These groups particularly exhorted African Americans to obtain high-level occupational success. During the eighteenth and nineteenth centuries, this meant especially encouraging African Americans to become ministers, which at that time was the highest status occupation. The Episcopal and other denominations also desired African Americans to advance in life (Wilson, 1977; Woodson & Wesley, 1962).

How Character Education in the Charity Schools Influenced the Public Schools

Because the public schools were basically converted charity schools, it logically follows that public schools adopted their curriculum in virtue. Consequently, there was no real dichotomy between the moral instruction that occurred in the era's public schools and that which was taught in church-based charity schools. Both were Bible-based and distinctly Christian in their content. Church schools were naturally more denominational in their orientation, but other than that the differences were minimal (Carter, 1969; Hunt & Maxson, 1981; Jones, 1964; Ulich, 1968; Yulish, 1980).

SUNDAY SCHOOL CHARACTER EDUCATION, A SUPPLEMENT

Donald Davis argues that "It's rather amazing that so little attention has been paid to the Sunday School by researchers." Sunday schools were another means of educating the masses free of charge. The Sunday school movement trained tens of thousands of mostly impecunious children. Charity schools and Sunday schools were often not totally distinct from one another. Thousands of churches sponsored both a Sunday school and a charity school program. Sunday schools usually made schooling an all-day affair. As one might expect, the instruction focused largely on religious and moral education. Accordingly, Vinovkis (1995, p. 81) states, "Sunday schools . . . encouraged the memorization of long passages from the Bible." Most children attended either a charity school or a Sunday school, but some attended both types of institutions (Eavey, 1964; Hunt & Maxson, 1981; Jones, 1964; Kliebard, 1969).

Robert Raikes (1735–1811) established the first Sunday school in Gloucester, England in 1780. The Sunday school movement soon arrived in the United States where it flourished, attracting thousands of poor children. The first Sunday school in the United States was started by William Elliot in Virginia in 1785 (Eavey, 1964). In 1786, the second Sunday school was established in Virginia by Francis Asbury, who desired to teach his slaves. Ministers of the era were very supportive of the Sunday school initiative. The Sunday school movement surged in popularity as a means to educate the neglected, slaves, the poor, and immigrants. The Sunday school movement continued to be a major force in educating the poor throughout the nineteenth century and into World War I (Eavey, 1964).

Sunday schools had considerably greater influence on character instruction than simply in the classroom. Sunday schools especially placed an emphasis on creating publications on character education. The curriculum that most American children were exposed to in the charity schools and other types of schools was also affected by the Sunday school movement. The Sunday school initiative should not be examined as an isolated movement, because those fostering the effort were heavily involved in producing some curricular material on character education. Vinovkis (1995, p. 81) asserted, "Evangelicals were particularly active in the Sunday school movement." Therefore, the publications possessed a large degree of Christian content. Many of these publications were purchased by school libraries and other public libraries. The libraries especially purchased a large number of religious books and tracts. Furthermore, many literary religious societies used the books promoting moral behavior in order to encourage literacy. Sunday school groups produced the following moral education publications: *Children's Magazine*, *The Children's Friend*, *The Child's Companion*, *Youth's Magazine*, and *Evangelical Miscellany* (Davis, 1997; Hovde, 1997; Tucker, 1997).

CHARACTER EDUCATION AT THE UNIVERSITY LEVEL

Most of the early schools at all levels continued to be founded by religious groups. As Charles and Mary Beard (1944, p. 65) assert, "It was mainly to religious motives that colleges, like elementary schools, owed their foundations." The members of these religious groups maintained that salvation and moral character were essential to keeping the nation together. The fact that nearly all of the nation's first 120 schools were founded by Christians helped ensure that character instruction would thrive in America's colleges. Some colleges were founded largely out of a concern about virtue and religious dedication. In fact, the founding of Yale University by the Puritans (Congregationalists) in 1701 was based on the notion the Harvard had departed from its previous theological conservatism. Of course, one must keep in mind that less than conservative in 1701 is considered quite conservative today (Hunt & Maxson, 1981; Kliebard, 1969; Marsden, 1994).

The Continuation of Spiritual Lineage of Jonathan Edwards and Its Effects at the College Level

As much as Jonathan Edwards of the Great Awakening period influenced America's colleges, especially Yale and Princeton, Edwards's influence extended into the late 1700s and early 1800s because he invested a considerable amount of time into his family and this yielded tremendous results. Not only did Jonathan Edwards, Jr., influence the spiritual atmosphere of the country, but Edwards's grandson Timothy Dwight had a phenomenal impact on American higher education in the late 1700s and early 1800s and eventually became president of Yale. Dwight graduated from Yale in 1769 and four years later became a pastor of a congregational church in Greenfield (now Southport), Connecticut. In his ministry, Timothy Dwight was quite concerned about educational reform and carried that emphasis to Yale (Hall, 1982).

Concurrent to serving as pastor of a church, Dwight also became the headmaster of a town school. Here he was able to experiment with his moral instruction curriculum. Dwight desired to end corporal punishment, if at all possible, and instead preferred discipline via guilt, shame, and the formation of good habits. Dwight's ultimate goal in moral education was to have the students open themselves to allow God to shape their attitudes. He believed that if the students allowed God to mold their attitudes, their behavior would ultimately change for the better. He believed that prayer and the study of the Bible were keys if any given youth was to allow God to change his or her attitudes (Hall, 1982).

It is difficult to underestimate the degree of influence that Timothy Dwight had on the spiritual atmosphere at Yale and spread of revival and character instruction throughout much of the country. Marsden notes that Timothy Dwight, "grandson of Jonathan Edwards," played a pivotal role in bringing in "spiritual revival." He continues by stating that "a major revival broke out, in which a third of the Yale students professed conversion" (Marsden, 1994, p. 82). The Yale revival helped inspire the Second Great Awakening of the 1790–1840 period. As a result, Yale College and Connecticut as a whole established missionary and reform societies with the intention of transforming the nation through an emphasis on love, prayer, and the teaching of the Bible (Marsden, 1982, 1994).

The Second Great Awakening had such a considerable impact that it influenced not only the halls of academe but penetrated Capitol Hill. The Federalist Party and later the Whig Party called for the advancement of morally responsible education in order to strengthen the country. The Federalist and Whig support for moral instruction was consistent with the fact that both political parties had their anchor of political support in the Bible Belt of the 1700s and 1800s, which was in New England and the Mid-Atlantic states (Jeynes, 2007; Marsden, 1994).

During his presidency at Yale, Timothy Dwight also maintained that character education was the main way to ensure that Yale's students would make an impact on society. Furthermore, he insisted that the college maintained certain standards of morality, etiquette, and other manifestations of proper behavior (Hall, 1982).

Timothy Dwight's reforms did not come to an end at his death in 1816. Dwight's replacement, Jeremiah Day went considerably farther than Dwight in making character a central theme at Yale. Timothy Dwight faithfully fulfilled Jonathan Edwards's desire to have spiritual revival and have a phenomenal impact on the academic sphere. Dwight and Day in their evangelical Christian zeal encouraged their College students not only to follow Christ but also to start other colleges and place moral instruction at the heart of the curriculum. As a result, their graduates were "instrumental" in founding Dartmouth, Columbia, Williams, NYU, Rutgers, Western Reserve, Illinois, Wisconsin, Missouri, California, Georgia, North

Carolina, Maryland, the U.S. Naval Academy, Alabama, and Mississippi. The fact that this list included both private religious and state colleges may surprise some, but the distinction between religious and state institutions was not that clear in the immediate post–Revolutionary War period. Certain schools that we now identify as state schools actually started as religious schools. The University of Tennessee, founded in 1794, started under the name Blount College and was founded by the Presbyterians. This was also true of Rutgers University, the eighth American college. It was founded in 1766 by the Dutch Reformed Church and did not become a state college until 1917. NYU was founded by Presbyterians in 1831 and the Congregationalists and Presbyterians founded UC-Berkeley in 1855 (Hall, 1982; Tewksbury, 1932).

Timothy Dwight and Jeremiah Day were most concerned with attracting godly individuals to Yale, no matter how much or how little they could pay. Consequently, during the first half of the eighteenth century, students who were exceptionally bright and wealthy went to Harvard and those who were very bright and poor went to Yale (Hall, 1982).

Dwight and Day viewed colleges as conduits through which character training could take place among the adult population and future leaders of the country. Their efforts were well planned, well funded, and well organized. At Yale there was an organization called the Moral Society, which as Hall (1982, p. 173) notes, "was viewed by Dwight as particularly useful in combating infidelity and misbehavior among students." Donors viewed the work of Dwight and Day as a true ministry. That fact was confirmed by the fact that the overwhelming number of college presidents were ministers. By 1850 the evangelical community had obtained considerable influence at the college level.

Throughout the 1800s the emphasis on character rested at the heart of an edifying and productive college education. Moral education at the college level was distinct from this instruction at the elementary and secondary school level in one very important way. This is, the emphasis at the college level was on self-control, whereas previously the moral control had always been from an external source. The official Harvard definition of a gentleman reflected this emphasis: "autonomy restrained by character" (Hall, 1982, p. 188). As Charles Eliot (1961, pp. 156–157), former Harvard president, observes, "In the absence of external control, which constitutes what is commonly called freedom, self-control becomes more and more important."

In addition to various college expectations regarding moral behavior, they also offered courses that at their core addressed issues of morality and stimulated thinking about issues of character. McClellan (1999, p. 28) affirmed, "Moral education appeared in a variety of places in the college curriculum, but formal instruction was most systematic in the course in moral philosophy, a virtually universal offering in the nineteenth century colleges. Moral Philosophy was often the capstone course in the curriculum and the men who taught it (including some college presidents) occupied a place of unique standing among nineteenth century academics." Although character instruction naturally took a different form at the college level than it did for either elementary or secondary school, its primacy nevertheless remained (Fay, 1966).

BOOKS

The schoolbooks of the period emphasized moral education. The two greatest forces influencing the books were the writings of Noah Webster and the revival called the Second Great Awakening. McClellan (1999) affirms that the books of this period generally presented truth in more black and white terms than was true in the 1700s and focused a great deal on moral education. Webster followed largely in the steps of the *New England Primer* (1690) and in fact updated the book in 1789. The *New England Primer* contained copious references to Jesus Christ and a religion-based moral instruction. For example, for letters A–C, Webster's *New England Primer* (1789) reads:

> In ADAM'S fall, we sinned all.
> Heaven to find, the BIBLE mind.
> CHRIST crucify'd, for Sinners dy'd (Ford, 1962, p. 23).

Noah Webster's writings were geared to character education, which most educators of the period believed formed the foundation of all constructive education. His books taught youth to be kind, compassionate, courageous, loyal, responsible, and filled with faith. His presentation of biblical morality had a tremendous effect. *A Grammatical Institute of the English Language*, Webster's most popular book, alone sold a total of 75 million copies by 1875. One of the reasons why Webster's books were so popular was because Webster did a masterful job of intertwining the spiritual, the moral, and the scholastic aspects of education. McClellan

(1999, p. 25) states, "Famous spellers and readers, like those of Noah Webster and William Holmes McGuffey, warned ominously of the dangers of drunkenness, luxury, self-pride, and deception, and promised handsome early rewards for courage, honesty, and respect for others." Among those schoolbooks that were written in the 1700s those that were most popular in the 1800s tended to have this orientation. In the early days of the nation after the Revolutionary War, Ellis Sandoz (2006, p. 6) notes, "Thought and speech were soaked in the Bible, with the Magna Carta and the Bible were quoted side by side and together with the classics . . . Political and religious liberty were seen to be all of the same piece." John Witherspoon (1776, p. 2) confirmed Sandoz's affirmation by stating, "There is not a single instance in history, in which civil liberty was lost, and religious liberty preserved entire." Even as Benjamin Rush declared that republicanism and faith went together, most of the fledgling nation's early leaders agreed with him. John Jay, the nation's first Chief Justice of the Supreme Court, asserted that a strong republic resulted from the fact that the citizens were of the same Christian faith (Gangel & Benson, 1983; Hiner, 1988; Hunt & Maxson, 1981; Sandoz, 2006; Spring, 2005; Yulish, 1980).

To the founders, it was of utmost importance that the United States be a virtuous country. David Ramsey summed up the lessons of the Revolutionary War experience well with these words, "Remember that there can be no political happiness without liberty, there can be no liberty without morality and no morality without religion" (Ramsey in Sandoz, 2006, p. 85). Sandoz examines the historical reality of republicanism and then concludes that there are five elements of republicanism, the most salient of which is "biblical faith" (Sandoz, 2006, p. 106).

As much as Americans esteemed the notion of a prosperous country, they valued a virtuous country even more. Americans also believed that personal virtue was impossible without the experience of personal salvation. It was the study of the central book of the post–Revolutionary War period, the Bible, which was the key for experiencing salvation and living a virtuous life. Jonathan Edwards had once defined "True virtue" as "the spontaneous overflowing of a purified soul" (Fiering, 1981, pp. 126, 128). Many people of the day, as well as many historians, regarded the essence of the American Revolution as striving for freedom based on religious revival. Benjamin Rush and others viewed the American Revolution as such and believed it was key for returning Americans to their biblical roots. Benjamin Rush, like most of the founders, desired to remind the nation of the linkage between religion and virtue. Sandoz (2006, p. 41) stated, "The only foundation for a useful education in a republic is to be laid in religion. Without this, there can be no virtue, and without virtue there can be no liberty." In the nation's early days, the Bible was the linkage between liberty, virtue, and religion. As Sandoz (p. 78) remarks, "Bible reading was ubiquitous in America throughout the period normally identified as 'the founding.'" During his State of the Union Address in 1796, Washington (1796) also highlighted the connection between religion and virtue, as he did during other times well (Rush, 1786, 1951; Sandoz, 2006; Tyler, 1878).

THE ORIGINAL MEANING OF THE FIRST AMENDMENT

The current debate over the First Amendment to the Constitution is one of the hottest debates occurring in America today. The First Amendment reads, "Congress shall make no law respecting an establishment of religion, or prohibiting the free exercise thereof." Much of the debate focuses on the concept of the phrase a "wall of separation between church and state." Unfortunately, both proponents of the use of this statement and those who think the statement has been improperly imputed to the First Amendment often only address this issue at a cursory level and therefore come to conclusions that are likely inaccurate and even unconstitutional. There are a number of truths that are essential to acknowledge. First, contrary to popular belief, the phrase "separation of church and state" does not appear in the Constitution. Surveys of the American populace indicate that 65 percent of Americans believe that this phrase does occur in the Constitution. This statistic is disconcerting because it demonstrates the degree to which Americans are not conversant with the Constitution and the Bill of Rights specifically. The phrase "wall of separation between church and state" was not used to apply to religious expression during the eighteenth century and in fact was not used in this way until early in the nineteenth century (Barton, 1995).

Second, what political leaders and judges who debate about this topic often ignore is the phrase "wall of separation" was a term sometimes used by prominent ministers throughout the ages. For example, Martin Luther (1483–1546) spoke of a "paper wall ... between the spiritual estate and the temporal estate" (Luther in Witte, 2006). John Calvin (1509–1564), in his *Institutes*, referred to a "wall of separation" between the "political kingdom" and the "spiritual kingdom" (Calvin, 1559). Within America's borders, Roger Williams (1604–1680) spoke of "a wall of separation between the garden of the church and the wilderness of the world" (Luther in Witte, 2006). The phrase "a wall of separation" was particularly well known among Baptists in early America, because Roger Williams was probably the most renowned early Baptist in the American colonial era. The phrase was a spiritual term used to refer to the extent that a Christian was to live a life separate and above worldly influence. When applied to the spiritual and political spheres, it meant that the church operated best when it functioned above the corruption frequently associated with politics (Witte, 2006).

Thomas Jefferson was the individual who used the phrase "the wall of separation between church and state" early in the nineteenth century. His use of the term is often used by individuals who are of a more restrictive persuasion regarding freedom of religion and who refer to Jefferson's words as if they appear in the Constitution. They often neglect to point out that Jefferson's words were in regards to a specific inquiry initiated by Danbury Baptists, that one must consider the interpretation of the First Amendment by other founders, and that one should also assess the actions (not merely the words) of the founders, including Jefferson's, and that Jefferson made other statements regarding the First Amendment in his second inaugural address that specify his views in an official capacity and are therefore more reliable than how he responded to one particular inquiry.

The Events That Made the First Amendment Possible

In order to apprehend the essence of the First Amendment to the Constitution, it is important that one become cognizant of the events leading up to its inclusion. In the period from 1607 to 1775, the 13 colonies differed in the extent to which each recognized an established church or whether numerous different denominations flourished. Generally speaking, the Mid-Atlantic colonies, such as New York, New Jersey, Pennsylvania, and Delaware, were the most flexible regarding the presence of an established church, and instead encouraged the growth of many different denominations. This fact was a key in helping to ensure freedom of religion in what would eventually become the United States because these states represented the middle to southern part of the Bible Belt of the period, which extended from northern New England to Maryland, and it was also the most populated and economically developed area of the United States. Therefore, because this freedom was the experience of a large number of Christians and the population at large, it facilitated the adoption of freedom of religion in the Bill of Rights (Estep, 1990; Noll, 2002; Wald, 1997).

It was in Virginia, however, that the most important battle for religious freedom was waged not only because the Anglican Church was essentially the official church of the colony but because James Madison, the primary author of the Constitution, was a Virginian and needed to be convinced regarding the need to definitively state a declaration regarding religious freedom. During the late 1760s and 1770s, the Baptists and Presbyterians were the two fastest growing non-state denominations in the state and they were often discriminated against (Estep, 1990; Semple, 1810). Virginia, as the oldest colony, was the most like England and as William Estep (1990, p. 121) notes, "The Anglican church in Virginia enjoyed a virtual monopoly over the religious affairs of the colony. It was by law the established church." During the 1770–1776 period, the Baptists regularly petitioned the House of Burgesses "for relief from the perverse interpretations of the Act of Toleration which had led to widespread oppression" (Estep, p. 129).

As Estep (1990, p. 131) observes:

> Up until August of 1775, the Baptist and Presbyterian petitioners had simply protested against the laws regulating dissenters. Freedom was in the air and they intended to make the most of it. Anticipating independence from England, the House of Burgesses called for the convening of a convention to make the transition from colony to state. This constituted a signal for the Separates to act. The Northern and Southern Districts of the Separate Baptists General Association met in August 1775 in DuPuy's meeting house (named for DuPuy, a former pastor), where the delegates decided to circulate petitions throughout the state addressed to the Virginia convention asking "that the church establishment should be abolished, and religion left to stand upon its own merits, and that all religious societies should be protected in the peaceable enjoyment of their own religious principles and modes of worship."

The Baptists felt so strongly about religious liberty that they joined the Revolutionary War effort for "fundamentally different reasons" than most groups, that is, for the purpose of procuring religious freedom (Estep, 1990, p. 132).

When James Madison first wrote most of the Constitution, it did not contain the Bill of Rights and it was not certain whether the states would ratify this important document. In order to convince the American people to approve the Constitution, John Jay, Alexander Hamilton, and James Madison together wrote the *Federalist Papers*. However, there was great concern about whether Virginia and New York would ratify the Constitution. Moreover, most believed that if these two heavily populated states refused to approve the document, other states would refuse as well and the Constitution would not be approved. In Virginia, where the Baptists and Presbyterians had often been harassed by government representatives, these religious groups would not support the Constitution unless an amendment was added guaranteeing freedom of religion. The Baptists and Presbyterians knew that they had the support of George Washington, who supported a specific guarantee of religious freedom. And because Washington, the most highly respected of the founders, backed them, they believed that Madison could eventually be convinced. Eventually Madison became convinced and so the First Amendment, along with nine others, was added. In order to underscore the original purpose of the First Amendment, it is important to note the central argument in favor of its inclusion was to keep the government out of the affairs of the church rather than the other way around. Virtually all denominations at the time insisted on its inclusion as a matter of religious freedom (Estep, 1990; Haynes, Chaltain, Ferguson, Hudson, & Thomas, 2003; Noll, 2002; Semple, 1810).

The Nature of the Danbury Baptist Inquiry and Jefferson's Response

In the early years following the birth of the United States, the Congregational Church, the denomination that the Puritans birthed, was the dominant church in New England and in the Northern Mid-Atlantic states which at that time was the upper section nation's Bible Belt. The Baptist denomination, which had been so concerned about the addition of the First Amendment to the Constitution, remained concerned about its survival as rumors swirled that the United States would name a church denomination as its official state church. The Baptist church in the United States was growing at this point but was badly outnumbered by the dominant Congregationalists. Not only were the Congregationalists foremost throughout the Northeast, but also they were dominant in education.

The nation's two best colleges, Harvard and Yale, were both Congregationalist institutions. Dartmouth College, a third Ivy League institution, was also a Congregationalist school. Many of the nation's future ministers, politicians, doctors, and lawyers were trained at these institutions. Whoever dominated America's best colleges likely would help determine the future direction of the country (Jeynes, 2007; Johnson, 1997; Tewksbury, 1932).

The Danbury Baptists felt totally outnumbered by the Congregationalists, largely because they were trying to prosper in the Congregationalist stronghold of Connecticut but were also located close to the Congregationalist educational beacon of Yale College. The Danbury Baptists heard rumors that the U.S. Government was about to name the Congregationalist Church the nation's official denomination. It is in this context that the Danbury church wrote to Thomas Jefferson. Jefferson replied that the First Amendment to the U.S. Constitution stipulated that there was to be no national church or denomination. Furthermore, Jefferson argued that under the Constitution the religious realm and the national government were two distinct institutions and therefore the fear the Baptists had for institutionalizing of a national denomination was not warranted. Nevertheless, Jefferson did not advocate separation *from* church and state, which appears to be the modern day rendering by some, but separation *of* church and state, that is, the church and state were to act independently from one another (Jefferson, 1802; Marshall & Manuel, 1977; Walker, 1990).

The Interpretation of the First Amendment by the Other Founders

The evaluation of the interpretation of the First Amendment is important not only in its own right but especially because although Jefferson was the primary author of the Declaration of Independence, in which he referred to God four times, he was not the primary author of the Constitution and especially did not play the major role in the writing of the First Amendment. In addition, Jefferson was probably the most liberal of the founders in his views regarding the First Amendment issues. His perspective on the First Amendment, even without the contortions initiated by modern day activists, was the exception rather than the rule. Therefore, to conclude that his perspective was representative of the founders' views would be naïve at best (Eidsmore, 1987). As Mark Noll (2002, p. 83) states, "Almost no one in the early United States took this separation of church and state to mean the absence of religious influence in public life." In fact, Thomas Jefferson was the only founder to use the term separation of church and state and this was many years after the Constitution was approved. None of the founders who worked on the *Federalist Papers*—John Jay, James Madison, and Alexander Hamilton—designed to communicate the principles of the Constitution use the term, nor did Fisher Ames who was one of the principal writers of the First Amendment (Eggleston, 1998; Eidsmore, 1987; Estep, 1990; Semple, 1810; Witte, 2006).

Jefferson's Official Statements Regarding the First Amendment in His Second Inaugural Address (1805)

The idea that one should place heavier weight on Jefferson's statements regarding the First Amendment in his official statements in his second inaugural address than on some statements he made regarding a particular situation seems so patent, one would seem almost obstinate to argue otherwise. Yet somehow this is often what is done and the result is that there are very few Americans who are even aware that he addresses this issue in his second inaugural. In this second inaugural address of his presidency, Jefferson made it clear that it was not his view that the *entire* government should be separated by a wall from religious institutions (Jefferson, 1805). Rather, he believed that the *state government* rather than the *federal government* should be the institution, along with the church, to make religious proclamations such as fasting and calls for prayer. This perspective was consistent with Jefferson's overall view that the center of power should be at the state government level rather than at the federal government level (Hutson, 2008). Jefferson was the most prominent leader of the Democratic-Republican Party whose chief tenet was a conviction that there were great risks in retrogressing into a near-monarchy if too much power was concentrated in the central government (Cremin, 1976, 1980; Stephens, 1872). It is only consistent with his overall belief that religious proclamations should be undertaken by politicians at the state level rather than the federal level, because he opined that the vast majority of government functions should take place at the state and not the federal level (Haynes, Chaltain, Ferguson, Hudson, & Thomas, 2003). Jefferson stated in his second inaugural address that "religious exercises" should be "under the direction and discipline of state or church" (Jefferson, 1805, p. 11).

President Jefferson affirmed this belief in a letter that he wrote to Samuel Miller in which he stated "religious matters" were "reserved to the states" (Jefferson in Hutson, 2008, p. 80).

The Actions of Jefferson Regarding Issues of Church and State

Consistent with his belief that religious exercises and proclamations should be a state initiative rather than a federal one, Jefferson as governor of Virginia was very active in announcing religious proclamations, but when Jefferson served as President he encouraged individual states to undertake these actions (Hutson, 2008). For example, in 1779, Governor Jefferson "issued a proclamation appointing a day of publick and solemn thanksgiving and prayer to Almighty God" (Jefferson, 1779, pp. 177–179).

In addition, in the 1770s, Thomas Jefferson, together with James Madison, introduced a bill that required that "Every minister of the gospel shall on each day so appointed attend and perform divine service and preach a sermon, or discourse, suited to the occasion in his church, on the pain of forfeiting fifty pounds for every failing, not having reasonable excuse." Although the Jefferson/Madison bill did not pass, the fact that they included a substantial fine for those ministers who did not comply highlights the extent to which Jefferson maintained that the state should be involved in stating various religious proclamations and practices. Moreover, in 1776 Jefferson served on the Committee of Revisors who was given the responsibility of writing the revised code for "A Bill for Appointing Days of Public Fasting and Thanksgiving" (Jefferson, 1784).

Jefferson's official words on the First Amendment in his second inaugural address, taken together with his involvement in religious proclamations at the state level, and an examination of the context of the Danbury interaction, lead one to conclude that it would be irresponsible to view Jefferson's Danbury letter in isolation from these other factors and to dismiss his public actions and explanations as secondary to a mere letter that is often removed from the context of the situation.

CONCLUSION

Character education in a broad list of settings and for various ages was almost omnipresent in post–Revolutionary War education. The founders of the nation saw moral instruction as a major prerequisite of the successful implementation of a democratic government in the United States. Therefore, in their speeches and writings, "morality" and "democracy" were often juxtaposed. The nation possessed many educators and writers who played major roles in assuring that character training would flourish in America's schools. Noah Webster and members of the Sunday school movement played major roles in developing a curriculum of moral instruction. Joseph Lancaster and DeWitt Clinton helped catapult the charity school initiative from being purely a Puritan-sponsored movement to being a nationwide effort schooling millions of children. There were family lines, such as those of Jonathan Edwards and Lyman Beecher, that were determined to play a major role in shaping the future of character education in the American school and college system. These individuals would likely have tremendous concern over the ways that many Americans interpret the First Amendment today. They would also likely express surprise over the lack of knowledge that Americans have regarding how the First Amendment came to be, the way most of the founders interpreted it, and how Thomas Jefferson himself interpreted and applied the First Amendment, particularly at the state level. The extent to which those who lived during this era desired character education to saturate every aspect of the instructional process is noteworthy and is a reminder of the extent to which they viewed moral instruction as having a central place in the curriculum at virtually all levels of education.

REFERENCES

Adams, J. (1756). *John Adam's diary.*

————. (1854). In C. Adams (Ed.), *The works of John Adams, second president of the United States* (Vol. IX). Boston, MA: Little Brown. Original statement, October 11, 1798.

Adams, S. (1794). A letter to the Massachusetts Legislature. January 17.

Andrews, C. C. (1969). *The history of the New York African free schools.* New York: Negro Universities Press.

Bailyn, B. (1960). *Education in the forming of American society.* Chapel Hill, NC: University of North Carolina Press.

Bark, O. T., & Lefler, H. T. (2004). Educating the youth throughout the New World. In M. C. Ryan (Ed.), *Living in colonial America* (pp. 93–110). San Diego, CA: Greenhaven Press.

Barton, D. (1995). *The myth of separation.* Aledo, TX: Wallbuilders.

Beard, C. A., & Beard, M. R. (1944). *A basic history of the United States*. New York: Doubleday, Doran, & Company.

Beecher, L. (1820). Address of Charitable Society for the Education of Indigent Pious Young Men for the Ministry of the Gospel. Concord: n.p.

———. (1828). Speech before American Sunday School Union.

———. (1835) *A plea for the West*. n.p.

———. (1874). *Educational reminiscences and suggestions*. New York: J. B. Ford.

Bell, A. (1807). *Extract of a sermon on the education of the poor*. London: Cadel & Davies.

Blinderman, B. F. (1976). *Three early champions of education*. Bloomington, IN: Phi Delta Kappa.

Bobbe, D. (1933). *DeWitt Clinton*. New York: Minton, Balch & Company.

Boles, D. E. (1965). *The Bible, religion, and the public schools*. Ames, IA: Iowa State University.

Bourne, W. O. (1870). *History of the Public School Society*. New York: Wood.

Brown, A. (1890). *The genesis of the United States*. Boston, MA: Houghton Mifflin.

Calvin, J. (1559). *Institutes of the Christian religion*. Geneva: O. Roberti Stephani.

Carter, J. G. (1969). *Letters on the free schools of New England*. New York: Arno Press.

Clinton, D. (1829) in Lincoln, C. Z. (Ed.), *Messages from the governors* (Vol. 5), p. 116. New York: State of New York Press.

Conforti, J. (2001). New England theology, from Edwards to Bushnell. In M. K. Cayton & W. Williams (Eds.), *The Encyclopedia of American cultural and intellectual history* (pp. 205–214). New York: Scribner.

Connecticut Record, Volume VII, 1726–1735. (1736).

Cornog, E. (1998). *The birth of empire: DeWitt Clinton & the American experience, 1769–1828*. New York: Oxford University Press.

Cousins, N. (1958). *In God we trust: The religious beliefs and ideas of American founding fathers*. New York: Harper & Brothers.

Cremin, L. A. (1970). *American education: The colonial experience, 1607–1783*. New York: Harper & Row.

———. (1976). *Traditions of American education*. New York: Basic Books.

———. (1980). *American Education: The national experience, 1783–1876*. New York: Harper & Row.

Cubberley, E. (1920). *The history of education*. Boston, MA: Houghton Mifflin.

———, ed. (1934). *Readings in public education in the United States: A collection of sources and readings to illustrate the history of educational practice and progress in the United States*. Cambridge, MA: Riverside Press.

Curran, F. X. (1954). *The churches and the schools*. Chicago, IL: Loyola University Press.

Current, R. N. (1964). The Dartmouth College case in J. A. Garrary (Ed.), *Quarrels that have shaped the Constitution* (pp. 21–36). New York: Harper & Row.

Davis, D. G., Jr. (1997). Bread upon the waters: Printed word in Sunday Schools in the 19th Century England and the United States. In D. G. Davis, Jr., D. M. Hovde, & J. M. Tucker (Eds.), *Reading for moral change* (pp. 5–18). Champaign, IL: University of Illinois Press.

Dowling, E. M., & Scarlett, W. G. (2006). *Encyclopedia of religious and spiritual development*. Thousand Oaks, CA: Sage Publications.

Eavey, C. B. (1964). *History of Christian education*. Chicago, IL: Moody Press.

Eggleston, E. (1998). *A history of the United States and its people*. Lake Wales, FL: Lost Classics Book Company.

Eidsmore, J. (1987). *Christianity and the constitution*. Grand Rapids, MI: Baker Book House.

Eisner, E. W. (1994). *Cognition and curriculum reconsidered*. New York: Teachers College Press.

Eliot, C. (1961). *Charles Eliot and popular education*. New York: Teachers College Press.

Estep, W. R. (1990). *Revolution within the revolution*. Grand Rapids, MI: Eerdmans.

Fay, J. W. (1966). *American psychology before William James*. New York: Octagon.

Fiering, N. (1981). *Jonathan Edwards's moral thought and its British context*. Chapel Hill, NC: University of North Carolina Press.

Fitzpatrick, E. A. (1969). *The educational views and influence of DeWitt Clinton*. New York: Arno Press.

Fogel, R. W. (2004). *The escape from hunger and premature death, 1700–2100*. New York: Cambridge University Press.

Ford, P. L., ed. (1962). *New England primer*. New York: Teacher's College Press.

Fraser, J. W. (2001). *The school in the United States*. Boston, MA: McGraw-Hill.

Gangel, K. O., & Benson, W. S. (1983). *Christian education: Its history and philosophy*. Chicago, IL: Moody.

Gerson, N. B. (1966). *Mr. Madison's war, 1812; the second war for independence*. New York: Messmer.

Gilpin, W. C. (1982). The creation of a new order: Colonial education and the Bible. In D. L. Barr & N. Piediscalzi (Eds.), *The Bible in American education* (pp. 5–23). Philadelphia, PA: Fortress Press.

Gutek, G. L. (1997). *Historical and philosophical foundations of education*. Upper Saddle River, NJ: Prentice Hall.

Hall, P. D. (1982). *The organization of American culture, 1700–1900*. New York: New York University Press.

Haynes, C. C., Chaltain, S. E., Ferguson, J. E., Hudson, D. L., & Thomas, O. (2003). *The First Amendment in schools*. Nashville, TN: First Amendment Center.

Hiner, N. R. (1988). The cry of Sodom enquired into: Educational analysis in seventeenth century New England. *The social history of American education*. Urbana, IL: University of Illinois Press.

Holmes, S. (2001). *God of grace and God of glory: An account of the theology of Jonathan Edwards*. Grand Rapids, MI: Eerdmans.

Holy Bible. (1973). Grand Rapids, MI: Zondervan.

Hovde, D. M. (1997). The library is a valuable hygienic appliance. In D. G. Davis, Jr., D. M. Hovde, & J. M. Tucker (Eds.), *Reading for moral change* (pp. 5–18). Champaign, IL: University of Illinois Press.

Howard, L. (1943). *The Connecticut wits*. Chicago, IL: University of Chicago Press.

Hunt, T., & Mullins, M. (2005). *Moral education in America's schools: The continuing challenge*. Greenwich, CT: Information Age Press.

Hunt, T. C., & Maxson, M. M. (1981). *Religion and morality in American schooling*. Washington, D.C.: University Press of America.

Hutson, J. H. (2008). *Religion & the new republic*. Lanham, MD: Rowman & Littlefield.

Jefferson in Thompson, D. L. (1991). *Moral values and higher education: A notion at risk*. Albany, NY: SUNY.

Jefferson, T. (1779). Proclamation appointing a Day of Thanksgiving Prayer, November 11, 1779. *Papers of Jefferson*, vol. 3, pp. 177–179.

———. (1784). Report of the Committee of Revisors by the General Assembly of Virginia in 1776 (pp. 59–60). Richmond, VA: Dixon & Holt.

———. (1802/2006). Letter to Danbury Baptists. *The essential Jefferson*. Indianapolis: Hacket Publishers.

———. (1805/2001). Second inaugural address. *The inaugural addresses of Thomas Jefferson, 1801 and 1805*. Columbia: University of Missouri Press.

Jensen, L. C., & Knight, R. S. (1981). *Moral education: Historical perspectives*. Washington, D.C.: University Press of America.

Jeynes, W. (2003). *Religion, education & academic success*. Greenwich, CT: Information Age Publishing.

———. (2007). *American educational history: School, society, and the common good*. Thousand Oaks, CA: Sage Publications.

Johnson, P. (1997). *A history of the American people*. New York: Harper Collins.

Jones, M. G. (1964). *The charity school movement: A study of eighteenth century Puritanism in action*. Cambridge, United Kingdom: Cambridge Books.

Kaestle, C. (1973). *Joseph Lancaster & the monitorial school movement.* New York: Teachers College Press.

———. (1983). *Pillars of the republic: Common schools and American society, 1780–1860.* New York: Hill & Wang.

Kamen, H. (2003). *How Spain became a world power, 1492–1763.* New York: Harper Collins.

Kennedy, R. (2001). Philosophy from Puritanism to the enlightenment. In M. K. Cayton & W. Williams (Eds.), *The encyclopedia of American cultural and intellectual history* (pp. 87–95). New York: Scribner.

Kidd, T. (2007). *The Great Awakening.* New Haven, CT: Yale University Press.

Kirk, R. (1953). *The conservative mind, from Burke to Santayana.* Chicago, IL: Regnery.

Kliebard, H. M. (1969). *Religion and education in America.* Scranton, PA: International Textbook Company.

Klinker, P. A., & Smith, R. M. (1999). *The unsteady march: The rise & decline of racial equality in America.* Chicago, IL: University of Chicago Press.

Lancaster, J. (1805). *Improvements in education.* Clifton, NJ: Kelly.

Lewy, G. (1996). *Why America needs religion.* Grand Rapids, MI: Eerdmans.

Marsden, G. M. (1982). *Fundamentalism and American culture.* New York: Oxford University Press.

———. (1994). *The soul of the American university.* New York: Oxford University Press.

Marshall, J. (1967). *John Marshall: Major opinions and other writings.* Indianapolis, IN: Bobbs-Merrill Company.

Marshall, P., & Manuel, D. (1977). *The light and the glory.* Grand Rapids, MI: Fleming Revell.

Mather, C. (1708). A master in our Israel. In W. Smith (Ed.), *Theories of education in early America* (pp. 9–24). Indianapolis: Bobbs-Merrill.

Matson, C. (2001). Liberalism and republicanism. In M. K. Cayton & W. Williams (Eds.), *The encyclopedia of American cultural and intellectual history* (pp. 169–175). New York: Scribner.

McClellan, B. E. (1999). *Moral education in America.* New York: Teachers College Press.

McClellan, B. E., & Reese, W. J. (1988). *The social history of American education* (pp. 6–10). Urbana, IL: University of Illinois Press.

McKay, D., & Scott, H. M. (1983). *The rise of the great powers, 1648–1815.* London: Longman.

Michaelsen, R. (1970). *Piety in the public school.* London: Macmillan.

Middleton, R. (2004). Religion and education. In M. C. Ryan (Ed.), *Living in colonial America* (pp. 65–74). San Diego, CA: Greenhaven Press.

Moss, J. (1984). *Noah Webster.* Boston, MA: Twayne.

Noll, M. A. (2002). *The old religion in a new world.* Grand Rapids, MI: Eerdmans.

Northwest Ordinance, 1787.

Orr, J. E. (1989). *The event of the century.* Wheaton, IL: International Awakening Press.

Prison Discipline Society. (1855). *Report of the Prison Discipline Society, 1832.* Boston: Boston Press of T. R. Marvin.

Pulliam, J. D., & Van Patten, J. J. (1991). *History of education in America.* Upper Saddle River, NJ: Merrill/Prentice Hall.

Raitt, J., & McGinn, B. (1987). *Christian spirituality: High middle ages and reformation.* New York: Crossroad.

Randell, K. (1988). *Luther and the German reformation, 1517–1555.* London: Edward Arnold.

Riley, J. C. (2001). *Rising life expectancy: A global history.* New York: Cambridge University Press.

Robson, D. W. (1985). *Educating republicans: The college in the era of the American revolution, 1750–1800.* Westport, CT: Greenwood.

Rollins, R. M. (1980). *The long journey of Noah Webster.* Philadelphia, PA: University of Pennsylvania Press.

Rothstein, S. W. (1994). *Schooling the poor: A social inquiry into the American educational experience.* Westport, CT: Bergin & Garvey.

Rush, B. (1786). *A plan for the establishment of public schools and the diffusion of knowledge in Pennsylvania.* Philadelphia: n.p.

————. (1798). *Essays, literacy, morals, and the philosophical.* Philadelphia, PA: Bradford.

————. (1951). Benjamin Rush letter to Richard Price, May 25, 1786. In L. H. Butterfield (Ed.), *Letters of Benjamin Rush, Vol. 1* (pp. 388–389). Princeton, NJ: Princeton University Press.

Sandoz, E. (2006). *Republicanism, religion and the soul of America.* Columbia, MO: University of Missouri.

Schreiner, S. A., Jr. (2003). *The passionate Beechers.* Hoboken, NJ: Wiley.

Semple, R. (1810). *History of the Baptists in Virginia.* Lafayette, TN: n.p.

Snyder, S. H. (1991). *Lyman Beecher and his children.* Brooklyn, NY: Carlson.

Somerville, M. (2002). *Tapestry of grace.* Gaithersburg, MD: Lampstand Press.

Spring, J. (2005). *The American school 1642–2004.* White Plains, NY: Longman.

Stephens, A. H. (1872). *History of the United States.* New York: Hale & Son.

Stewart, G., Jr. (1969). *A history of religious education in Connecticut.* New York: Arno Press & the New York Times.

Stoll, M. (2001). The transformation of American religion, 1776–1838. In M. K. Cayton & W. Williams (Eds.), *The Encyclopedia of American cultural and intellectual history* (pp. 215–225). New York: Scribner.

Tewksbury, S. (1932). *Founding of American colleges and universities before the Civil War.* New York: Teachers College Press.

Thompson, D. L. (1991). *Moral values and higher education: A notion at risk.* Albany, NY: SUNY.

Tucker, J. M. (1997). Wide awakening. In D. G. Davis, Jr., D. M. Hovde, & J. M. Tucker (Eds.), *Reading for moral change* (pp. 5–18). Champaign, IL: University of Illinois Press.

Tyler, M. C. (1878). *A history of American literature.* New York: Putnam.

Ulich, R. (1968). *A history of religious education.* New York: New York University Press.

Unger, H. G. (1998). *Noah Webster: The life and times of an American patriot.* New York: Wiley.

Urban, W., & Wagoner, J. (2000). *American education: A history.* Boston, MA: McGraw-Hill.

Vinovkis, M. A. (1995). *Education, society and economic opportunity.* New Haven, CT: Yale University Press.

Wald, K. D. (1997). *Religion and politics in the United States.* Washington, D.C.: CQ Press.

Walker, S. (1990). *In defense of American liberties: A history of the ACLU.* New York: Oxford University Press.

Waller, G. M. (1950). *Puritanism in early America.* Boston, MA: Heath.

Washington, B. T. (1969). *A new Negro for a new century.* Miami, FL: Mnemosyne.

Washington, G. (1779/1988). Farewell address. In W. B. Allen (Ed.), *George Washington: A collection* (pp. 521–522). Indianapolis: Liberty Classics.

Washington, G. (1796). *Farewell address,* September 19.

Webster, N. (1789). *New England Primer.* New York: Patterson.

———. (1807). *Education of youth in the United States.* New Haven, CT: n.p.

———. (1834). *Value of the Bible, and the excellence of the Christian religion. For use of families and schools.* New Haven, CT: Durrie & Peck.

Wilson, P. (1977). Discrimination against blacks in education: An historical perspective. In W. T. Blackstone & R. D. Heslep (Eds.), *Social justice and preferential treatment* (pp. 161–175). Athens, GA: University of Georgia.

Witherspoon, J. (1776). *The dominion of providence over the passions of men.* Indianapolis, IN: Liberty Fund.

Witte, J., Jr. (2006). *God's joust, God's justice.* Grand Rapids, MI: Eerdmans.

Woodson, C. G. (1968). *The education of the Negro prior to 1861.* Washington, D.C.: Associated Publishers.

Woodson, C. G., & Wesley, C. H. (1962). *The Negro in our history.* Washington, D.C.: Associated Publishers.

Yulish, S. M. (1980). *The search for a civic religion.* Washington, D.C.: University Press of America.

5

———◆◦◆◦◆———

PRAYER AND MORAL EDUCATION IN THE EYES OF THE FOUNDERS OF THE MODERN DAY PUBLIC SCHOOL

The nation's emphasis on moral education was not simply limited to the first 200–250 years of its European roots. The foundation of the public school system was based on character education. The growth and spread of the public school movement possessed as its central theme, a moral emphasis. The renowned educational historian Ellwood Cubberley (1909, p. 68) remarked, "The work of public education is with us . . . to a large degree, a piece of religious work." Moral education was an important component of education in Mann's day. Stephen Yulish (1980, p. 80) sums up this truth well:

> The concept of moral education has always been a crucial underpinning of
> the American notion of a virtuous republic. Throughout its development,
> American leaders in education have strenuously sought to condemn mere
> intellectual training. Whether it was the phrenological justifications of
> Horace Mann for training pupils in proper laws of health and morals or
> the widespread perception of a need for moral training to inculcate respect
> for authority and law and order, the notion of moral education has histori-
> cally been a crucial factor in the American experience. The deep-felt need to
> control behavior and conduct by moral training was undertaken by the
> schools alongside the instruction of the church and the home.

The fact that the common schools were the focal point of American education was in stark contrast to the European orientation, which emphasized the presence of a wide variety of private religious schools. In the United States, the emphasis was on teaching "nonsectarian Christianity at public expense" (McClellan, 1999, p. 31).

It is important to understand that character education at the time was not limited to a certain portion of the school day but was intricately woven into every subject. Moral education in the nineteenth century permeated many aspects of the curriculum. As McClellan (1999, p. 25) points out, "Moral lessons suffused nineteenth-century textbooks not just readers but spellers and arithmetic books as well." The reason why teachers, principals, and district leaders did this was to demonstrate to the children that living a life of integrity ultimately affects every avenue of one's life (Barnard, 1842; Barnard & Lannie, 1974; Mann, 1846, 1848, 1849; Ramsey, 2006; Yulish, 1980).

THE INGREDIENTS IN CHARACTER EDUCATION THAT THE AMERICAN PEOPLE DESIRED

Judeo-Christian Truth

One truth that was patent throughout the 1700s, 1800s, and most of the 1900s is that not only did educators favor moral instruction but also they nearly always envisioned a particular type of this instruction. One of the reasons for this fact is that Americans acknowledged that character training not only benefited individuals but also society as a whole. Charles DeGarmo, for example, who played the primary role in bringing Pestalozzian/Herbartian educational theorems to the United States opposed any sense of subjective individualistic morality, because it lent itself to relativism. Rather, DeGarmo espoused "the tradition of moral education of implanting a certain body of doctrine and their fixing of approximate habits" (Yulish, 1980, p. 10). He therefore believed that encouraging students to develop their own moral edicts and boundaries was profligate and, in fact, deleterious, because it was based on a subjective relativism that was prone to error. Instead DeGarmo and nearly all of his contemporaries believed that Judeo-Christian truths provided the moral compass that children needed to mature into loving, civil, and responsible human beings.

DeGarmo maintained that upholding these values had certain discernable advantages. First, they were the values maintained by God Himself. Therefore, they were true, eternal, and essential for the success of the human race. Most of these traits included those that ministers, educators, and other societal leaders considered foundational for a person's character such as kindness, responsibility, honesty, and sincerity. Second, there was also a commonly held belief that instructors could emphasize clearly identifiable behaviors that although in some cases were of less importance, were considered significant enough to address. Yulish (1980, p. 19) observes, "Eating candy, smoking, and drinking coffee were not viewed as physically harmful, but were seen to indicate a growing desire for mere stimulation of the nervous system and thus morally wrong." The character curriculum of the era generally emphasized traditional Protestant morality and good citizenship. Throughout the late 1700s and 1800s, the vast majority of spellers and readers gave admonishments against many wrongs, including drunkenness, obsession with luxury, pride, and lying. In contrast, they praised such qualities as responsibility and honesty.

Beyond these qualities, however, Americans looked to character education to instruct children in physical hygiene, literacy, and personality development. Overall, many educational psychologists looked to moral instruction to help develop adjusted youth. Americans also expected schools to teach students to abstain from alcohol. As one might expect, this was the orientation in American schools during prohibition. This preference, however, continued even after prohibition was overturned. Even by 1961 abstinence from alcohol was still taught in the public schools (Setran, 2006; Zimmerman, 2006).

Third, character education could help students make ethical decisions about right and wrong. Moral education in the nineteenth century was presented in a more "black and white" fashion than was so in the past. Character instruction was emphasized more than government and politics. In the eyes of educators, however, this degree of emphasis was worth the price, because the reward was social stability (Barnard, 1842; Barnard & Lannie, 1974; Mann, 1846, 1848, 1849; McClellan, 1999; Yulish, 1980).

Judeo-Christian Principles and Immigrants

A considerable amount of the moral instruction during the mid-to-late 1800s focused on acquainting immigrants with the Judeo-Christian values practiced in the United States. Americanization as many often called it helped immigrants comprehend and internalize the mores prevalent in the United States. Americanization involved inculcating immigrants regarding the evils of slavery, the salience of national unity, civility, and responsibility, among other traits. Some of these traits were intrinsically geared toward creating reliable citizens who could contribute to the health of the republic. Other traits, however, focused on the moral fiber that it was necessary for youth to possess (Barnard, 1842; Barnard & Lannie, 1974; Mann, 1846, 1848, 1849).

Character Education Focusing on Individual Responsibility

The character instruction of the 1800s focused on the individual much more than they did on the nation level. The consensus among most at the time was that most of society's problems were rooted in individual problems rather than in societal issues. Consequently, when schools addressed questions of maladjustments and behavioral ills, it did not eschew the individual ramifications of the importance of avoiding these activities. Rather, schools deliberately highlighted steps that a person could take to avoid inappropriate behavior and maximize edifying actions. Teachers placed much more emphasis on this than how the nation could maximize productive activities from coast to coast.

In the eyes of Americans during the mid-to-late 1800s, there was no need for intellectual and moral education to be antipodean. Each one could be incorporated within the curriculum and each could compliment the other. In fact, school leaders asserted that each pillar was insufficient without the other and that one could not be completely successful without either component. One of the primary reasons why parents sent their children to school was not only for their intellectual development but also for their moral edification. Numerical evidence, in fact, indicates that those schools that offered the most moral education instruction had higher attendance rates than those that emphasized moral instruction less (Rury, 2006; Yulish, 1980).

Character instruction during the mid-to-late 1800s was designed to cover a wide range of topics. Although the Bible and other morally oriented books were used as the primary texts, they were used to address a wide range of issues. The writings of various school officials during the mid-to-late 1800s indicate the extent to which education in the Bible via reading, reciting, and studying the Bible in other ways yielded a copious number of benefits both morally and intellectually. As one might expect, many educators averred that character instruction would have moral benefits. Similarly, as one might expect, teachers also claimed that character education would make children into better democratic citizens (Butts, 2006; Sandoz, 2006).

HORACE MANN AND HIS EMPHASIS ON MORAL EDUCATION

Background

There were a number of principal figures in the public school movement, all of whom emphasized moral education. However, it is Horace Mann who is known as the father of the common school movement, who therefore exercised the greatest influence over the presence of moral education in the public schools.

Horace Mann was born in Franklin, Massachusetts in the year 1796 and educated at Brown University. From his youth, Mann wanted to make an impact on society. Consequently, in the early days of his adulthood, he studied law. However, once he had practiced law for a time, he became disillusioned. Mann asserted that education was a superior means to improve the nation rather than through the law. This was Mann's view, because the law dealt with adults, who were already established in their ways. Education dealt with children and therefore had more potential to produce change. Mann (1907, p. 13) averred, "Men are cast-iron, but children are wax." Mann claimed that the means for extricating humans from evil rested not in the law, but in education (Messerli, 1972).

In 1837 Mann became the first secretary of the Massachusetts Board of Education. Through his writings in academic journals and other publications, especially during the 1837–1849 period, Mann became widely known and eventually became the most prominent educator of his day. Specifically, Mann's writings in the *Massachusetts Common School* and his reports became the most cited works on the schools (Bobbe, 1933; Bourne, 1870; Spring, 1997).

Mann Believed that Moral Education Must Be the Primary Focus of Education

Mann was a strong proponent of moral education. Mann (1840, 1846, 1849) believed that moral education was the cornerstone of any effective education program. Without the presence of moral education, Mann claimed that any attempt by teachers to enhance society was futile.

Although his writings on moral education in the 1830s did impact the education world, his "Twelfth Annual Report," in 1849, had the fullest effect. In this report, Mann posited that it was moral edification, far more than the education of the mind, which was the key for transforming the nation. Mann (1957, p. 100, citing Proverbs 22:6) claimed that the most vital focus that educators should have is "best expressed in these few and simple words from the Bible: 'Train up a child in the way he should go, and when he is old he will not depart from it.' " This biblical adage best summarizes Horace Mann's educational worldview. Urban and Wagoner (2000, p. 107) observe, "For Horace Mann and the other common school reformers, moral education was the heart of the curriculum." In Mann's (1849) "Twelfth Annual Report," which educators assert summarizes the essence of his educational philosophy, he declared,

> But, it will be said that this great result, in Practical Morals, is a consummation of blessedness that can never be attained without religion; and that no community will ever be religious without a Religious Education. Both of these propositions, I regard as eternal and immutable truths. Devoid of religious principles and religious affections the race can never fall so low that it may sink still lower. (as cited in Kliebard, 1969, p. 73)

Filler (1965, p. ix) adds, "The essence of Mann's program was moral. He believed not only that education carried moral responsibilities, but prosecuted without them, it could only produce more evil than it had ever inherited." Mann believed that just as mental and physical abilities increased via exercise, one's morality increased in the same way. Therefore, he argued that schools should give children the opportunity to exercise their moral facilities (Mann, 1845, 1849, 1969).

The emphasis that Mann placed on moral education was not unique to himself, but it reflected a pervasive belief in the United States at the time that the state of one's heart and whether a person was an individual of compassion, justice, and faithfulness was of even greater importance than how intelligent a person was. Consequently, virtually every educational leader of the time was a strong proponent of the presence of moral and religious education. Reflecting this fact, Hunt and Mullins (2005, p. 39) stated, "Mann credited the State Board with contributing to the moral training of children." Mann (in Hunt & Mullins, 2005, p. 39) noted that "Directly and indirectly, the influences of the Board of Education have been the means of increasing, to a great extent, the amount of religious instruction given in our schools." Whether one was a parent, school board member, educational administrator, school leader, or teacher, Americans expected moral education to possess the central place in the common school curriculum (Bourne, 1870; Cubberley, 1909; Mann, 1849). In fact, Horace Mann frequently expressed great joy over the fact that state boards of education were often at the forefront of prompting moral education. Mann observes, "Nothing has given me so much pleasure as reading the Reports of the school committees that have given prominence" to the "subject of Moral Education."

Horace Mann's annual reports that he wrote as the Massachusetts Secretary are usually the most transparent regarding his views on moral education. In several of Mann's annual reports, he places more of an emphasis on moral education than on any other topic. This tendency is especially ostensible in the latter two-thirds of Mann's annual reports. Hunt and Mullins (2005, p. 37) note that in his annual reports Mann focused "his attention on moral education in 1840" and beyond. They observe, "The year 1840 also witnessed several lectures that Mann gave on education in which he emphasized the moral character off education. In one he maintained that education was carrying on God's Word" (p. 37).

In his ninth annual report Mann (1846, p. 86) stated, "If securing the goodwill of scholars is preliminary to their attainment of knowledge, far more important it is to the cultivation of their moral sentiments and to good habits." Lawrence Cremin (in Mann, 1959, p. 3) observes that the principal theme of Mann's ninth annual report was the "primacy of moral over intellectual education."

Mann's emphasis on moral education is no more apparent than in his twelfth annual report, which stands as his final and most celebrated annual report. The primary reason that the twelfth annual report is so frequently cited and lauded is because Mann uses this report to summarize the essence of his educational beliefs. In fact the nature and structure of Mann's twelfth annual report is decidedly different than most of his earlier annual reports particularly (Mann, 1849).

Thomas Hunt and Marilyn Maxson (1981, p. 14) note, "For Mann, then, moral education was the key; it was a major reason for the existence of the common school and for significantly expanding its function." Charles and Mary Beard (1944, p. 238) state, "To the grand end of a happy and virtuous life for the individual and the progress of civilization in

American society Horace Mann subordinated all other aims of education." Cremin (in Mann, 1957) adds that Mann viewed "public education as a moral enterprise."

Mann Emphasized the Pursuit of Truth in Education

To Horace Mann the best kind of instruction involved the pursuit of truth. This consisted of first and foremost a pursuit of moral truth and also intellectual truth (Beard & Beard, 1944; Hunt & Maxson, 1981; Yulish, 1980). Mann (1855, p. 1) averred,

> Sacred regard for truth; to keep them unspotted from the world, that is uncontaminated by its vices; to train them up to the love of God and the love of man; to make the perfect example of Jesus Christ lovely in their eyes.

Mann (1969) contended that one of the vital functions of the common schools was to teach children a love for the truth and that love for the truth should have as its objects both intellectual and moral truths. He was so dedicated to the importance of these truths that he was convinced that without them, we in American society not only cannot weather a storm but that "we cannot weather a calm" (Mann, 1969, p. 125). Mann believed that the Bible was an essential text to inculcate youth in fundamental moral truths. He contended that the universe was filled with absolute truths that teachers must teach children in order to ensure a vibrant future society. In Mann's mind, the universe was filled with interminable examples of absolute truths. The square root of 2, π, and 8 squared have certain unalterable values that cannot be gainsaid. Various scientific laws, whether they were discovered before or after Mann's time, such as the speed of light and the laws of thermodynamics cannot be changed simply on the basis of capricious individual opinions. Furthermore, although Mann acknowledged that people possessed differences of opinion about historical facts, there are many historical facts that either did or did not happen. Granted, the divulging of precisely what these facts are might be more difficult than in the case of mathematical and scientific facts. However, Mann and nearly all of his contemporaries believed that these were historical facts nevertheless (Beard & Beard, 1944; Hunt & Maxson, 1981; Jeynes, 2003a; Yulish, 1980).

With this perspective in mind, Mann adhered to the belief that one of the purposes of the common school was to teach children certain core values. This goal applied not only to religious values but to political values as well. Mann (1844) contended that teachers should eschew the controversial political debates of the day. Nevertheless, he believed that Americans shared certain values on which the nation was based. Mann believed it would nourish America if teachers taught these values. He affirmed that a core set of values would fortify the nation as a whole and reduce crime and personal injury (Beard & Beard, 1944; Hunt & Maxson, 1981; Jeynes, 2003a; Kaestle & Vinovkis, 1980; Yulish, 1980).

The orientation of Horace Mann was not his alone. Mann's successors continued the same orientation. For example, one of Mann's successors as the secretary of the Massachusetts Board of Education, George Boutwell (1860, p. 61) said in his 1860 Annual Report, "I am, however, of the opinion that in a number of cases so great … the criminal character is developed in consequence of neglect of mental and moral training." Myriad Americans embraced Mann's common value orientation, especially after the conclusion of the Civil War, because at this juncture, many citizens became cognizant of the exigent need of adhering to a common set of values, because the nation had previously been so deeply divided (Kaestle & Vinovkis, 1980).

Mann Believed in the Teaching of Religious Education

To Horace Mann, moral education meant that teachers would give children religious instruction. Hunt and Mullins (2005, p. 53) note, "To Mann, religion and morality were inseparable." Mann (1846, p. 86) asserted in his ninth annual report that "No community can long subsist unless it has religious principle as the foundation of moral action, nor unless it has moral action as the superstructure of religious principle." Horace Mann, according to Maris Vinovkis (1995, p. 47), "believed that education and religion could and should coexist in the classroom." Mann was "deeply religious" (p. 47) and believed that it was imperative that religious and character institution have prominent place in the curriculum. According to Vinovkis (p. 47), "Mann frequently discussed the value of moral and religious education in his annual reports. He was enthusiastic about the ability of moral education to eliminate crime."

In Mann's view, morality and religion were inextricably connected. To him, one needed to possess a consistent and eternal reason for living a moral life or else the righteousness would not last. In addition, Mann noted that both religion and morality were rooted in obedience. If one was obedient to God, that person would also live a moral life. As Mann declared, "By religion I mean the great ideas and affections pertaining to human brotherhood and to practical obedience to the precepts of the Gospel of Jesus Christ" (Mann, 1854, p. 425). Mann believed it was essentially impossible to expect children to live righteous lives without the teaching of the Bible. To Mann, the Bible was the perfect instrument to ensure virtue among students. He believed that school leaders could read and present the Bible in a nonsectarian way so that one did not have to address specific theological differences. As Mann (in McCluskey, 1958, p. 94) asserted, "The Bible without note or interpreter is the means par excellence of realizing this primary aim of education because it breathes God's laws and presents illustrious examples of conduct, above all that of Jesus Christ."

Horace Mann believed that the study of the Word of God encouraged personal depth. Mann averred, therefore, that people ought to submit themselves to God's ways. He states one should be "fashioning our moral nature into some resemblance to its divine original—subordinating our propensities to the law of duty, expanding our benevolence into a sentiment of universal brotherhood, and lifting our hearts to the grateful and devout contemplation of God" (Mann, 1848, in McCluskey, 1958, p. 36). Mann was so convinced of the necessity of the presence of religious teaching, especially using the Bible, and prayer in the schools, that he believed that the future of civilized society was dependent on its inclusion (Filler, 1965; Mann, 1848, 1849).

Mann believed that in the Bible rested humanity's hope for securing a civilized society (Hunt & Mullins, 2005). He believed that without having instruction in the Bible as an integral part of the common school experience, human beings would regress into animalistic tendencies. Mann (1974/1838, p. 55) maintained that it was the responsibility of teachers to "cultivate moral behavior and advance morals and religious sentiments into ascendancy and control over animal and selfish propensities."

Horace Mann believed that truth, particularly moral and religious truth, should not only be understood but also acted upon. Even near the end of his life Mann was a strong believer in the need for people to obey God's law. At Antioch he said that he professed belief "not only in the Ten Commandments but in ten thousand. He lives, and wherever He rules there is law and a law of God is a command. All the kingdom of nature around us—the inorganic which exists, and the organic which lives, and the sentient which feels—are pervaded by God's laws. We also in our powers, faculties, and susceptibilities are subject of God's laws" (Mann in McCluskey, 1958, p. 21).

In Mann's view it was important that students develop morally, particularly in two ways, demonstrating love to others and obedience to God and His moral code. He asserted part of true education was "subordinating our propensities to the law of duty, expanding our benevolence into a sentiment of universal brotherhood, and lifting our hearts to the grateful and devout contemplation of God" (Mann, 1848, p. 23).

Mann's emphasis on godliness, love, and other virtues was inextricably connected with his view of the ideal society. As much as Mann valued the importance of an intelligent society, he cherished a civilized and compassionate society even more. In a letter to Reverend D. Wright, Jr., on April 28, 1848, Mann wrote, "Moral qualifications, and the ability to inculcate and enforce the Christian virtues, I consider to be even of greater moment than literacy attainments." Horace Mann, the father of the common school movement, was completely unapologetic about the prominence of character and religious instruction in the curriculum. Horace Mann, like nearly all Americans of the time, believed that the cultural and philosophical foundation of the United States came from the Judeo-Christian and Greco-Roman traditions. He maintained that America's moral compass could be found in these two traditions. Dunn notes that the degree of Christian teaching was great during the Mann epoch (Dunn, 1955; Jencks & Riesman, 1968; McCluskey, 1958).

Mann viewed religion as the foundation of moral living. This perspective was hardly revolutionary. Moreover, it has been the overwhelming view of Americans from the days of the earliest settlers through the George Washington era and throughout the Horace Mann period. Given this emphasis, it is no surprise that, as McCluskey (1958, p. 18) observes, Mann "had nothing but scorn for all species of atheism." Mann expressed his assertion of the relationship between morality and religion in the following: "fashioning our moral nature into some resemblance to its divine original—subordinating our propensities to the law of duty, expanding our benevolence into a sentiment of universal brotherhood, and lifting our hearts to the grateful and devout contemplation of God" (Hunt & Maxson, 1981; Jeynes, 2007; Mann, 1848, 1854; McClellan, 1999).

Horace Mann believed, as most Americans at the time did, that the Bible should be a primary basis for those common values, as well as the moral instruction that was presented in the schools. He was nevertheless careful to include the Bible in such a way that would not produce friction between religious denominations. Mann (1849, p. 6) claimed that "The laws of Massachusetts required the teaching of the basic moral doctrines of Christianity." He believed that the common schools needed a nonsectarian use of the Bible in which the aspects of the Bible that all denominations taught could be emphasized. This view of the place of the Bible in the public school curriculum was well received and practiced in American schools until the early 1960s (Blanshard, 1963; Kliebard, 1969; Mann, 1844, 1849).

Mann's strong belief in the primacy of religion and morality helped solidify the prominent presence of each in America's public schools. Mann (1974/1838, n.p.) stated,

> As piety is the discharge of our duty to God, and as that duty cannot be discharged, without a knowledge of his character and attributes, it follows that to teach the principles of piety, we must teach that character and those attributes.

Americans during this time concurred with Mann's insistence that schools possess a religious orientation, because the United States was a thoroughly Christian nation at the time. During his journeys to America in 1831 and 1832, Tocqueville (1966, p. 268) had declared, "There is no other country in the world where the Christian religion retains a greater influence over the souls of men than in America." Horace Mann viewed education as a necessary supplement and complement to the church in terms of addressing the ills of society and offering spiritual and moral medicine for those afflictions. Mann declared:

> The more I see of our present civilization and of the only remedies for its evils, the more I dread intellectual eminence when separated from virtue. We are in a sick world, for whose maladies, the knowledge of truth, and obedience to it, are the only healing. (Mann, as cited in Filler, 1965, p. iii)

The extent of Mann's convictions along these lines is summarized well in his writing in the *Common School Journal*. Mann states, "A man is not educated, because he buys a book nor is he educated because he reads a book, though it should be the wisest book that ever was written, and should enumerate and unfold all the laws of God. He only is educated, who practices according to the laws of God." Furthermore, in a letter he wrote to Reverend Wright, Mann averred, "Moral qualifications, and the ability to inculcate and enforce the Christian virtues, I consider to be even of greater moment than literacy attainments."

One who observes these statements might ask why it was that Mann stressed the development of virtue even more than intellectual prowess. Mann (1854, pp. 367–368) averred, "The moral and religious part of man's nature is the highest part. Of right it has sovereignty and dominion over all the rest." Mann contended that humans were first and foremost spiritual beings. Humans, according to Mann, were also intellectual in nature, but this was designed to be deferential to one's moral dimension. In the summer of 1846, Mann wrote a marvelous letter to New York state children communicating the following, "You were made to be moral and religious. Morality consists primarily in the performance of our duties to our fellow-men; religion in the performance of our duties to God" (Mann, 1854, p. 271).

Mann's Emphasis on Personal Example

To Mann and the prominent school leaders of the time, not only was instruction in character education important, but so was the need for teachers to establish good moral examples for the children. From Mann's perspective, the teaching of character was most efficacious when it proceeded from people of character. Horace Mann believed that the primacy of moral education emerged not only as a curricular matter but also as a matter of personal example. Consistent with this conviction, Mann preferred female teachers over male teachers because he believed that women were better than men at managing children and were more virtuous than their male counterparts. Horace Mann, the father of the common school, believed that moral education was the centerpiece of the curriculum. The overwhelming majority of teachers in the mid-1800s agreed with Mann's philosophy. McClellan (1999, p. 23) observes, "Nothing revealed the importance of moral education in the public school so clearly as the overwhelming preference for women teachers." Mann and other of his contemporaries believed that women were morally superior to men and more nurturing than their male counterparts (Elsbree, 1939; Jeynes, 2007; Mann, 1846, 1849; Spring, 1997; Vinovkis, 1995).

As a result, beginning in the late 1830s, the percentage of the teaching force that was female steadily grew so that by 1865, female teachers outnumbered male teachers for the first time. Moreover, since that time the numerical constitution of the teaching force has always favored females (Elsbree, 1939; U.S. Department of Education, 2007). The nation's dedication to the notion of female educators was so substantial that one organization alone, the National Board of Popular Education, sent 600 single women to the West in order to make certain that the children from these new territories had access to a "proper Christian culture" (McClellan, 1999, p. 24).

Mann's Orientation Reflected the Culture and Changes of the Time

Christian Revivals: The Second Great Awakening (1790–1840) and the Late 1850s

Mann's emphasis on character education particularly thrived partially because it reflected the cultural emphasis of the time. During the period just prior to Mann's ascension to power, moral education had a prominent place in American society. Addressing the 1750–1820 period, McClellan (1999, p. 10) observed that the "root of the . . . moral tone was the extraordinary stability of the family and community life in towns, cities, and plantations along the eastern seaboard where most Americans still lived." The social support for character instruction increased during the 1830s and 1840s due to "the revival of evangelical Christianity" (McClellan, 1999, p. 19). The view of the church was that character training was the combined responsibility of the family, the school, and the church. This perspective translated into the church supporting character instruction both in faith-based schools and public schools (Jeynes, 2007; McClellan, 1999).

Most of the curriculum and "modes of organization" of American public schools had its roots in Protestantism. Schools often recruited Protestant clergy to teach and help organize the schools. Americans viewed common schools as a means of spreading the Christian faith and concurrently facilitating social stability and harmony (McClellan, 1999).

The presence of character instruction in the public schools was greatly influenced by the revival of the late 1850s. This revival accomplished a number of breakthroughs, including: (1) a renewed emphasis on spirituality and maturity; (2) a call for character education classes; and (3) addressing social and moral ills, for example, slavery. Therefore, as a consequence of the succession of great revivals, Americans felt very comfortable with Mann's perspective on the relationship between character and intellectual development (McClellan, 1999). Character education, in Mann's view, was at the heart of the curriculum particularly because the ultimate goal of schooling was to produce virtuous, caring, and faithful human beings as opposed to simply focusing on intellectual capabilities. According to McCluskey (1958, p. 70), "Mann says that the intellectual faculties are cultivated so that we may know God's attributes and His world and harmonize our conduct with its laws."

Changes in the Family and Community

There were changes beginning to emerge on the American landscape. There were two changes that were taking place, in addition to the revival of evangelical Christianity. First, during the 1830s and 1840s, more fathers were working away from home. Hence, mothers now played a heightened role in moral training versus the father's role than was so previously. Before this time, fathers were frequently the main source for character education. Second, as the United States began to move away from being an agrarian community, parents had to prepare their children to move away from home (Hiner, 1988; Jeynes, 2007; McClellan, 1999).

Due to the above trends, even though Americans always viewed character education as one of the functions of the schools, with the new developments ostensible in the first 50 or 60 years of the nineteenth century, parents increasingly were depending on the schools to supplement the character training that children received in their homes. During this time, the Sunday school emerged as one of the most aggressive efforts to provide moral tutelage that children needed (McClellan, 1999).

Although the Sunday school played an important role in training youth, parents ideally wanted this type of training to be available to students during each day of the school week. It is insightful to note that parents not only wanted character training to be made available to their children but to other youth as well. The fathers and mothers comprehended the reality that the United States was regarded as a land of liberty to both the native and the immigrant. George Washington's conclusion that liberty and democracy could eventually yield an "unbridled democracy" was a perspective maintained by the vast majority of nineteenth-century Americans as well. Consistent with this understanding, the general belief was that character training, concurrently made available in the homes, the churches, and the schools, would help ensure that the nation's liberty would not lead to anarchy. The role of moral training in the schools would provide this value not only at the individual level but also at the corporate level. That is, such instruction not only would provide order to individual lives but would also be instrumental in providing order and harmony at the societal level (McClellan, 1999).

The fact that virtually all Americans valued character education in the nineteenth century significantly facilitated the teaching of character. In other words, character instruction saturated many aspects of a child's school life, including the teaching, school activities, and the textbooks themselves. McClellan (1999, p. 25) notes, "Moral lessons suffused nineteenth century textbooks—not just readers, but spellers and arithmetic books as well."

Daniel Blake Smith (1980, p. 15) comments on the nature of the context of these textbooks.

> The values themselves were a blend of traditional protestant morality and nineteenth century conceptions of good citizenship. Textbooks taught love of country, love of God, duty to parents, the necessity to develop habits of thrift, honesty, and hard work in order to accumulate property, the certainty of progress and the perfection of the United States.

During the 1800s, moral instruction took myriad forms and came from a variety of sources, which they believed that together would produce a large population of virtuous youth. Parents viewed these sources as helping to support the others. For example, parents generally believed that Sunday schools and common schools complimented one another. In addition, other groups formed to promote moral values as well. These groups included 4-H clubs, the Camp Fire Girls, and the Boy Scouts (McClellan, 1999).

Mann and Catholicism

Over time therefore, Americans developed a consensus regarding the Christian values that could be taught, while acknowledging the rights of individuals to maintain certain specific doctrines. Although Horace Mann and his contemporaries sought to construct a Protestant-based curriculum, Mann and many of contemporaries hoped that Catholics would be drawn in as well. Most educational textbooks emphasize the conflicts that emerged between Protestant and Catholic leaders. Nevertheless, more often than not

Protestants and Catholics tried to compromise and accommodate one another. One of the most heated controversies involved the Catholic desire to read their version of the Bible, the Douay Version, rather than the version(s) preferred by Protestants. Although there were many cases in which both Protestants and Catholics were adamant in their position and demonstrated no willingness to compromise with the other group, there were compromises. Frequently, however, at least one of the groups would express a willingness to compromise. Often in order to attract more Catholics into the public schools, school leaders would either allow the reading of the Douay Version of the Bible or release time so that students could study elements of the Catholic faith. Nevertheless, Catholics desired their youth to attend schools that were as deeply founded in the Catholic tradition as public schools were routed in Protestantism (McClellan, 1999; Tyack, 1974).

Mann's views regarding the place of religion and moral instruction in the public schools were typical of the day. American Jewish people generally supported this orientation. Jewish people did establish some parochial schools as early as the 1700s, but most of them were founded between 1840 and 1860. Although many Catholics were also supportive of the common schools, others formed parochial schools. There were three primary reasons for this action by some Catholics. First, they wanted more of an emphasis on religious instruction than the common schools were willing to offer. Second, they wanted more of a Catholic orientation in the curriculum. Third, they wanted more of a pro-Catholic atmosphere in the classroom (Brereton, 1982).

As much as Horace Mann emphasized character education, and as influential as he was, moral instruction could not have enjoyed the centrality that it did without the dedication of countless educators who placed immense value on instruction in character. With this in mind, in the next section of this chapter, we look at some of the contributions of Mann's contemporaries.

CONTEMPORARIES OF HORACE MANN IN THE COMMON SCHOOL MOVEMENT

Henry Barnard

Henry Barnard (1811–1900) was a contemporary of Horace Mann and emerged as the second most influential educator of his time. Barnard was born into a "deeply religious family" and was inspired by "the Puritan work ethic" (Barnard & Lannie, 1974, p. 1). Barnard was Mann's counterpart for the state of Connecticut, serving as the Secretary of the Board of Education for that state. Barnard shared Mann's emphasis on moral education. Henry Barnard believed that common school instructors should teach Christian virtues, peace, civility, and self-control (Barnard, 1842, 1855; Barnard & Lannie, 1974; MacMullen, 1991).

Barnard and Mann became close friends and often corresponded with each other. In their letters to each other, it is patent that both of these leaders viewed education as a kind of ministry and a call from God with moral implications for all attendees. Mann's assertion in the letter below is typical of their correspondence.

In the same letter, Mann wrote about the deep conviction that he had about the necessity and importance of common school education:

> I have long been accustomed to look at the great movement of education as part of the providence of God, by which the human race is to be redeemed. It is my conviction, it constitutes part of the Divine ordinances. I throw myself forward into the coming contest and see that the work has prospered. I regard it as more than a prophecy, as a fact . . . Good-bye, my dear friend and fellow laborer in the holiest of causes. (Mann, 1840, p. 1)

Calvin Stowe

Calvin Stowe significantly facilitated the founding and maturation of common schools in the Midwest. His influence over education in Ohio was similar to Mann's leadership in Massachusetts (Rippa, 1997). Stowe served as a professor of New Testament at Lane Theological Seminary in Cincinnati. He was the husband of Harriet Beecher Stowe, the author of *Uncle Tom's Cabin*. At this time, the United States greatly admired European practices and often emulated their educational theories and disciplines. Stowe facilitated this by traveling to Europe in 1836 and reporting on European school practices. He noted that European teachers adhered to the teachings of the Bible in order for moral instruction to take place. He asserted that the European emphasis on Christianity was bringing civilization to the remote parts of Europe. He credited this punctuation with much of Europe's educational success. Stowe, like Mann and Barnard, viewed moral instruction as indispensable to the efficacy of education. He stated,

> To leave the moral faculty uninstructed was to leave the most important part of the human mind undeveloped, and to strip education of almost

every thing that can make it valuable; and that the Bible, independently of the interest attending it, as containing the most ancient and influential writings ever recorded by human hands, and comprising the religious system of almost the whole of the civilized world, is in itself the best book that can be put into the hands of children to interest, to exercise, and to unfold their intellectual and moral powers (Stowe, 1837, pp. 18–19).

Samuel Seelye

Samuel Seelye was another influential educator in the early days of the common school. He said that "Christianity is essential to education" (Seelye, 1864, p. 3). He added that a loving and moral environment was necessary in the classroom. He believed that the more educators taught about God, the more the youth would develop in holiness (Seelye, 1864).

Johann Herbart

Johann Herbart (1776–1841) was a German psychologist and was a major influence in education, although much of his impact occurred after he died. Charles DeGarmo first introduced the Herbartian orientation to American schools in the 1880s and 1890s (Dunkel, 1970).

Herbart maintained that character education was the primary goal of the school (Dunkel, 1970; Graves, 1912). Graves (1912, p. 177) observes, "The making of the morally religious man is, therefore, Herbart's idea of the end of education." Herbart (1852, p. 7) even titled one of the chapters in his book, "Morality: The Sole and Total Task of Education." In that book, he stated, "Education is not merely to make man 'better' in some sense, but is to make him 'morally good.' The aim of education is virtue, morality."

JOHANN PESTALOZZI AND THE MATERNAL ROLE OF THE SCHOOLS

Johann Pestalozzi (1746–1827) was born in Zurich, Switzerland and became one of the most influential educators of his era. Not only did his beliefs impact education directly, but they also helped mold the educational philosophies of Johann Herbert and Friedrich Froebel, and facilitated the adoption of the common school model in the United States. John Griscom, a well-known American educator, was largely responsible for bringing Pestalozzian practices to the United States. By the 1840s, myriad teachers and scholars became familiar with Pestalozzian principles, but it was the Oswego Normal School, founded in 1861, that was most active in disseminating his ideas throughout the United States (Downs, 1975; Gutek, 1968; Spring, 1997).

Overall, Johann Pestalozzi was a moderate in his instructional philosophy. He believed that schooling needed to become more child-centered than in the past. However, he also passionately asserted that moral education stood as the central part of the curriculum and that this instruction was inherently religious. Kinloch (1969, p. 89) notes that Pestalozzi was "a profoundly religious man who said in his first published book that man's relationship to God is the nearest of all his relationships and he was convinced that education must be essentially religious." In fact, Pestalozzi propounded six principles of education, the two foremost of which were that education must be essentially religious and that schooling must develop people as a whole (Kinloch, 1969; Pestalozzi, 1898, 1916).

Pestalozzi believed that schooling must appeal not only to the mind but also to the spirit. Pestalozzi, however, possessed a strategy different from most educators of his day. He believed that in instructional incipiency, a teacher's instruction should focus on appealing to a child's senses. Although modern day liberals find this aspect of Pestalozzi's teaching appealing, they often remove this orientation from its proper context. Although Pestalozzi viewed appealing to the senses as appropriate rudimentary education, he nevertheless asserted that once this foundation is laid teaching must then urge children ascend to the realm of judgment. From Pestalozzi's perspective, a person's senses could deceive one. He especially believed that this was true with regard to moral teaching. This is why it is so important for a teacher to guide a child from the rudimentary experience of the senses to the realm of truth and justice and right and wrong. Consequently, according to Pestalozzi, although the nature of limited development of young children dictated that instruction begin at the level of the senses, teachers must ensure that it will not remain at this simplistic level (Kinloch, 1969).

In Pestalozzi's view the essence of education was religious. He averred that the natural process of edification required that children from an early age rely on their parents and on their senses. As children matured, however, Pestalozzi contended that this process necessitated that this prior reliance give way to a reliance on God and wise judgment (Ulich, 1968).

This period of transference was of utmost importance. During this period, it was vital that a child be instructed to transfer that faith in the mother to a faith in God. Pestalozzi (1801, pp. 313–315) asserted:

> It asks that we develop humanely and understandably the loving and faithful state of mind the truth and blessing of which the innocent child has so far enjoyed unconsciously in his relation to the mother. For sooner or later this state of innocence, the faith in the mother, will weaken and vacillate. Nature then demands new means of faith. And unless we plant faith in God deeply into the child's soul, we create the danger of cutting the natural links of human development. However, in the state of early childhood, this desirable continuity can be achieved only by appeal to the child's natural sensitive faculty. The motivations of faith in God must be already provided before the child's sensuous and natural attachment to the mother is fading. Faith in God, as it were, must be melted into the maturing relation to the mother. Here is the only chance for a pure, continuous, and natural development from the innocence of childhood toward human morality, for the latter grows from the first. Only this process of growth leads to real faith and love, the lifting of sensuous affection toward the level of moral and spiritual maturity.

Pestalozzi claimed that the nurturing qualities of a mother were indispensable in terms of drawing a child into a reliance on God. Furthermore, Pestalozzi (1801) opined that an efficacious teacher must also exhibit those identical maternal qualities in order to help fabricate an irremovable foundation for child development and spawn in the child a ripening reliance on God. With this background in mind, it is not surprising that Pestalozzi in his most renowned work, *Leonard and Gertrude*, emphasizes the role of the loving mother in the story who reads the Bible to her children, prays with them, and observes the Sabbath (Kinloch, 1969). Kinloch (p. 99) notes, "Pestalozzi always maintained that the whole of his curriculum was religious."

In Pestalozzi's writings, he often made a strong distinction between the heart and the mind. Pestalozzi's views reflected the conventional views of his time in that he believed that it was inconceivable to approach instruction as only a means to improve the mind. Pestalozzi believed the words of Cicero, the great statesman and orator, who believed that the most dangerous man alive was one who was intelligent, but not virtuous. Centuries later, Martin Luther King would echo almost these precise words.

Nevertheless, Pestalozzi maintained an interesting perspective regarding the mind and the heart. He did not view them as antipodal nor did he claim that they were mutually exclusive. Rather, he believed that they were inextricably connected. Pestalozzi posited that the ultimate goal of teachers should be to lead the heart in the way of love and to lead the mind in the way of truth (Downs, 1975; Dupuis, 1966; Jeynes, 2007; Kinloch, 1969).

Pestalozzi asserted that the quest for truth and love was so interwoven simply because "love and truth are but two different names for God" (Kinloch, 1969, p. 99). Religious instruction and the Bible, according to Pestalozzi, were best suited to this blended type of teaching because Christianity and the Bible directed the reader to seek both truth and love. What Pestalozzi refers to when he states that love and truth are names for God are Bible verses such as "God is love" (I John 4:8) and when Jesus states "I am the way, the truth, and the life" (John 14:6a). Therefore, in Pestalozzi's view, the Bible offered the perfect balance in education by offering instruction that was edifying both to the mind and to the heart (Kinloch, 1969).

Pestalozzi believed that discipline was a salient part of moral education (Castle, 1962). Castle (p. 158) notes that "Pestalozzi's attitude toward discipline is best understood against the background of his view of man as primarily a moral being." Although Pestalozzi read Rousseau's works and agreed with some of his views, he clearly had some disagreements with him. He particularly had objections to the lack of personal boundaries evident in Rousseau's book *Emile*. Castle (p. 158) observes, "The parent or teacher is to enter more deliberately into disciplinary action than Emile's tutor would have deemed necessary. The most definite break with Rousseau is seen in Pestalozzi's insistence on obedience."

Pestalozzi contended that obedience together with love, thankfulness, trust, and confidence produced "the first germ of conscience" (Castle, 1962, p. 158). Pestalozzi asserts that it is wrong for a child to struggle against the loving mother or teacher. He also believes that families and schools should teach children in such a way that these young people comprehend that they are not the center of the world. Selfishness is antipodal to love. In order to mature into a loving and caring individual, each child needs to comprehend that the mother is also dedicated to the welfare of other individuals, most notably her husband and her other children. Similarly, the youth also needs to appreciate the fact that his or her father and teacher are also dedicated to the welfare of a spouse, their children, and other significant individuals (Castle, 1962).

In Pestalozzi's mind, the extent of character education was vast. He averred that children ought to be taught appropriate attitudes and behaviors toward God, their family, their teachers, their neighbors, and broader society. To Pestalozzi, moral education was not only crucial, but he affirmed that all other forms of education were dependent on its presence as the centerpiece of the curriculum.

Pestalozzi's emphasis on moral education was never more clear than in his book, *Leonard and Gertrude*. The essence of the book is that practicing the maternal influence of the home in the school can produce constructive moral change. Ulich (1968, p. 230) describes the book the following way:

> It pictures the rottenness of the life in a poor Swiss village, where Gertrude, the pious wife of a mason . . . is the only source of educational wisdom and inspiration . . . Observing how Gertrude brings up her children he and his friends realize the interdependence between family spirit and the spirit of the community, of religion and education and also of physical welfare and human dignity.

Pestalozzi (1898, 1916) averred that it is the maternal nature of the mother that enables the home to function as a warm sanctuary for most children. Furthermore, he propounded a belief that if teachers exuded the same degree of maternal charity, children could view the school as a place of comfort as well. Pestalozzi believed that in this type of loving environment, a child could flourish. He wanted to make the schoolroom a place of love and psychological nourishment, just like their homes were, in which children could excel and reach their highest potential. Gerald Gutek (1968, pp. 61–62) notes, "Pestalozzi was deeply impressed by the mother's crucial role in the kindling of love." Gutek also notes, "In developing educational theory Pestalozzi affirmed the crucial importance of the home circle as the origin of all education" (pp. 24–25). Therefore, he believed that teachers should seek to apply many of the approaches used by parents. Pestalozzi maintained that the maternal emphasis would yield not only intellectual benefits but character-building ones as well. In fact, he believed that these two qualities were often juxtaposed in the sense that children of character also excelled the most intellectually. Pestalozzi affirmed that parents and teachers should, in essence, work as partners to foster a child's healthy relationship with God. Pestalozzi maintained that as a child received God's love from his or her mother and teacher, the potential would be spawned for that child to have a love relationship with God also.

In Pestalozzi's view, children learned best in the home because the home was a place of love. Gutek (1968) observes, "If a child is given love and care by the mother, the child's idea of benevolence will be activated. If he continues to experience tender loving care, the child will grow into a person who is capable of giving and receiving love."

Pestalozzi contended that education has deviated from its biblical roots and needed to return to a Christian focus, in other words, the love of God and neighbor, which Christ declared were the two most prominent commandments. On this issue, Pestalozzi (1801, p. 423) asserts,

> Thus it is evident that the truth of fundamental and organic education and the totality of its means issues from the divine spark which is planted into human nature and harmonizes with the spirit of Christianity. On the other hand, it is equally evident that our present education with all its artificiality, corruption and routine does not spring from the divine spark in the depth of man, but from his brutal and sensuous desires. Consequently, it contradicts the spirit and evidence of Christianity and can have no other effect but to undermine it.

In many respects, Pestalozzi's teachings reflected the views of other great educators that preceded him, including Plato, Cicero, Augustine, and especially Comenius. Comenius (1592–1670) was a Czech educator and religious leader who aided in school reform in Sweden, Poland, and England (Kinloch, 1969; Sadler, 1966). Pestalozzi agreed with Comenius in that he espoused the primacy of a religious foundation. When comparing Comenius and Pestalozzi, Robert Ulich (1968, p. 30) observed:

> Both Pestalozzi and Comenius were so intrinsically religious that their piety shines through every one of their works. They could not speak of nature without thinking of God as its creator; they could not speak of the human being without sensing the divine in even the poorest soul. For both parental love and the good family were the reflection of the fatherly love of God on the level of human relations . . . Finally, for both, education was not merely a way of teaching and learning, but the human attempt to participate in the divine plan to unfold the best in individual man and in humanity as a whole.

FRIEDRICH FROEBEL AND HIS VISION FOR THE KINDERGARTEN

Friedrich Froebel (1782–1852) is best known for being the founder of the kindergarten. He conceived of the kindergarten as being fundamentally distinct from the elementary school. He saw the kindergarten as foundational for the remainder of the schooling experience (Doherty, 1977; Downs, 1975; Slight, 1961). He believed that an emphasis on moral character that was necessary to emerge as a compassionate, righteous, and intelligent human being must precede a focus on intellectual development (Doherty, 1977; Downs, 1975; Slight, 1961).

Froebel maintained that the essence of the kindergarten was to enable children grow up, like a garden, and experience unity with God and the individuals around them. His vision for the kindergarten was what he envisioned a mixture of the best combinations of the conservative and liberals schools of educational thought. From the conservative vantage point, he believed that the primary orientation of the kindergarten should be on moral education. From the liberal perspective, he opined that education should be child centered. Although Froebel died in 1852, his ideas soon spread to the United States. Carl and Margarethe Schurz established the first kindergarten in the United States in Watertown, Wisconsin in 1855, although kindergartens were not very common in America in the 1850s (Baylor, 1965; Beatty, 1995; Doherty, 1977; Downs, 1975; Slight, 1961).

To Froebel, the key to all positive moral and intellectual development found its source in unity with God. Froebel declared, "All things have come from the Divine Unity, from God, and have their origin in the Divine Unity, in God alone" (Froebel in Von Bulow, 1894, p. 211). Fruhling (1952, p. 22) notes, "This bringing of one's mind to the unity of God is to Froebel the beginning of all knowledge." Froebel believed that the purpose of the kindergarten was to unite children to God and to each other (Doherty, 1977). Froebel asserted that only through God could this unifying process take place. He stated, "Education consists in leading man as a thinking, intelligent being growing into a self-conscious and free representation of the inner law of Divine Unity, and in teaching him ways and means thereto" (as cited in Doherty, 1977, p. 5).

Friedrich Froebel had deep personal Christian roots. He was a minister and the son of a Lutheran pastor. Fruhling (p. 30) observes, "He [Froebel] viewed the Christian religion as the conviction that God must reveal himself in a three-fold way as creator, preserver, and ruler." Fruhling (p. 31) adds, "Froebel's deep religious sense showed in all facets of his writing." Appreciating Froebel's Christian orientation is paramount if one is truly to fathom the purpose and essence of Froebel's original kindergarten paradigm. In Froebel's mind, unity with God was the natural place to begin the educational process because he believed that "the human quest for truth is inborn, because the consciousness of God is imminent in every soul" (Froebel in Von Bulow, 1894, p. 182). Froebel maintained that since God is truth and possesses all truth, to experience unity with God was the natural place for the educational process to begin (Fruhling, 1952; Slight, 1961).

In his autobiography, Froebel did a remarkable job of explicating how unity with God unleashed the experience of God's truth and inaugurated the educational experience.

> I desire to educate men whose feet shall stand on God's earth, rooted fast in Nature, while their head towers up the heaven, and reads its secrets with steady gaze, whose heart shall embrace both earth and heaven, shall enjoy the life of earth and nature with all its wealth of forms, and at the same time shall recognize the purity and peace of heaven, that unites in its love God's earth with God's heaven. (Froebel, 1889, p. 58)

In Froebel's kindergarten paradigm, as one directs children into experiencing unity with God, the teacher's primary focus becomes God-likeness in the children. In the *Education of Man*, Froebel (1898, p. 59) asserts, "And God-likeness is and ought to be man's highest aim in thought and deed." For Froebel the good, the perfect, and the image of God were the only possible results if men follow their destiny and God's will.

Froebel definitely possessed an academic component to his kindergarten rubric. Nevertheless, he believed that one should gear instruction to the whole child. His hope was that education would transform children and that these individuals, especially as they grew older, would change the world into a far more harmonious and loving environment. As Fruhling (1952, p. 43) notes, "Froebel felt that man's main duty is to develop and promote the realization of God's ideal in humanity." From Froebel's perspective, although intellectual prowess could improve the world in some ways, his conviction was that most of the world's ills were character-based. With this perspective in mind, Froebel contended that it was more important for a person to manifest good character than it was for that person to emerge as an intellectual giant (Beatty, 1995; Hughes, 1897; Jeynes, 2006; Ulich, 1957; Wolfe, 2000).

Although Froebel esteemed character more than he did intellect, he nevertheless maintained that the loving environment and individual self-discipline that would result from strength of character that burgeoned from the kindergarten's moral emphasis would yield cerebral benefits as well (Deboer, 2002; Jeynes, 2006; Ulich, 1957).

Although Froebel wrote and spoke emphatically about the need for teachers to emphasize moral education, he was unwavering in his belief that parents were the primary instructors of children both with regards to character and education in the broadest sense. Froebel, Castle (1962, p. 216) notes, "regard[ed] the family as the place where education begins." According to Liebschner (1992, p. 66), "The child aims at mounding his own life in its purity, harmony, and efficiency, on the mode he finds in the family." In Froebel's view the teacher's function was to complement the influence of the family. Froebel believed that it was imperative that the teacher in no way attempt to usurp the role of the parent. As much as Froebel esteemed the role of schooling, like virtually all academics and other educators of his time, he viewed the school's role as not only secondary to the role of parents but subordinate to their desires. Froebel averred that if what schools taught purposely contradicted parental values, then teachers violated a covenant of trust with parents. Sending their children was an act of trust on the part of parents. These family members were leaving their precious children in the hands of teachers that they might or might not have known previously. In fact, with the ascendancy of industrialization with each passing year, parents typically knew less about their children's teachers than they did the year before. Given the trust that parents were expressing in school officials by sending their children to schools, Froebel believed that it is unconscionable for educators to undermine parental values (Jeynes, 2006, 2007; Lascarides & Hinitz, 2000; Snider, 1900).

Given that Froebel maintained that the home was the pivotal place of education, he cherished the place of parental involvement in facilitating positive academic and behavioral outcomes. He believed that parents could not assume their proper role as primary educators unless they doughtily assumed that function and enjoyed that privilege. One should also note that naturally most people of that era assumed that parents would be engaged in their children's education. In most households, both mothers and fathers spent more time at home than is true in contemporary society. Largely, because of this fact, fathers and mothers were typically considerably more engaged in their children's schooling than one commonly witnesses today. Consequently, in the nineteenth and early twentieth centuries, academics almost never engaged in a debate about the efficacy of parental involvement. At that time, parental involvement was present and people believed that it was indispensable for success in life and school (Jeynes, 2003b, 2005, 2006, 2007, 2010; Ulich, 1957).

With Froebel's perspective of the role of the family and the school in mind, it is not surprising that Froebel was an early ambassador for the establishment of family-school partnerships. Froebel opined that it was of paramount importance that parents and teachers be unified in purpose and strategy when it came to the education of the child, including instruction in character. This unity was facilitated by the fact that it was a common practice in the United States and Europe for teachers to visit the homes of their students prior to the commencement of the school year. This practice was particularly common at the elementary school level. In this way teachers familiarized themselves with the strengths and weaknesses of each individual student. In addition, via this manifestation of love by the teacher, parents procured an understanding of the extent to which the teacher cared. Through this expression of charity and the accretion in knowledge that it fostered, parent-teacher partnerships were fostered and enhanced (Castle, 1962; Jeynes, 2006, 2007; Lascarides & Hinitz, 2000; Snider, 1900).

A second way that the unity between parent and teacher could be augmented and realized was for each to rely on God in establishing an educational and curricular strategy for the child. Froebel asserted, "The way of parent and teacher, therefore, must be the way of the Divine Creator who energizes, guides, protects, but leaves each part of His creation to acquire its own perfection by developing according to its own nature" (Liebschner, 1992, p. 66). As a minister and the son of a minister, Froebel believed in the Christian philosophy of striving for unity between people and God, in the purity of the child's spirit, and in combining these beliefs in the kindergarten (Castle, 1962; Ulich, 1968).

H. A. Hamilton (1969, p. 178) notes, "There has, indeed, been a response to Froebel in . . . America . . . primarily because of his clear religious emphasis. Some have found that they could accept an educational theory which saw the goal in terms of unity with God." Froebel believed that it was very important that the school day always begin and end by praying and giving praise to God, especially by singing hymns. He generally allotted over an hour to Bible reading and praise. Froebel believed that although the academic had some place in the American kindergarten, the spiritual and moral foundation created was what was of greatest import (Slight, 1961).

Other Leaders in the Kindergarten Movement

From the mid-1800s onward, character instruction in schools started at the kindergarten level. Although Friedrich Froebel was the German founder of the kindergarten, it is also true that Elizabeth Peabody and Mrs. Horace Mann were two of the most influential advocates for the kindergarten within the United States (Mann & Peabody, 1864).

Mann and Peabody (1864) argued that kindergarten should provide a moral foundation on which children's entire personalities can be built. They opined that it was essential that young children feel secure in this new world to which they were being exposed (Mann & Peabody, 1864). They believed that the key to this taking place was each child's acknowledgment of a Godhead of Providence. They asserted:

> If a timid child cannot be taught that he is under the eye of a tender and watchful Providence, his childhood may be one long terror as I have known to be the case. (Mann & Peabody, 1864, p. 153)

Mann and Peabody (1864, p. 178) emphasize the depths to which goes their conviction about character instruction when they stated, "I know no higher motive to be given to a child or to a man than that the more he obeys the voice of conscience, the more tender it becomes."

MORAL EDUCATION AT OTHER AGE LEVELS AND DIMENSIONS

Although common schools were the major vehicle through which school-based character education took place, it was not the only means. Americans, in fact, believed that character education should take place at as young an age as possible. As a result, the presence of infant schools designed to instruct children from the age of 18 months to preschool gained some degree of popularity. The first school was founded in 1816 in Scotland by Robert Owen. The United States was generally very willing to incorporate educational advances in Great Britain. Therefore, in 1827 in Hartford, Connecticut, the first infant school in America was developed. Most Americans, however, were not enthusiastic about infant schools as some believed that early childhood education was the responsibility of the parents and that through infant schools, the educational establishment was overextending its bounds. By the 1850s, there emerged a renewed interest in early education. This renewed interest was kindled via the writings and practices of Friedrich Froebel and Johann Pestalozzi. Americans received well the views of Froebel and Pestalozzi because they addressed the training of children beginning at the age of five, rather than children as young as the age of 18 months. Froebel was both a minister and the son of a minister and believed that character education should be at the heart of the kindergarten curriculum. Americans tended to be very amenable to character education at the kindergarten level. They agreed with Froebel that it was imperative that character instruction should be central to the curriculum for five- and six-year-olds. Concurrently, they also felt more comfortable with schooling for five- and six-year-olds than they did for toddlers. Froebel and Pestalozzi were of the belief that the best way one could encourage the rise of scholastically proficient youth was by providing a potent spiritual and moral foundation. This foundation would enable youth to develop many of the qualities necessary to flourish intellectually at later stages of development (Vinovkis, 1995).

In addition to infant schools and kindergarten, Sunday schools also provided schooling opportunities, particularly for impoverished youth. Sunday schools were first introduced to the United States in the 1790s. Sunday schools not only instructed poor youth but also taught adults. Sunday schools emphasized two themes in particular, literacy and Bible memorization. African Americans were some of the chief beneficiaries of the presence of Sunday schools. For example, African Americans made up 25 percent of the pupils in the New York City Sunday school union society's network of schools (Boylan, 1988; Vinovkis, 1995).

McClellan (1999, p. 22) states,

> The emergence of the Sunday school was one important indication of the quest for formal agencies to assist parents in the task of moral education.

The main emphases of Sunday schools were to provide moral edification and instruction in reading and writing. Evangelicalism soon became the major driving force behind the Sunday school movement. As evangelicals became more instrumental in guiding the Sunday school movement, character education became the paramount emphasis in the curriculum (McClellan, 1999).

The Sunday school movement sought to reach children of all backgrounds. Although Sunday schools particularly focused on reaching the poor, as the Sunday school movement expanded instruction reached a multitude of youth across social class and race and in both urban and rural areas (McClellan, 1999).

As one might expect from its title, Sunday school was designed as a supplement to the instruction that normally took place in the schools. This was true of the character component of the curriculum as well. McClellan (1999, p. 22) asserts, "As much as Protestant Americans in the nineteenth century valued Sunday school, they never believed that it could serve as more than an adjunct, in the case of moral education ... it was the common daily school that Americans turned to find primary support for the early educational efforts of the family."

The Sunday school had a considerable amount of influence on public schools, because the latter sought to apply the use of character education as one of the foundations of common schools. The common schools were particularly interested in the self-restraint component of moral education. Consequently, common schools came to emphasize character instruction as much as did the private religious schools (McClellan, 1999).

CONCLUSION

It is undeniable that moral education represented not only the primary foundation of America's schooling system in the early days of the settlements but remained the principal emphasis throughout the formative years of America's public school system. To leaders such as Horace Mann, Henry Barnard, Friedrich Froebel, and Johann Pestalozzi, it was unconscionable to have the continuance of a system of primary and secondary schools without moral education as the centerpiece. This orientation not only shaped American schools but helped mold American society. These educators believed that for a civil and successful society to exist virtue, kindness, honesty, compassion, accountability, and responsibility all had to coexist among a nation's people. Without this prerequisite people could not trust each other in economic transactions, could not believe in other people to keep their promises, and generally could not expect to receive acts of kindness. In other words, without the practice of morality, ultimately much of what creates a civilized state falls apart into a plague of covetousness, lasciviousness, licentiousness, and cynicism. These school leaders believed that moral education enabled the most deleterious human qualities to abate and the most ethereal ones to prevail. In the minds of these educators, by successfully founding the public school system on moral education they had helped facilitate the ultimate success of American civilization for at least the remainder of the nineteenth century and likely early into the twentieth century as well. Through their personal vision and the victories they won on behalf of moral education, the future leaders of America would be well grounded in loving, righteous, and humane behavior.

REFERENCES

Barnard, H. (1842). Manuscript collection of Trinity College Watkinson Library. Hartford, CT.

———. (1855). *American Journal of Education, 1* (1), 1.

Barnard, H., & Lannie, V. P. (1974). *Henry Barnard, American educator.* New York: Teachers College Press.

Baylor, R. M. (1965). *Elizabeth Palmer Peabody: Kindergarten pioneer.* Philadelphia: University of Pennsylvania Press.

Beard, C. A., & Beard, M. R. (1944). *A basic history of the United States.* New York: Doubleday, Doran, & Company.

Beatty, B. (1995). *Preschool education in America: The culture of young children from the colonial era to the present.* New Haven, CT: Yale University Press.

Blanshard, P. (1963). *Religion and the schools.* Boston, MA: Beacon Press.

Bobbe, D. (1933). *DeWitt Clinton.* New York: Minton, Balch & Company.

Bourne, W. O. (1870). *History of the Public School Society.* New York: Wood.

Boutwell, G. S. (1860). *Thoughts of educational topics and institutions.* Boston: Brown & Taggard.

Boylan, A. M. (1988). *Sunday school: The formation of an American institution.* New Haven, CT: Yale University Press.

Brereton, V. L. (1982). The public schools are not enough: The Bible and private schools. In D. L. Barr & N. Piediscalzi (Eds.), *The Bible in American education* (pp. 41–75). Philadelphia, PA: Fortress Press.

Butts, R. F. (2006). The politics of civic and moral education. In D. Warren & J. J. Patrick (Eds.), *Civic and moral learning in America* (pp. 7–19). New York: Palgrave MacMillan.

Castle, E. B. (1962). *Educating the good man: Moral education in Christian times*. New York: Collier.

Cubberley, E. P. (1909). *Changing conceptions of education*. New York: Houghton Mifflin.

Deboer, G. E. (2002). Student-centered teaching in a standards-based world. *Science & Education*, 11, 405–417.

Doherty, C. H. (1977). *Kindergarten and early schooling*. New York: Prentice Hall.

Downs, R. B. (1975). *Heinrich Pestalozzi: Father of modern pedagogy*. Boston, MA: Twayne.

Dunkel, H. B. (1970). *Herbart & Herbartanism: An educational ghost story*. Chicago, IL: University of Chicago Press.

Dunn, J. (1955). *Retreat from learning*. New York: David McKay Company.

Dupuis, A. M. (1966). *Philosophy of education in historical perspective*. Chicago, IL: Rand McNally.

Elsbree, W. (1939). *The American teacher: Evolution of a profession in a democracy*. New York: American Book Company.

Filler, L. (1965). *Horace Mann on the crisis in education*. Yellow Springs, OH: Antioch Press.

Froebel, F. (1889). *Reminiscences of Friedrich Froebel*. New York: Dillilingham.

———. (1898). *The education of man*. New York: Appleton & Company.

Fruhling, D. (1952). *The conception of religion in Friedrich Froebel's educational thought* (unpublished doctoral dissertation, University of California, Berkeley, CA), AG 21737815.

Graves, F. P. (1912). *Great educators of three centuries*. New York: Freeport.

Gutek, G. L. (1968). *Pestalozzi and education*. New York: Random House.

Hamilton, H. A. (1969). The religious roots of Froebel's philosophy. In E. Lawrence (Ed.), *Friedrich Froebel and English education* (pp. 156–168). New York: Schocken Books.

Herbart, J. (1852). *Samtliche werke*. Leipzig: n.p.

Hiner, N. R. (1988). The cry of Sodom enquired into: Educational analysis in seventeenth century New England. In *The social history of American education*. Urbana: University of Illinois Press.

Hughes, J. L. (1897). *Froebel's educational laws for all teachers*. New York: Appleton.

Hunt, T. C., & Maxson, M. M. (1981). *Religion and morality in American schooling*. Washington, D.C.: University Press of America.

Hunt, T. C., & Mullins, M. (2005). *Moral education in America's schools: The continuing challenge*. Greenwich, CT: Information Age Press.

Jencks, C., & Riesman, D. (1968). *The academic revolution*. Garden City, NY: Doubleday, Doran, & Company.

Jeynes, W. (2003a). *Religion, education & academic success*. Greenwich: Information Age Publishing.

———. (2003b). A meta-analysis: The effects of parental involvement on minority children's academic achievement. *Education & Urban Society*, 35 (2), 202–218.

———. (2005). A meta-analysis of the relation of parental involvement to urban elementary school student achievement. *Urban Education*, 49 (3), 237–269.

———. (2006). Standardized tests and Froebel's original kindergarten model. *Teachers College Record*, 108 (10), 1937–1959.

———. (2007). *American educational history: School, society, and the common good*. Thousand Oaks, CA: Sage Publications.

———. (2010, in press). The salience of the subtle aspects of parental involvement and encouraging that involvement: Implications for school-based programs. *Teachers College Record*.

Kaestle, C. F., & Vinovkis, M. (1980). *Education & social change in nineteenth-century Massachusetts*. New York: Cambridge University Press.

Kinloch, T. (1969). *Pioneers of religious education*. Freeport, NY: Books for Libraries Press. Textbook Company.

Kliebard, H. M. (1969). *Religion and education in America*. Scranton, PA: International Textbook Company.

Lascarides, V. C., & Hinitz, B. F. (2000). *History of childhood education*. New York: Falmer Press.

Liebschner, J. (1992). *A child's work: Freedom & play in Froebel's educational theory and practice*. Cambridge: Lutterworth Press.

MacMullen, E. N. (1991). *In the cause of true education reform: Henry Barnard & nineteenth century school reform*. New Haven, CT: Yale University Press.

Mann, H. (1840). *Third annual report*. Boston, MA: Dutton & Wentworth.

———. (1844). *Seventh annual report*. Boston, MA: Dutton & Wentworth.

———. (1845). *Eighth annual report*. Dutton & Wentworth.

———. (1846). *Ninth annual report*. Boston, MA: Dutton & Wentworth.

———. (1848). *Eleventh annual report*. Boston, MA: Dutton & Wentworth.

———. (1849). *Twelfth annual report*. Boston, MA: Dutton & Wentworth.

———. (1854). Dedication of Antioch College. Yellow Springs: A. S. Dean.

———. (1855). *Lectures on education*. Boston: Ide & Dutton.

———. (1957). *The republic and the school: Horace Mann on the education of free men*. New York: Teachers College, Columbia University.

———. (1959). *Last essays*. New York: Knopf.

———. (1969). *Lectures on education*. New York: Arno.

————. (1974). The perspective of the common school journal. (1838). In
S. Cohn (Ed.), *Education in the United States: A documentary history*
(Vol. II). New York: Random House.

Mann, M., & Peabody, E. (1864). *Moral culture of infancy, kindergarten guide*.
Boston, MA: Burham.

Mann, M. P., ed. (1907). *Life of Horace Mann*. Washington, D.C.: National
Education Association.

McClellan, B. E. (1999). *Moral education in America*. New York: Teachers College
Press.

McCluskey, N. G. (1958). *Public schools and moral education*. New York:
Columbia University.

Messerli, J. (1972). *Horace Mann: A biography*. New York: Knopf.

Pestalozzi, J. (1801). *Leonard and Gertrude*. Philadelphia, PA: Groff.

————. (1898). *How Gertrude teaches her children: An attempt to help mothers to
teach their own children and an account of the method*. Translated by
L. Holland & F. Turner. Syracuse: Bardeen.

————. (1916). How a child is led to God through maternal love. In J. A. Green
(Ed.), *Pestalozzi's educational writings*. London: Edward Arnold.

Rippa, S. A. (1997). *Education in a free society*. White Plains, NY: Longman.

Rury, J. L. (2006). Social capital and the common schools. In D. Warren &
J. J. Patrick (Eds.), *Civic and moral learning in America* (pp. 69–86).
New York: Palgrave Macmillan.

Sadler, J. E. (1966). *J. A. Comenius and the concept of universal education*.
New York: Barnes & Noble.

Sandoz, E. (2006). *Republicanism, religion and the soul of America*. Columbia,
MO: University of Missouri.

Seelye, S. T. (1864). Discourses by Rev. Samuel T. Seelye and Calvin E. Stowe
delivered at Lowell, Massachusetts and Hartford, Connecticut. New York:
Gray & Green.

Setran, D. P. (2006). Character and the clinic: The shift from character to person-
ality in American character education. In D. Warren & J. J. Patrick (Eds.),
Civic and moral learning in America (pp. 173–190). New York: Palgrave
Macmillan.

Slight, J. P. (1961). Froebel and the English primary school of today. In
E. Lawrence (Ed.), *Friedrich Froebel and English education* (pp. 95–124).
London: Routledge.

Smith, D. B. (1980). *Inside the great house planter: Family life in the eighteenth
century*. Ithaca, NY: Cornell University Press.

Snider. (1900). *The life of Friedrich Froebel, founder of the kindergarten*. Chicago:
Sigma.

Spring, J. (1997). *The American school 1642–1996*. White Plains, NY: Longman.

Stowe, C. E. (1837). *Report on elementary public instruction in Europe made to the thirty-sixth General Assembly of the state of Ohio, December 19, 1837*. Harrisburg: Packer, Barrett & Parker.

Tocqueville, A. (1966). *Democracy in America*. New York: Harper & Row.

Tyack, D. (1974). *The one best system*. Cambridge, MA: Harvard University Press.

Ulich, R. (1957). *Three thousand years of educational wisdom*. Cambridge, MA: Harvard University Press.

———. (1968). *A history of religious education*. New York: New York University Press.

Urban, W., & Wagoner, J. (2000). *American education: A history*. Boston, MA: McGraw-Hill.

U.S. Department of Education. (2007). *Digest of education statistics, 2006*. Washington, D.C.: Department of Education.

Vinovkis, M. A. (1995). *Education, society and economic opportunity*. New Haven, CT: Yale University Press.

Von Bulow, M. (1894). *Reminiscences of Froebel*. Tr. Mary Mann. Boston: Lee & Shepard Publishers.

Wolfe, J. (2000). *Learning from the past: Historical voices in early childhood education*. Mayerthorpe, Canada: Piney Branch Press.

Yulish, S. M. (1980). *The search for a civic religion*. Washington, D.C.: University Press of America.

Zimmerman, J. (2006). Sex, drugs, and right 'n' wrong: Or, the passion of Joycelyn Elders. In D. Warren & J. J. Patrick (Eds.), *Civic and moral learning in America* (pp. 191–206). New York: Palgrave Macmillan.

6

THE PRACTICE OF CHARACTER EDUCATION FROM THE MID-1800S UNTIL 1962

The period from the mid-1800s until 1962 was a period of time in which character education continued to flourish in most American schools, but one in which challenges began to emerge to the teaching of character instruction. Concurrently, character education also continued to flourish overseas. Several East Asian countries emulated the West in order to develop economically and a number of their leaders viewed Western-style character education as a means to that end, as well as valuable in its own right. No single educator had the impact on character education during this period that did McGuffey.

THE MCGUFFEY READERS

William McGuffey was a minister and leading Christian intellectual who wrote the McGuffey Readers, which sold 120 million books between 1836 and 1920. This makes McGuffey's Readers some of the top four selling books in American history. McGuffey arose as an important writer because common school leaders wanted to locate an author who could supply a common curriculum that would help define the common schools. McGuffey was chosen because it was believed that because of his religious faith, his writing abilities, and his intellectual capacities as a professor, he was the ideal person to write these readers (Hunt & Mullins, 2005; Jeynes, 2007; Ruggles, 1950).

The McGuffey Readers constitute one of the most influential collection of books in American history. Each successive reader was a little bit more difficult than the previous one. William McGuffey was both a spiritually and academically oriented individual. He was a minister, a professor of biblical ancient languages, and a college president. Although the University of Virginia was a less religious college than the private institutions, William McGuffey, a very religious minister and writer, was the college's most well-known professor (Cremin, 1976; Cubberley, 1920; Marsden, 1994; Westerhoff, 1978).

During the rise of the common schools, from the mid-1830s until the remainder of the century, William McGuffey did more to shape the moral instruction in the common schools than any other individual, with the possible exception of Horace Mann. In McGuffey's mind, as well as in the views of most Americans, character education proceeded from a religious foundation. In addition, McGuffey believed that moral training arose as the most vital type of instruction. Yes, intellectual training was important, but character development was even more important. As Westerhoff (1978, p. 103) asserts, "First religion, then morality, and last knowledge that was the focus of their content. We should not be surprised, therefore, to learn that McGuffey's Readers read more like a theology textbook than a children's elementary schoolbook. Life is God-conscious and God-centered in McGuffey's Readers."

McGuffey's focus on character education was not merely his own emphasis but reflected the orientation of American society in the nineteenth century. Westerhoff (1978, p. 22) remarks, "What do Americans expect of their public schools? They expect that there will be reading, writing, and arithmetic surely, but much more. For most of the two hundred years of America's natural life, schools have been expected to instill piety, mold character, and transmit community values."

The Bible Providing Moral Instruction

The McGuffey Readers utilized the Bible as a means of moral edification in two ways. First, many of McGuffey's writings directly focused on the Bible as a primary source of character instruction. Second, McGuffey also often threaded the Bible and moral education throughout the academic curriculum (Hunt & Mullins, 2005; Ruggles, 1950).

The Bible as a Direct Source of Character Instruction

McGuffey was not at all averse to share the essence of the message of the Scriptures in his books. Westerhoff (1978, p. 76) notes that McGuffey's Readers possess a patent message that "God sent his Word for our eternal benefit. Within the pages of the Bible, God reveals himself, the mystery of creation, the nature of human life and death, and all that he requires us to know, believe, and do. Most important, in the Bible we learn that God uniquely reveals himself in the life, death, and resurrection of Jesus Christ. Without which our lives would have no meaning or purpose."

To McGuffey, it was vital to establish who Christ is so that students would understand that morality is not some capricious and nebulous concept that lacks consistency. Rather, morality is well rooted in eternal principles that have meaning and transcend space and time. Consequently, one can fabricate his or her life around these principles (Hunt & Mullins, 2005).

McGuffey drew many of his books' teachings from biblical accounts. Nevertheless, McGuffey also wrote stories that taught children to acknowledge God and depend upon Him in their daily lives. There was an assumption on McGuffey's part that if children did this, they would be more likely to submit to His precepts. In a story entitled "The Sun Is Up" in McGuffey's first reader, it states, "Though I do not see the wind, yet it blows round me on all sides; so God is with me at all times though I see him not" (McGuffey, 1835, p. 15). In another story entitled "About the Moon," it reads, "God is good to us. In gratitude, we ought to obey Him." And "If we do His will, he will love us and be our God" (McGuffey, 1835, p. 35). McGuffey not only asserted that if one acknowledged God, he or she will be righteous. He goes beyond this to assert that if one experiences salvation, that person will be righteous. The world that McGuffey presents is "God-conscious, God-centered" and to the extent that one exhibits this type of orientation, he will live a life of righteousness. McGuffey is careful to point out that this life of righteousness is only possible if one experiences salvation in Christ. Therefore, it is McGuffey's view that although individuals have a propensity to commit evil acts, hope exists because of Christ's offer of salvation. Once a person experiences salvation, the abundant virtuous life can emerge (Hunt & Mullins, 2005; McGuffey, 1835, 1836; Ruggles, 1950).

As much as McGuffey desired the children who read his book to develop into intelligent human beings, he particularly desired the students to become virtuous. A majority of McGuffey's lessons had values as their primary theme. The values that McGuffey addressed the most were, first, salvation and, second, righteousness followed by piety, kindness, and patriotism (Westerhoff, 1978). McGuffey's definition of righteousness began with loving God and loving one's neighbor, which Christ asserted were the two greatest commandments. To McGuffey, the key to manifesting love and kindness to others was remembering God's love and kindness. In McGuffey's selection entitled "Time to Get Up," it reads, "Never forget before you leave your room to thank God for His kindness. He is indeed kinder to us than an earthly parent" (McGuffey, 1836, pp. 10–11).

McGuffey also emphasized the fact that God sees everything as an incentive for children to be righteous. In his reading entitled "More about the Little Chimney Sweep," it states, "You cannot steal the smallest pit without being seen by that eye which never sleeps" (McGuffey, 1835, p. 66). Westerhoff (1978, p. 103) further observes, "Basically, the McGuffey Readers directed persons to live for salvation—the eternal life with God in another world—a life goal closely connected to righteousness. The modes of conduct most expressive of righteousness are the love of country, love of neighbor, and love of God. It is the last value—piety—that is the most important for indeed all the other depend on it."

McGuffey also spent a considerable amount of time teaching about God's providence. He believed that thankfulness was one aspect of virtue. Thankfulness demonstrated a humble and appreciative heart. One excerpt from John Jones in the first reader exemplifies this emphasis on thanksgiving.

> John, you must always bear in mind that it is God who made you and who gave you all that you have and all that you hope for. He gave you life and food and a home to live in. All who take care of you and keep you were sent by God. He sent his son to show you His will and to die for your sake. He gave you his word to let you know what he has done for you and what He bids you to do. (from McGuffey, "John Jones," *First Reader*, 1835, p. 32)

McGuffey also considered thankfulness to be a vital type of virtue because that gratitude led to obedience (Westerhoff, 1978).

Although McGuffey focused on some values more than others, he dealt with a full gamut of values that reflect the extent to which he believed the Christian lifestyle should penetrate one's being. McGuffey emphasized compassion in "The Poor Old Man," lying in "More about the Little Boy Who Told a Lie." He addressed prayer, forgiveness, profanity, diligence, patience, humility, and a wide range of other topics.

The Bible as an Indirect Source of Moral Instruction

McGuffey also used the Bible as an indirect source of moral instruction. Often the gist of a lesson would be academic, but McGuffey would include a reference to God meant to instill character. For example, McGuffey would include a lesson about wool coming from sheep to make people warm and that this was evidence of God's love for humanity and that one should remember God's wisdom and kindness.

On many occasions when McGuffey teaches scientific facts, he does so in a way that features a moral principle. It might be a truth that emphasizes the hard working nature of ants, the cooperation of bees, the interplay of birds, flowers, and bees, or the resourcefulness of other animals. Nevertheless, McGuffey examines the outstanding characteristics of these creatures not only in their own right but as it relates to moral principles. He makes it clear in his books that there is a designer that enables scientific principles to work the way that they do. McGuffey wanted to communicate to children that God acted lovingly and provided for human beings (Mosier, 1965; Ruggles, 1950).

McGuffey also taught that God made the universe according to His design and therefore there was a divinely based order (Hunt & Mullins, 2005; Ruggles, 1950). One of the passages that McGuffey used to convey is called the "story of George Washington." In this passage, George Washington observed that the cabbages were arranged in such a way that it spelled out his name. George approached his father, having concluded that his father must have planted the seeds in such a way to make this possible. His father then praised George and said that he planted the seeds and in this way to teach George a lesson. He stated that just as the order of the cabbage led George to the conclusion that there was "a designer" for the cabbage, the natural order of the universe leads one to the conclusion that there is "a designer" who created and has sustained the world (McGuffey, 1835, p. 130).

MCGUFFEY'S BIBLICAL ORIENTATION

Although the McGuffey Readers certainly offer intellectual stimulation, McGuffey's primary concern at a general level was providing character education to the students. More specifically, his goal was that the students commit their lives to Jesus Christ. Westerhoff (1978, pp. 91–92) states, "McGuffey's Readers placed salvation first among all possible terminal values, with righteousness close behind."

McGuffey's moral instruction was highly religious in nature. McGuffey believed that religion and morality were inseparable (Westerhoff, 1978). Robert Wood Lynn (1973, p. 7) stated that McGuffey's Readers "embodied a vision of piety, justice, and the commonwealth, a form of patriotic party which still appeals to some folk living amidst our current crisis of loyalty." Like most of his educational contemporaries, McGuffey averred that the primary function of public school instruction was moral in nature. John Westerhoff (1978, p. 18) observes:

> On the basis of McGuffey's life history, his writings and his personally complied Readers, it is reasonable to say that he was a theological and pedagogical conservative. He understood the purpose of public schooling in terms of moral and spiritual education.

Consistent with McGuffey's conviction that religion and morality are inseparable, his perchance for Bible instruction in his books is not surprising (McGuffey, 1836). Westerhoff (1978, p. 76) notes, "It is difficult to conceive of William H. McGuffey compiling schoolbooks for children in which God is not central . . . Indeed, the mind and spirit of McGuffey cannot be understood apart from his understanding of God. Neither can his readers." Consistent with this approach it is clear that to McGuffey, "No book is more important than the Bible" (Westerhoff, 1978, p. 77). If one was to live a life of integrity, one should also be a person of faith (McGuffey, 1836, 1837; Ruggles, 1950). Westerhoff (1978, p. 23) states, "W. H. McGuffey, maintaining the inseparability of morality and religion, provides us, in his Readers, with . . . a religious value system."

According to McGuffey, salvation and righteousness were key to living moral lives. As Westerhoff (1978, p. 91) observes, "More than half the lessons in McGuffey's Readers have values as their dominant theme . . . salvation and righteousness are the most frequently mentioned life goals; piety, kindness, and patriotism (in that order) the most frequently occurring modes of conduct." McGuffey's Christian worldview naturally presents an incentive for moral behavior, that is, the existence of an afterlife. He spoke of the reality of the grace and mercy of God on the one hand,

and the judgment of God on the other (Hunt & Mullins, 2005; Ruggles, 1950; Westerhoff, 1978).

Given McGuffey's emphasis on God and salvation, it is only logical that McGuffey's teaching on character education was rooted in the Bible and in the deity. McGuffey taught that the Bible was the most important book that one could study. Therefore, McGuffey included many lessons from the Old and New Testaments. McGuffey emphasized the character traits of God, not only to help the students know who God was, but in order to establish what moral traits the youth should pursue. McGuffey also used the Ten Commandments and other biblical commandments to serve as a model, which students can follow (Hester, 2003; Hunt & Mullins, 2005; Ruggles, 1950).

THE CHARACTER TRAITS THAT MCGUFFEY EMPHASIZED THE MOST

Overall, McGuffey emphasized a full gamut of character traits that enabled students to receive a broad character education, which certainly contributed to the ongoing popularity of the readers. To whatever extent, certain parents wanted particular character traits emphasized, an overwhelming majority of parents were satisfied.

One of the qualities that McGuffey emphasized in his work was diligence. As one might imagine this trait was especially supportive of many of the academic emphases of the school. McGuffey taught about the rewards of hard work. He would share that hard work often required substantial sacrifice. But he also shared that if one was willing to make that sacrifice, there would be rich rewards over time. On numerous occasions, McGuffey emphasized one character trait in conjunction with another. For example, in his story "The Good Boy Whose Parents Are Poor," he described a boy who rises early each morning to help his father and mother. In this case, McGuffey combined diligence, love, and honoring one's parents (Hunt & Mullins, 2005; McGuffey, 1920b).

Other traits that McGuffey emphasized include love, kindness, and piety. McGuffey averred that these traits often went together. McGuffey affirmed that two of these traits, love and kindness, proceeded from piety. In his view, religious dedication led people to embrace righteousness and to refrain from every form of evil. McGuffey took very seriously Christ's declaration that the two greatest commandments were love of God and love of neighbor. He attempted to instill within students the understanding that some character traits were more important and these were two of them (Hunt & Mullins, 2005; Ruggles, 1950).

McGuffey not only addressed the quality of love in a general sense but also in both his fictional and nonfictional accounts he gave specific examples. In his *First Reader* McGuffey penned the story "John Jones," which focuses on the fact that people need to respond to God's love manifested in Jesus Christ to therefore love one another (McGuffey, 1920a). McGuffey also instructed youth about the importance of helping the poor.

In McGuffey's mind, applying the two most prominent commandments, love of God and love of neighbor, went together. In addition, McGuffey insisted that one aspect of love of God and neighbor was the love of country, that is, patriotism acknowledges God's love, providence, and kindness in creating this country. One way that the love of God fostered the love of neighbor was through prayer. McGuffey believed that prayer sensitized people to the mind of God. Once this happened, McGuffey believed, people would be released to reach out to others in love. McGuffey's Readers exhorted young people to pray both in the morning and at night (Hunt & Mullins, 2005; Ruggles, 1950; Westerhoff, 1978).

There were other qualities that McGuffey emphasized as well, and he believed that these qualities were essential to developing lives of integrity. Among these were honesty, obedience, and industry. McGuffey dedicated fairly substantial parts of his books to the advantages of honesty and the disadvantages of lying. To McGuffey, honesty in many ways formed one of the pillars of society, because without people trusting one another, society could not thrive (Hunt & Mullins, 2005; Westerhoff, 1978). McGuffey stated that "Honesty is the best policy" (Mosier, 1965, p. 115).

Related to lying, McGuffey Readers also teach against stealing (McGuffey, 1920a). In his story "More about the Little Chimney Sweep," McGuffey asserts, "You cannot steal the smallest pit without being seen by that eye which never sleeps" (McGuffey, p. 66).

McGuffey's Readers also emphasized a tenderness of heart that resulted in myriad desirable traits. First, "McGuffey readers were unalterably opposed to war" (Mosier, 1965, p. 44). McGuffey particularly encouraged both the United States and the Native Americans to lay down their arms and make peace (Mosier, 1965). And although McGuffey highly esteemed absolute values, he also advocated being tolerant of people with different backgrounds, ethnicities, and lifestyles. He also taught that God blessed some with money so that they could give to the poor. He therefore thought that generosity was very important (McGuffey, 1920a, 1920b, 1920c, 1920d; Mosier, 1965).

McGuffey also wanted youth to have a peace that the world was a comforting place to live. McGuffey's Readers generally trended in the same direction as the common school movement. The common schools first arose as a potent national force in the mid-to-late 1830s. This was also true of the McGuffey Readers. From 1836 to 1861 the spread of the common schools and the McGuffey Readers was especially prominent in the North. The primary reason why the spread of the readers and the common school movement was primarily a northern national phenomenon is because each of these movements was initiated and supported especially by people from the Whig Party. The two major political parties of that time were the Whigs and the Democrats. The Whigs were dominant in the North and the Democrats had a major advantage in the South. Horace Mann and Henry Barnard, the primary founders of the common schools, were both Whigs. William McGuffey was also a Whig. The political beliefs of the Whigs differed from those of their Southern counterparts. The most notable difference in terms of moral beliefs were that the Whigs were against slavery (or using today's terminology, pro-life) and the Democrats believed that any decisions regarding the morality of slavery should be left up to the state or the individual pro-choice. The Whigs also favored temperance, a movement started by Lyman Beecher, a renowned northern preacher also well known for his antislavery position. Lyman Beecher was the father of Harriet Beecher Stowe, the author of *Uncle Tom's Cabin*, and the well-known minister, Henry Ward Beecher (Beecher, 1864; Earle, 1996; Eggleston, 1998; Gutek, 1991; Howe, 1973, 1979; Jeynes, 2007; Johnson, 1997; Mann, 1848; Mondale & Patton, 2001; Schreiner, 2003; Snyder, 1991; Spring, 2005).

Because the Whig perspective was so different from the typical southern view point, before the Civil War, common schools and therefore the McGuffey Readers made less progress reaching students in the South than they did in the North. However, after the Civil War, the South also recognized the need for common moral values to be taught in the common schools. Therefore, the popularity of the common schools and the McGuffey Readers soared after the Civil War. The nation was now becoming more united than it had been previously. The McGuffey Readers would play in unifying the nation further through moral education (Earle, 1996; Jeynes, 2007).

WHY MCGUFFEY'S READERS WERE SO POPULAR

In the 1836–1920 period during which McGuffey's Readers were so popular, Americans generally wanted their books to confirm the strong relationship between faith and morality. In other words, McGuffey's Readers reflected the values of American society at the time and the populace wanted these values highlighted. There were, as one might expect, other readers that were available at the same time as McGuffey's. Some of these included *Sander's Readers* by Charles Sanders, the *University Series* by George Holmes, the *Appleton Readers* by William Torrey Harris, and the *Hillard Readers* by George S. Hillard (1808–1879). In spite of the availability of these readers, McGuffey's Readers were far more popular than the other books, largely because it had an emphasis on character education. Generally speaking, among the school textbooks that were used during the mid-1800s, the more religious and morally based were the books, the more demand for these books are. Consistent with this trend, the McGuffey Readers were the most popular of all in response to its "emphasis on moral and religious culture" (Mosier, 1965, p. 23). McGuffey synthesized religious and middle-class values. McGuffey's Readers contained more Bible readings than nearly all the textbooks of the period (Earle, 1996; Jeynes, 2007; McGuffey, 1920a, 1920b, 1920c, 1920d; Ruggles, 1950; Westerhoff, 1978).

There were several other reasons, besides the content of the readers, which made it likely that McGuffey's Readers should be popular. First, McGuffey was a very popular minister and professor both at Miami of Ohio University and the University of Virginia. Second, McGuffey, as both a minister and a professor, functioned in this very acceptable dual capacity. During this period, most Americans still viewed education as primarily the church's responsibility. Therefore, Americans generally believed that McGuffey was an ideal person to write the readers. That is because he was a church leader and a man of great intelligence operating in the educational sphere. In McGuffey's era, people valued character instruction and expected schools to provide it in a Christian context. Americans wanted schools to "instill piety" and "mold character" (Westerhoff, 1978, p. 22). Third, McGuffey also supported Horace Mann's vision of the common schools. This helped ensure that his writings would spread with the expansion of the common schools. Fourth, McGuffey was an eloquent speaker who was able to rally support for his perspective (Earle, 1996; Ruggles, 1950;

Westerhoff, 1978). All in all, as Pringle and Pringle (1955, p. 30) assert, "McGuffey probably did more to mold American thinking than any other single influence except the Bible."

DARWIN

Darwin's theory of evolution had profound implications for moral education, but these were largely realized through the efforts of Herbert Spencer. It was actually Herbert Spencer who coined the phrase "survival of the fittest" (Tobach, 1974). Originally, Spencer used this term to refer to different cultures, but as Tobach (1974, p. 99) notes, "was adopted by Darwin to explicate the process of natural selection."

The combination of Darwin's influence in the biology discipline and Spencer's in the discipline of sociology and education yielded a movement that had a large degree of influence on school and university curriculum. First, Herbert Spencer did believe that moral education should be practiced in school, but neither he nor Darwin opined that it should have the prominent role that it currently had in American schools. Both Spencer and Darwin believed that human beings emerged as a species purely by chance. They also claimed that humans and apes came form a common ape-like ancestor. That is, the teaching of evolution was not that human beings were made in the image of God, but instead they arose by chance. The change in emphasis has profound implications for moral education. When society emphasizes that humans are made in the image of God, the focus becomes one in which one should live up to that elevated position. In contrast, when the emphasis is that one has an animal ancestry, the place of morality becomes less important (Jackson & Weidman, 2004; Lugg, 1996; Weikart, 2004).

Second, Darwin, Spencer, and other evolutionists believed that this process occurs by chance. The emphasis is not on one's purpose, but on chance. Character education is rooted, at least in part, in discerning one's purpose in life and acting on that purpose in order to benefit others and society as a whole. In fact, placed in a religious context, one's purpose can also be living to glorify God (Weikart, 2004).

Third, evolutionists viewed several character traits as undermining the advancement of the species. Darwin and Spencer were very concerned that compassion for those, for example, with special needs would thwart the development of a stronger species. Spencer (1966) argued that the aim of schools was to improve the human species. Consequently, teachers should concentrate their efforts on training the fittest individuals so that these people could carry on the species to the next level. Such an orientation would accelerate the evolutionary process. Spencer believed that neither public schools nor special education furthered this goal. He asserted that special education would neutralize the positive effects of evolution. Moreover, he called public schools "a monopoly for mediocrity" (Hawkins, 1997; Spencer, 1851, 1908, 1963, 1966; Weikart, 2004).

Spencer's perspective created considerable friction between evolutionists and Christians. The Darwinist emphasis on instructing the elite ran contrary to the Christian tradition of attempting to educate all. This Christian tradition is based on the biblical edict that God created all people equal, which is totally at odds with the intellectual hierarchy that is inherent in Darwinist belief (Dupuis, 1966; Marrou, 1956). Evolutionists also viewed the care of the mentally handicapped differently than did Christians. Nicole Rafter (2004, p. 234) states, "Herbert Spencer and other so-called Darwinists advised that specially problematic groups should be left to die out, like inferior species." Consistent with this declaration Herbert Spencer (1851, pp. 323–324) declared, "Under the natural order of things society is constantly excreting its unhealthy, imbecile, slow, vacillating, faithless members." He further asserted, "to aid the unfit would merely thwart this purifying process of extinction."

Darwin and his followers had a very low opinion of students with special needs. In his book, *The Descent of Man, and Selection in Relation to Sex*, Darwin (1874, p. 495) averred, "We may trace a perfect graduation from the mind of an utter idiot, lower than that of an animal low in the scale, to the mind of Newton." In Darwin's eyes, those with special needs had an intelligence that was beneath that of "low" animals.

To evolutionists, the compassion of Christians toward those with special needs under-minded the evolutionary progress of humanity. Darwinists claimed that Christians appeared more interested in helping the weak than in acting in the best interests of the species. Christians were concerned about what they perceived as a lack of compassion and insensitivity among the evolutionists. The Christians were offended by the attack by Darwinists on the public schools, largely because Christians were behind the common school/public school movement (Cubberley, 1920; Monroe, 1940).

After the Civil War, a large majority of textbooks emphasized the evils of slavery and racial discrimination. Advocates of character education believed that school textbooks should dissuade students from engaging in acts of racism (Jeynes, 2007). Concurrent to this emphasis, evolutionists were making statements that, in contrast, were fanning the flames of racism. The full title of Darwin's well-known 1859 book often referred to as the *Origin of Species* is actually *On the Origin of Species by Means of Natural Selection, or the Preservation of Favoured Races in the Struggle for Life.* Darwin's title means exactly what one thinks. He was concerned with issues of racial superiority. Darwin contended that the smallest gap between ape and human kind was between gorilla and blacks (Gould, 1981). Darwin (1871, p. 201) asserts, "The break will then be rendered wider, for it will intervene between man in a more civilized state, as we may hope, than the Caucasian, and some ape as low as a baboon, instead of at the present between the Negro or Australian and the gorilla." As Jackson and Weidman (2004, p. 69) observe, "Darwin admitted that the gap in intelligence and moral sense between civilized people and animals was a great one. But one could look to the lower races to fill that gap."

Darwin's assertions set the stage for at least a century's worth of racist remarks and hypotheses by Darwin's followers. For example, in D. K. Shute's 1896 (p. 124) article in the *American Anthropologist*, he averred, "These characters are siminoid and the races possessing them in largest number and development are lowest in the scale. Measured by these criteria the Caucasian stands at the head of the racial scale and the Negro stands at its bottom." D. Colin Wells (1907, p. 700) insisted that blind and deaf-mutes were inferior and bemoaned the fact that in the United States, "We train deaf-mutes and the blind to become self-supporting and able to marry." G. Stanley Hall, the renowned child psychologist and dedicated evolutionist, viewed people of color as "adolescent races" and averred that "their faults and their virtues are those of childhood and youth" (Hall, 1908, p. 715). And Charles Davenport (1914), an avid Darwinist, stated that races lowest on the scale do not have the self-control to allow the general populace to permit these groups to mate, based on their own choices. He asserted that these people of color have "neither intelligence nor self-control enough to justify the State to leave its mating in their own hands" (Davenport, p. 3).

Darwin and his followers were very concerned about Christian efforts to educate those with special needs and to give greater freedom to people with regard to marriage and mating. Darwin did believe that ultimately there would be the "extermination of the inferior races by the superior" (Jackson & Weidman, 2004, p. 71). Christians, however, found the remarks of Darwinists toward people of color to be highly insulting in nature and they claimed this would undermine the positive effects of character instruction, part of the success of which depended on whether students felt confident that they could be virtuous people. By excoriating and demeaning people of color the way that Darwinists did, Christians believed that they undermined that confidence. Evolutionists such as Francis Galton and Alfred Ploetz drew connections between race and such traits as intelligence and hygiene. Galton went too far to claim that the smartest dog was more intelligent than the dumbest humans. Most Christians were outraged by these teachings (Cogdell, 2004; Graves, 2001; Jackson & Weidman, 2004).

Darwinists were also patent in their assertions that certain racial groups were not only intellectually inferior but also morally inferior. The evolutionists claimed that savages in Africa and the New World constituted the missing link between the ape-like ancestors of humans and modern Homo sapiens. Most evolutionists believed that there was such a wide chasm between the moral convictions of the West and those other people in the world that such a gap could only partially be bridged. In other words, because these differences were due to the forces of natural selection, there was very little one could do to countervail those trends. The Christians of the era also possessed a frame of mind that believed that almost anyone could become a moral and civil individual if he or she tried and maintained that Darwinists leaned too heavily on a biological determinism perspective for Christians to feel comfortable. For example, evolutionists often pointed to the smaller brain capacities of blacks around the world and certain ape-like features of certain groups that indicated to them that there was a "hierarchy of races" (MacMaster, 2001, p. 144). Many Christians averred that maintaining this type of an attitude doomed many people of color to failure morally and intellectually, simply because expectations are placed so low (Anderson, 2007; Ferguson, 2005; Fluehr-Lobban, 2006; Wake, 1867; Wolpoff & Caspar, 1997).

In many ways, evolution set the stage for the undermining of moral education many years later. Students were learning to think of themselves as biological animals with strong emotional drives that were not much different from other animals. And students of color wrestled with the supposed racial hierarchy that relegated them to a lower status, all inveterately rooted in so-called scientific evidence.

OTHER LEADERS IN CHARACTER EDUCATION

There were many other leading advocates of moral education during the late 1800s and the early 1900s. The vast majority of them sought to broaden the reach of character education or to increase its efficacy.

Joseph Lee and Henry Curtis

For example, Joseph Lee and Henry Curtis were active in education during the late 1800s and early 1900s and were the founders of the play movement. Both of these individuals argued that play was necessary for children's moral development in terms of learning to obey rules, cooperate, and so forth. They advocated the building of playgrounds in schoolyards all across the country. Joseph Lee (1915, p. 2) asserted, "The thing that most needs to be understood about play is that it is not a luxury but a necessity. It is not simply something that a child *likes* to have; it is something that he *must* have if he is ever to grow up." Lee (1925) claimed that play helps children to stay out of trouble. Regarding play Lee (1925, p. 17) claimed, "When conducted under wholesome conditions, it has great educational and social values."

Johann Herbart

Johann Herbart (1776–1841) was a German psychologist who had his greatest influence on American education in the late 1800s after Charles DeGarmo first introduced Herbart's perspective to the United States in the 1880s and 1890s. Herbart's greatest contribution was the lesson plan, which secured him a great deal of attention and admiration in the United States. However, it was not the lesson plan that Herbart thought was the most important component of schooling. Herbart averred that character education was the primary task of the school (Dunkel, 1970; Graves, 1912). Graves (1912, p. 177) observed, "The making of the morally religious man is, therefore, Herbart's idea of the end of education." Herbart even titled one of the chapters in his book, "Morality: The Sole and Total Task of Education" (Herbart, 1852). Herbart (1852, p. 7) stated, "Education is not merely to make man 'better' in some sense, but is to make him 'morally good.' The aim of education is virtue, morality."

Colin Scott

Colin Scott was an educator primarily from the early 1900s who believed that schools should work to teach students how to work for the betterment of society. He also believed that instructors needed to teach youth how to solve problems by working together. This procedure gained an increasing amount of support from the business community, because companies appreciated the practical value of working in groups. Scott established the Social Education Association (1906) in order to realize these goals. Colin Scott helped popularize group activity among students (Scott, 1908).

Maria Montessori and William James

Maria Montessori and William James came from entirely different educational perspectives, but on the issue of moral instruction they both agreed that the formation of salubrious moral habits was a major key in developing good character. Maria Montessori (1870–1952) was an exceptional person who became the first female in Italy to graduate from medical school, as well as that nation's first woman doctor. As time advanced her work increasingly involved special education students, who were mentally handicapped (Appelbaum, 1971; Kramer, 1976). The more Montessori experienced success with special education youth, the more she acknowledged that her techniques would work well and in 1907 applied her methods with more typical children as well (Kramer, 1976; Lillard, 1972; Montessori, 1956, 1965; Standing, 1957).

As a devout Roman Catholic, Montessori highly esteemed character education (Montessori, 1964). She asserted that religion should play a major part in the operations of the class, especially with regards to the teaching of right and wrong and good manners. Montessori claimed that moral education was especially important if children were to learn self-discipline and if the world was ever to experience future peace (Montessori, 1964; Standing, 1957).

William James (1958) claimed that the key to a fecund moral education program was to develop good habits in students. He believed that establishing habits was also the key to plenteous positive results emerging from scholarly education. James maintained that moral training was a more for-midable task because of "the peculiarity of moral habits contradistin-guishing them from intellectual acquisitions" in that it deals with "two hostile powers" of Good and Evil (James, 1958, p. 59). Nevertheless, James believed that it was important for a teacher to try.

JOHN DEWEY'S CHALLENGE TO MORAL EDUCATION

Although the key events and dates regarding character education were a series of U.S. Supreme Court decisions in 1962 and 1963 removing Bible reading and prayer from the schools, there were certain developments prior to these decisions that helped set the stage for these decisions to occur.

Dewey's concept of morality was very different from the American con-ception that preceded him. Dewey maintained that moral failure had nothing to do with decisions regarding right and wrong, but was limited to whether or not one applied the scientific method. He also averred that moral principle only applied to unique situations. Therefore, there were no consistent moral principles that applied to many situations. Although Dewey was an atheist, McCluskey observes that "anti-theist" might be even a more accurate description of Dewey, because he was very critical of people of faith. Therefore, Dewey believed that all ethical and moral values should not be drawn from enduring values, but should originate in society (Dewey, 1902, 1910, 1915, 1920, 1990; McCluskey, 1958).

Progressives, like Dewey, believed that absolute values were not longer applicable to modern day society. Dewey believed in a relativistic set of values in which there was only the right and wrong action to take in a given situation. As a result, Dewey and his followers viewed moral instruc-tion only in terms of social improvement. Dewey believed that individuals should assess the "social consequences of actions" (McClellan, 1999, p. 58). Nevertheless, teachers generally had a difficult time instructing chil-dren about social improvement in the way that liberals dictated, without reference to absolute values. In the view of most teachers, it was virtually impossible to direct students about how to make a difference socially with-out making reference to some interminable values on which the students could base their decisions (McClellan, 1999).

Although Dewey's influence was rising, there were nevertheless still movements in place that ensured that the moral orientation of most Americans would remain in place and thrive. For example, in 1911 the

Character Education Association was founded and headed up by Milton Fairchild. In addition, in 1917 William Hutchins published the book, *The Children's Morality Code* (McClellan, 1999).

H. H. Horne

H. H. Horne (1931) was a professor of education at NYU. He was concerned that Dewey was directing education away from many of its moral foundations: a belief in definite right and wrongs, an emphasis on the teacher's heart of love toward the child, and the moral example of the teacher. Horne (1923, p. vii) noted, "Educating is the purposeful providing of an environment . . . it is personality in and behind the environment that counts most." Horne affirmed that Dewey and his followers made schooling into a mechanical process that focused more on effective pedagogy than the individual teacher and child. Horne (1931, p. 48) maintained that Dewey and Spencer's theories "separate the process of education from the process of complete living."

Three Trends in Character Education in the Mid-1800s and Early 1900s

Educational Psychology's Effect on the Teaching of Moral Instruction

During the first half of the twentieth century, moral education continued to maintain a prominent role in the American public school curriculum. School leaders wanted to preserve the traditional place that character education enjoyed within the curriculum. Nevertheless, they also wanted to occasionally incorporate some of the additional advances in character instruction. For example, because there were some advances in educational psychology in the late 1800s and early 1900s, some school leaders averred that these advances should influence the way in which character education was taught (Doherty, 1977; Yulish, 1980). However, school officials also did not want to simply mimic some of the psychological advances incorporated by the Germans. However, German Freudian psychology applied to the classroom was called by some American school leaders "psychology without a soul" (Yulish, 1980, p. 530).

The emphasis on the peace component of moral education also became more organized beginning in the early 1900s. The National Peace Conference was founded in 1907 with the goal of promoting peace. Peace had been a salient component of moral education for some time, but under the auspices of the National Peace Conference it became much more defined (Yulish, 1980).

The National Institution for Moral Instruction, later called the Character Education Institute, provided funding for research in character education. Throughout the first half of the twentieth century, there were three threads of emphasis in America's character education curriculum. The first thread was that of love, encompassing both the love of God and humanity. A second thread focused on faith, and a third thread focused on living moral lives and good citizenship. Americans supported these emphases in the public schools because they believed such teaching yielded productive and loyal patriots and would reduce crime. The American populace and educations alike were convinced that schools could have similar ameliorative effects to that of churches. Nevertheless, they also averred that in order to enjoy that degree of influence, the character teaching needed to parallel the instruction of the church as much as was feasible in the public schools. Americans also maintained that moral instruction would also help prepare American youth to anticipate and prepare for their future roles in society. These roles were not defined so much on the basis of occupation, but instead addressed how one could strengthen the country through honoring God, helping others, and fulfilling one's duties to the country and society (Gangel & Benson, 1983; Ulich, 1968; Yulish, 1980).

The curriculum of the late 1800s and early 1900s tended to be proactive and emphasized the positive differences that one could make in society. Most of the nation's leaders, across a large gamut of disciplines, asserted that if one provided tutelage in encouraging constructive behavior, delinquent behavior would be far less likely. Nevertheless, the era's leaders also believed that youth needed adults to specifically address what were deleterious behaviors that should be avoided. A growing body of research on delinquency emerged during the late 1800s and early 1900s, which fortified the delivery of sermons, warning Americans about the dangers of delinquency (Jeynes, 2007; Yulish, 1980). Consequently, the character education movement continued to flourish throughout this period. The World War I also "convinced Americans that intellect without a moral idea was potentially evil" (Yulish, 1980, p. 256).

During the early 1900s, psychologists also developed social intelligence tests to assess how well a person could handle social and interactive situations. This was a major development to make character education more scientifically based. There is a considerable amount of disagreement, however, regarding whether the move toward additional testing generally was a positive or negative development. In fact, much of the time period in the school day that had been reserved for character instruction by the mid-1960s was inundated with both the administration of tests and preparation for them (Jeynes, 2006).

MORAL EDUCATION FOR AFRICAN AMERICANS BEFORE THE CIVIL WAR

In the mid-1600s, missionaries had established schools for African Americans and taught them moral education. Puritans and the Quakers were the earliest to undertake these initiatives. These efforts at character instruction were in the context of broader schooling efforts that were extremely successful in the North but faced considerable resistance in the South. The efforts by these and other groups as time passed led to high literacy rates among African Americans in the far Northern states but lower rates as one neared the border with the South. By 1850 most major Northern cities had African American literacy rates between 64 and 97 percent. In contrast, the literacy rate of slaves in the South was much lower. In the eyes of essentially all the churches that provided character education for African Americans, moral instruction and literacy were linked. First, the churches used the Bible as the primary source of moral schooling and therefore the ability to read it was vital for spiritual growth. Second, Christians viewed increasing the number of literate freed and enslaved African Americans as a major prerequisite for emancipation to take place (Bergman & Bergman, 1969; Bullock, 1970; Harrison, 1893; Jeynes, 2007; Wilson, 1977; Woodson, 1915).

Once the Civil War concluded, the schools started by these religious societies emphasized two principles, in particular, in their tutelage of African Americans. First, they focused on the salience of literacy to help the newly liberated secure a job and a place in American society. Second, they taught a great deal of moral education in order to provide African Americans with the necessary foundation to thrive in the free society to which they now had access (Dilworth, 2006).

Black churches were also involved in providing moral instruction for their parishioners who attended church and also to a wider scope of people through schooling. As Dilworth (2006, p. 107) states, "Black church historians agree that in the United States the role of the black church in civic and social reform cannot be overstated . . . After Emancipation, the church played a significant role in promoting civic and moral learning as critical path for racial uplift. It became a site for developing black leadership skills that were granted in fostering moral courage and civic responsibility." W. E. B. DuBois (1993, p. 214) in his book, *The Souls of Black Folk*, confirms this perspective and affirms that black churches provided "one expression of the higher life."

To both African American leaders and white proponents of civil rights both before and after the Civil War, education for African Americans needed to simultaneously emphasize literacy and character education. Booker T. Washington called for a union of the head, heart, and hands in promoting advancement for African Americans. There was a general belief that in order for African Americans to succeed in the United States, they needed moral fortitude, the intellectual qualification, success, and the opportunities to express what they could accomplish.

Although many people esteemed the vital role of character instruction as a major contributing factor to individual African American success, religious leaders, educators, African American spokespeople, and abolitionists also viewed the two-pronged emphasis on character education and literacy as vital in the quest for equality overall. These people believed that in order for African Americans to be respected, it was important they be seen as moral people who were actively contributing to society. In this way, lawmakers and the general public would be more likely to grant them equal opportunities. In addition, if African Americans were to successfully argue their point in the "halls of public opinion," it would be essential for them to be able to make their case from a moral high ground.

Stating one's case from the position of a moral high ground was particularly important in the 1800s because during this era people frequently assessed arguments not merely on the basis of their intellectual merits but also considered the moral underpinnings of the assertions. This acknowledgment of the primacy of moral fortitude would not only serve African Americans well in the period immediately following the Civil War but also play a vital role in the meritorious successes of the civil rights movement of the 1960s under Martin Luther King (Dupuis, 1966; King, 1998).

MORAL EDUCATION OVERSEAS

Europe

Virtually every nation in the world that possessed a schooling system in the 1800s maintained a program of moral education. Europe, whose schooling system the United States had emulated in the 1600s and 1700s, continued to have a character education program similar to that of the United States. Bible instruction was a central part of the curriculum and even today has a much larger role in the curriculum than is commonly found in the United States. The reasons that European school systems, such as found in Britain, France, Germany, and Russia, gave for including Bible teaching in the schools in the 1800s were to facilitate the moral development of students and to encourage the development of a mature faith. Today, these same nations continue the practice of Bible instruction both for the moral benefits that result and, in the case of some Western European nations, as part of an expression of multiculturalism in which these nations consider the Christian religion a vital part (Glenn, 1989, 2000; Jones, 1964; Kwiran, 2001).

Moral education in various European countries was generally quite demonstrative. In England and Wales it took the form of school worship services that consisted of singing hymns and Bible-based character instruction. In both Germany and Russia until World War I (in the case of Germany) and the Bolshevik Revolution (in the case of Russia), there was a conviction in each of these countries that teaching religion and values had a positive effect on the culture. Consequently, during this time each of these nations emphasized moral instruction. However, the traumas of geopolitical events in Germany and Communist rule in Russia caused each of these nations to drift away from the character emphasis during the 1914–1945 and 1917–1992 periods, respectively. Poland, even during the time it virtually disintegrated from the European landscape and was dominated by other European nations, had a moral instruction program that was inextricably connected with Catholicism (Davies & Evans, 2001; Kwiran, 2001; Tomiak, 2001).

Japan

In East Asia, by the mid-late 1800s the structure of moral education changed from its traditional Confucian, Buddhist, or Shintoist orientation to a considerably more organized Western orientation (Khan, 1997; Watanabe, 1996). Japan was the first of these nations to change. As Hiroshi Watanabe (1996, p. 129) observes, "Before introduction to the West, Japan followed China. Therefore, once they acknowledged Western superiority over China and Japan in technology and science, and even in morality and politics, it was not very difficult for them to change their model from ancient China to the contemporary West."

In the case of many Asian countries, a formal education system really did not exist until there was extensive exposure to Western educational influence. Levine & White (1986, pp. 96–97) note that "In 1853, the beginning of Japan's modern contact with the West, Japan had no centralized or uniform national schooling." And in other cases, for example, China, the education system that existed was only geared toward the training of the governmental ruling elite. In the cases of Japan, China, and even to a greater degree in the other East Asian countries, character instruction was considerably less organized than in the United States and Europe and was largely based in less formal education provided by houses of worship and families (Khan, 1997; Shimizu, 1992).

Japan was the first nation to base its educational rubric on the Western model. In 1868, Emperor Meiji assumed the throne and argued that unless Japan adopted certain Western modern ways, Japanese society could not thrive. In the 1870s Meiji initiated a plethora of reforms and called for a radical level of Western-style reforms that involved everything from adopting the Christian calendar to hiring hundreds of American and other Western educators to construct the Japanese education system. Meiji asked several of these educators to head up the project (Hood, 2001; Shimizu, 1992).

Emperor Meiji therefore asked several Western educators to come to Japan and construct a Japanese education system that would be based on the Western model. These educators were led by David Murray from Rutgers College, who became the Superintendent of Schools and served in that capacity from 1873 to 1878 (Amano, 1990). Murray and his colleagues helped put in place a moral educational program that taught 20 moral traits. Khan (1997, p. 65) notes that while "the reality of Western moral education was used . . . the actual principles were Confucian in nature." Confucian principles were taught because Japanese educators wanted to support the values taught in the home. Murray's influence was so profound that, Keenleyside & Thomas (1937, p. 92) assert,

"Dr. Murray himself probably did more than any other one man to influence the trend of educational development in Japan." The Japanese, like the United States, developed a system of character instruction that was designed to support the moral values of the parents. At the time, both Japan and the United States believed that character schooling could only thrive in an environment in which the parents and teachers worked as partners. To reach this goal Murray incorporated in Japan the American practice, in place since the days of Puritans, of the elementary school teachers visiting the homes of the students before the school year started. The practice of teachers visiting student homes declined in America shortly before the practice of doctors making house calls (Amano, 1990; Chamberlin, 1961; Gangel & Benson, 1983; Hood, 2001; Jeynes, 2005; Keenleyside & Thomas, 1937; Khan, 1997; Morgan, 1986).

Korea

Shortly after these changes in Japan, American and European missionaries also started Western-style schools in Korea, which had a heavy emphasis on moral education. Western missionaries founded a large number of Korea's finest universities and elementary and secondary schools. South Korea, like Japan, was influenced by Western educational traditions more than other East Asian nations. The Euro-American influence was due to different factors than those at work in Japan. South Korea has been far more amenable to Western missionary influence than its East Asian counterparts and this facilitated the influence of Western missionaries on education. As in the case of Japan, Koreans did their best to weave Korean cultural distinctions with Western educational traditions. The schools sought to be supportive of the family and the values taught at the home (Chamberlin, 1961; Cho, 1989; Duke University, 2002; Monroe, 1940; Sah-Myung, 1983).

China

Initially, China did not pursue the Western model of character education as aggressively as the Japanese. That changed when China suffered a stunning defeat in the Sino-Japanese War of 1894–1895 (Pepper, 1990). Suzanne Pepper (1990, p. 10) observes:

> Thereafter China could no longer maintain even the pretense of its ancient superiority as the center of the East Asian world.

The Chinese elite were cognizant of the fact that Japan had adopted Western technology and education and they were well aware that this fact had given Japan the edge (Pepper, 1990, p. 10). Consequently, China "suddenly abandoned" with "unprecedented imperial haste" its previous system of education which trained only a small number of the Chinese elite and instead embraced a Western model (Pepper, 1990, pp. 10–11). Robert Morrison (1782–1834) was the first Protestant missionary to China and had exposed the Chinese to "mission schools" in China. As a result, the Chinese were familiar with the Western model of character education. Soon Western mission schools blossomed all over the country. American, British, and Swiss mission schools were doubling in number every 5–10 years. By 1920 there were 6,301 mission elementary schools in China. These mission elementary schools placed the Bible and character education at the forefront of the curriculum. The Communist revolution discontinued many of these practices, although the remembrance of these teachings remained in a number of circles (Cui, 2001; Reynolds, 2001; Thorgerson, 1990).

Other East Asian Countries

Among the nations or provinces of China, Taiwan, Singapore, and Hong Kong, Western character educational influences were more substantial in the latter three cases. Hong Kong and Singapore were influenced via the establishment of British colonies there. Taiwan was influenced by Western character education more than China, largely because Chiang-Kai-shek and his wife were both of the Christian faith and therefore, like the Koreans, were open to Western practices (Lee, 1991; Miller, 1943).

CONCLUSION

The period from the mid-1800s until 1962 was a period during which the influence of character instruction broadened. The McGuffey Readers caused character instruction to become one of the pillars of the public schools. New educators widened the definition of moral education to include play, psychological development, and being active in wider society. Character education also became more organized, defined, and widespread around the world. At the same time, certain challenges to character education emerged that would facilitate a major setback in 1962.

REFERENCES

Amano, I. (1990). *Education and examination in modern Japan*. Tokyo: University of Tokyo Press.

Anderson, K. (2007). *Race and the crisis of humanism*. London: Routledge.

Appelbaum, P. (1971). The growth of the Montessori movement in the United States, 1909–1970 (Ph.D. dissertation: New York University). *Dissertation Abstracts International* 7211442.

Beecher, L. (1864). *Autobiography*. Cambridge: Belknap Press of Harvard University Press.

Bergman, P. M., & Bergman, M. N. (1969). *The chronological history of the Negro in America*. New York: Harper & Row.

Bullock, H. A. (1970). *A history of Negro education in the south: From 1619 to the present*. New York: Praeger.

Chamberlin, G. J. (1961). *Parents and religion*. Philadelphia, PA: Westminster Press.

Cho, P. (1989). *Ordeal and glory through the 30-year history of Yoido Full Gospel Church*. Seoul: Yoido Full Gospel Church.

Cogdell, C. (2004). *Eugenic design*. Philadelphia, PA: University of Pennsylvania Press.

Cremin, L. A. (1976). *Traditions of American education*. New York: Basic Books.

Cubberley, E. (1920). *The history of education*. Boston, MA: Houghton Mifflin.

Cui, D. (2001). British Protestant educational activities and nationalism of Chinese education in the 1920s. In G. Peterson, R. Hayhoe, & L. Yongling (Eds.), *Education, culture, and identity in twentieth century China* (pp. 137–160). Ann Arbor, MI: University of Michigan.

Darwin, C. (1859). *On the origin of species by means of natural selection, or the preservation of favoured races in the struggle for life*. London: Murray.

———. (1871). *Descent of man*. London: Murray.

———. (1874). *The descent of man*. New York: Burt.

Davenport, C. (1914). The eugenics programme and progress in its achievement. In L. J. Wilson (Ed.), *Eugenics: Twelve university lectures* (pp. 1–14). New York: Dodd, Mead & Company.

Davies, B., & Evans, J. (2001). In J. Cairns, D. Lawton, & R. Gardner (Eds.), *Values, culture, and education* (pp. 190–205). London: Kogan Page.

Dewey, J. (1902). *The child and the curriculum*. Chicago, IL: University of Chicago Press.

———. (1910). *The influence of Darwin on philosophy*. New York: Holt.

———. (1915). *The school and society*. Chicago, IL: University of Chicago Press.

———. (1920). *Reconstruction in philosophy*. New York: Holt.

————. (1990). *The school and society/The child and the curriculum*. Chicago, IL: University of Chicago Press.

Dilworth, P. P. (2006). Widening the circle: African American perspectives on moral and civic learning. In D. Warren & J. J. Patrick (Eds.), *Civic and moral learning in America* (pp. 103–117). New York: Palgrave Macmillan.

Doherty, C. H. (1977). *Kindergarten and early schooling*. New York: Prentice Hall.

DuBois, W. E. B. (1993). *The souls of black folk*. New York: Knopf.

Duke University. (2002). *Big list of Korean universities* (Web page). Durham, NC: Duke University. Retrieved June 11, 2003 fromwww.duke.edu/myhan/c _biku.html.

Dunkel, H. B. (1970). *Herbart & Herbartanism: An educational ghost story*. Chicago, IL: University of Chicago Press.

Dupuis, A. M. (1966). *Philosophy of education in historical perspective*. Chicago, IL: Rand McNally.

Earle, J. F. (1996). *The McGuffey readers and civil religion, 1918–1963* (Unpublished doctoral Dissertation at the University of Minnesota).

Eggleston, E. (1998). *A history of the United States and its people*. Lake Wales, FL: Lost Classics Book Company.

Ferguson, R. F. (2005). Teachers' perceptions and expectations and black-white test score gap. In O. S. Fashola (Ed.), *Educating African American males*. Thousand Oakes, CA: Corwin Press.

Fluehr-Lobban, C. (2006). *Race and racism: An introduction*. Lanham, MD: Rowman & Littlefield.

Gangel, K. O., & Benson, W. S. (1983). *Christian education: Its history and philosophy*. Chicago, IL: Moody.

Glenn, C. (1989). *Choice of schools in six nations*. Washington, D.C.: U.S. Department of Education.

————. (2000). *The ambiguous embrace*. Princeton, NJ: Princeton University Press.

Gould, S. J. (1981). *The mismeasure of man*. New York: Norton.

Graves, F. P. (1912). *Great educators of three centuries*. New York: Freeport.

Graves, J. L. (2001). *The emperor's new clothes: Biological theories of race at the millennium*. New Brunswick, NJ: Rutgers University Press.

Gutek, G. L. (1991). *Education in the United States: An historical perspective*. Boston, MA: Allyn & Bacon.

Hall, G. S. (1908). Adolescent races and their treatment. *Adolescent psychology and its relations to physiology, anthropology, sociology, sex, crime, religion, and education, Vol. II*. New York: Appleton.

Harrison, W. P. (1893). *The gospel among the slaves*. Nashville: M. E. Church.

Hawkins, M. (1997). *Social Darwinism in European & American thought, 1860– 1945*. New York: Cambridge University.

Herbart, J. (1852). *Samtliche werke*. Leipzig: n.p.

Hester, J. P. (2003). *The ten commandments*. Jefferson, NC: McFarland.

Hood, C. (2001). *Japanese education reform: Nakasone's legacy*. London: Routledge.

Horne, H. H. (1923). *Idealism in education or first principles of making men and women*. New York: Macmillan.

———. (1931). *The essentials of leadership*. New York: Macmillan.

Howe, D. W. (1973). *The American Whigs: An anthology*. New York: Wiley & Sons.

———. (1979). *The political culture of the American Whigs*. Chicago: University of Chicago Press.

Hunt, T., & Mullins, M. (2005). *Moral education in America's schools*. Greenwich, CT: Information Age Press.

Jackson, J. P., Jr., & Weidman, N. M. (2004). *Race, racism, and science*. Santa Barbara, CA: ABC-CLIO.

James, W. (1958). *Talks to teachers on psychology and to students on some of life's ideals*. New York: Norton.

Jeynes, W. (2005). Parental involvement in East Asian schools. In D. B. Hiatt-Michael (Ed.), *Promising practices for family involvement in schooling across the continents* (pp. 153–179). Greenwich, CT: Information Age Press.

———. (2006). Standardized tests and Froebel's original kindergarten model. *Teachers College Record, 108* (10), 1937–1959.

———. (2007). *American educational history: School, society, and the common good*. Thousand Oaks, CA: Sage Publications.

Johnson, P. (1997). *A history of the American people*. New York: Harper Collins.

Jones, M. G. (1964). *The charity school movement: A study of eighteenth century Puritanism in action*. Cambridge, United Kingdom: Cambridge Books.

Keenleyside, H. L., & Thomas, A. F. (1937). *History of Japanese education and present educational system*. Tokyo: Hokuseido Press.

Khan, Y. (1997). *Japanese moral education: Past and present*. Madison, NJ: Fairleigh Dickinson University Press.

King, M. L. (1998). In C. Carson (Ed.), *The autobiography of Martin Luther King*. New York: Warner.

Kramer, R. (1976). *Maria Montessori: A biography*. New York: Putnam.

Kwiran, M. (2001). In J. Cairns, D. Lawton, & R. Gardner (Eds.), *Values, culture, and education* (pp. 219–232). London: Kogan Page.

Lee, J. (1915). *Play & playgrounds*. New York: Playground and Recreation Center of America.

———. (1925). *The normal course in play*. Washington, D.C.: McGrath.

Lee, W. O. (1991). *Social change and educational problems in Japan, Singapore, and Hong Kong*. New York: St. Matthew's Press.

Levine, J. A., & White, M. (1986). *Human conditions: The cultural basis of educational development.* New York: Routledge.

Lillard, P. P. (1972). *Maria Montessori: A modern approach.* New York: Schoken.

Lugg, C. (1996). *For God & country.* New York: Peter Lang.

Lynn, R. W. (1973). Civil catechetics in Mid-Victorian America: Some notes about American civil religion: Past and present. *Religious Education, 68* (1), 5–27.

MacMaster, N. (2001). *Racism in Europe.* New York: Palgrave.

Mann, H. (1848). *Eleventh annual report.* Dutton & Wentworth.

Marrou, H. I. (1956). *A history of education in antiquity.* New York: Sheed & Ward.

Marsden, G. M. (1994). *The soul of the American university.* New York: Oxford University Press.

McClellan, B. E. (1999). *Moral education in America.* New York: Teachers College Press.

McCluskey, N. G. (1958). *Public schools and moral education.* New York: Columbia University.

McGuffey, W. (1835). *First eclectic reader.* Cincinnati: Truman & Smith.

———. (1836). *Second eclectic reader.* Cincinnati: Truman & Smith.

———. (1837). *Third eclectic reader.* Cincinnati: Truman & Smith.

———. (1920a). *McGuffey's first eclectic reader.* New York: America Books.

———. (1920b). *McGuffey's second eclectic reader.* New York: America Books.

———. (1920c). *McGuffey's third eclectic reader.* New York: America Books.

———. (1920d). *McGuffey's fourth eclectic reader.* New York: America Books.

Miller, B. W. (1943). *Generalissimo and Madame Chiang Kai-shek: Christian liberators of China.* Grand Rapids, MI: Zondervan.

Mondale, S., & Patton, S. B. (2001). *School, the story of American public school education.* Boston, MA: Beacon Press.

Monroe, P. (1940). *Founding of the American public school system.* New York: Macmillan.

Montessori, M. (1956). *The child in the family.* Translated by N. R. Cirillo. Chicago, IL: Henry Regnery.

———. (1964). *The Montessori's method.* New York: Schocken Press.

———. (1965). *Dr. Montessori's own handbook.* New York: Schocken Press.

Morgan, J. (1986). *Godly learning: Puritan attitudes towards religion, learning, and education.* New York: Cambridge University Press.

Mosier, R. D. (1965). *Making the American mind: Social and moral ideas in the McGuffey readers.* New York: Russell.

Pepper, S. (1990). *China's education reform in the 1908s.* Berkeley, CA: Regents of the University of California.

Pringle, H. F., & Pringle, K. (1955). He scared the devil out of grandpa. *The Saturday Evening post, 227,* 30.

Rafter, N. (2004). The criminalization of mental retardation. In S. Noll & J. W. Trent, Jr. (Eds.), *Mental retardation in America.* New York: New York University Press.

Reynolds, D. R. (2001). Christian mission schools and Japan's to-a-dobun shoin: Comparisons and legacies. In G. Peterson, R. Hayhoe, & Y. Lu (Eds.), *Education, culture, and identity in twentieth century China* (pp. 82–108). Ann Arbor, MI: University of Michigan. New York: Cambridge University Press.

Ruggles, A. M. (1950). *The story of the McGuffeys.* New York: American Book Company.

Sah-Myung, H. (1983). The Republic of Korea. In R. M. Thomas & T. N. Postlethwaite (Eds.), *Schooling in East Asia* (pp. 204–235). Oxford: Pergamon Press .

Schreiner, S. A., Jr. (2003). *The passionate Beechers.* Hoboken, NJ: Wiley & Sons.

Scott, C. (1908). *Social education.* Boston, MA: Ginn & Company.

Shimizu, K. (1992). Shido: Education and selection in Japanese middle school. *Comparative Education, 28* (2), 114–125.

Shute, D. K. (1896). Racial anatomical peculiarities. *The American Anthropologist, 9* (2), 123–127.

Snyder, S. H. (1991). *Lyman Beecher and his children.* Brooklyn, New York: Carlson.

Spencer, H. (1851). *Social statics or the conditions essential to happiness specified, and the first of them developed.* London: John Chapman.

————, in Duncan, D. (1908). *Life and letters of Herbert Spencer.* New York: Appleton.

————. (1963). *Education: Intellectual, moral, and physical.* Paterson, NJ: Littlefield & Adams.

————. (1966). *The works of Herbert Spencer.* New York: Appleton (originally published in 1904).

Spring, J. (2005). *The American School 1642–2004.* Boston: McGraw Hill.

Standing, E. M. (1957). *Maria Montessori: Her life and work.* New York: New American.

Thorgerson, S. (1990). *Secondary education in China after Mao.* Denmark: Aarhus University Press.

Tobach, E. (1974). Social Darwinism rides again. In E. Tobach, J. Gianutsos, & H. R. Tapoff (Eds.), *The four horsemen: Racism, sexism, militarism & social Darwinism* (pp. 97–123). New York: Behavioral Publications.

Tomiak, J. (2001). In J. Cairns, D. Lawton, & R. Gardner (Eds.), *Values, culture, and education* (pp. 258–267). London: Kogan Page.

Ulich, R. (1968). *A history of religious education*. New York: New York University Press.

Wake, C. S. (1867). On the antiquity of man and comparative geology. *Journal of the Anthropological Society*, 5, 105–106.

Watanabe, H. (1996). Confucian eyes in nineteenth-century Japan. In W. Tu (Ed.), *Confucian traditions in East Asian modernity* (pp. 119–131). Cambridge, MA: Harvard University Press.

Weikart, R. (2004). *From Darwin to Hitler*. New York: Palgrave Macmillan.

Wells, D. C. (1907). Social Darwinism. *The American Journal of Sociology*, 12 (4), 695–716.

Westerhoff, J. H. (1978). *McGuffey and his readers*. Nashville, TN: Abingdon Press.

Wilson, P. E. (1977). Discrimination against blacks: A historical perspective. In W. T. Blackstone & R. D. Heslep (Eds.), *Social justice and preferential treatment* (pp. 161–175). Athens, GA: University of Georgia.

Wolpoff, M., & Caspar, R. (1997). *Race and human evolution*. New York: Simon & Schuster.

Woodson, C. G. (1915). *The education of the Negro prior to 1861*. New York: Knickerbocker Press.

Yulish, S. M. (1980). *The search for a civic religion*. Washington, D.C.: University Press of America.

7

THE NEW PHILOSOPHY OF EDUCATION BEGINNING IN 1962 AND 1963

THE REMOVAL OF PRAYER AND BIBLE READING FROM THE SCHOOLS

In the 1950s and early 1960s, the United States was in the midst of spiritual revival and its economic zenith. Statistics on morality and spirituality were encouraging. By 1960, 69 percent of Americans were members of a church, which was one of the highest percentages in the nation's history. Many social scientists referred to the 1950s as the "Eisenhower revival." It was a period in which Billy Graham was drawing millions of people to his crusades and toy stores made prayer dolls that could pray out loud. Concurrent to these facts was the cherishing of America's religious freedoms because of the contrast that existed between the United States and the Communist nations Soviet Union and China, where religious oppression was horrific. The government was also quick to point out to Americans that three atheistic leaders, who had no tolerance for religious liberty—Josef Stalin, Adolf Hitler, and Mao Tse Tung—ordered the slaying of scores of millions of civilians, more than all other centuries combined. Americans realized the antireligious bigotry for what it was. In the aftermath of the holocaust and the extermination of many eastern European and Asian Christians by Adolf Hitler, Josef Stalin, and Mao Tse Tung, Americans apprehended the value of freedom of religious expression in as great a way as ever before. The Great Depression (1929–1941) had also significantly altered the nation's priorities, causing materialism to decline and church attendance to steadily rise. In the 1950s and 1960s the civil rights movement, founded strongly in the nation's religious traditions, was also busily achieving copious victories for African Americans (Cremin, 1977; Klein, 2004; Lambert, 2008; Smith, 2006; Sweet, 1950).

The economic situation in the United States was equally impressive. Although the United States had only 5–6 percent of the world's population, it produced 55 percent of the world's goods. In the 1950s, based on this economic prowess, the United States also possessed a military advantage over its rivals that some historians considered unprecedented in world history. The United States had the overwhelming majority of the world's automobiles, television sets, and advanced electronic products. The wealth and standard of living advantage that the United States enjoyed over other nations was probably unprecedented in global history (Johnson, 1997; U.S. Bureau of the Census, 1975).

In this context, one might not expect that actions were about to be undertaken that would help dramatically change the spiritual and moral ambience of the country. And yet, if one in retrospect examines the scenario at that time, the situation in the 1950s and early 1960s invited complacency and mobilized antireligious forces that resented the fact that the United States was experiencing a period of spiritual renewal. The complacency and optimism of the 1950s and early 1960s were reflected in the terms used during the era. Americans referred to Camelot and the Great Society. Such optimism would be unfathomable today. Clearly, the nation was in a different era. The optimism and complacency perhaps contributed to Americans being overly optimistic regarding other issues as well, most notably the Vietnam War, the generation gap, and race relations (Johnson, 1997; Smith, 2006).

Soon, however, the nation was to be stunned by the removal of prayer and Bible reading from the schools, the enigmatic assassination of President Kennedy, the Vietnam War, and the government's lies and deceit regarding the war. The U.S. Supreme Court, in three 1962–1963 decisions, removed prayer and Bible reading from the public schools. *Engel v. Vitale* (1962) was the first of these Supreme Court decisions and involved the forbidding of school prayer. *Murray v. Curlett* (1963) not only prohibited school prayer and Bible reading but caused schools to steer clear of character education for fear of lawsuits (Murray, 1982). Following this case, Madalyn Murray O'Hare emerged as the most well-known atheistic leader in the country. Her son, Bill who was the child directly involved in the case, later came to feel remorse over his role in the case. He wrote a letter of apology to the American people in a Baltimore newspaper, where the family had lived. He later converted to Christianity (Blanshard, 1963; Kliebard, 1969; Louisell, 1964; Michaelsen, 1970; Murray, 1982; Sikorski, 1993; VanDeMark, 1991).

The Engel case involved a prayer that the Board of Regents of New York State encouraged schools to use as part of New York State's program of moral education that was entitled "Statement on Moral and Spiritual Training in the Schools" (Kliebard, 1969, p. 198). The prayer read as follows:

> Almighty God, we acknowledge our dependence upon Thee, and we beg Thy blessings upon us, our parents, our teachers, and our country. (Kliebard, 1969, p. 198)

No student was compelled to say the prayer. Any child who so desired did not have to participate (*Engel v. Vitale*, 1962). The prayer was doubly voluntary because not only could parents opt out of the prayer but local school boards could also opt out (Blanshard, 1963). Justice Douglas also specifically stated that this prayer certainly did not establish a religion (*Engel v. Vitale*, 1962). Despite these facts, the Supreme Court disallowed the prayer. In his dissent, Judge Stewart stated that the decision resulted in "the establishment of a religion of secularism" (*Abington School District v. Schempp*, 1963).

The Engel decision was enigmatic and stunned many Americans not only because of the decision itself but also because of unprecedented procedural deficits. Michaelsen (1970, p. 199) explains one reason why many American legal analysts were so shocked: "In a most unusual fashion, Justice Black, in writing the opinion of the Court in Engel, did not appeal to a single court case as precedent setting." In this Engel decision and in the 1963 case of *Abington v. Schempp*, Black and the other Supreme Court justices who agreed with him based their decisions on the "separation principle," which created an imbroglio for many constitutional because the phrase never occurred in the constitution (see Chapter 4; *Engel v. Vitale*, 1962).

The controversy about the Supreme Court's decisions were exacerbated by the fact that a number of judicial experts pointed out that the court had the lowest amount of judicial experience in the history of the Supreme Court. Therefore, the justices were not qualified to grapple with the legal issues involved and were insufficiently experienced to be cognizant of all the pertinent prior cases that would serve as a precedent for any eventual decision by the court. In virtually every case the justices were appointed to the Supreme Court following a long history of political rather than judicial experience. Prior to their appointment to the Supreme Court Justice Hugo Black had been a U.S. Senator for 10 years; Chief Justice Earl Warren had served as Governor of California for 10 years; Justice William Douglas was chairman of the Security and Exchange Commission; Justice Arthur Goldberg served as Secretary of Labor; and Justice Felix Frankfurter was an assistant to the Secretary of Labor and served as a founding member of the ACLU. It is intriguing to note that the lone justice with capacious federal Constitutional experience before he began his service on the U.S. Supreme Court, Justice Potter Stewart, was also the only justice to oppose the removal of prayer and Bible reading (*McCollum v. Board of Education*, 1948; Michaelsen, 1970).

The reaction by the American public and its leadership was not positive. Dwight Eisenhower, who opened each of his cabinet meetings with prayer and prayed for God's guidance in the selection of the timing of D-day (DiCianni, 2004; Smith, 2006), reacted by stating:

> I always thought that this nation was essentially a religious one. I realize, of course, that the Declaration of Independence antedates the Constitution, but the fact remains that the Declaration was our certificate of national birth. It specifically asserts that we as individuals possess certain rights as an endowment from our Creator—a religious concept. (*New York Times*, 1962)

The U.S. Congress strongly deprecated the Court's decision. In the *Congressional Record* for the following day, there was not one member of Congress who defended the Court's decision. Congressman Frank Becker, a Catholic, called the Engel decision "the most tragic in the history of the United States" (Congressional Record, 1962). Senator Eugene Talmadege asserted that "the Supreme Court has set up atheism as a new religion" (hearings before the Committee on the Judiciary, 1962, p. 140). There were myriad earnest points of view voiced by both religious and political leaders in the days immediately following the Supreme Court's Engel decision in June of 1962 (Blanshard, 1963).

Former President Hoover said the Supreme Court decision constituted "a disintegration of a sacred American heritage." He added, "The Congress should at once submit an amendment to the Constitution which establishes the right to religious devotion in all government agencies—national, state, or local" (National Catholic Almanac, 1963, p. 69). A Gallup Poll in 1963 indicated that Americans were opposed to the Engel, Murray, and Schempp decisions by a 3-1 margin (Gallup Poll, 2005). Even the newspaper media, often criticized for being left of center politically, was about twice as likely to express opposition to the Engel decision. Feelings were so intense that congressional leaders initiated an unsuccessful movement started to impeach the Supreme Court Chief Justice Earl Warren (Blanshard, 1963; Sikorski, 1993).

In the second relevant case, *Abington v. Schempp* (1963), the Supreme Court heard a case regarding the reading of the Bible in the classroom. Pennsylvania possessed a law that stated, "At least ten verses from the Holy Bible shall be read, without comment, at the opening of each public school on each school day. Any child shall be excused from such Bible reading or attending such Bible reading, upon the written request of a parent or guardian" (Pennsylvania Statute). The *Murray v. Curlett* (1963) case involved a similar situation. In this case, the Board of School Commissioners of Baltimore allowed for the opening exercises of a school to include primarily the "reading, without comment, of a chapter in the Holy Bible and/or the use of the Lord's Prayer" (Kliebard, 1969, p. 213). The three decisions had a considerable impact on school practices. A study indicated that in four eastern states (New Jersey, Pennsylvania, Maine, and Massachusetts), 96 percent of the schools *did* have Bible reading before 1962 and 97 percent *did not* have Bible reading after 1962. The Engel, Schempp, and Murray court decisions eradicated public school prayer, religious released-time taking place on school premises, and school-sponsored group prayer (Michaelsen, 1970; Sikorski, 1993).

The Views of Some in Favor of the Supreme Court Decision

It should be noted that there were some people who supported the Supreme Court decisions. These people generally either thought character instruction should solely take place in the home or they feel that the presence of any form of religious expression in the schools is equivalent to the establishment of religion, as dictated by the government. This perspective was later articulated in Ronald Flowers's book *That Godless Court?* (Flowers, 1994).

The Misapplication of the Supreme Court Decisions

A number of social scientists and educational leaders have been quick to point out that it is inappropriate to lay all the blame for the absence of school prayer, Bible reading, and moral instruction in the public schools on the Supreme Court. These individuals point out that the paucity of these practices is due as much to the ignorance and personal biases of school officials as to the content of the judicial decisions themselves (Flowers, 1994; Jeynes, 1998). Whether it was due to vacuous school personnel, personal prejudice, and lack of cognizance about the law, the problem of discrimination against people of faith became sufficiently extensive so that eventually government hearings would be convened to examine these issues. These hearings will be addressed later in the chapter.

THE POSSIBLE PRICE OF TAKING PRAYER AND MORAL EDUCATION OUT OF THE SCHOOLS

Both the practices of schools regarding prayer and moral education and statistical trends suggest that the removal of vocal prayer and Bible reading from the public schools had a baleful impact on the teaching of moral education in the public schools. Prior to 1962, character education was founded on the Bible. Once Bible reading was forbidden, schools no longer emphasized moral teachings like "turning the other cheek," "you should not covet," and "honoring your mother and father" for fear that many would interpret these as religious and moral teachings.

The removal of teaching on virtue from the public schools quickly became associated with a religious and moral decline in the nation as a whole. It is challenging to determine how much of this decline resulted from the removal of vocal prayer and Bible reading from the school and how much the moral decline influenced the Supreme Court decisions on this matter. The direction of causality is probably in both directions. There is little doubt, however, the removal of Bible reading and verbal prayer had a substantial impact on the extent to which teachers dared address moral education (Sikorski, 1993). Vitz (1994) also notes that following 1962, public school textbook manufacturers substantially reduced the number of moral lessons that had previously been a recurring thread in many American textbooks.

If one looks at government statistics, it is patent that beginning in 1963, American juveniles experienced a sudden surge in immoral behavior.

How much of this considerable increase was due to America's overall moral problems and how much was due to the absence of many moral teachings in the public schools is debatable. There were several factors involved. Theoretically, the increase in immoral behavior could have been entirely coincidental. However, very few people think it was merely coincidental. Here are some interesting statistically based facts. When one compares the late 1990s with 1962, one finds the following.

1. Murder arrests among 13–18-year-olds are nearly five times their 1962 levels.
2. Murders by girls are also five times their 1962 levels.
3. Aggravated assaults by girls 13–15 are up five times since 1962.
4. Rape arrests among 13–14-year-old boys are three times their 1962 levels.
5. Teenage pregnancies among unwed girls are up seven times since 1962.
6. Half of sexually active adolescent males had their first sexual experience between the ages of 11 and 13.
7. Teenage pregnancies—about 80 percent of the girls end up on welfare. Nearly 50 percent of all people on consistent welfare started there as unwed teens (U.S. Department of Health and Human Services, 1998; U.S. Department of Justice, 1999).

Could it all be coincidence that each of these surges started in 1963? Most people think that it is not. Granted, there were certain other factors that were involved. One should realize that removing prayer out of the schools was not only a cause but also an effect. That is, it resulted partially from a decreased emphasis on morality and discipline in the country as a whole. It is difficult to determine the forces of cause and effect of this behavioral change pattern but there seems little doubt that these trends are part of a larger moral and religious puzzle. The removal of vocal prayer and Bible-based moral teaching is likely an important component of this puzzle. As previously mentioned, there were other pieces of evidence indicating an overall national moral decline. Illegal drug use surged beginning in the early to mid-1960s. In addition, the divorce rate, which had been in slight decline since 1948, suddenly began to soar in precisely 1963. The divorce rate then peaked in 1980 and since then has remained slightly under the 1980 level. To the extent that parents and schools are the two institutions that impact children the most, it is difficult to fathom that the moral decline present in each of these institutions, especially evident following 1962, did not impact juvenile behavior (Glenn, 1999; Jeynes, 2004; U.S. Department of Health and Human Services, 1992; U.S. Department of Justice, 1993).

KEY EVENTS AND COURT CASES FOLLOWING SUPREME COURT DECISIONS OF 1962–1963

To the degree that the U.S. Supreme Court decisions of 1962 and 1963 dramatically changed the nation's attitude toward religion and moral instruction, subsequent decisions expanded the pervasive nature of these decisions and complicated the imbroglio that those who viewed themselves as defenders of freedom of religious expression faced. The fact that in 1962 both President Kennedy and some facets of the Christian community, most notably the editors of *Christianity Today* in the evangelical community and mainline Protestant denominations, called on Americans to restrain themselves from inaugurating any attempt to construct a constitutional amendment to turn back the Supreme Court decisions on prayer neutered any efforts to pass a constitutional amendment permitting a moment of silence of prayer in the schools. Combined, these developments deflated what might have been a legislative victory that could have overturned the 1962 and 1963 decisions of the Supreme Court. These events likely made inevitable the failure of a 1966 Senate effort to propose a constitutional amendment that would permit *voluntary* school prayer (Alley, 1994; Andryszewski, 1997; Fedwick, 1989; Greenawalt, 2005; Jeynes, 2007; Sparks, 2002).

Lemon v. Kurtman (1971)

In the *Lemon v. Kurtman* (1971) case, the U.S. Supreme Court propounded a three-part test that emerged as the most frequently utilized standard for whether a law was permitted by the establishment clause (Andryszewski, 1997). "First the statute must have a secular or legislative purpose; second its principal or primary purpose must be one that neither advances nor inhibits religion . . . Finally, the statute must not foster an excessive government entanglement with religion" (*Lemon v. Kurtman*, 1971).

President Ronald Reagan and Prayer

When Ronald Reagan assumed the presidency in January of 1981, the United States faced a moral crisis. Beginning in 1963, juvenile crime rates soared and average SAT scores dropped for 17 consecutive years and divorce rates after falling somewhat from 1948 to 1962 had also surged for 17 consecutive years (U.S. Department of Education, 2005; U.S. Department of Justice, 1999). President Reagan believed that the dearth of character education, the removal of prayer from the public schools, and the deterioration of the family were three of the factors that had contributed to these trends. Although family trends and dynamics were arduous to control, Reagan maintained that the government could attempt to foster ameliorative trends in the schools. He therefore urged the return of character education and prayer in the schools. In May of 1982 President Reagan called on the Senate to pass a constitutional amendment allowing prayer in the public schools (Andryszewski, 1997; Jeynes, 2007). The proposed amendment read as follows: "Nothing in this Constitution shall be construed to prohibit individual or group prayer in public schools or other institutions. No person shall be required by the United States to participate in prayer" (in Andryszewski, 1997, pp. 54–55).

The Senate debated about the proposed amendment in 1982 and 1983. In the summer of 1983, a phrase was added to the proposed amendment that read "Neither the United States nor a state shall compose the words of any prayer to be said in the public schools" (in Andryszewski, 1997, p. 55). Although the amendment enjoyed the support of a majority of the senators, the extent of that majority was not enough for passage so that the process toward amending the Constitution could be started.

By the 1980s and 1990s the religious rights and freedom of expression movement had been reduced to haggling over pretty straightforward cases of discrimination. Under Reagan the emphasis of religious freedom of expression advocates focused on equal access legislation that was designed to make certain that people of faith and faith-based groups had the same access to school facilities that other individuals and groups had. The fact that people of faith even had to be concerned about this issue at all is indicative of the extent to which the attitude of the courts toward the non-secular realm had changed over the last 22 years. Those concerned about America's moral climate were now aware of this. Rather than argue about anything that was substantial and could improve the environment for non-secular freedom in the public sphere, the aim was to "stop the bleeding" so that discrimination against people of faith would not reach levels greater than was already apparent (Andryszewski, 1997; Fedwick, 1989).

Although the "equal access" initiatives clearly revealed the extent to which religious freedom advocates had now taken a defensive posture, nevertheless these advocates were still not certain that these efforts would yield victory. They believed that there had now emerged a court-sponsored bias against religion that could work to preclude any fair-minded assessment of discrimination against religious groups. Nevertheless, proponents of religious expression believed that addressing issues of discrimination against religious groups via equal access issues, albeit a defensive strategy, was the best way to proceed, given the cases (Andryszewski, 1997; Fedwick, 1989).

In 1984, Congress passed the Equal Access Act, the key clause of which read as follows:

> It shall be unlawful for any public secondary school which receives Federal financial assistance and which has a limited open forum to deny equal access or fair opportunity to, or discriminate against, any students who wish to conduct a meeting within that limited open forum on the basis of the religious, political, philosophical, or other content of the speech at such meeting.

Wallace v. Jaffree (1985)

After the Supreme Court decisions of the 1960s, myriad Americans looked for alternative ways to allow for religious freedom of speech within the confines of the parameters dictated by the court. One ostensibly logical approach was to allow the youth to have a moment of silence instead of a verbalized prayer. The major advantage of this approach was that the students could meditate or pray according to their own preferences. If a child was an atheist, he or she could meditate in a direction that was without any religious content whatsoever. Similarly, youth from the full gamut of global faiths could pray or meditate according to their own free will and the ways proscribed by their faith. This approach appeared to be an act of tolerance that would also not inhibit religious freedom (Fedwick, 1989; Greenawalt, 2005; Jeynes, 2007).

Although religious freedom advocates recommended this approach for some time, it was not fully tested at the U.S. Supreme Court level until years later in the *Wallace v. Jaffree* case. In 1978 the Alabama state legislature passed a state that required schools to have a moment of silence to begin each day. Had that 1978 statute been the edict that the Supreme Court assessed, the court may have had no objection to the Alabama decision. This original version stated that the purpose of the statute was for meditation. Three years later, however, the Alabama legislature added three words to the statute and it is likely that these three words were what raised the concerns of what was a left-leaning Supreme Court. In 1981 the Alabama state legislature replaced the phrase "for meditation or voluntary prayer." The Supreme Court ruled that the statute violated the establishment clause of the First Amendment (Andryszewski, 1997; Fedwick, 1989; Greenawalt, 2005).

The 1985 U.S. Supreme Court decision was an important one especially because by this time 25 states permitted or provided for such moments of silence in the public schools. The court's decision made many Americans conscious of the fact that court was very intolerant of any expression that was not secularist. The fact that the nation's justices would not even tolerate one minute set aside for silent meditation in a school day that was typically 360–400 minutes long in the eyes of many political leaders and parents divulged the extent to which the court desired to marginalize non-secular thought and freedom of expression. Many Americans were shocked that the courts could object to a moment of silence and felt that such a decision infringed upon their First Amendment rights. They also now comprehended that the so-called tolerance that was advocated by the courts was not the inclusive type advocated in Europe that included religion under an umbrella that encouraged religious expression, diversity, and dialogue. Instead, advocates of a moment of silence believed that the courts advocated only a tolerance toward the secular and an intolerance toward the non-secular (Andryszewski, 1997; Blakeman, 2005; Fedwick, 1989; Glenn, 2000; Greenawalt, 2005).

Whether or not this conclusion was justified, this belief patently changed the entire strategy and perception of the religious community. If there was a doubt about an antireligious judicial agenda in the Supreme Court decisions of 1962 and 1963, to Protestants and Catholics in particular such an agenda was apparent now. Consequently, rather than seek to increase the court's and public schools' tolerance toward religion, people who favored a place for tolerance for religious people decided to take a much more defensive posture. They decided to focus on cases of discrimination against religious groups in which they were denied "equal access" to public facilities (Andryszewski, 1997; Blakeman, 2005; Blanshard, 1963; Fedwick, 1989; Jeynes, 2009a, 2009b; Sparks, 2002).

Board of Education of the Westside Community Schools v. Mergens (1990)

The key issue in *Board of Education of the Westside Community Schools v. Mergens* (1990) dealt with allowing students to join various groups sponsored by faculty members to meet after school hours, "while disallowing groups sponsored by political or religious organization" (Andryszewski, 1997, p. 64). Justice Sandra Day O'Conner wrote the majority opinion for the Supreme Court, stating that the prevention of the formation of a religious club in a public school was a violation of the Equal Access Act (Andryszewski, 1997).

Lee v. Weisman (1992) and *Santa Fe Independent School District v. Doe* (2000)

Andryszewski (1997, p. 69) declared, "On June 24, 1992, the Supreme Court ruled in Lee v. Weisman that including clergy who offer prayers as part of an official public school graduation ceremony is forbidden by the Establishment Clause" (Harrison & Gilbert, 1996). In the case, Robert Lee represented both himself and Nathan Bishop Middle School, as its principal (*Lee v. Weisman*, 1992). The *Lee v. Weisman* case transpired when Daniel Weisman, who was Jewish and the father of Deborah Weisman, a student at a public school in Rhode Island, objected to the verbal expression of any prayers at his daughter's middle school graduation ceremony (Andryszewski, 1997). In June 1992 the Supreme Court ruled in *Lee v. Weisman* that "including clergy who offer prayers as part of an official public school graduation ceremony is forbidden by the Establishment Clause" (*Lee v. Weisman*, 1992). In this decision and a similar decision, *Santa Fe Independent School District v. Doe* (2000), the U.S. Supreme Court "extended its bar on prayers to graduation ceremonies and football games" (*Santa Fe Independent School District v. Doe*, 2000).

Jones v. Clear Creek Independent School District (1993)

"Only a year after Lee v. Weisman in June, 1993, the Supreme Court let stand (approved without writing a detailed plan of its own) a federal appeals court ruling permitting student-led prayer at graduation. In this case, *Jones v. Clear Creek Independent School District*, the school allowed high-school seniors to vote on whether not to include 'nonsectarian and nonproselytizing prayer' to be written and spoken by a student volunteer at their graduation ceremony" (Andryszewski, 1997, p. 75).

The Knox Controversy

In many respects, the prayer debate reached critical mass in the case of a Mississippi principal named Bishop Knox. In November 1993 a Jackson,

Mississippi high school dismissed Bishop Knox from his position as principal for on three occasions allowing a student to recite a prayer over the public address system. These prayers were the idea of a set of students, who approached Principal Bishop Knox. The student body then voted in favor of allowing the prayers by a vote of 490–96 (Andryszewski, 1997). The principal then permitted the students to go ahead with the plan.

As a result of Knox's approval of this student initiative, the school suspended Knox pending further investigation. However, parents, students, and other concerned citizens protested how Knox was treated by the school district. Thousands of demonstrators gathered at the state capital to express their support for Bishop Knox. In April 1994, the governor of Mississippi signed an edict allowing student-led prayer in the public schools. Later that month a county court ordered that the school district restore Knox's job to him (Andryszewski, 1997).

In spite of these developments, in December 1994 in a separate case a Mississippi federal court declared the governor's law unconstitutional. The court asserted that student-led prayer was only permissible at special events (Andryszewski, 1997).

Two Constitutional Amendments

In late 1995 Congress introduced two constitutional amendments pertaining to school prayer. The first one was known as the Religious Equality Amendment and was introduced by Congressman Henry Hyde. This amendment read, "Neither the United States nor any state shall deny benefits to or otherwise discriminate against any private person or group on account of religious expression, belief, or identity, nor shall the prohibition on laws respecting an establishment of religion be construed to require such discrimination" (Andryszewski, 1997, pp. 91–92).

The second amendment was introduced by Republican Congressman Ernest Istook, Jr. This piece of legislation was known as the Istook amendment and specifically focused on school prayer.

> To secure the people's right to acknowledge God according to the dictates of conscience. Nothing in this constitution shall prohibit acknowledgements of the religious heritage, beliefs, or traditions of the people, or prohibit student-sponsored prayer in public schools. Neither the United States nor any state shall compose any official prayer or compel in joining

in prayer, discriminate against religious expression or belief. (Andryszew-ski, 1997, p. 92)

These efforts to amend the Constitution served as reminders to the sponsors just how difficult it is to successfully amend the Constitution. Once again, the efforts to amend the Constitution fell short.

Reconsidering What the Supreme Court Decisions Do Allow For

As the U.S. Supreme Court decisions continued to be handed down and those who supported the freedom of religious expression continued to complain about judicial activism, there was a growing change in orientation among defenders of religious liberty. Instead of allowing the courts to choose the judicial battles regarding what religious expression could not be done, the focus became identifying certain practices that could be done. This transformation in orientation resulted from two conclusions about the trends that had been in place over the last several decades regarding the curtailing of religious expression and character education, especially that which in any way related to religious literature. First, the evidence was becoming increasingly palpable that myriad schools were overreacting and misapplying the edicts of the U.S. Supreme Court (Jeynes, 2007). There was therefore a need to accurately explicate to and instruct school leaders regarding how to apply those decisions. Second, those who sought to create an aegis in support of religious liberty sensed a new urgency to meticulously examine the past court decision and via those decisions define those aspects of religious expression that were still permissible (Jeynes, 2007, 2009b, 2009c, in press).

Schools Were Overreacting and Misapplying the Edicts of the U.S. Supreme Court

In late June of 1995 the Committee on the Judiciary of the House of Representatives convened to hold hearings on the issue discriminating against people of faith, by either ignorantly or misapplying the U.S. Supreme Court decisions regarding prayer, Bible reading, and character education. The committee examined actions such as school authorities suspending students who bring Bibles to school, who pray individually, and who engage in other religious activities such as wearing religious clothing. One of the cases that arose during these hearings was that of April Fiore. Ms. Fiore's daughter, Rebecca, and two of her friends sometimes carried Bibles in the school. The school admonished them to stop bringing their Bibles to school or they would be suspended from school for 10 days (the same punishment as for possession of illegal drugs). The girls claimed that they were being denied their rights of freedom of religion. When they were caught holding their Bibles on another occasion, they were suspended from school for 10 days and the school officials strongly urged the parents to send their children to another school (House Committee on the Judiciary, 1995).

The hearings before the House Committee on the Judiciary produced such a stir that shortly after the conclusion of the hearings, on July 12, 1995, President Bill Clinton decided to speak on the issue of religious freedom in the public schools. In a speech at James Madison High School in Vienna, Virginia, Clinton stated, "nothing in the First Amendment converts our public schools to religion-free zones or requires all religious expression to be left at the schoolhouse door" (Religious Tolerance, 2002).

In spite of Clinton's remarks a considerable number of reports continue to emerge of students who feel that they have had their rights to religious freedom of speech violated. On May 19, 2000 a teacher at Lynn Lucas Middle School in Texas threw the Bibles of Angela and Amber Harbison in the trash asserting, "This is garbage!" Praying in school and Bible reading still remain the most frequent types of religious expressions that are punished by suspension. A first grader at Haines Elementary School was sent to the principal's office for reading a Bible passage, even though the teacher had asked the students to read aloud any literature passage of their choice (Dominion School, 2002; Libertocracy, 2002; Religious Tolerance, 2002).

Religious clothing has also been an area of concern. In 1997, school officials told two Texas students that they could not wear rosaries. An Alabama school blocked students from wearing crosses. A girl, the Anti-Defamation League (2002) only refers to as Ann, was suspended for wearing a Star of David necklace. Another student was forbidden from wearing a shirt that promoted family values. Various and sundry examples of discrimination against people of faith have emerged both before and since the 1995 Clinton oration. In February 2000 a principal forbade a Bible Club from using the cross as a club symbol. Incidents such as these mentioned in the last few paragraphs are numerous and many social scientists and political leaders believe that these actions restrict the freedom of religion (Jeremiah Project, 2002; *Maranatha Christian Journal*, 1999; Religious Tolerance, 2002; World Net Daily, 2002).

Concurrently, a number of political leaders took notice of these complaints and acted accordingly. House Speaker Newt Gingrich announced that they would hold nationwide hearings regarding a constitutional school prayer amendment. In response to this initiative, President Bill Clinton said that he might be willing to consider a moment of reflection. In July of 1995, Bill Clinton established a set of guidelines for religious expression in the public schools, including school prayer. He declared that students could voluntarily participate in school prayer as long as they did not compel others to join them. Clinton averred, "Nothing in the First Amendment converts our public schools to religion-free zones or requires all religious expression to be left at the schoolhouse door. The First Amendment permits and projects a greater degree of religious expression in public schools than many Americans now understand" (Clinton in Andryszewski, 1997). Newt Gingrich's (in Andryszewski, 1997, p. 84) initiatives were consistent with his assertions in a speech he gave before the Heritage Foundation on October 5, 1994:

> The country is on the edge of historic victories. And I believe that school prayer will be one of the seminal fights of the decade. School prayer is important in itself because we should have the right to pray voluntarily in the school and have student-led prayers.

These various court decisions attenuate the expressions of people of faith in the classroom. Nevertheless, there were certain activities involving religion that were still allowed. First, the objective study of teaching about religion was also permitted. Second, there could be religious released-time off school premises. In a 1952 case (*Zorach v. Clauson*) this type of religious expression was allowed as long as it was not done on public school property. Third, ceremonies that were patriotic or civic in purpose with religious references were also acceptable (Michaelsen, 1970).

Defining Those Aspects of Religious Expression That Were Still Permissible

Teaching the Bible as Literature

For decades defenders of religious expression viewed the *Abington v. Schempp* (1963) case, as well as the two other court decisions of the period, as almost an anathema and possessed no desire to cite the case or parse its contents. In recent years, however, these people have taken an exhaustive look at *Abington v. Schempp* (1963) and realized that for years the case contained some important assertions that have been largely overlooked. For example, in *Abington v. Schempp* the court declares:

> In addition, it might be well said that one's education is not complete without a study of comparative religion or in the history of religion and its relationship to the advancement of civilization. It certainly may be said that the Bible is worthy of study for its literary and historic qualities. Nothing we have said here indicates that such study of the Bible or of religion, when presented objectively as part of a secular program of education, may not be effected consistent with the First Amendment. (*Abington v. Schempp*, 1963)

Examining the specific wording of the 1962 and 1963 U.S. Supreme Court decisions led religious liberty advocates to recognize that the justices actually appeared to encourage the academic study of the Bible as long as it was done in an objective way. The reanalysis of these decisions spawned initiatives to reintroduce the Bible back into the schools both for its historical value and as a tome of great literary import (Jeynes, 2009b).

Literary experts pointed out that for countless centuries the authors of books from most of the world's continents, Europe, North America, South America, and Australia, wrote with assumption that the reader would have a working knowledge of the Bible. Consequently, many of the great books of the world have themes, titles, and references to the Bible. William Shakespeare alone cites the Bible about 1,300 times. Moreover, such books as *War and Peace, Grapes of Wrath, East of Eden*, and a host of others cannot be fully comprehended unless one has a significant knowledge of the Bible. The Bible is not only easily the best-selling book in the history of humanity, but it has been the world's best-selling book each and every year in recorded history and has remained so to this day. It would be virtually impossible to argue that an American is educated without a strong working knowledge of the Bible.

In addition, historians pointed out that American and world history has also been profoundly influenced by the Bible. Whether one reads about George Washington's miraculous eschewing of certain death during the French and Indian War that had such a dramatic impact on his Christian commitment, or the Puritans and Quakers teaching the slaves the truths of the Bible, or the role of the Bible in the women's suffrage and civil rights movements, knowing the Bible is essential to understanding American history.

Recent research, particularly a meta-analysis, confirms that Bible literacy is strongly associated with higher academic outcomes and better social behavior among students. These results help justify offering courses in the Bible as literature in hundreds of school districts across the country. Some states have even passed legislation so that these courses are offered as electives across their state and a myriad of school districts offer the Bible as literature as an elective course. The *Bible Literacy Project* and other efforts are underway to encourage the instruction of the Bible as literature in public schools. Given that these efforts do not entail a devotional use of the Bible, which the Court struck down in 1962 and 1963, and instead emphasize the teaching of the historical and literary significance of the Bible, which those Court decisions actually encouraged, at this point the availability of these courses is increasing (Jeynes, 2009a, 2009c, in press).

CONCLUSION

It has now been a number of decades since the Supreme Court decisions of 1962 and 1963. Nevertheless, Gallup and Harris polls indicate that about 75 percent of Americans do want voluntary prayer in the schools. A large majority of Americans believe that there should be a moment of silence given to children, whatever their religious or personal beliefs, during which they can pray or just simply collect their thoughts. There are also efforts to teach the Bible in a way that is permissible by the Supreme Court. The decisions of the U.S. Supreme Court over the last few decades and some school leaders' interpretation of them have been major obstacles to the practice of character education in America. And indeed statistics suggest the United States has quite possibly paid a major price for the absence of moral instruction in the public schools (Barton, 1990).

REFERENCES

Abington School District v. Schempp, 374 U.S. 225 (1963).

Alley, R. S. (1994). *Schoolprayer*. Buffalo, NY: Prometheus.

Andryszewski, T. (1997). *School prayer: History of the debate*. Springfield, NJ: Enslow.

Anti-Defamation League. (2002). *Ann*. Retrieved June 11, 2002 from www.adl.org/religion_ps/dress_codes.asp.

Barton, D. (1990). *Our Godly heritage (video)*. Aledo, TX: Wallbuilders.

Blakeman, J. C. (2005). *The Bible in the park: Religious expression, public forums, and federal district courts*. Akron, OH: University of Akron Press.

Blanshard, P. (1963). *Religion and the schools*. Boston, MA: Beacon Press.

Congressional Record. (1962). June 26. 11719.

Cremin, L. A. (1977). *Traditions of American education*. New York: Basic Books.

DiCianni, R. (2004). *The faith of the presidents: Our national leaders in prayer*. Lake Mary, FL: Charsma House.

Dominion School. (2002), n.t. Retrieved June 11, 2002 from www.dominion school.com/mewstud.pdf.

Engel v. Vitale, 370 U.S. 421 (1962).

Fedwick, L. B. (1989). *Should the children pray?* Waco, TX: Markham Press Fund.

Flowers, R. (1994). *That Godless Court?* Louisville, KY: Westminster John Knox Press.

Gallup Poll. (2005). *Surveys from 1960–2005*. Washington, D.C.: Gallup (www.Gallup.com).

Glenn, C. L. (2000). *The ambiguous embrace*. Princeton, NJ: Princeton University Press.

Glenn, N. D. (1999). Further discussion on the effects of no-fault divorce on divorce rates. *Journal of Marriage and the Family, 61* (3), 800–802.

Greenawalt, K. (2005). *Does God belong in the public schools?* Princeton, NJ: Princeton University Press.

Harrison, M., & Gilbert, S. (1996). *Freedom of religion decisions of the United States Supreme Court*. San Diego, CA: Excellent Books.

House Committee on the Judiciary. (1962). Hearings before the Committee on the Judiciary, 1962, p. 140.

———. (1995). Hearings on Religious Freedom in the Schools. Washington, D.C.: U.S. House of Representatives.

Jeremiah Project. (2002). Available at http://www.jeremiahproject.com. Retrieved July 27, 2004.

Jeynes, W. (1998). Are America's public educational institutions anti-religious? *Education, 119* (1), 172–175.

———. (2004). Immigration in the United States and the golden years of education: Was Ravitch right? *Educational Studies, 35* (3), 248–270.

———. (2007). *American educational history: School, society, and the common good*. Thousand Oaks: Sage Publications.

———. (2009a). The Bible in the public schools. In *The handbook of religion and education* (pp. 91–102). New York: Praeger.

———. (2009b). Prayer in the public schools. In *The handbook of religion and education* (pp. 350–357). New York: Praeger.

————. (2009c, in press). The relationship between Bible literacy and behavioral and academic outcomes in urban areas: A meta-analysis. *Education and Urban Society.*

Johnson, P. (1997). *A history of the American people.* New York: Harper Collins.

Klein, S. (2004). *The most evil dictators in history.* New York: Barnes & Noble.

Kliebard, H. M. (1969). *Religion and education in America.* Scranton, PA: International Textbook Company.

Lambert, F. (2008). *Religion in American politics: A short history.* Princeton, NJ: Princeton University Press.

Lee v. Weisman, 505 U.S. 577 (1992).

Lemon v. Kurtman, 403 U.S. 602 (1971).

Libertocracy. (2002). *Web essays.* Retrieved June 11, 2002 from www.libertocracy .com/webessays/religion/persecution.

Louisell, D. W. (1964). The man and the mountain: Douglas on religious freedom. *Yale Law Journal, 73,* 975–988.

Maranatha Christian Journal. (1999). *Alabama school stops student from wearing cross* (www.mcjonline.com).

McCollum v. Board of Education, Dist. 71, 333 U.S. 203 (1948).

Michaelsen, R. (1970). *Piety in the public school.* London: Macmillan.

Murray, W. (1982). *My life without God.* Nashville, TN: Thomas Nelson.

National Catholic Almanac, 1963.

New York Times. (1962). June 28, p. 1.

Religious Tolerance. (2002). *News* (www.religioustolerance.org).

Santa Fe Independent School District v. Doe, 530 U.S. 290 (2000).

Sikorski, R. (1993). *Controversies in constitutional law.* New York: Garland.

Smith, G. S. (2006). *Faith and the presidency.* New York: Oxford University Press.

Sparks, A. (December 2002). *Engel v. Vitale:* Legacy of a landmark (Unpublished master's thesis: Pennsylvania State University).

Sweet, W. W. (1950). *The story of religion in America.* New York: Harper.

U.S. Bureau of the Census. (1975). *Historical statistics of the United States.* Washington, D.C.: U.S. Government Printing Office.

U.S. Department of Education. (2005). *Digest of education statistics, 2004.* Washington, D.C.: U.S. Department of Education.

U.S. Department of Health and Human Services. (1992). *Statistical abstracts of the United States.* Washington, D.C.: Department of Health and Human Services.

————. (1998). *Statistical abstracts of the United States.* Washington, D.C.: Department of Health and Human Services.

U.S. Department of Justice. (1993). *Report to the nation on crime and justice.* Washington, D.C.: U.S. Department of Justice.

————. (1999). *Age-specific arrest rate and race-specific arrest rates for selected offenses, 1965–1992*. Washington, D.C.: U.S. Department of Justice.

VanDeMark, B. (1991). *Into the quagmire: Lyndon Johnson and the escalation of the Vietnam War*. New York: Oxford University Press.

Vitz, P. (1994). In J. Kennedy (Ed.), *The hidden agenda (video)*. Ft. Lauderdale, FL: Coral Ridge Presbyterian Church.

World Net Daily. (2002). *News* (www.worldnetdaily.com/nes/article.asp/ ARTICLE_ID=22891).

8

AMERICA HAS LOST ITS WAY

SCHOOL SHOOTINGS

It really was not until 1996 that Americans began to focus on the carnage that was resulting from school shootings. National statistics indicate that school shootings were almost unheard of prior to the 1960s, but they started to become a periodic phenomenon beginning at that point. If the reader was alive at that point, the reader will probably recall that school shootings began to appear in the news in the early 1960s, but did not receive anything close to the publicity that accompanied the shootings of the 1996–2001 period. This is largely because the shootings that transpired during the 1962–1995 period were nearly always in America's urban areas, which were already riddled with high crime rates, gangs, and dastardly murderous deeds. Therefore, the shootings came as no surprise (Coleman, 2004; Lieberman, 2006, 2008).

The media has a tendency to report the shocking and the sensational. Apparently, the members of the media did not believe that student deaths resulting from the shootings of the 1960s, 1970s, and 1980s, and early 1990s had the shock value that similar events in suburbs would have. There is little doubt that the mode of selectivity chosen by the media reveals a deleterious bias that contributes to a double standard that many members of the public have. That is, when the public hears of a school shooting in a major city such as Los Angeles, Philadelphia, or Detroit, their typical response is something like "That shooting is too bad, but well, you know Los Angeles, you know Philadelphia." However, if many Americans hear of a school shooting in well-known suburb or a major city, such as Mount Prospect, Illinois, Scarsdale, New York, or Mission Viejo, California, their response is more likely to be along the lines of "Oh my goodness, I can't believe it! What is this world coming to?" (Cohen, 2000; Dobbs, 2006; Jeynes, 2007; Krajicek, 1998)

The different ways the media often reports school crimes in urban versus suburban areas contribute to the existence of this double standard. Typically, if there is a school shooting, television reporters will convey the story in a demeanor that is along the following lines, "In Los Angeles today, three students were killed and four others injured when an armed middle school student opened fire. The identity of the assailant is being withheld until . . . " In contrast, when there is a school shooting takes place in a suburban or rural area, the way the story is reported reaches almost histrionic proportions and frequently begins with, "This is a special report from CNN: School shooting in . . . " In a number of cases, these incidents received all-day coverage, which would have been unheard of if the incident had occurred in a large crime-ridden city. It is also true that even without media influence, Americans do typically respond to a school shooting in a low-crime area differently than in a high-crime area. Nevertheless, the media contributes to this double standard (Esbensen & Deschenes, 1998; Jeynes, 2007; Ladson-Billings, 2000; Lal, Lal, & Achilles, 1993; Lieberman, 2006, 2008).

In many respects, it is a tragedy that the American people did not become fully engaged in the horror of the school shootings when they first erupted in the early 1960s, but instead waited until 1996 to really become aware of the gravity of the problem. Most Americans began to become concerned only after the culture of adolescent violence was so inveterate in the fabric of the country that youth could not be easily extricated from self-destructive spirals of grudges, anger, hateful music, and obsession with violence. Nevertheless, it is helpful to review some of the highlights in the recent trends of school shootings in order to remind Americans about how serious the problem has become and why it is that so many students, in response, either go to school in fear or carry concealed weapons or both (Jeynes, 2007; Lieberman, 2006, 2008).

Although 1996 was not the first year of the school shootings, it was the time when these events came to suburban and rural America. On February 2, 1996 Barry Loukaitis, a 14-year-old from Moses Lake, Washington, slew two students and a math teacher. Loukaitis stated that he was greatly influenced by the Stephen King novel entitled *Rage*, which was about a school killing (Coleman, 2004). Loukaitis quoted the book at the time of the killing saying, "It sure beats algebra, doesn't it?" Loukaitis also claimed that he was influenced by Pearl Jam's video *Jeremy*, as well as the movies *Natural Born Killers* by Oliver Stone and *The Basketball Diaries* (Coleman, 2004). Coleman (p. 4) notes that "Today, Stephen King says he wishes that he had never written *Rage*."

In October of 1997 in Pearl, Mississippi a boy who was a Satan worshipper and was enraged at his former girl friend stabbed his brother to death and killed the ex-girlfriend and another student. He was a member of a gang called the Kroth (Matera, 2001). A substantial number of the school shootings, including the one at Columbine, involve a breakup with a girlfriend, who decides to date another guy. In Beth, Alaska, Evan Ramsey said he thought it would be "cool" to gun down people and then proceeded to shoot his principal and a classmate (Matera, 2001).

In late 1997 and the first half of 1998 the school rampages continued. In West Paducah, Kentucky on December 1, Michael Carneal barged in on a prayer meeting before school and shot eight students, killing three. The shooting in Jonesboro, Arkansas in March 1998 was perhaps the most publicized shootings before Columbine (Matera, 2001). In Jonesboro two boys, ages 11 and 14, opened fire on the school students killing 4 classmates and a teacher and wounding 10 other students. The boys shared that their motive was that they wanted to scare people. This incident received a tremendous amount of publicity for a number of reasons that include: it took place in the open air where the slayings could easily be televised, the perturbing nature of the children's motives, and the extent of the injuries. The day after this incident a student shot himself in Coldwater, Michigan and six days after the Jonesboro shooting a female student in Chapel Hill, North Carolina shot herself. Within two months after the Jonesboro shooting three major shootings took place. On April 24, 1998 a boy shot his teacher. On May 19, in Fayetteville, Tennessee a boy shot another boy who dated his ex-girlfriend. On May 21 a boy in Springfield, Oregon killed one student, wounded 23 others, and then shot and killed his parents (Coleman, 2004; Matera, 2001).

Other school shootings occurred in Stamps, Arkansas, Conyers, Georgia, Deming, New Mexico, Fort Gibson, Oklahoma, Mount Morris Township, Michigan, El Cajon, California, Santee, California, Lake Worth, Florida, and dozens of other locations. Most states have been affected (Matera, 2001).

The slaughter at Columbine High School in Littleton, Colorado constitutes the most infamous school shooting episode that took place. In April 1999, Eric Harris and Dylan Kliebold exploded 30 bombs and blasted 188 shots culminating in the death of 15 students and the wounding of 14 others. As gruesome as these results were, this tally actually fell well short of their goal because two massive 20-pound propane bombs in the cafeteria failed to detonate. Had they completed their initial plan, "authorities believe that 488 people in the bustling lunchroom would have perished, as well as 56 who were quietly studying in the library one floor above" (Matera, 2001, p. 2). It is not only the number that were killed that elevated the Columbine tragedy in the minds of Americans, but the scope of the plot (Brown & Merritt, 2002; Carlston, 2004; Matera, 2001; Scott & Nimmo, 2000; Zoba, 2000).

Harris and Kliebold loved the music of Marilyn Manson and played violent video games and evidence indicates that a majority of the assailants in the nation's school shootings beginning in 1996 had a proclivity to engage in these activities. In addition, Eric was hurt by a girl he had once dated, and he sought revenge against her (Brown & Merritt, 2002). One student said, "Eric held grudges and never let them go" (Brown & Merritt, p. 75). School athletes also bullied them (Brown & Merritt, 2002).

There were many warnings that Harris and Kliebold were planning a horrific attack and had a level of hate, egocentrism, and unmitigated anger that was very repugnant. Harris had a Web site that declared his beliefs and intentions. On his Web site Harris declared, "My belief is that if I say something, it goes. I am the law, if you don't like it you die. If I don't like you or I don't like what you want me to do, you die" (Brown & Merritt, 2002, p. 84). He also stated, "I will rig up explosives all over a town and detonate each of them at will after I mow down the whole (expletive) area" (Scott & Nimmo, 2000, p. 150). Harris wrote in Dylan's handbook, "God I can't wait until they die. I can taste the blood now ... You know what I hate? MANKIND! Kill everything ... Kill everything" (Brown & Merritt, 2002, p. 94).

Following Columbine, there was an increase in the number of school shootings planned, but a decrease in the number of those succeeding. The failure of several of planned attacks is due largely to increased vigilance by school authorities, the FBI, and the police. Some of the plans, if successful, would have made the Columbine shootings seem meager (Newman, 2004). For example, officers of the law intercepted an e-mail the day before a planned series of multiple explosions and shootings that, if successful, would have blown up an entire school in New Bedford, Massachusetts in 2001 (Coleman, 2004; Gahr, 2002; Kaufman et al., 2000; Matera, 2001; Newman, 2004; Snyder & Sickmund, 1995; Stevens, 2001).

REASONS FOR THE SHOOTINGS

Clearly, those who committed these violent acts were malicious and bitter people. Nevertheless, the causes of them being so enraged varied. Many of the students were obsessed with guns and violence. Some recently had their girlfriends break up with them. Others were bullied or teased. A number of them received a failing grade at school. Some of the students just simply wanted to scare people and get reactions. Generally speaking, the attitudes of the shooters had more commonalities than they had shared experiences. The youth tended to idolize guns and listened to and watched media that condoned violence. Newman (2004) notes that all the students tended to be low on the totem poll of the student hierarchy (Armstrong, 2002; Bennett, 1983; Brown & Merritt, 2002; Burns et al., 1998; California League of Middle Schools, 2004; Casella, 2003; Celano & Neuman, 2000; Clinton, 1995; Coleman, 2004; Coleman & Ganong, 1990; Eisenstadt, 1967; Matera, 2001; Newman, 2004).

CHARACTER EDUCATION: AN IMPORTANT SOLUTION GIVEN FOR SCHOOL SHOOTINGS

One of the most common solutions to school shootings that social scientists and national leaders propose is character education. When character instruction had a much more salient role in American education, teachers taught more proactively about love, the golden rule, forgiveness, managing anger, and not picking on any one who is different for any reason. Those who espouse this position believe that increasing the number of metal detectors, zero-tolerance programs, and other initiatives only deal with the symptoms of the problem, when it is the condition of the human heart that must be addressed (Coleman, 2004).

MUSIC

There is a plethora of research available regarding how music affects its listeners. Plato maintained that music possessed such a cogent impact that he classified it as a type of moral education. There is no question that music affects the decision-making and moral convictions that children have. There are many testimonies of youth engaging in a certain behavior as a direct consequence of being influenced by the music to which they have listened. There is considerable evidence that school shootings, suicides, and many other less extreme acts have directly resulted from the influence of the media, particularly music (Jeynes, 2007; Kuntz, Brownback, & Lieberman, 2000; Plato, 2000, 2004; Tomasino, 2005; Wilson, 2008).

The significance of the influence of music is particularly salient with regard to moral education in two ways. First, to whatever degree music is a type of moral education, as Plato envisioned, it serves as a competitor of moral education. Second, with the removal of prayer and the vast majority of character instruction from the schools in 1962 and 1963, music has in many respects replaced character instruction as a molder of behaviors. The 1962 and 1963 decisions created a mammoth void in the public school curriculum. Within the school itself that void has largely been replaced making children feel good about themselves and raise their self-esteem. Both of these new emphases have deep roots in Piagetian educational psychology (Fleege, Charlesworth, & Burts, 1992; James & Tanner, 1993; Jeynes, 2006; Leary, 2008; Perrone, 1990; Sykes, 1995; Twerski, 1995).

Music as a Competitor of Moral Education

Music is not only a competitor for moral education, it is a competitor in the most negative way, that is, it undermines moral instruction (Tomasino, 2005). Anna Tomasino (p. 33) asserts, "Music . . . has been blamed for corrupting young people and having an immoral influence on the young." Many social scientists such as Allan Brown blame the music industry for corrupting the youth and causing parents to lose control of their young. Bloom, who bemoans the overall decline in the quality of education in America, goes so far to claim that the music industry reduces their desire for education (Bloom, 2005). Bloom (p. 42) adds, "Rock music provides premature ecstasy and, in this respect, is like the drugs with which it is allied."

A number of social scientists and other leaders assert that rock, hip-hop, and rap music appeal to the emotions. Myriad individuals aver that the music industry and rock groups are encouraging adolescents to become emotionally driven beings. Increasingly, the music industry is urging the young to cast aside serious thoughts and instead focus on what they feel in their emotions. It contributes to a nation and also reflects a society, which increasingly values subjective emotions more than thoughtful thinking and analysis. In a sense, such an orientation should not surprise the reader, because the nation as whole is increasingly valuing what a person feels over objective facts that can be divulged by the use of one's mind. In America's schools and in the centers of debate in American society today, generally it is personal experience and subjective viewpoints that are valued rather than intellectual depth and the rules of logic and debate. The reality is that facts are not emphasized as much as they once were and no longer possess the central place in debate that they once did. Instead, it is the individual's or group's perception of those facts that are regarded as fundamental. Supposedly, there are little in the way of objective facts, because each person possesses such a widely different perspective. The fact that much of modern music, expressed in rock, hip-hop, rap, and other forms of music emphasizes emotion almost solely at the expense of the rational mind only contributes to society's orientation toward the emotional (Bloom, 2005; Kuntz, Brownback, & Lieberman, 2000; Tomasino, 2005; Wilson, 2008).

In contrast, character education involves the whole person, including the mind and the will. In fact, the most efficacious moral instruction is one that trains individuals for their will to triumph over their most negative emotions.

Modern Day Music Often Replaces Character Education

As has been pointed out, the removal of prayer, most religious expression, and character education from the public schools left a tremendous void in the curriculum. To the degree that there were extensive changes taking place in the American family that also created a moral void, one can see how it was only natural that an alternative source fill that void (Jeynes, 2006).

Unfortunately, a number of forms of contemporary music have filled the voids, but they have filled them with a set of values that undermine virtue, religion, and objective truth (Kuntz, Brownback, & Lieberman, 2000; Merritt, 2000). The lyrics from a good number of these songs clearly reflect this fact. For example, in Marilyn Manson's "The Reflecting God" from the CD entitled *Antichrist Superstar*, some of the words state, "No salvation, no forgiveness, no salvation."

Many leaders along a variety of disciplines have expressed concern that the values vacuum that developed after 1962 and 1963 has created a "naked public square," to use Richard Neuhaus's term (Neuhaus, 1984, pp. 17–33). Neuhaus asserts that this "naked public square," as Kuntz, Brownback, & Lieberman (2000, p. 47) point out, "describes the extent to which we in our country . . . have . . . pushed out of the public square acceptance and respect of one of the major sources of values and discipline in our culture traditionally which is religion." Kuntz, Brownback, and Lieberman (p. 47) then continue by averring "that what happens then when the public square is naked is that something else fills it. And too often in our time what is filling it is this abominable culture, music, TV, movies." They conclude that the nation's music and movies are "giving our kids exactly the wrong message" (Kuntz, Brownback, & Lieberman, 2000, p. 47).

The effects of such musical venues as heavy metal, rap music, hip-hop, and other types of rock music are somewhat complex. Clearly, these musical expressions influence youth. There is also a certain degree of research that indicates that these types of musical expressions also attract rebellious youth as listeners (Carpenter, Knobloch, & Zillmann, 2003; Kirsh, 2006).

It is interesting to note that a great deal of these controversial types of music expanded significantly in the 1960s and 1970s relatively soon after the U.S. Supreme Court decisions of 1962 and 1963. Heavy metal music has roots going all the way back to Led Zeppelin and Black Sabbath. Rap music started with the Sugar Hill Gang's release of the song, "Rapper's Delight" (Kirsh, 2006).

Heavy metal, rap, hip-hop, and a number of other types of rock music often encourage all kinds of harmful or antisocial behavior. The lyrics often encourage, "Drug use, casual sex, reckless driving, and other sensation related behaviors" (Kirsh, 2006, p. 190). It is quite possible that this type of music influences all types of adolescents. However, Carpenter and his colleagues (2003) contend that this type of music attracts rebellious youth who are attracted to defiant and antisocial music, because it helps define their identity.

The body of research appears to suggest that among the negative qualities ostensible in all these expressions of music, it is the violent aspects even more than the sexual aspects that appear to affect adolescents the most. Part of this is accentuated by the fact that the music industry, the media, and video games glamorize violence. Hence, the void has not been filled by the music industry alone, but by several media manifestations (Hamerlinck, 2005; Hansen & Hansen, 1990; U.S. Senate Subcommittee on the Judiciary, 2005).

There are a copious number of "death metal" and "gangsta rap" groups that promote violence, death, racism, hate, and intolerance. Heavy metal groups such as Morbid Angel, Cannibal Corpse, and Dying Fetus encourage death, violence, and hatred. Some titles from some of the foremost heavy metal artists include "Irresponsible Hate Anthem" by Marilyn Manson, "Highway to Hell" by AC/DC, and "Appetite for Self-Destruction" (Thomson, 2008; Wilson, 2008). Concurrently, gangsta rap glorifies the "mythology of black gangs and the violence in which they engage" (Wilson, 2008, p. 68).

Heavy metal music has a strong relationship with school shootings. Nearly all the students who initiated the school shootings listened to heavy metal music. The trends elaborated on in this section are likely to continue until character education and prayer are restored in the schools. Only if the vacuum of moral education is filled can these trends begin reverse (Jeynes, 2007; Wilson, 2008).

CORPORATE CORRUPTION

The extent of corporate corruption that started to become manifest in the late 1990s and has persisted since that time appears to have exceeded the scope of anything that the nation has experienced previously. During the period of the late 1990s until about 2009, never had so many major corporations been inundated with greed, corruption, and succumbed to senseless Washington pressure to produce such widespread corporate failure as in this period. The consequences were enormous. Never in American history had so many prodigious companies with such a pervasive degree of worldwide influence undergone such widespread failure. Some of the most influential companies in America such as Enron, Worldcom, Lehman Brothers, AIG, Fannie Mae, Freddie Mac, and Merrill Lynch collapsed and brought the U.S. economy to its knees. Because so many companies were corrupt, the U.S. government was able to bail out some companies but allowed others to fail. Indeed, in retrospect it was probably the government's decision to allow Lehman Brothers to fail that caused the U.S. and global economy to spiral out of control (Brenkert, 2004; Goldstein & Henry, 2008; Morris & McGann, 2008; Muolo & Padilla, 2008; Wempe & Donaldson, 2004). In fact, in Asia and Europe, politicians and economists refer to economic crisis as "Lehman shock" (Craig et al., 2008).

One of the most intriguing aspects of the economic crisis is that virtually no one called the CEOs of these failing companies stupid. In fact, there is a general assumption among most business analysts and economists that the overwhelming majority of the CEOs of the nation's largest companies are quite intelligent. The cause of these companies failing had little to do with the lack of intelligence of these CEOs. Rather, most of the nation's leaders and analysts place the blame on the dearth of such qualities as integrity responsibility, compassion, and being accountable and a plethora of such traits as greed, deceptiveness, selfishness, and egotism. So nearly unanimous was this conclusion that many individuals called for the punishment and even the imprisonment of many of these CEOs. Some pundits even blame McCain's election defeat of 2008 on his failure to plug into the anger of the American people over the corruption and audacity of these CEOs (Goldberg, 2008; Morris & McGann, 2008; Muolo & Padilla, 2008; Wempe & Donaldson, 2004).

Clearly, some of these CEOs, CFOs, COOs, and other business leaders were punished and/or sentenced to imprisonment for their pernicious behavior (Wempe & Donaldson, 2004). Business leaders from Enron and Adelphia are examples of some degree of action being taken against such individuals (Wempe & Donaldson, 2004). Other companies, such as Tyco, had their business leaders publicly humiliated as a result of intense media scrutiny (Muolo & Padilla, 2008). Nevertheless, too many CEOs walked away from their bankrupted or nearly impecunious company with hundreds of millions of dollars in golden parachute benefits while emptying the retirement account of many of their employees and investors. Moreover, the selfish greed of a number of these CEOs affected a large population of people all across the nation. Myriad Americans lost their jobs not only within the failing companies but all across the full gamut of business dependent on these failing financial institutions. With the bankruptcy and government bailout of other companies headed toward bankruptcy such as Lehman Brothers, AIG, Fannie Mae, and Freddie Mac, other financial institutions had to act quickly to preclude financial ruin. Citibank, Morgan Stanley, and Goldman Sachs, which were considered blue chip companies only a few months before, were threatened by extinction unless they either sold off some of their assets or quickly found partners or investors to help prop up their stock prices which were falling precipitously (Hudson, 2009; Morris & McGann, 2008; Muolo & Padilla, 2008; Van Luijk, 2004).

The fallout from the greed and irresponsibility of these CEOs extended well beyond the financial sector. The housing market plummeted further because the financial crisis caused banks to lend only to their most reliable clients. Many potential buyers could not obtain a loan and consequently the housing market suffered and home values dropped significantly (Brenkert, 2004; Muolo & Padilla, 2008; Shiskin, 2009).

Because the purchase of a house represents the largest purchase that most people will make it is only logical that the evaporation of bank funds would affect the housing industry first. It is also true, however, that the second largest purchase that most people make is the purchase of a car. It therefore should come as no surprise that the American automobile industry was also greatly affected by the collapse of a number of America's largest financial institutions. In November and December, America's Big Three automakers, General Motors, Ford, and Chrysler, reported that they had to turn away hundreds of thousands of people who wanted to buy their cars but could not obtain financing (Kiviat, 2008; Muolo & Padilla, 2008).

The effects of the selfishness and greed of a number of these CEOs of financial companies ultimately had devastating ramifications for the economy. The fact that so many Americans called for the punishment of these CEOs demonstrates the extent to which the populace was cognizant of the fact that this was a moral problem (Muolo & Padilla, 2008; Van Luijk, 2004; Wempe & Donaldson, 2004).

Had moral transgressions of these CEOs been isolated and rare events with limited consequences, most Americans would have dismissed the wrongs as manifestations of the periodic failings of humanity that fall within the bounds of common human failings of character. However, it was rampant nature of corruption reaching many of the major corners of the banking world that initially stunned the nation and opened the eyes of the citizenry to the extent of major character problems that inundated some of the nation's largest financial companies. In addition, because of the dire economic consequences of their blatant selfishness and irresponsibility, the public became more aware of the depth of the problems that can result from major character flaws that are allowed to go unchecked (Morris & McGann, 2008; Muolo & Padilla, 2008; Van Luijk, 2004; Wempe & Donaldson, 2004).

Naturally, the public realized that not all of the economic problems of the late 1990s and 2008 and beyond could be blamed on the character voids manifested in a number of company CEOs. The seeds and roots of the disaster from an economic standpoint probably go back to the defining year of 1973. In that year the Organization of the Petroleum Exporting Countries (OPEC) initiated an oil embargo designed to change the West's policy toward Israel. The embargo caused gas prices to triple and as a result Americans increasingly turned to cheap and gas-preserving foreign cars. The cheap imported cars helped whet the American appetite for imported products and the nation's trade deficit started to soar. Other developments emerged concurrently that also contributed to an environment that would cause economic decline. First, federal budget deficits also surged beginning in about 1973. Finally, in 1973 federal laws were passed pressuring banks and other financial institutions to grant house loans to people who normally would be unable to afford qualifying for the loan. Community Reinvestment Acts passed in the 1980s and 1990s further pressured banks to loan money to people who could not afford to repay their loans (Considine & Tarr-Whelan, 1991; Jeynes, 2007; Muolo & Padilla, 2008; Thygerson, 1973; U.S. Congress, 2000; Wempe & Donaldson, 2004).

No one denies that other factors, beyond corporate greed and self-absorption, are included among the deleterious economic events beginning in 1973. Nevertheless, one might conclude that just as economics that started decades ago and continued for decades, there were also moral trends that were initiated decades ago and continued for years. One could argue that the moral transgressions by the business leaders of some of America's leading companies were inevitable because these were the first generation of business leaders to be raised without character education in the schools. Given that in 1962 and 1963 the U.S. Supreme Court acted to remove prayer and Bible reading from the schools, it also removed the character education that was based in Judeo-Christian traditions (Andryszewski, 1997; Jeynes, 2007; Morris & McGann, 2008).

Responsible for Vast Sums of Money

Today's corporate leaders are responsible for vast sums of money. Anderson, Cavanagh, and Lee (2000) note that in 2000, 51 of the 100 largest economic entities were corporations and not nations. With such power at their disposal, it is vital that CEOs, CFOs, COOs, and other leaders live lives of integrity and be accountable for how they handle money. As Ronald Berenberm (2004, p. 15) observes, "If companies and their leaders were not accountable for making ethical choices, there would be no such thing as business ethics."

The reality is, however, that too many business leaders do not practice accountability and live lives of integrity to the extent that they should. Instead, Americans are regularly hearing of a steady stream of "corporate Watergates" such as Tyco, Global Crossing, Worldcom, and Enron. Wempe & Donaldson (2004, p. 24) assert that "These corporate Watergates 'have shaken the foundations of trade and industry.' " Of course, corporate greed and corruption are not new. What is unprecedented, however, is the number, extent of breadth, and depth of the scandals. Although the media publicized the Enron debate for more than it did other corporate scandals, the activities at other companies such as Worldcom and Tyco were blatant, horrific, self-serving, and scandalous. At Worldcom, for example, the company included millions of dollars of stealth charges for its customers and manipulated profits. Tyco held corporate luxury gatherings that treated its leaders like Middle Eastern emirs and sometimes included promiscuous diversions (Muolo & Padilla, 2008; Van Luijk, 2004; Wempe & Donaldson, 2004).

Although the most blatant corruption of certain corporations receives the greatest publicity, corporations often suffer from more subtle expressions of insensitivity and excess. Many corporations contribute to national problems such as obesity, disease, and even death with very little indication of remorse, or even the hint of personal or social responsibility. Many food products are unnecessarily inundated with fat and sugar, contributing to obesity and the physical problems that often result. Other corporations contribute to cigarette and alcohol consumption. In the midst of the frequent revelations of corporate corruption in the form of alarming scandals grounded in greed, excess, and self-centeredness emerged a growing awareness of these qualities in other corporations that were manifested in more subtle ways. These tendencies were not only evident in the types of products that they sold but in the exorbitant amount that many CEOs were paid compared to those who served in other countries. The remuneration that CEOs receive relative to the average workers of their companies is of particular interest especially because the relative compensation that people receive at various companies often reveals the priorities and values of the CEOs and other leaders. O'Higgins (2004) notes that among companies around the world with $500 million or more in revenue, the compensation of American CEOs is considerably higher in the United States than it is in any other country around the world. Among these countries, the United States ranked first in terms of the greatest compensation for its CEOs, $1.93 million. Mexico ranked at distant second at $879,000, followed by Argentina at $866,000 and Canada at $787,000. Other nations generally pay their CEOs at a considerably lower rate than either the United States or the other nations whose CEO compensation ranks in the top four (O'Higgins, 2004; Rochlin, 2004).

In the United States, the average CEO makes between 200 and 475 times more than the average worker, depending on the estimate that one uses. This is in tremendous contrast to the United Kingdom, Japan, and Germany, where CEOs make 16, 15, and 13 times as much as the average worker, respectively. American CEOs also receive much more in severance pay than their counterparts in either Europe or Asia (Brenkert, 2004; O'Higgins, 2004; Wempe & Donaldson, 2004).

Typically, part of the justification that American corporate leaders give for the unbalanced salary figures is that they desire to give the CEOs, CFOs, and COOs sufficient incentive to perform well as measured by increased profit and revenue. As a matter of ethics, however, one wonders why it is that the United States places such an emphasis on profits and revenue rather than how a corporation benefits humanity (O'Higgins, 2004).

In addition to salaries and severance pay, executives often receive "golden parachutes" which are often in the form of stock options, insider trades, and other executive advantages. These golden parachutes may be sometimes morally objectionable to begin with, because they provide such a boon to the CEOs or other company officers often without benefiting the overwhelming majority of company employees. Nevertheless, it is also true the companies provide golden parachutes even when stock prices are plummeting and millions of investors are losing substantial portions of their investments. Some of the worst offending companies of the early 2000s include Quest, Broadcom, and AOL Time Warner. Executives from

Quest received $2.26 million in golden parachutes even as the NASDAQ 100 plummeted 85%. Broadcom executives received $2.08 million in garden parachutes followed by AOL Time Warner at $1.79 million and Gateway at $1.27 million (Brenkert, 2004; Hightower, 2003; Morris & McGann, 2008; Wempe & Donaldson, 2004).

Corporations place such an emphasis on providing incentives for CEOs to work hard, but companies place much further down on the priority list the need to encourage workers to achieve higher performance levels. This is in marked contrast to East Asian and European nations, which focus on worker incentives more than those at the CEO level (O'Higgins, 2004).

At the heart of morality is the notion that one should constantly consider the feelings of others. Therefore, a compassionate CEO should be concerned with how to best reward the company's workers so that they can attain their highest potential at the company. Therefore, a CEO who truly cares about the employees will likely be far more supportive of employee incentives than benefit oneself (Brenkert, 2004; Muolo & Padilla, 2008).

An Issue of Trust: Conflicts of Interest

Another reason why many Americans have concerns about corporate corruption and have suspicions about the accuracy of company financial statements is because they are aware of the relationship of convenience the auditors often have with those that they audit and vice versa (Van Luijk, 2004). During the stock market boom of the 1990s and early 2000s, increasingly many investors began to see the relationship between various companies and their auditors as problematic. Norman Bowie (2004, p. 59) states it well:

> The Enron scandal was the prelude to a seemingly endless string of scandals that stretches throughout 2002 and well into 2003. It is not too far fetched to say that the stock market decline in the first six months of 2002 was almost entirely the result of investor distrust in the integrity of the financial reports of many of America's major corporations. The boom of the late 90s was a mirage, not the result of irrational exuberance as Alan Greenspan said, but rather a house built on lies and deception that could not stand once exposed to the light.

As a result of Enron fiasco, Americans became cognizant of the conflicts of interest that existed between the clients and their auditors.

In 2002 *Business Week* produced a special issue for January 28 addressing the crisis in accounting. A month later *Business Week* released another special issue entitled "The Betrayed Investor" declaring that the conflicts of interest had caused investors to conclude that the earnings of various major corporations were considerably stronger than they actually were (Bowie, 2004; Nussbaum, 2002; Victors & McNamee, 2002).

In the 1990s and early 2000s, there was patently a lack of auditor independence. Auditors realized that as long as they issued positive financial reports, they would be hired to undertake further audits. George Enderle (2004, p. 88) asserts that "Before the Enron and Anderson scandals, relatively little public attention was paid to the truthfulness of financial reporting." He accurately declares that Americans must be able to trust financial reporting or the investment world cannot thrive. A number of business leaders assert that this issue of lack of auditor independence is a critical ethical issue (Dunfee, Glazer, Jaenicke, McGrath, & Sieyal, 2004; Enderle, 2004; Weil, Barrionvevo, & Bryan-Law, 2002). There is sufficient concern for this issue that Dunfee and his colleagues have offered "An ethical framework for auditor independence."

The Solution: Character Education in Business Ethics and General Moral Education

The problems regarding dearth in business integrity are so vast that a growing number of people in business and education are calling for schools and colleges to offer moral education and business ethics courses to train future business leaders to pursue lives of integrity that they will carry into the business world. Vogl (2004, p. 6) avers that due to a spirit of denial and "business as usual" it would be nearly impossible for the business community to initiate this type of reform on its own (DeGeorge, 2004; Muolo & Padilla, 2008; Van Luijk, 2004; Vogl, 2004).

John Deinhart (2004) asserts that the only solution to the lack of business integrity is to intervene well before an individual enters the corporate domain. Deinhart claims that the most efficacious type of character education is one that begins early in a person's development and continues through high school and college. He argues that moral education is the key to changing CEO behavior. Deinhart claims that this character instruction is vital if the moral climate in the United States is to be transformed. Rochlin (2004) concurs with Deinhart as well as Vogl and asserts that schools must do more than deal with a student's acumen but also with the compassion and integrity of one's heart.

FOREIGN POLICY

Increasingly, America's foreign policy does not reflect virtue and Judeo-Christian values. From its earliest days as a nation, the United States had tried to fashion its foreign policy in a way that reflected integrity, justice, and biblical truth (Blinderman, 1976; Kirk, 1953; Lewy, 1996; Matson, 2001; McClellan, 1999; Weil, Barrionvevo, & Bryan-Law, 2002).

From its incipiency, the United States attempted to act as a defender of the oppressed and a herald of freedom and democracy. Clearly, there were times when the United States fell short of these objectives. Nevertheless, the nation would ultimately return after erring, because the objectives remained the same. For example, both Presidents George Washington and John Adams called for the United States not to get excessively entangled in foreign disputes nor to seek the overthrow of every monarch or dictator with whom the country disagreed. Consequently, for many decades the United States tended to "mind its own business" in foreign affairs. In addition, the United States did not view its mission as purging the world of unrighteous monarchs or dictators that had little influence on everyday American life (Eggleston, 1998; Jeynes, 2007; Johnson, 1997; Washington, 1796).

The United States, under the Monroe Doctrine, assigned themselves to the role of protecting South America and much of the Western Hemisphere. The United States was cognizant of the fact that the European powers were far more puissant than the fledgling nations of the Western Hemisphere. The United States was well aware from its own history how Great Britain, France, and Spain had tried to dominate it and bring its various colonies, states, and territories in submission (Johnson, 1997; May, 1975; McKay & Scott, 1983; Perkins, 1955; Washington, 1796).

The United States was also well aware of the expansionist propensities of most of the powerful countries in the world. The nations naturally included the European powers of Great Britain, France, Spain, and Portugal. However, the United States was also aware that in other areas of the world, outside of Europe and North America, the strong tended to dominate the weak. China and Japan had frequently attacked their neighbors. Historically, this trend appeared equally ostensible. The Mongols, Romans, and

Egyptians were expansionists (Benson, 1995; Eckert & Yi, 1990; Wright, 2001).

Under the Monroe Doctrine, the United States proclaimed that it was the defender of freedom and of the oppressed. One might have debated at the time whether the Monroe Doctrine was really in the United States' best interests. After all, the policy could involve the United States in a number of foreign wars in the hemisphere, which could potentially weaken the nation. The Monroe Doctrine established the United States as the benevolent big brother. It helped establish the nation's foreign policy as one of integrity, loyalty, and fairness (Cunningham, 1996; Johnson, 1997; May, 1975; Perkins, 1955; Shermer, 2004).

The Good Neighbor Policy under President Franklin D. Roosevelt continued this attitude of helpfulness, especially toward other nations in the Western Hemisphere. Once again, through this policy the United States enhanced its reputation of faithfulness and responsibility. The fact that the United States was key in saving Europe in World War I and World War II also enhanced its reputation as a defender of freedom and a guardian for the oppressed (Ahlstrom, 1972; Guerrant, 1950; Johnson, 1997; Shermer, 2004; Wood, 1961).

As mentioned earlier, naturally, over such a long period of time, the United States had some foreign policy shortcomings. Perhaps two of the most notable failures were Andrew Jackson's reversal of George Washington's stated policy toward Native Americans and Franklin Roosevelt's internment of Japanese Americans during World War II (although some might define the latter as domestic policy, the fact is that this was done as a result of a foreign war). Nevertheless, for the period from the Revolutionary War until just before the Vietnam War, the United States earned the trust of a large part of the world. Many nations looked to the United States as an important facilitator in world affairs (Ahlstrom, 1972; Jeynes, 2007; Robar, 2000; Robinson, 2001).

After the removal of prayer and moral instruction from the public schools in 1962 and 1963, the foreign policy of the nation was heavily criticized, especially during the decade-long Vietnam conflict and the second Iraq War. Certainly, the decline of moral education both in the schools and in the family was not entirely or even mostly responsible for this trend. Nevertheless, it is quite possible that these developments may have been partially a result of the nation's moral decline (Bork, 1996; Nye, 2007; VanDeMark, 1991; Will, 1982).

It is quite logical that the absence of moral instruction may have influenced American foreign policy along fronts. First, many people serving in Vietnam and Iraq went to war with little or no school-based character education. This was the first time this had taken place since the nation's founding. During the Vietnam War there were more reported instances of massacres and similar misdeeds committed by American service people than during any previous foreign military conflict. The most publicized massacre was the My Lai massacre lead by Lieutenant Calley. The slaying of the civilians was witnessed by many people, some of whom testified against Calley during his military trial. There is some evidence to indicate that there were other similar slayings of civilians in Vietnam. It is only fair to mention that the nature of the Vietnam War was such that it was not always possible to distinguish between innocent civilians and Vietcong, true enemies, who were simply disguised as civilians. It is also likely that with these circumstances in mind, mistakes could be made more easily (Beldler, 2004; Corfield, 2008; Hester, 2003; Holzer, 2004; Nye, 2007; VanDeMark, 1991).

Nevertheless, it is patent that such military crimes were a good deal more frequent during the Vietnam War than they been during previous wars. Self-discipline reflects the degree of moral fiber that one obtains through moral education procured either at school or at home. Clearly, the trends beginning in 1963 indicated an abrupt decline in moral tutelage both at home and in the public school curriculum. One of the ways that the effects of that decline were manifesting itself was in the increased incidence of unmitigated and inappropriate military violence (Beldler, 2004; Hester, 2003; Jeynes, 2007; Nye, 2007; Stone, 2008; Wirtz, 1977).

By the time of the second Iraq War, even a higher percentage of American soldiers served in armed services with virtually no exposure to a character education public school curriculum. Once again the misdeeds of certain members of the American military served to embarrass the United States and fan the flames of terrorist propaganda and recruitment. The mistreatment of certain prisoners at Abu Ghraib grossly harmed America's reputation as a civilized nation and leader of the free world. When one heard of the outrageous ways that some of the Americans who operated the prison acted, one could not help but react by wondering where these military people had received their moral training. The reputation of the United States had been more than sullied but rather has been badly damaged. During the 1607–1962 period, the nation enjoyed a character curriculum that strengthened its people. However, as long as the nation turned its back on the value of character instruction, it was only to be expected that there would be an increase in the number of service people exhibiting behavior that is unbecoming to an officer (Beldler, 2004; Hersch, 2004; Hester, 2003; Holzer, 2004; Jeynes, 2007; Judis, 2007; Love, 2008; Nye, 2007; Stone, 2008; VanDeMark, 1991).

Second, by the time the United States reached the 1990s, most of the nation's political leaders had been raised in a public school system that was devoid of a curriculum that was filled with moral tutelage. Hence, many of the foreign policy political decisions made regarding Kosovo and Iraq were made by those who were not schooled in strong character education program (Hester, 2003; Holzer, 2004; Judis, 2007; Love, 2008).

Third, in the absence of moral education, training America's contemporary leaders were not raised in America's public schools to be trained to understand the extent to which the United States is a nation that defends the defenseless. Millions of people around the world despise the United States. One of the primary reasons why is because they no longer view us as a nation that defends the weak. Instead they see the United States as endorsing oppressive political leaders, promoting a loose American culture that millions of people find debasing and offensive, and funding abortion procedures that fail to protect the most defenseless humans, those still in the womb. Whereas, before the early 1960s, most people in the world viewed American foreign policy as acting for the common good, over the last several decades resentment toward the United States has grown because individuals around the world have come to view the United States as a nation that forces its will on other countries. Character education would have taught contemporary American leaders that such behavior is totally inappropriate (Beckwith, 1993; Brennan, 1986; Edwards, 1986; Ikenberry, 2007; Love, 2008; MacNair, 2008; MacNair & Zunes, 2008; Meehan, 2008; Sechser, 2007; Shettles & Rorvik, 1986).

CONCLUSION

It is clear that the United States is paying a price for the lack of moral integrity at so many levels. Consequently, the nation needs a moral compass. Of course, although it is helpful to focus on particular aspects of this dilemma, it is important that one comprehend the pervasive nature of this challenge. For example, it is easy for politicians and the general public to blame companies such as AIG, Fannie Mae, Freddie Mac, Merrill Lynch, Lehman Brothers, and Countrywide Credit for the economic crisis of the present day. However, one should note that politicians and many Americans motivated by greed probably bear equal responsibility. For example, two of the congressional leaders in charge of leading the effort to reign in these corporations were some of the people whose campaigns received the most money from these companies and who had resisted calls to reform Fannie Mae and Freddie Mac in 2005. In addition, millions of Americans falsified information on home loan applications and became greedy in their efforts to live beyond their means. The moral problems that this nation faces are widespread and the indications are plain that the United States has lost its way.

REFERENCES

Ahlstrom, S. E. (1972). *A religious history of the American people*. New Haven, CT: Yale University Press.

Anderson, S., Cavanagh, J., & Lee, T. (2000). *The field guide to the global economy*. New York: New Press.

Andryszwewski, T. (1997). *School prayer: A history of the debate*. Springfield, NJ: Enslow.

Armstrong, A. (2002). Guns have been wrongfully blamed for school shootings. In Egendorf (Ed.), *School shootings* (pp. 36–39). San Diego, CA: Greenhaven Press.

Beckwith, F. (1993). *Politically correct death*. Grand Rapids, MI: Baker Books.

Beldler, P. D. (2004). *Late thoughts on an old war*. Athens, GA: University of Georgia.

Bennett, W. J. (1983). Authority, discipline, excellence. In R. Reagan, W. Bennett, & E. W. Lefever (Eds.), *Reinvigorating our schools*. Washington, D.C.: Ethics & Public Policy Center.

Benson, D. S. (1995). *Six emperors: Mongolian aggression in the thirteenth century*. Chicago, IL: Benson.

Berenberm, R. (2004). Wiggenstein's bedrock. In G. G. Brenkert (Ed.), *Corporate integrity and accountability* (pp. 15–18). Thousand Oaks, CA: Sage Publications.

Blinderman, B. F. (1976). *Three early champions of education*. Bloomington, IN: Phi Delta Kappa.

Bloom, A. (2005). Music. In A. Tomasino (Ed.), *Music and culture* (pp. 35–41). New York: Pearson.

Bork, R. H. (1996). *Slouching towards Gomorrah*. New York: Regan.

Bowie, N. E. (2004). Why conflicts of interest and abuse of information asymmetry are keys to lack of integrity and what should be done about it. In G. G. Brenkert (Ed.), *Corporate integrity and accountability* (pp. 59–71). Thousand Oaks, CA: Sage Publications.

Brenkert, G. G. (2004). The need for corporate integrity. In G. G. Brenkert (Ed.), *Corporate integrity and accountability* (pp. 1–10). Thousand Oaks, CA: Sage Publications.

Brennan, W. (1986). Advancing medical technology proves fetal viability. In D. L. Bender (Ed.), *Abortion: Opposing viewpoints* (pp. 29–33). St. Paul, MN: Greenhaven Press.

Brown, B., & Merritt, R. (2002). *No easy answers: The truth behind death at Columbine.* New York: Lantern Books.

Burns, S., McArthur, E., Heaviside, S., Rowand, C., Williams, C., & Farris, E. (1998). *Violence & discipline problems in U.S. public schools: 1996–97.* Washington, D.C.: U.S. Department of Education.

California League of Middle Schools. (2004). *Legislative Update.* July 21. Retrieved July 23, 2006 from www.clms.net/legislation/leg0704.htm.

Carlston, L. (2004). *Surviving Columbine.* Salt Lake City, UT: Deseret.

Carpenter, F. D., Knobloch, S., & Zillman, D. (2003). Rock, rap, and rebellious comparisons of traits predicting selective exposure to defiant music. *Personality & Individual Differences, 35,* 1643–1655.

Casella, R. (2003). Zero tolerance policy in schools: Rationale, consequences, and alternatives. *Teachers College Record, 105* (5), 872–892.

Celano, D., & Neuman, S. B. (2000). Channel one: Time for a TV break. *Phi Delta Kappan, 76* (6), 444–446.

Clinton, B. (1995). *Proposed legislation: The Gun Free Zones Amendments Act of 1995.* Washington, D. C.: U.S. Government Printing Office.

Cohen, D. (2000). *Yellow journalism: Scandal, sensationalism, and gossip in the media.* Brookfield, CT: Twenty-first Century Books.

Coleman, L. (2004). *The copycat effect.* New York: Paraview.

Coleman, M., & Ganong, L. (1990). Remarriage and stepfamily research in the 1980s: Increased interest in an old family form. *Journal of Marriage and the Family, 52,* 925–940.

Considine, J. M., & Tarr-Whelan, L. (1991). How banks can help children. *New York Times,* June 22, p. 23.

Corfield, J. J. (2008). *The history of Vietnam.* Westport, CT: Greenfield.

Craig, S., McCracken, J., Hilsenrath, J., Solomon, D., Karnitschnig, M., Lattman, P., Gullipalli, D., Ng, S., Lauricella, T., Rappaport, L., & McKay, P. A. (2008). AIG, Lehman shock hits world markets. *Wall Street Journal, 252* (65), A1–A2.

Cunningham, N. E. (1996). *The presidency of James Monroe*. Lawrence, KS: University of Kansas Press.

DeGeorge, R. (2004). Law, accountability, and globalization. In G. G. Brenkert (Ed.), *Corporate integrity and accountability* (pp. 166–176). Thousand Oaks, CA: Sage Publications.

Deinhart, J. (2004). Global business ethics and sustainability. In G. G. Brenkert (Ed.), *Corporate integrity and accountability* (pp. 186–201). Thousand Oaks, CA: Sage Publications.

Dobbs, L. (2006). *War on the middle class*. New York: Viking.

Dunfee, T. W., Glazer, A. S., Jaenicke, H. R., McGrath, S., & Sieyal, A. (2004). In G. G. Brenkert (Ed.), *Corporate integrity and accountability* (pp. 72–86). Thousand Oaks, CA: Sage Publications.

Eckert, C. J., & Yi, K. (1990). *Korea old and new: A history*. Cambridge, MA: Harvard University Press.

Edwards, J. (1986). "The silent scream" proves the fetus is human. In D. L. Bender (Ed.), *Abortion: Opposing viewpoints* (pp. 38–41). St. Paul, MN: Greenhaven Press.

Eggleston, E. (1998). *A history of the United States and its people*. Lake Wales, FL: Lost Classics Book Company.

Eisenstadt, S. N. (1967). *The decline of empires*. Englewood Cliffs, NJ: Prentice Hall.

Enderle, G. (2004). The ethics of financial reporting, the global reporting initiatives, and the balanced concept of the firm. In G. G. Brenkert (Ed.), *Corporate integrity and accountability* (pp. 87–99). Thousand Oaks, CA: Sage Publications.

Esbensen, F., & Deschenes, E. P. (1998). A multisite examination of youth gang membership: Does gender matter? *Criminology, 36* (4), 799–828.

Fleege, P. O., Charlesworth, R., & Burts, D. C. (1992). Stress begins in kindergarten: A look at behavior during standardized testing. *Journal of Research in Childhood Education, 7* (1), 20–26.

Gahr, E. (2002). Access to guns can lead to school shootings. In Egendorf (Ed.), *School shootings* (pp. 33–35). San Diego, CA: Greenhaven Press.

Goldberg, J. (2008). Exit stage right. *National Review, 60* (22), 8–12.

Goldstein, M., & Henry, D. (2008). A money mystery at Lehman. *Business Week, 4104* (October 22), 34–35.

Guerrant, E. O. (1950). *Roosevelt's good neighbor policy*. Albuquerque, NM: University of New Mexico Press.

Hamerlinck, J. (2005). MTV and morality. In A. Tomasino (Ed.), *Music and culture* (pp. 43–46). New York: Pearson.

Hansen, C. H., & Hansen, R. D. (1990). The influence on sex and violence on the appeal of rock music videos. *Communication Research, 17*, 212–234.

Hersch, S. M. (2004). *Chain of command: The road from 9/11 to Abu Ghraib*. New York: Harper Collins.

Hester, J. P. (2003). *The ten commandments*. Jefferson, NC: McFarland.

Hightower, J. (2003). *Thieves in high places*. New York: Viking.

Holzer, H. (2004). Why Lincoln matters. Orlando, FL: Harcourt.

Hudson, K. (2009). Loan deadline passes for general growth. *Wall Street Journal*, *253* (28), C13.

Ikenberry, G. J. (2007). Is American multilateralism in decline? In *Paradoxes of power: U.S. foreign policy in a changing world* (pp. 63–71). Boulder, CO: Paradigm.

James, J. C., & Tanner, C. K. (1993). Standardized testing of young children. *Journal of Research and Development in Education*, *26* (3), 143–152.

Jeynes, W. (2006). Standardized tests and Froebel's original kindergarten model. *Teachers College Record*, *108* (10), 1937–1959.

———. (2007). *American educational history: School, society, and the common good*. Thousand Oaks, CA: Sage Publications.

Johnson, P. (1997). *A history of the American people*. New York: Harper Collins.

Judis, J. (2007). What Woodrow Wilson can teach today's imperialists. In D. Skidmore (Ed.), *Paradoxes of power: U.S. foreign policy in a changing world* (pp. 63–71). Boulder, CO: Paradigm.

Kaufman, P., Chen, X., Choy, S. P., Ruddy, S. A., Miller, A. K., & Fleury, J. K. (2000). *Indicators of school crime & safety 2000*. Washington, D.C.: U.S. Department of Justice.

Kirk, R. (1953). *The conservative mind, from Burke to Santayana*. Chicago: Regnery Company.

Kirsh, S. J. (2006). *Children, adolescents and media violence*. Thousand Oaks, CA: Sage Publications.

Kiviat, B. (2008). Need a loan? *Time*, *172* (15), 40–41.

Krajicek, D. J. (1998). *Scopped*. New York: Columbia University Press.

Kuntz, R., Brownback, S., & Lieberman, J. (2000). Heavy metal music contributes to teen suicide. In T. L. Roleff (Ed.), *Teen suicide* (pp. 9–12). San Diego, CA: Greenhaven Press.

Ladson-Billings, G. (2000). Fighting for our lives: Preparing teachers to teach African American students. *Journal of Teacher Education*, *51* (3), 206–214.

Lal, S. R., Lal, D., & Achilles, C. M. (1993). *Handbook on gangs in schools: Strategies to reduce gang-related activities*. Thousand Oaks, CA: Corwin Press.

Leary, D. (2008). *Why we suck: A feel good guide to staying fat, loud, lazy, and stupid*. New York: Viking.

Lewy, G. (1996). *Why America needs religion*. Grand Rapids, MI: Eerdmans.

Lieberman, J. (2006). *The shooting game: The making of school shooters.* Santa Ana, CA: Seven Locks Press.

————. (2008). *School shootings: What every parent and educator needs to know to protect our children.* New York: Citadel Press.

Love, J. (2008). Contested morality in U.S. foreign policy. In D. K. Lennard (Ed.), *Enemy combatants, terrorism, and armed conflict* (pp. 51–63). Westport, CT: Praeger.

MacNair, R. M. (2008). Introduction: The power of being consistent. In R. M. MacNair (Ed.), *Consistently opposing killing* (pp. 1–8). Westport, CT: Praeger.

MacNair, R. M., & Zunes, S. (2008). The direct killing of racism and poverty. In R. M. MacNair (Ed.), *Consistently opposing killing* (pp. 55–60). Westport, CT: Praeger.

Matera, D. (2001). *A cry for character.* Paramus, NJ: Prentice Hall.

Matson, C. (2001). Liberalism and republicanism. In M. K. Cayton & W. Williams (Eds.), *The Encyclopedia of American cultural and intellectual history* (pp. 169–175). New York: Scribner.

May, E. R. (1975). *The making of the Monroe doctrine.* Cambridge, MA: Harvard University Press.

McClellan, B. E. (1999). *Moral education in America.* New York: Teachers College Press.

McKay, D., & Scott, H. M. (1983). *The rise of the great powers, 1648–1815.* London: Longman.

Meehan, M. (2008). The left has betrayed the sanctity of life: Consistency demands concern for the unborn. In R. M. MacNair (Ed.), *Consistently opposing killing* (pp. 19–24). Westport, CT: Praeger.

Merritt, N. (2000). Teen suicide is a serious problem. In T. L. Roleff (Ed.), *Teen suicide* (pp. 9–12). San Diego, CA: Greenhaven Press.

Morris, D., & McGann, E. (2008). *Fleeced.* New York: Harper.

Muolo, P., & Padilla, M. (2008). *Chain of blame: How Wall Street caused the mortgage and credit crisis.* Hoboken, NJ: Wiley & Sons.

Neuhaus, R. J. (1984). *The naked public square: Religion and democracy in America.* Grand Rapids, MI: Eerdmans.

Newman, K. S. (2004). *Rampage: The social roots of school shootings.* New York: Basic Books.

Nussbaum, B. (2002). Can you trust ANYBODY anymore? *Business Week,* January 28, p. 30.

Nye, J. S., Jr. (2007). *Paradoxes of power: U.S. foreign policy in a changing world,* edited by D. Skidmore (pp. 27–32). Boulder, CO: Paradigm.

O'Higgins, R. E. (2004). CEO compensation. In G. G. Brenkert (Ed.), *Corporate integrity and accountability* (pp. 218–237). Thousand Oaks, CA: Sage Publications.

Perkins, D. (1955). *A history of the Monroe Doctrine.* Boston, MA: Little Brown.

Perrone, V. (1990). How did we get here? Testing in the early grades: The games grown-ups play. In C. Kamii (Ed.), *Testing in the early grades* (pp. 1–13). Washington, D.C.: National Association for the Education of Young Children.

Plato. (2000). *The republic.* Cambridge, MA: Cambridge University Press.

———. (2004). *Protagoras and Meno.* Ithaca, NY: Cornell University Press.

Robar, K. (2000). *Intelligence, internment, and relocating: Roosevelt's executive order 9066.* Seattle, WA: Kikar.

Robinson, G. (2001). *By order of the president: FDR and the internment of Japanese Americans.* Cambridge, MA: Harvard University Press.

Rochlin, S. A. (2004). Principles with process. In G. G. Brenkert (Ed.), *Corporate integrity and accountability* (pp. 207–217). Thousand Oaks, CA: Sage Publications.

Scott, D., & Nimmo, B. (2000). *Rachel's tears.* Nashville, TN: Thomas Nelson.

Sechser, T. S. (2007). The effects of September 11: A rift between Europe and America. In D. Skidmore (Ed.), *Paradoxes of power: U.S. foreign policy in a changing world* (pp. 27–32). Boulder, CO: Paradigm.

Shermer, M. (2004). *The science of good and evil.* New York: New York Times.

Shettles, L. B., & Rorvik, D. (1986). Human life begins at conception. In D. L. Bender (Ed.), *Abortion: Opposing viewpoints* (pp. 16–22). St. Paul, MN: Greenhaven Press.

Shiskin, P. (2009). When "rescue" means eviction. *Wall Street Journal, 253* (46), D1–D3.

Snyder, H. N., & Sickmund, M. (1995). *Juvenile offenders and victims: A focus on violence.* Pittsburgh, PA: National Center for Juvenile Justice.

Stevens, M. L. (2001). *Kingdom of children.* Princeton, NJ: Princeton University Press.

Stone, R. H. (2008). *Moral reflections on foreign policy in a religious war.* Lanham, MD: Rowman & Littlefield.

Sykes, C. J. (1995). *Dumbing down our kids: Why America's children feel good about themselves, but can't read, write, or add.* New York: St. Martin's Press.

Thomson, G. (2008). *I shot a man in Reno.* New York: Continuum.

Thygerson, K. J. (1973). *The effect of government housing and mortgage credit programs on savings and loan associations.* Chicago, IL: U.S. Savings and Loan League.

Tomasino, A. (2005). *Music and culture.* New York: Pearson.

Twerski, A. J. (1995). *Life's too short: Pull the plug on self-defeating behavior and turn on the power of self-esteem*. New York: St. Martin's Press.

U.S. Congress. (2000). *OPEC's policies: A threat to the U.S. economy*. Washington, D.C.: U.S. Congress.

U.S. Senate Subcommittee on the Judiciary. (2005). Children, violence, and the media: A report for parents and policy makers. In A. Tomasino (Ed.), *Music and culture* (pp. 62–80). New York: Pearson.

VanDeMark, B. (1991). *Into the quagmire: Lyndon Johnson and the escalation of the Vietnam War*. New York: Oxford University Press.

Van Luijk, H. (2004). Integrity in the private, the public, and corporate domain. In G. G. Brenkert (Ed.), *Corporate integrity and accountability* (pp. 38–54). Thousand Oaks, CA: Sage Publications.

Victors, M., & McNamee, M. (2002). The betrayed investor. *Business Week*, February 25, pp. 105–115.

Vogl, F. (2004). The U.S. business scandals. In G. G. Brenkert (Ed.), *Corporate integrity and accountability* (pp. 133–147). Thousand Oaks, CA: Sage Publications.

Washington, G. (1796). *Farewell address*, September 19.

Weil, J., Barrionvevo, A., & Bryan-Law, C. (2002). Anderson wins, lifts U.S. Enron case. *Wall Street Journal*, June 17, p. A1.

Wempe, J., & Donaldson, T. (2004). The practicality of pluralism. In G. G. Brenkert (Ed.), *Corporate integrity and accountability* (pp. 24–37). Thousand Oaks, CA: Sage Publications.

Will, G. (1982). *The pursuit of virtue*. New York: Simon & Schuster.

Wilson, S. (2008). *Great Satan's rage: American negativity and rap/metal in the age of supernationalism*. Manchester: Manchester University Press.

Wirtz, W. (1977). *On further examination*. New York: College Entrance Examination Board.

Wood, B. (1961). *The making of the good neighbor policy*. New York: Columbia University Press.

Wright, D. C. (2001). *The history of China*. Westport, CT: Greenwood.

Zoba, W. M. (2000). *Day of reckoning: Columbine & the search for the American soul*. Grand Rapids, MI: Brazos Press.

9

———❖———

A NATION WITHOUT
ABSOLUTE VALUES

There is little question that one of the overriding trends that has taken place in American culture since the removal of prayer, Bible instruction, and most character training from the public schools is the rise of an emphasis on relativism and a decline in the cherishing of certain absolute values. Such a plethora of social scientists have noted this trend such that its reality is virtually undeniable. This is not to say that this trend is purely a consequence of the 1962 and 1963 Supreme Court decisions. There were a myriad of concurrent trends, especially in the family, that also contributed to the decline in an emphasis on absolute values. Soaring divorce rates, which started in exactly 1963, surging consumption of illegal drugs that started at almost exactly the same time, and the tumultuous cultural turmoil produced by the Vietnam War and the hippie movement were also salient factors. Moreover, these factors likely acted upon each other in contributing to the decline in an adherence to absolute values. It is also incontrovertible that the majority of the Supreme Court justices serving on the bench when they handed down the 1962 and 1963 decisions were considerably farther to the left than the American public as a whole. Nevertheless, it is hard to imagine that the removal of character instruction from what had historically been such a main source, that is, the schools, of that education would not influence student character in much the same way that the removal of math instruction would impact the average mathematical abilities of children in that school. To argue that the removal of character instruction from the public schools would not have much of an impact contradicts the innumerable host of educators who worked so diligently to ensure it would maintain its central place in the curriculum because they believed that it did make such an indelible impact. In short, one could easily assert that to maintain that somehow the removal of a considerable portion of moral instruction from the schools would have only a perfunctory impact, whereas somehow the removal of an academic subject would have a considerable influence appears naïve at best and understates the vital role that teachers have in the lives of their students. To insist that teacher influence is limited only to certain subjects is contrary to common sense and does not find support in the research literature (Barnard, 1843; Blanshard, 1963; Bloom, 1987; Jeynes, 2007a, 2007b, 2010; Kliebard, 1969; Likona, 1976; Mann, 1849; Michaelsen, 1970; Ruggles, 1950; Sikorski, 1993).

In one sense, it is easy to understand how relativism grew in the United States. There were a number of factors that were evident. First, the fact that the country is an amalgamation of people from different cultures necessitates some degree of acceptance by the members of the general populace. Second, it is also true that one can adhere to absolute values to an excessive degree so that the gray areas of life are underemphasized to an unrealistic extent. This tendency almost guarantees that there will be pendulum swings in the opposite direction from time to time. Third, historically, as nations have become wealthier they have tended to focus on money and pleasure more and less on life's more intrinsic values such as love, truth, justice, and family. Notwithstanding, the unmitigated degree to which many Americans dismiss absolute values or at least insist that they do is unfathomable. Although within this context, one would be wise to concur with Plato's assertion that he had met many people who claimed to be relativists, but he never actually met one. Plato asserted that everyone has some absolute values whether they confess that they do or not (Eisenstadt, 1967; Feyerabend, 1987; Jeynes, 2007a; Nardo, 2000, 2001; Plato, 2000, 2004).

Nevertheless, it is patent that Americans do not adhere to absolute moral truths the way that they once did. This seems particularly difficult to comprehend because the more the nation has developed technologically, the more it is axiomatic that the universe is replete with absolute truths and in fact its daily function is infinitely dependent on the operation of many of these truths. The prime numbers are the same now as they were in 1876 and 1776 and AD 30. The same holds for the square root of 3, the square root of 2, and the hypotenuse of a right triangle with a base of 4 and a height of 3. The speed of sound is what it is at sea level with slight variations due to atmospheric conditions and the speed of light is what it is. High tide and low tides are amazingly predictable, as are eclipses and the times of the sunrise and sunset. The world appears much more dominated by the intricate workings of absolute principles than relativistic ones. Does it not seem likely that there exist absolute principles in the moral realm as well? Surely, there is room for situational factors in considering questions of morals and ethics. However, it would seem wise and discerning to admit that a person who does not acknowledge the existence of absolute values, asserting that everything is relative, is being just as intransigent and insular as one who does not acknowledge the presence of gray areas that at times exist between the white and the black (Carter, 1993; Feyerabend, 1987; Reed, 1994).

Over the past five decades, the American people have not sought a proper balance between adhering to absolute and relativistic values. Instead, they have often sought out a personal philosophy that is devoid of any sense of absolute right and wrong. The reality of the matter, however, is that relativism and absolute values are at antipodes. As Joseph Margolis (1989, p. 236) asserts, "Relativism obliges us to retreat from bipolar truth values." If historical precedent is any indication, when such a retreat takes place even the most potent societies decay from within (Carter, 1993; Feyerabend, 1987; Reed, 1994).

RELATIVISM, TOLERANCE, AND SELF-CONTRADICTIONS

Some philosophers and social scientists argue in favor of relativism on the basis of the need for tolerance. However, there is nothing contradictory about maintaining absolute values and demonstrating tolerance toward those of other opinions. In fact, the irony is that tolerance is actually more consistent with those who espouse absolute values than those who are relativists. Those who esteem absolute values can easily argue that tolerance is an absolute value, worthy of impassioned pursuit. Relativists, in contrast, are in the awkward and seemingly self-contradictory position of arguing favor of relativism by asserting that tolerance is an unalterable value. In other words, relativists are in the unavoidable position of frequently appealing to a person's sense of absolute right and wrong in order to convince people of the accuracy of a relativistic perspective (Arkes, 1986; Harman & Thomson, 1996; Holzer, 2004; Kaufman, 1960; McCarthy, 1989; Schaeffer & Koop, 1979). McCarthy (p. 262) states that just because a person acknowledges the fact that different people have distinct points of view does not mean that "you overlook that some views are better than others."

One of the greatest weaknesses of relativism, generally, is that it is self-contradictory. That is, those who espouse relativism assert that relativism is absolutely true (Arkes, 1986; Kaufman, 1960). In other words, advocates of this viewpoint use arguments normally propounded to support absolute values to contend that relativism is the right perspective. Kaufman notes, "The criticism here usually takes the following form: Relativism is logically inconsistent and self-contradictory in that, on the one hand, it presupposes certain logical criteria as of exclusive significance in formulating its own theory, while on the other hand, the theory itself is directed precisely to showing that these criteria are not of exclusive significance." Kaufman (p. 9) continues by stating, "This charge that relativism is finally self-contradictory is really the most fundamental problem with which relativistic theory must deal."

THE DANGERS OF RELATIVIST THINKING

To some, on the surface, the notion of relativism appears harmless. However, as one examines the potential ramifications of relativistic beliefs, the eventual consequences can be substantial. Kaufman (1960, p. 4) states, "And when men can no longer bring themselves to take a position on issues of truth and value, human culture cannot long survive." Francis Schaeffer and C. Everett Koop make an interesting observation along these lines. They assert that whether one maintains absolute values, especially when it pertains to loving one another, often determines the extent and the worth of that society. They aver, "The final measure of mankind's humanity is how humanly people treat one another" (Schaeffer & Koop, 1979, p. 15). Schaeffer and Koop believe that the United States and the West have veered away from their Judeo-Christian roots and have incorporated a more relativistic approach. They declare, "Why has our society changed? The answer is clear. The consensus of our society no longer rests on a Judeo-Christian base, but rather on a humanistic one . . . It puts men rather than God as the center of all things" (Schaeffer & Koop, 1979, p. 20).

DO CULTURAL DIFFERENCES AND CULTURAL RELATIVISM DEMAND RELATIVISM RATHER THAN ABSOLUTE VALUES?

A great deal of the argument for relativism rests in disputes about the place of cultural relativism. The idea behind cultural relativism is that virtually everyone is significantly influenced by the culture in which he or she was reared (Herskovits, 1972; Hutchings, 1972; Kasich, 2006; Kaufman, 1960). Many social scientists are convinced "of the overwhelming importance of culture in determining human personality" (Herskovits, 1972, p. vii). In fact, on this basis Herskovits (p. v) was convinced that one needed to treat "anthropology as one of the humanities rather than as a science." Many social scientists believe that this is an appropriate approach. In fact, some social scientists have embraced this approach to such an extent that they take for granted the "relativity of truth" and view it as "a demonstrated fact" (Kaufman, 1960, p. 3).

Those who advocate the relativist approach sometimes overlook the fact that to maintain that "everything is relative" can lead to illogical conclusions. As Alasdaiv MacIntyre (1989, p. 183) observes, relativists can often paint themselves into a corner if they say it "seems true to such and such persons." Joseph Margolis (1989, p. 236) adds, "Relativism obliges us to retreat from bipolar truth-values." To reject all absolute values or even the vast majority of them, Mohanty (1989, p. 339) asserts, is "ill-conceived" and "indefensible." Mohanty (p. 339) makes a profound point when he avers, "Ethical standards found in different cultures are only in apparent conflict with each other. Plurality exists only at the surface. At some deeper level there is only one set of moral standards to which everybody should conform, and it is possible to discover this singular standard of universal morality through rational means."

It is, of course, one thing to declare that there are *some* matters that are relative. Those who espouse the existence of absolute values are quick to admit this. Differences in taste, perspectives, and circumstances necessarily leave room for some degree of differences by culture. This acknowledgment facilitates mutual respect and thwarts judgmental attitudes (Herskovits, 1972).

Some people assert that there must be cultural relativism in order for there to be mutual respect among people from different cultures. However, to declare that cultural relativism is a prerequisite for mutual respect is equivalent to asserting that in order for there to be mutual respect one must eliminate any consideration of right and wrong. This approach appears to assume that human pride is so entrenched that one is unable to admit that his or her nation has been wrong at times. No nation or culture has even approached perfection. It would appear to be more within the scope of realism to admit that one's home nation has at times erred rather than to assert a parochial declaration that values are all relative (Herskovits, 1972).

Cultural relativism not only appears to suggest that people have difficulty swallowing their pride and admitting their nation's faults but also appears to exacerbate pride's presence in cultural dialogue. If one espouses the cultural relativism perspective, then it is easy for one to contend that one's nation acted consistently with its cultural values and therefore, at least according to its own cultural milieu, acted in the right way. What frequently results is that both sides leave their dialogue convinced that his or her nation acted appropriately, with little sense of needed humility which is so helpful in intercultural dialogue. Rather, most frequently there is simply an agreement to disagree. Although such conclusions to intercultural discussions are often not disastrous, they do not encourage the improvement of intercultural relations (Feyerabend, 1987).

Nevertheless, cultural relativism has its advocates because, as Melville Herskovits (1972, p. 93) avers, "The values by which men live are relative to the particular kind of cultural learning they have experienced." The problem with this statement is that while it may be true, at least in part, that the values that they live by are relative to what they have learned in their given culture, it assumes a dichotomous "yes" or "no" when the reality is that people learn their values from a variety of sources. Each of these sources may or may not be in congruence with one's culture. It is even quite possible that one's own family might instruct a child in ways that are contrary to the culture. In fact, there is a considerable amount of research that parental and cultural values are often at odds (Carter, 1993; Jeynes, 2005, 2007a).

The Intersection of Absolute Truth and Cultural Teaching

One of the mistakes that advocates of cultural relativism make is that they contend that if one comprehends cultural teaching, then one will be able to adequately measure people's moral behavior. However, the reality is that cultural teaching only gives one some insight into a person's behavior. Cultural teaching does provide some useful insight into value-based behavior and people who promote absolute values should not overlook this fact.

The interaction of absolute values and cultural teaching can be best summarized in Table 9.1 (Herskovits, 1972).

As one can see in Table 9.1, cultural teaching plays a major role in determining moral behavior in cells A and B. Hence, there is no question that cultural teaching does impact moral behavior. Nevertheless, it is also true that there are both positive and negative behaviors that people engage in that either is not culturally taught (C and D) or a given culture may actually teach against (E and F). In fact, the moral behavior that most people tend to admire the most is positive moral behavior that is done contrary to cultural norms (Branch, 1988; King, 1998).

From this grid, one can compute that appreciating the influence of cultural norms of moral behavior is fundamental if one is to apprehend the value-based behavior that a given individual engages in. An understanding of these norms also contributes to an understanding of why people behave the way that they do. It is patent, however, that appreciating these cultural norms is hardly sufficient for understanding an individual's behavior nor the reasoning that rests behind that behavior. If one examines Bronfenbrenner's Ecological Systems Model, one appreciates the fact that culture is but one factor in a litany of them (Bronfenbrenner, 1979).

Table 9.1 Interaction of Cultural Teaching and Moral Behavior in Helping to Explain Value-Based Behavior

	Right	Wrong
Promotes	Positive moral behavior encouraged by culture (A)	Negative moral behavior encouraged by culture (B)
Does not promote	Positive moral behavior practiced by individual without cultural support (C)	Negative moral behavior practiced by individual without cultural support (D)
Discourages	Positive moral behavior practiced by individual against the prevailing culture (E)	Negative moral behavior practiced by individual against the prevailing culture (F)

ABSOLUTE VALUES AND FAMILY AND CHILDREN

One of the areas in which the removal of absolute values has had the greatest impact is that of family issues. For centuries, people around the world have assumed that a child living with its two biological parents was the ideal environment in which that child was to be raised. Historically, individuals have concluded based primarily on observation and interpersonal facts that the physical, emotional, and spiritual oneness that results from marriage is most likely to produce a healthy environment for children. The belief was that if both parents were physically related to the child, they would possess the love, compassion, and natural intimacy to consistently act in the child's best interests and, most importantly, provide that loving environment that the child so desperately needs. It was asserted that the physical bond of marriage and the stability of that relationship were extremely salient if the child was to live up to his or her potential (Cherlin, 1992; Jeynes, 2002; McLanahan & Sandefur, 1994; Wallerstein & Blakeslee, 1989; Zill & Nord, 2004).

When the divorce rate suddenly began to surge in 1963, the overwhelming number of Americans believed that this trend was a negative one. However, by the time that a significant number of social scientists began to examine the effects of divorce in the late 1970s, absolute values were not in vogue while relative values were. The result is that numerous researchers concluded that parental divorce had virtually no impact on children and that family structure was of little or no consequence when it came to the psychological and educational welfare of youth. The conclusion by many in the research community that parental family structure has little influence on young children and adolescents had a profound influence on the advice that psychologists and family counselors gave their clients. Unlike in past generations, myriad counselors did not discourage spouses who were considering divorce to proceed with the breakup. Moreover, some psychologists even encouraged marital dissolution with the assumption that it was better to initiate a marital breakup than it was for they and their children to live in an atmosphere of tension and strife (Beer, 1992; Herzog & Sudia, 1971; Jeynes, 2002; McLanahan & Sandefur, 1994).

In addition, psychologists concluded that parental remarriage was preferred over remaining in the divorced single-parent family structure not only for the couple but also for the children. They surmised that the presence of two caregivers was better than one, even if one of them was not biologically related to the child. They further opined that the major advantage of the two-parent family over the single-parent one was that there were two people serving the needs of the children. The fact that there were two workers tending to the welfare of the children would make the reconstituted family resulting from remarriage of equal utility to that was made up of two biological parents (Zaslow, 1988, 1989).

Although the influence of a relativistic framework contributed to the hypotheses and conclusions that many social scientists made regarding the influence of family structure, many of the writings of these individuals were not based on scientific fact, but rather were based on theorizing and conjecture (Zaslow, 1988, 1989).

During the 1980s, 1990s, and 2000s, a considerable amount of research based on statistical research indicated that parental family structure had substantial psychological and educational effects on youth. For example, children from intact families on average outperform their counterparts in divorced single-parent and divorced remarried families. In fact, generally speaking, the further a student's parental family structure is from that of a biological intact family, the more of a negative impact it has on children's academic outcomes. For example, research indicates that on average students from single-parent never-married families do not perform as well as students from single-parent divorced families. This is largely because children from a singe-parent divorced family, on average, have had considerably more access to their noncustodial parent, usually the father, than their counterparts in single-parent never-remarried families. Divorces may occur when the children are four, eight, twelve, sixteen, or a wide variety of other ages. Because of this, the children involved in the divorce have often had a fairly extensive exposure to their fathers during the years prior to their divorce. In addition, children from divorced families often have access to their fathers after the divorce has taken place. In contrast, children from never-married single-parent families often do not even know who their father is. Estimates are that between five and ten million Americans do not know who their father is. Because of this, there are various programs designed to help identify who the father of children is (Diamond, 2006; Hetherington & Clingempeel, 1992; Jeynes, 2000, 2002; Wallerstein & Blakeslee, 1989).

The fact that the farther one departs from an intact family, the greater the negative impact on children also likely helps explain why children from divorced remarried families do more poorly in school and have more behavioral problems than youth from divorced single-parent families. In addition, children from cohabiting families also do not do as well in school as children in divorced remarried families. This fact also supports the notion that the amount of time one spends with one's parents influences outcomes for children. The number of family transitions is another factor that likely influences the relationship between parental family structure and the educational outcomes of children. Each change that a family encounters requires a certain degree of adjustment on the part of children. Considering this additional factor would explain why when adjusted for socioeconomic status children from cohabiting families do not do as well as children from never-married single-parent families, and why children from remarried divorced families do not do as well as their counterparts in divorced single-parent families (Hetherington & Clingempeel, 1992; Heyman, 1992; Jeynes, 2002, 2006a, 2006b).

Similar tendencies to those just delineated for academic data also exist for specific behavioral trends. For example, adolescents differ considerably in their propensity for taking illegal drugs and alcohol. As in the case with scholastic outcomes, generally speaking, the farther one departs from the intact family structure, the more likely an adolescent is to partake of illegal drugs. The same pattern holds for the adolescent consumption of alcohol and cigarettes. Once again, those youth from family structures that are most associated with less access to the biological parents are the most likely to consume drugs and to do so fairly regularly. Research studies also indicate that youth from nontraditional family structures are more likely to engage in premarital sex, have promiscuous attitudes, and behave inappropriately in schools (Jeynes, 2006a, 2006b; Wallerstein & Blakeslee, 1989).

The evidence that youth from single-parent families are less likely to excel academically and behaviorally is undeniably strong. It is patent that for youth on the whole it is best for them to have two biological parents in the home. Yet in spite of this evidence, those who espouse a relativistic view assert that all family structures have equal utility (Jeynes, 2002, 2006a, 2006b; Zill & Nord, 1994).

ABSOLUTE VALUES AND THE VALUE OF LIFE

One of the convictions most closely associated with absolute values is the inherent worth of life. The exhortation not to murder is one of the

Ten Commandments and has equivalents in nearly all of the major religions in the world. Exhortations not to murder exist in Hinduism, Buddhism, Islam, and Mormonism (Beckwith, 1993; Cooper, 2003; Edwards, 1986; Meehan, 2008; Sharma, 1994).

The emphasis on the value of life applies to a plethora of different issues, including one-on-one murder, manslaughter, gun control, abortion, war, and capital punishment. Historically, absolute values have been based on religious teaching and have taught that each person is unique and precious. The Buddhist teaching is that each person is so precious that the ultimate goal of life should be to enter nirvana, which is a state without pain. According to Buddhist thought, in order to obtain this state one must empty oneself of desire. This is because it is frustrated desires that produce pain (Marrou, 1956; Sharma, 1994).

In Christian thought, each person is made in the image of God, which makes each person inherently valuable and potentially having a divine purpose. Islam also views each person as a creation of God (Marrou, 1956).

The inherent value of each human being is key in addressing each of the issues addressed below. Unfortunately, however, with the increase of relativism, people frequently see humans differently than they did before. There may be a number of contributing factors to this, including the rise of the teaching of evolution which instructs people to believe that they evolved from an ape-like ancestor rather than image of God. Although those who believe in theistic evolution assert that there need not be any inherent contradiction between evolution and believing that one is made in the image of God, there are a vast number of other factors that may have contributed to the rise of relativism and less value being placed on each human being. Urbanization may have been such a factor. Urbanization means that people are exposed to a wide range of ideas, which may enhance any trends toward relativism. The very presence of crowds might also make people more irritable and less compassionate toward specific individuals. Some of the other potential reasons will be addressed under the points listed below (Myers, 2000; Noll, 2002).

Murder

Many social scientists argue that the murder of one individual by another is not taken with the degree of shock and seriousness that it once was. Murder is still regarded as morally wrong by general American populace, but one can argue that two trends have emerged that indicate that people's attitudes toward murder is changing. First, people witness many more news reports of murder than they did in past generations. Some contend that the rife reporting of murders has yielded callous hearts, which have become less sensitized to the gruesome nature of this act. Second, over the last four decades, myriad people are more likely to feel for the assailant, particularly if the aggressor pleads insanity or is young (Lieberman, 2006, 2008; Newman, 2004).

One of the most incisive examples of the above trends occurred with the school shootings. First, one can argue that as time has gone on, people's hearts have become somewhat hardened to the suffering that results from these shootings. For example, school shooting emerged as major problem in the 1960s, but they were limited to urban settings. Hence, these events did not receive more than a minimal degree of national publicity. A considerable degree of the reason for this is because individuals often respond differently to urban violence as opposed to suburban and rural violence (Coleman, 2004; Jeynes, 2007a; Lieberman, 2006, 2008). Often when one hears of urban violence, his or her response is along the lines of "Well, that is too bad. But those kind of things happen in L.A. You know L.A." In contrast, when one hears of an identical event taking place in a wealthy U.S. suburb, such as Mission Viejo, California, the reaction is more like this: "Mission Viejo? Mission Viejo? What is this world coming to?"

Some have complained that there is a double standard between the way urban and suburban or rural school shootings are reported. The media tends to report urban shootings along the following lines: "In the news today, eight children were killed and eleven injured when two adolescents . . ." In contrast, when a school shooting occurs in a suburban or rural area, a typical report begins, "This is a special report . . ."

In addition, presently even when there are school shootings in suburban or rural areas, the media gives less attention to these events and the general populace appears more inured to these events than before (Lieberman, 2006, 2008).

A second trend evident in the school shootings is that some people treat the aggressors as victims, asserting that they were bullied, underachievers, and so forth. Those who focus on the value of life assert that this perception of the assailants as victims is overdone and diminishes the loss inflicted on families as a result of the murders. In addition, examination of the Web sites of the assailants and interviews with those acquainted with them indicate that the aggressors have a plethora of malicious anger and bitterness (Brown & Merritt, 2002; Newman, 2004; Scott & Nimmo, 2000).

Gun Control

Death or injury by gunfire frequently occurs when the one holding the gun accidentally fires the revolver or when it is done out of anger, rage, or bitterness. Because of this the plethora of guns is often associated with higher rates of death for such actions as murder, manslaughter, self-defense, and accident. Estimates of just how many guns there are in the United States vary considerably, especially because some are obtained illegally. Estimates are that there are between 250 and 300 million guns in the United States. With the vast number of guns that there are in the United States, the potential for gun-related deaths is astronomical (Davidson, 1993; Diaz, 1999; Fuectman, 1988).

There are some who contend that the availability of guns actually reduces the likelihood of death (Goldberg, 2007; Lott, 1998). They argue that shooting rampages such as those that took place at Virginia Tech would have been preventable or at least containable if someone with a gun had been on hand (Goldberg, 2007; Kellner, 2008). And indeed, it is probably so in the case of wide-scale shootings if right-minded people possess a pistol, fewer people will be slain. Nevertheless, this likelihood must be balanced out with the fact there would be fewer accidents and passionate actions that involve guns if there were fewer guns available. The reality is that when a person is inundated with feelings of anger and bitterness to the point of doing something violent, an aggressor will often seek the most lethal and effective weapon available. It would seem that fewer guns would save lives in most cases. Although hunters are quick to point out that the constitutional right to bear arms should be respected and indeed they should be, there are many kinds of weapons such as submachine guns that are purely killing machines that should be outlawed. Although the leisurely pursuits of hunters are worthy of discussion, the primary focus of such discussions should be on trying to preserve life. When most people speak of pro-life, they refer to a position in the abortion debate. However, the debate surrounding gun control should be regarded as part of a pro-life philosophy as well (Davidson, 1993; Diaz, 1999; Fuectman, 1988).

Abortion

Most people acknowledge deep down in their hearts that a baby in the womb is a living individual. The child has a heartbeat by four weeks in the womb, sucks its thumb by 9 weeks, and as much as possible even flees for his or her life when the doctor initiates an abortion. To many the issue of abortion is complicated by the possibility of rape and incest. However, if one allows for abortion under such instances, this accounts for only 1 percent or 2 percent of abortions. Births sacrificing the life of the mother are also rare (Bajema, 1974; Beckwith, 1993; Faundes & Barzelatto, 2006; Fuectman, 1988; Saunders, 2006).

Beyond this, the primary debate then becomes one between a baby's life and a woman's right to choose. Indeed, a woman does have a right to choose, but the choice is at the time of intercourse. Beyond this, the life of the child must be considered before the situation of the mother. Increasingly, individuals want the blessing of a new life in the womb without accepting the responsibility of caring for that new life. Since the passage of *Roe v. Wade* in 1973, an average of between 1 and 1½ million abortions are performed each year. Abortion is one of the greatest examples of taking life too lightly (Beckwith, 1993; Faundes & Barzelatto, 2006; Fuectman, 1988; Lowe, 1987; MacNair, 2008).

Most of the largest religious bodies of the world oppose abortion. These groups assert that individuals need to act more responsibly before they decide to have sexual intercourse. If an additional child will be an inconvenience or a financial burden, then those engaging in intercourse need to consider these issues before having a physical relationship. This needs to be done in sensitivity to any potential baby's life (Bajema, 1974; Beckwith, 1993; Faundes & Barzelatto, 2006; Fuectman, 1988; Herring, 2003).

War

Many experts argue that Americans do not take warfare quite as seriously as they used to in the past. In modern days of video games in which computerized individuals clash creating pool of mechanized blood, many social scientists believe the act of war has been minimized and dehumanized. Consequently, according to these arguments in actual warfare, the death or suffering of the participants is no longer taken as seriously as it once was. Researchers believe that this fact especially applies to death and injury of the opponent soldiers. The assertion is therefore that many Americans, especially younger ones brought up in the video game era, do not have the compassion that they should toward those who die in war. Beyond this, there has been a particular insensitivity toward victims who are America's opponents. Somehow, there are some who assume that the lives of people from certain nations possess less value (Brock & Young, 1999; Cahill, 1994).

Increasingly, political, religious, and academic leaders have pointed out that for generations the United States was very reluctant to go to war. The United States generally did not go to war unless it was fired upon first or severely provoked. Since the Vietnam War, however, it appears that many Americans have changed their attitude toward war. War is supposedly more easily justifiable than it used to be. Americans appear to be less reluctant to go to war than was so in past generations. In the 1700s and 1800s and the first decades of the 1900s, American warfare was rare. However, beginning in the mid-1900s, the United States started to engage in warfare in increasing frequency, engaging in a major war every decade with the exception of the 1980s. It may be that Americans are weary of war when it comes to the possibility of losing their own lives, but may not take the loss of life among other nations as seriously as they should (Brock, 1998; Brock & Young, 1999; Cahill, 1994; Jeynes, 2007a; Johnson, 1997; Weddle, 2001).

ABSOLUTE VALUES AND CHARACTER EDUCATION IN THE EXEMPLARY SCHOOLS OF EAST ASIA

The leaders of the United States frequently point to East Asian systems of schooling as the best systems of elementary and secondary school education in the world. Although Americans have emphasized East Asian academic prowess and the tendency of their students to score about two years ahead of Americans, an increasing number of social scientists are focusing on the fact that their systems of character education are worthy of emulation as well. Unlike the contemporary situation in the United States, the Japanese still concentrate on teaching absolute values in their character education program. In contrast, Japan, for example, is seeking to increase its emphasis on moral education, concluding that those years when teachers significantly reduced their moral instruction resulted in sudden increases in juvenile crime (Cummings, 2003; Fitzpatrick, 1997; Jeynes, 2008; Levine & White, 1986; Stevenson & Stigler, 1992; White, 1987).

In most East Asian entities, that is, Japan, China, South Korea, Singapore, and Taiwan, the practice of character education is much like it was in the United States and other nations in the last third of the nineteenth century, when these Asian countries emulated educational practices in the West. The strategy that East Asian countries generally employ is to focus heavily on character instruction in the early years of a child's education. This emphasis emerges because the teachers and principals in these nations believe that the character training that occurs in these formative years establishes the foundation for academic and psychological development for many years to come. Although the structure of these moral education programs is American in nature, the actual content varies considerably by nation. In Japan and Singapore the content of the moral education is Confucian, in China it is based on the Communist worldview, in the Philippines it is Christian, and in South Korea it is mostly Christian and Buddhist. Of all of these nations, the mode of character education has changed the most in China and South Korea over the last 100 years. This is largely because of the Communist revolution in China in 1949 and the phenomenal growth of Christianity in South Korea since the Korean War. The number of Christians in South Korea is about the same as the number of Buddhists. South Korea hosts the largest church in the world, with a membership of about 750,000 and an average Sunday attendance of about 450,000. In each of these countries and their schools, absolute values are emphasized much more than is the case in the American society (Cho, 1989; Jeynes, 2006a, 2006b; Khan, 1997; Thorgerson, 1990).

ABSOLUTE VALUES AND THE DECLINE
OF ACADEMIC ACHIEVEMENT

For centuries educators believed the belief and attention to absolute values helped youth to perform well in school. The assertion was that a child's attention to absolute values and religion would give him or her a sense of purpose. This purpose in turn would produce a determination to excel in life in all things pertaining to the fulfillment of that purpose. Many social scientists believe that the infamous academic decline of the 1963–1980 period, particularly measured in SAT scores, was partially due to the decline in the teaching of absolute moral values in the school. During this period, SAT scores dropped for 17 consecutive years. Previous to this time, scores had never even dropped in two consecutive years in the history of the administration of the SAT. The decline in test scores was substantial enough (about 90 points on two sections combined) so that the Educational Testing Service (ETS), the designers of the SAT, undertook a major analysis of the test score decline to apprehend its root causes. Because of the controversy surrounding the achievement test score decline generally and the SAT score decline specifically, the ETS initiated the largest organized effort ever amassed to assess standardized test score trends. In 1977, because of the extensive debate surrounding the SAT decline, the College Board organized a panel of approximately 20–25 renowned educational researchers to address the question of what caused the protracted decline in SAT scores (Lipsitz, 1977; Marco, 1994; U.S. Department of Education, 2000; Will, 1982; Wirtz, 1977).

One of the first hypotheses that the ETS tested was to see if the SAT had somehow become more arduous during the years in question, despite their frequently lauded statistical efforts to make the test quite consistent throughout time. To the amazement of the College Board, the results indicated that the test had actually become 20 points easier. Hence, the 90-point drop was actually a 110-point drop. Once the ETS had determined that there was a 110-point decline, they undertook further analysis to determine the causes of this decline. Using statistical analysis, they determined that some of the decline was due to changes in the composition of students taking the SAT and the remainder of the decline was due to real academic change (Wirtz, 1977). Their investigation determined that the SAT score decline was due to both compositional and real academic factors to the extent listed in Table 9.2.

Table 9.2 Factors Contributing to the SAT Score Decline

	Compositional factors	Factors affecting academics
1963–1970	22.7 points (71%)	9.3 points (29%)
1970–1977	12.25 points (25%)	36.75 points (75%)
1977–1980	0 points	10.00 points
Test change	*7.6 points*	*12.4 points*
	42.55 points (37.7%)	68.45 points (62.3%)

The 42.55 points of compositional change was due to a higher percentage of students taking the exam, which would tend to somewhat depress the overall cohort average and a higher number of disadvantaged students taking the exam. The remainder of the 110-point decline, 68.45 points, was due to real academic decline. There were a number of factors that indicated that a large part of the decline in SAT scores was due to real academic factors (Wirtz, 1977).

First, beginning around 1963, other achievement tests showed commensurate declines during the same period. This includes almost every other major standardized test, including the ACT, the GRE, the ITBS, the ITED, and the Stanford Achievement Test (U.S. Department of Education, 2000). The Stanford Achievement Test comparing 1964 and 1973 achievement for grades 1–8 also demonstrates a trend similar to that of the ITBS. Reading and math scores showed slight increases for grades 1 and 2. Scores for 1973 dropped for grades 3–8, with the greatest decreases coming in the highest grades (see Table 9.3; Clearly & McCandless, 1976; U.S. Department of Education, 2000).

Second, the performance of American students on international comparison tests also suggests a decline, because the U.S. students fell further behind their international counterparts during the 1960s, 1970s, and 1980s.

Table 9.3 Decline in Academic Achievement on the Stanford Achievement Test, 1964–1973 (unit of measure is months of loss; Cooperman, 1985)

Grade	Reading	Math
8	−8	−18
7	−5	−14
6	−7	−12
5	−4	−9
4	−5	−4
3	−4	−2
2	+1	+4
1	+3	Not available

The decline was substantial enough so that by 1988 in the International Assessment of Educational Progress, the United States finished 12th out of the 12 nations that participated. Third, a decline in literacy rates in the United States during the 1970s and 1980s also confirmed an academic decline (Jeynes, 2007a; National Center for Education Statistics, 2001).

The decline in scores has remained largely intact, although it is less ostensible today because the ETS re-normed the SAT scores in 1995. The results of the verbal and math scores, though totaling in the low 900s at that time, were re-normed to equal 1,000. Most people were not aware of the re-norming, which was the hope of the ETS, and given that the scores were artificially elevated, complaints about chronically low nationwide average SAT scores abated over time (Fineberg, 1995; Young, 1995).

Possible Explanations the ETS Gave for the Real Academic Achievement Decline

Decline in Character Education in Society at Large

The ETS noted (Wirtz, 1977, pp. 42, 43) that one can "attribute the decline to a 'growing rejection of traditional Western religions' and . . . concern about a crisis in values is widely expressed . . . a revolution in values, including a decline in the Protestant work ethic . . . In general we find the sum of these contributions substantially helpful in suggesting the character of a period, covered by the score decline, which has been an unusually hard one to grow up in." The ETS (Wirtz, 1977, p. 41) panel observes:

> Although the panel's attention has been directed repeatedly to the facts of increased school ground violence and crime and juvenile alcoholism and drug addiction, we can add nothing here to what common knowledge and common sense already establish. These aberrations obviously affect not only the individuals directly involved, but the broader educational process, and they have been increasing as the SAT scores have been going down . . . What is causing the delinquent behavior?

A Decline in the Work Ethic

The College Board maintains that there was a decline in the work ethic during the 1963–1980 period. It maintains that there is "observable evidence of diminished seriousness of purpose" in students of the post-1963 era (Wirtz, 1977, p. 48). The College Board panel contends, "For whatever combination of reasons, there has been an apparent marked diminution in young people's learning motivation" (Wirtz, p. 48). The ETS suggests that the availability of the television played a major role in this trend (Schramm, 1977; Winn, 2002). However, the ETS acknowledges that the declining work ethic is probably not only a cause but also a result of other broader factors at work in society. It concludes, "It can hardly be coincidence that problems of discipline and absenteeism appear at a time when changing life styles and values in adult society, earlier physical maturity, higher mobility, drugs, and the pill are all interacting" (Wirtz, 1977, p. 35).

The Decline of the Family

The College Board observed that divorce rates, which had been in a decline from 1948 to 1962, suddenly started to soar in precisely 1963. Precisely, just as SAT scores declined 17 consecutive years before bottoming out in 1980, divorce rates rose 17 consecutive years, topping out in 1980 (U.S. Census Bureau, 2001; U.S. Department of Education, 2000). Regarding these trends, the College Board concluded, "There is probably more than coincidence between the decline in SAT scores and the drop in the number of children living in two-parent homes" (Wirtz, 1977, p. 34). Given this confluence of statistics, most social scientists agree that the decline of the family impacted achievement test scores during the 1963–1980 period. The panel adds, "Yet if the question is why those scores have been going down, few would respond without recognizing that part of the answer is almost certainly hidden in these gaps in present knowledge—about the effects of change on the whole meaning of family and youth decline" (Wirtz, 1977, p. 35).

CONCLUSION

Historically, where character education is practiced, there is almost always the assumption of the existence of absolute values. Because there has been a dearth of character instruction since 1962, it only follows that ultimately this will influence the percentage of Americans who adhere to absolute values. When one does not possess any or hardly any absolute values, one of the first areas that is influenced is the attitude that he or she has toward life. In fact, it is reasonable to conclude that it is on issues of life that one sees manifested the ultimate absolute values. Few would deny that many situations in life involve the application of relative values, but what will this world look like if humans insist on living in a self-determined world totally or largely without absolute values?

REFERENCES

Arkes, H. (1986). *First things.* Princeton, NJ: Princeton University Press.

Bajema, C. E. (1974). *Abortion and the meaning of personhood.* Grand Rapids, MI: Baker Book House.

Barnard, H. (1843). *Papers of Henry Barnard.* Manuscript collection of Trinity College Watkinson Library, Hartford, CT.

Beckwith, F. (1993). *Politically correct death.* Grand Rapids, MI: Baker Books.

Beer, W. R. (1992). *American stepfamilies.* New Brunswick, NJ: Transaction Publishers.

Blanshard, P. (1963). *Religion and the schools.* Boston, MA: Beacon Press.

Bloom, A. (1987). *The closing of the American mind.* New York: Simon & Schuster.

Branch, T. (1988). *Parting the waters: America in the King years, 1954–1963.* New York: Simon & Schuster.

Brock, P. (1998). *Varieties of pacifism.* Syracuse, NY: Syracuse University Press.

Brock, P., & Young, N. (1999). *Pacifism in the twentieth century.* Syracuse, NY: Syracuse University Press.

Bronfenbrenner, U. (1979). *The ecology of human development.* Cambridge, MA: Harvard University Press.

Brown, B., & Merritt, R. (2002). *No easy answers: The truth behind death at Columbine.* New York: Lantern Books.

Cahill, L. S. (1994). *Love your enemies: Discipleship, pacifism, and just war theory.* Minneapolis, MN: Fortress Press.

Carter, S. L. (1993). *The culture of disbelief.* Grand Rapids, MI: Baker Book House.

Cherlin, A. (1992). *Marriage, divorce and remarriage.* Cambridge, MA: Harvard University Press.

Cho, P. (1989). Ordeal and glory through the 30-year history of Yoido Full Gospel Church. Seoul: Yoido Full Gospel Church.

Clearly, T. A., & McCandless, S. A. (1976). *Summary of score changes (in other tests).* Princeton, NJ: Educational Testing Service.

Coleman, L. (2004). *The copycat effect.* New York: Paraview.

Cooper, D. E. (2003). *World philosophies: An historical introduction.* Malden, MA: Blackwell.

Cooperman, P., in National Committee on Excellence in Education. (1985). A nation at risk. In B. & R. Gross (Eds.), *The great school debate.* New York: Simon & Schuster.

Cummings, W. (2003). *The institutions of education: A comparative study of educational development in the six core nations.* Oxford: Symposium Books.

Davidson, O. G. (1993). *Under fire: The NRA and the battle for gun control.* New York: Holt.

Diamond, J. (2006). *Fatherless sons.* Hoboken, NJ: Wiley.

Diaz, T. (1999). *Making a killing.* New York: New Press.

Edwards, J. (1986). "The silent scream" proves the fetus is human. In D. L. Bender (Ed.), *Abortion: Opposing viewpoints* (pp. 38–41). St. Paul, MN: Greenhaven Press.

Eisenstadt, S. N. (1967). *The decline of empires.* Englewood Cliffs, NJ: Prentice Hall.

Faundes, A., & Barzelatto, J. (2006). *The human drama of abortion.* Nashville, TN: Vanderbilt University Press.

Feyerabend, P. (1987). *Farewell to reason.* London: Verso.

Fineberg, L. (1995). A new center for the SAT. *College Board Review,* 174, 8–13, 31–32.

Fitzpatrick, M. (1997). Severed heads adds to crime fears. *Times Educational Supplement,* no. 4232, p. 11.

Fuectman, T. G. (1988). *Consistent ethic of life: Cardinal Joseph Bernadin.* Chicago, IL: Loyola Press.

Goldberg, J. (2007). *Liberal fascism.* New York: Doubleday, Doran, & Company.

Harman, G., & Thomson, J. J. (1996). *Moral relativity and moral objectivity.* Cambridge, MA: Blackwell.

Herring, M. Y. (2003). *The pro-life/choice debate.* Westport, CT: Greenwood.

Herskovits, M. J. (1972). *Cultural relativism: Perspectives in cultural relativism.* New York: Random House.

Herzog & Sudia. (1971). *Boys in fatherless families.* Washington, D.C.: U.S. Department of Health, Education & Welfare.

Hetherington, E. M., & Clingempeel, W. G. (Eds.). Coping with marital transitions: A family systems perspective. *Monographs on the Society for Research in Child Development,* 57 (3/4), 1–242.

Heyman, J. R. (1992). The relationship between family structure as defined by parental marital status, family structure histories, gender, and various academic outcomes for seventh grade students in private schools (doctoral dissertation, University of San Francisco), abstract in *Dissertation Abstracts International,* AAG 9316055.

Holzer, H. (2004). *Why Lincoln matters.* Orlando, FL: Harcourt.

Hutchings, P. (1972). *Kant on absolute value.* Detroit, MI: Wayne State University.

Jeynes, W. (2000). The effects of several of the most common family structures on the academic achievement of eighth graders. *Marriage & Family Review,* 30 (1/2), 73–97.

———. (2002). *Divorce, family structure, and the academic success of children.* Binghamton, NY: Haworth Press.

———. (2005). A meta-analysis of the relation of parental involvement to urban elementary school student academic achievement. *Urban Education, 40* (3), 237–269.

———. (2006a). The impact of parental remarriage on children: A meta-analysis. *Marriage & Family Review, 40* (4), 75–102.

———. (2006b). The predictive nature of parental family structure on attitudes regarding premarital pregnancy and the consumption of marijuana. *Journal of Human Behavior in the Social Environment, 6* (1), 1–16.

———. (2007a). *American educational history: School, society, and the common good.* Thousand Oaks, CA: Sage Publications.

———. (2007b). The relationship between parental involvement and urban secondary school academic achievement: A meta-analysis. *Urban Education, 42* (1), 82–110.

———. (2008). What we should and should not learn from the Japanese and other East Asian education systems. *Educational Policy, 22* (6), 900–927.

———. (2010, in press). *The salience of the subtle aspects of parental involvement: Implications for school-based programs.* Teachers College Record.

Johnson, P. (1997). *A history of the American people.* New York: HarperCollins.

Kasich, J. (2006). *Stand for something: The battle for America's soul.* New York: Warner.

Kaufman, G. D. (1960). *Relativism, knowledge, and faith.* Chicago, IL: University of Chicago Press.

Kellner, D. (2008). *Guys and guns amok.* Boulder, CO: Paradigm.

Khan, Y. (1997). *Japanese moral education: Past and present.* Madison, NJ: Fairleigh Dickinson University Press.

King, M. L. (1998). In C. Carson (Ed.), *The autobiography of Martin Luther King, Jr.* New York: Warner.

Kliebard, H. M. (1969). *Religion and education in America.* Scranton, PA: International Textbook Company.

Levine, R. A., & White, M. (1986). *Human conditions: The cultural basis of educational development.* New York: Rutledge.

Lieberman, J. (2006). *The shooting game: The making of school shooters.* Santa Ana, CA: Seven Locks Press.

———. (2008). *School shootings: What every parent and educator needs to know to protect our children.* New York: Citadel Press.

Likona, T. (1976). *Moral development.* New York: Holt, Rinehart & Winston.

Lipsitz, L. (1977). *The test score decline: Meaning and issues.* Englewood Cliffs, NJ: Educational Technology Publications.

Lott, J. R. (1998). *More guns, less crime.* Chicago, IL: University of Chicago Press.

Lowe, J. M. (1987). Teaching self-worth and the sanctity of life. In J. K. Hoffmeier (Ed.), *Abortion* (pp. 139–148). Grand Rapids, MI: Baker Book House.

MacIntyre, A. (1989). Relativism, power, philosophy. In M. Krausz (Ed.), *Relativism: Interpretation and Confrontation* (pp. 182–204). Notre Dame: Notre Dame University.

MacNair, R. M. (2008). Introduction: The power of being consistent. In R. M. MacNair & S. Zunes (Eds.), *Consistently opposing killing* (pp. 1–8). Westport, CT: Praeger.

Mann, H. (1849). *Twelfth annual report.* Boston, MA: Dutton & Wentworth.

Marco, G. (1994). Statistician for the Educational Testing Service. Personal Interview. November 2.

Margolis, J. (1989). The truth about relativism. In M. Krausz (Ed.), *Relativism: Interpretation and Confrontation* (pp. 232–255). Notre Dame: Notre Dame University.

Marrou, H. I. (1956). *A history of education in antiquity.* New York: Sheed & Ward.

McCarthy, T. (1989). Contra-relativism: A thought experiment. In M. Krausz (Ed.), *Relativism: Interpretation and Confrontation* (pp. 256–271). Notre Dame: Notre Dame University.

McLanahan, S., & Sandefur, G. (1994). *Growing up with a single parent: What hurts, what helps.* Cambridge, MA: Harvard University Press.

Meehan, M. (2008). The left has betrayed the sanctity of life: Consistency demands concern for the unborn. In R. M. MacNair (Ed.), *Consistently opposing killing* (pp. 19–24). Westport, CT: Praeger.

Michaelsen, R. (1970). *Piety in the public school.* London: Macmillan.

Mohanty, J. N. (1989). Ethical relativism & confrontation of culture. In M. Krausz (Ed.), *Relativism: Interpretation and Confrontation* (pp. 339–362). Notre Dame: Notre Dame University.

Myers, D. G. (2000). *The American paradox.* New Haven, CT: Yale University Press.

Nardo, D. (2000). *Classical Greece and Rome.* San Diego, CA: Greenhaven Press.

———. (2001). *The end of ancient Rome.* San Diego, CA: Greenhaven Press.

National Center for Education Statistics. (2001). *Progress in International Reading Literacy Study (PIRLS) of 2001.* Washington, D.C.: National Center for Education Statistics.

Newman, K. S. (2004). *Rampage: The social roots of school shootings.* New York: Basic Books.

Noll, M. A. (2002). *The old religion in a new world.* Grand Rapids, MI: Eerdmans.

Plato. (2000). *The republic.* Cambridge, MA: Cambridge University Press.

————. (2004). *Protagoras and Meno*. Ithaca, NY: Cornell University Press.

Reed, R. (1994). *Politically incorrect*. Dallas, TX: Word Publishing.

Ruggles, A. M. (1950). *The story of the McGuffeys*. New York: American Book Company.

Saunders, W. P. (2006). Abortion is immoral. In J. D. Torr (Ed.), *Abortion: Opposing viewpoints* (pp. 15–19). Detroit, MI: Greenhaven Press.

Schaeffer, F. A., & Koop, C. E. (1979). *Whatever happened to the human race?* Old Tappan, NJ: Revell.

Schramm, W. L. (1977). *Television and test scores*. Princeton, NJ: College Board.

Scott, D., & Nimmo, B. (2000). *Rachel's tears*. Nashville, TN: Thomas Nelson.

Sharma, S. N. (1994). *Buddhist social and moral education*. Delhi: Parimal.

Sikorski, R. (1993). *Controversies in constitutional law*. New York, Garland.

Stevenson, H. W., & Stigler, J. W. (1992). *The learning gap*. New York, NY: Summit Books.

Thorgerson, S. (1990). *Secondary education in China after Mao*. Denmark: Aarhus University Press.

U.S. Census Bureau. (2001). *Census 2000*. Washington, D.C.: U.S. Census Bureau.

U.S. Department of Education. (2000). *Digest of education statistics*. Washington, D.C.: U.S. Department of Education.

————. (2004). *Digest of education statistics*. Washington, D.C.: U.S. Department of Education.

Wallerstein, J., & Blakeslee, S. (1989). *Second chances: Men, women, and children a decade after divorce*. New York: Tichnor & Fields.

Weddle, M. B. (2001). *Walking in the way of peace*. Oxford: Oxford University Press.

White, M. (1987). *The Japanese educational challenge: A commitment to children*. New York, NY: Free Press.

Will, G. (1982). *The pursuit of virtue*. New York: Simon & Schuster.

Winn, M. (2002). *Television, computers and family life*. New York: Penguin.

Wirtz, W. (1977). *On further examination*. New York: College Entrance Examination Board.

Young, J. W. (1995). Recentering the SAT score scale. *College & University, 70* (2), 60–62.

Zaslow, M. J. (1988). Sex differences in children's response to parental divorce: Research methodology and predivorce family forms. *American Journal of Orthopsychiatry, 58* (3), 355–378.

————. (1989). Sex differences in children's response to parental divorce: Samples, variables, and sources. *American Journal of Orthopsychiatry, 59* (1), 118–141.

Zill, N., & Nord, C. W. (1994). *Running in place*. Washington, D.C.: Child Trends.

10

MOST OF AMERICA'S PROBLEMS
ARE NOT ECONOMIC AND
ACADEMIC IN NATURE

American leaders these days frequently talk about the need to address economic and educational problems, as if these are the two most prominent issues that the country ever faces. The reality of the matter, however, is that the country faces challenges that, while they frequently drastically impact the economic and educational welfare of the nation, are rooted in moral problems (Felsenheimer & Gisdakis, 2008; McLean & Elkind, 2003).

When the economy collapsed under major problems at some of the nation's largest financial institutions in 2008, virtually no one called the CEOs of these companies stupid. Rather, the far more common assertion of the American public and economic experts was that these leaders lacked the moral fiber necessary to be efficacious leaders, for example, they were greedy and selfish. Similarly, although students attending American schools these days are achieving at subpar levels academically, most of the complaints about today's youth have little to do with low levels of academic achievement and much more to with issues of character, immorality, and the inability of students from varying backgrounds to get along. Students from differing racial backgrounds have been engaging in racial fights. Moreover, these encounters are becoming more frequent as adolescents from different cultures are being exposed to each other for the very first time. With school violence present as a stark reality in many American schools, one can argue that these students require guidance in anger management, compassion, and sensitivity even more than they need to excel academically. In fact, there is a copious amount of evidence that suggests that students filled with anger and frustration over a variety of situations (e.g., family circumstances) do not do as well academically as their less frustrated counterparts (Blakeman, 2005; Felsenheimer & Gisdakis, 2008; Jeynes, 2009; Lal, Lal, & Achilles, 1993; Leary, 2008; Lewy, 1996; Likona, 1976; Winn, 2002).

What one needs to emphasize, however, is that character instruction not only benefits the youth who receive it but also has effects that often last a lifetime. The reality is that today's children and adolescents are the politicians, CEOs, lawyers, and used car salespeople of tomorrow. Consequently, when character education and prayer were removed from the public schools in 1962 and 1963, one could expect to see serious ramifications not only for the youth immediately, affected at the time, but for these same individuals throughout their lives (Blanshard, 1963; Kliebard, 1969; Michaelsen, 1970; Sikorski, 1993).

Because it has been a number of decades since moral education and prayer were removed from the public schools, most of the adult working population in the United States were raised in schools in which character education and voluntary public prayer were absent (Jeynes, 2007a). Furthermore, most social scientists would agree that concurrent to this trend was the fact that the moral foundation of the family was also eroding over the same period. For example, divorce rates surged in precisely 1963. For the period immediately before then, 1948–1962, the divorce rate in the United States was actually in decline. Since 1963, however, the stability of the family has been deteriorating. The developments in myriad American families together with the dearth of tolerance of religious expression and character education have had a baleful impact on the individuals growing up during this period (Andryszewski, 1997; Blakeman, 2005; Jeynes, 2002a, 2007a; McLanahan & Sandefur, 1994; U.S. Census Bureau, 2001; Wallerstein & Blakeslee, 1989).

To the extent that we are cognizant of the fact that the removal of character instruction from the schools and the dearth of it had a detrimental impact that lasted many decades, one can easily understand numerous problems that the United States faces from a very different perspective.

THE MORAL HIGH GROUND IN THE WAR AGAINST TERROR

Immediately following September 11, 2001, it appeared that the United States was on the proper trajectory toward experiencing a moral and spiritual revival. Americans returned in great numbers to churches, synagogues, and other houses of worship. Schools erected banners encouraging people to pray. Americans reached out to others with acts of love, sensitivity, and compassion. Americans had a renewed appreciation for patriotism (Ford, 2002; Giunta & Stephenson, 2002; Tuttle, 2006).

When President Bush and Mayor Rudolph Guilianni stood on Grand Zero, the former site of the World Trade Center, they inspired the American people by their strength and leadership in the midst of crisis. George Bush then initiated a widely popular policy toward Afghanistan, in which he asked them to hand over Osama Bin Laden who instigated the September 11 attacks. America's initial response to 9/11 was consistent with American behavior throughout much of its history, that is, the United States has generally been hesitant to engage in a war unless it was initiated by a hostile foreign power. Consequently, the United States enjoyed a great deal of support from its European and Asian allies for its initial handling of Afghanistan-based crisis. The United States even found limited support among some nations in the Middle East, including Libya's Momar Kadafy's declaration that the United States had a right to defend itself (Ashcroft, 2006; Ford, 2002; Jeynes, 2007a; Johnson, 1997; Williams, 2003).

President Bush's initial response to the September 11 attacks appeared to be measured with wisdom and cooperation in much the same way that his father rallied international port to liberate Kuwait from Iraqi aggression. However, the decision by President Bush to engage in a preemptive strike against Iraq, in order to divulge previously hidden weapons of mass destruction, appeared inconsistent with the just war criteria that the United States generally used to decide whether to enter a war. Traditionally, the United States has generally waited until it was fired upon or at least thought it was fired on before declaring war on another country (Ashcroft, 2006; Howard, 1971; Johnson, 1997; Williams, 2003; Woodward, 2004).

Rather than exhibit the patience that President George H. W. Bush exhibited during the first Iraq War, George W. Bush settled for a smaller coalition and moved ahead more briskly than his father did. Some of the reasons for the brisk nature of Bush include the fact that Saddam Hussein ordered the assassination of his father, the 41st president, and Bush's conviction that representatives from Al Qaeda and Iraq met in Prague, Czechoslovakia to jointly plan the 9/11 attacks and that there were weapons of mass destruction residing in Iraq that might be given to terrorists or used by Iraq against the United States. However, American's European allies appeared to cringe when it became apparent that the United States seemed intent on resorting to war to resolve the conflict against the objections of most of the nations that the United States had previously worked with as partners in the first Iraq War (Nye, 2007).

Rather than attempting to adhere to the usual rules associated with just war theory, in which one of the qualifications is to view war only as a last resort, the United States launched a preemptive strike. Another qualification to meet the just war criterion is that the military action be out of self-defense. Unfortunately, the United States did not act out of self-defense, but initiated a preemptive strike. The concept of a preemptive strike had previously been an anathema to American foreign policy. Many Americans grieved that after centuries of at least seeking to satisfy the requirements of what constitutes a just war, those requirements were relegated to a secondary position (Holmes, 1989; Nye, 2007; Teichman, 1986; Williams, 2003; Woodward, 2004).

By initiating a preemptive strike, the United States lost the moral high ground in the war on terror. This was a grievous development, particularly because it should not have been difficult for the United States to procure the moral high ground. The primary reason why it should not have been difficult is because terrorists are nearly always filled with hate. The verbiage of the terrorists is virulent, racist, and malicious. They possess virtually no tolerance for those who live different lifestyles, are from unique cultures, and especially for the existence of the nation of Israel. To anyone with any sense of objectivity, the terrorists are hate-filled, Jew-obsessed, xenophobic killers who should concern any person who values life, justice, and civilization. And yet because of various actions that were ill-advised, presumptuous, and headstrong, the United States soon found itself losing the public relations battle in the Middle East, Asia, and even in Europe (Bacevich, 2007; Bennett, 2002; Nye, 2007).

The current perception of the American-initiated war on terror depends on what nation's perspective one chooses to examine. Nevertheless, one trend is quite patent: since the maturation of the U.S. policy toward Iraq, world opinion of the veracity and the worthiness of the U.S. war against terror has declined. It is clear that the moral high ground which the United

States should enjoy has evaporated over time. The evanescent moral edge that the United States enjoyed in the initial days and weeks following September 11 was lost because the nation did not act in a way that was consistent with the Judeo-Christian and biblical ethos on which it was established (Bacevich, 2007; Nye, 2007; Williams, 2003; Woodward, 2004).

The nation's refusal to act in accordance with its ethical roots not only caused countries with differing philosophical foundations to reject the new and alternative American approach that eschewed its Judeo-Christian roots but caused other nations, particularly in Europe, with similar roots, to rebuff the new American approach. It was the European opposition to the American strategy that was particularly devastating to American credibility both within and beyond its own borders. The reason why the European resistance was so important is because they possessed many of the same philosophical roots as the United States. Therefore, they had learned what to anticipate from the United States and had insight into the motives and goals of the United States to a degree that most other nations of the world did not (Andreani, 2006; Bertram, 2006; Kotzias & Liacouras, 2006; Pfaff, 2006; Sechser, 2007).

European nations and other American allies began to perceive that the United States was not acting in accordance with the mores and worldview with which other nations were accustomed. Europeans perceived a number of changes in the U.S. international policies that represented a considerable departure from the past. First, Europeans perceived that the United States did not act in a spirit of self-restraint. Instead, what they perceived was a nation that had reacted emotionally to September 11 and Saddam Hussein's plot to assassinate President George H. W. Bush. Ironically, for most of the twentieth century, until the Vietnam War, Europeans had perpetually been critical of America's reluctance to enter into major military conflicts. For decades many Europeans complained that the U.S. hesitancy to enter World War I and World War II literally cost millions of lives. Since the Vietnam War, however, the European perception has been that the United States has lacked self-restraint in this regard. This trend started under Presidents Kennedy and Johnson and has affected certain presidents since then, particularly George W. Bush. In the view of Europeans and much of the world, the United States needs to return to the conviction of self-restraint that it practiced for so many years before Vietnam War (Bacevich, 2007; Jeynes, 2007a; Kotzias & Liacouras, 2006; Nye, 2007; Pfaff, 2006; Sechser, 2007; VanDeMark, 1991).

Second, Europeans and other nations perceive that the United States did not collaborate with other nations when it entered the second Iraq War in the way that it generally has over the course of its history. Rather, it tends to act unilaterally often without obtaining adequate council and advice from its allies. In the eyes of America's allies, the United States use to be adept in the area of communication, but that is no longer the case. Therefore, the United States needs to return to its emphasis on communication if it really wants to maximize the influence of its power (Ikenberry, 2008; Kotzias & Liacouras, 2006; Pfaff, 2006).

Third, the United States needs to be more cautious about engaging in activities that are inconsistent with its value system. Instances of torture and inappropriate treatment of POWs during the second Iraq War have tarnished America's reputation. In addition, these actions have caused many nations to question the extent to which the United States really intends to live according to its philosophical roots (Ikenberry, 2008; Kotzias & Liacouras, 2006; Love, 2008).

CRIME AND TRUST

In the minds of many, the causes of crime are nearly all rooted in the depths of issues of socioeconomic status (SES). In other words, where there is economic desperation and deprivation crime rates are likely to soar. There is certainly some evidence to support this notion, especially if one only examines the research at a cursory level. For example, research appears to support the notion that poor inner city area are more likely to have more elevated rates of crime than that exists in most suburbs. The vast majority of community leaders and social scientists acknowledge that low SES is responsible for at least part of this difference (Agnew, Matthews, & Bucher, 2008; Jeynes, 1999; Johnson, Jang, & Li, 2000; Johnson, Jang, Larson, & Li, 2001).

Equipped with data regarding differences in crime between suburbs and urban area, some researchers assume that they possess the ultimate proof of the root cause of crime. Unfortunately, the presence of other national statistics and research seriously undermines this assumption. First, the poorest sections of the United States tend to be rural areas, where the crime rate is, on average, much lower than in urban area. Second, the United States is often regarded as one of the nations in the world with a standard of living that elicits a great deal of envy among other nations. Yet, in spite of this the United States has the highest crime rate in the industrialized world and the highest rate of incarceration of any nation in the world. If crime and low SES are almost inextricably connected as proponents of socioeconomic theory suggest, then one would certainly not expect these types of statistics. Third, urbanization associated with the industrialization of a given area is usually accompanied by an increase, not a decrease, in the crime rate. If crime is, in essence, a socioeconomic phenomenon, one would expect just the opposite trend (Agnew, Matthews, & Bucher, 2008; Jeynes, 1999, 2002b, 2007b; United Nations, 2005).

The presentation of the above three trends is not meant to totally refute the existence of a relationship between crime and SES. Instead, what appears more likely is the existence of two realities. First, SES is one of several factors that have an influence on the crime rate. Second, a portion of the relationship between SES and crime is triangular. That is, a good part of the relationship between SES and crime is not causal but mostly correlational; and the relationship is largely explained because both variables are related to other factors. For example, people who have moral problems are considerably more likely to be of low SES and are also more likely to commit crime. Among these moral problems that are generally associated with lower SES are alcoholism, illegal drug addiction, unmarried teen pregnancies, extramarital affairs, and school suspensions. People who engage in these activities are all more likely to commit a crime and be of lower SES than other people (Chad & York, 1969; Davis, 1996; Dombrink & Hillyard, 2007; Hills, 1971; Jeynes, 2002c).

The fact that the relationship between SES and crime is somewhat dubious and that part of that relationship may be triangular in nature leads one to conclude that they play a more prominent role in explaining the extent of the crime rate (Johnson, Jang, & Li, 2000; Johnson, Jang, Larson, & Li, 2001).

There is a considerable amount of historical and contemporary research that indicates that there is a salient relationship between personal character and crime. Although financial stress can increase the likelihood that a person will commit a crime, there are patent character traits that separate the person who will commit a crime under financial duress and the one who will not (Buchanon, 1994; Jeynes, 2007a; Orr, 1989).

Historically, one of the great predictors of a drop in the crime rate is religious revival. At various times and places throughout history, religious revival has been followed by a reduction in the crime rate, the closing of bars, and a drop in prostitution (Marsden, 1994; Orr, 1989).

Based on these historical data and the personal observations of many, myriad community leaders, social workers, politicians, and psychologists called for the establishment of churches in the old west as a means of bringing a civilizing influence and in the inner city as a means of preventing the exponential growth of gang infestation and crime (Beecher, 1835; Fraser, 2001; Jeynes, 2007a).

One of the original purposes of moral instruction during colonial and post–Revolutionary War times was to reduce crime. This emphasis was particularly strong with single-parent children, because so many parents had died due to disease and even war. Virtually all the East Asian countries are convinced that their programs of moral education are key in reducing crime. They have not only noticed that moral instruction has ameliorative effects on student behavior in the classroom but observed that when character education is reduced or eliminated, the juvenile crime rates were affected (Beard & Beard, 1944; Cubberley, 1920, 1934; Duke, 1986, 1991; Hiner, 1988; Jeynes, 2007a; Lee, 1991; Levine & White, 1986; Lewis, 1995).

For centuries, teachers taught character education in the schools with the belief that character education was essential to support the foundations of society. One of those foundations is trust. Trust creates the kind of atmosphere that is the antithesis of what exists in a world of crime. Crime creates an atmosphere in which trust does not reside. Where children are taught trust, society will thrive. Productive and healthy business transactions, close friendships, strong marriages and families, faithful neighbors, and loyal business-customer relationships are all built on the quality of trust. Within a framework of trust, society thrives. Where there is a lack of trust, civilization crumbles (Berman, 2000; Chad & York, 1969).

For centuries, America's leaders chose to create a society of trust. In 1962 and 1963 the U.S. Supreme Court, in a series of three decisions, chose to remove the moral and religious exercises that were the basis of creating the society of trust. Many cultural experts and social scientists believe that it is no accident that juvenile crime started to surge in exactly 1963. Both many Americans and foreigners believe that America's high crime rate represents one of its greatest problems. Yet in 1962 and 1963 the U.S. Supreme Court ruled in a way that encouraged a nation high in crime and one that would inevitably become low in trust.

ISSUES OF RACE AND CHARACTER EDUCATION

In spite of all the laws that have been passed, designed to discourage racism, the reality is that legal restrictions alone will not eliminate racism. Ultimately, racism reflects the state of one's heart. Therefore, the only way to address the root causes of racism is to deal with the heart. Consequently, character instruction, which deals with the heart, is perhaps the best way to confront the realities of racism, as well as address the attitudes, beliefs, and emotions that are necessary to overcome racism (Jeynes, 2007a; King, 1998).

The relative salience of character training versus legal solutions is ostensible throughout the course of American history. Throughout history there have been various and sundry attempts to address the disease of racism. Abraham Lincoln made one of the most valorous attempts when he signed the Emancipation Proclamation in 1863. Although through this means Lincoln declared liberation for the slaves, the South certainly did not immediately set the slaves free (Essig, 1999; Hardman, 1987; McKivigan, 1999).

After the Civil War the U.S. government passed the 13th amendment designed to emphatically assert that the African Americans were equal under the law and possessed the same rights as white people did. The government initiatives were done with every intention of resolving the problem of racism in America. The government leaders had every expectation that by amending the Constitution in this way, the racism issue will have finally been resolved. There is no question that these amendments ameliorated the status of African Americans. The amendments were needed to communicate to former slaveholders and to all Americans that African Americans not only possessed the same God-given rights as whites but were also legally equal and should be regarded as equal (Jeynes, 2007a; Washington, 1969).

Through the years, lawmakers and court justices have passed various laws and court decisions that have been designed to ensure that African Americans and other racial minorities receive the equal treatment that they are entitled to under the law. Among the most significant events was the *Brown v. Board of Education* decision in 1954. This ended years of segregation in the Southeast in particular, where school officials separated students into schools on the basis of race. In the *Brown v. Board of Education* court case, the justices decided to end forced segregation in the South and overturn the foolish decision of *Plessy v. Ferguson* (1896), which allowed segregation as long as the facilities (in this case schools) were of equal quality. The problem is that facilities that are separate are rarely equal (Jeynes, 2007a; Richardson, 1986).

During the process of *Brown v. Board of Education*, a number of social scientists both directly involved in the proceedings and those offering commentary on the case claimed that calling for the desegregation of schools in the South or wherever such an order applied would substantially reduce the achievement gap and give African Americans the boost they needed to excel in schools (King & Washington, 1968).

Naturally, *Brown v. Board of Education* was the right decision for the Supreme Court to make and the 9-0 vote helped reinforce the wisdom of the decision. It was the appropriate decision because it was the morally right action to take. Unfortunately, in spite of the Brown decision, there was essentially no reduction in the achievement gap over the next generation (about 20 years; Jeynes, 2007a).

The *Brown v. Board of Education* decision did little to reduce the level of racism in the country. The fact that desegregation did little to reduce the achievement gap also meant that on another dimension racism was not reduced. To whatever extent some people's racism might decline if the achievement gap narrowed, *Brown v. Board of Education* did not appear to contribute to a reduction in racism (Johnson, 1997).

By the time the civil rights movement of the late 1950s and early 1960s emerged, racism was still evident on the American landscape. Since the Civil War about a century beforehand, countless laws had been passed in order to address racism; many people still held this embittered racist attitudes toward individuals of different colors than themselves (Jeynes, 2007a; King, 1998).

What had the greatest impact on racism was the ministry of Martin Luther King (1998). Although King sought to have American laws changed, he was sufficiently discerning to realize that the true key to procuring civil rights victories was to aim at the transformation of the human heart. In his I Have a Dream speech, it is clear that although Martin Luther King (1998) is concerned about cashing in the "promissory note" given by the United States to the African American people following the Civil War, he is most concerned about the transformation of human hearts. This was in fact apparent in myriad of his speeches and writings. King posited that the presence of sin went deep into people and that these individuals needed to experience dramatic change in one's heart in order to overcome racism. In fact, the essence of Martin Luther King's teaching was character instruction (Branch, 1998; King, 1998; King & Washington, 1968).

Martin Luther King was cognizant of the fact that the key component of his ministry that would most likely yield success was his emphasis on character training, based on the truths of the Bible. First, he trained the members of his congregation and other followers to engage in a loving attitude of passive resistance. Although, an attitude of passive resistance appears antithetical to the natural inclinations of most human beings, King possessed confidence that once exposed to this practice of taking the moral high ground people would respond positively. Second, King opined that if those who followed him in the civil rights movement would practice passive resistance in the midst of stubborn segregationalist practices and occasional police brutality, Americans would see this and side with African Americans. As the civil rights movement intensified under King's leadership, many Americans were touched by the moral example established by Martin Luther King and his followers. The actions of the civil rights marchers appeared to match the spiritual preaching of Reverend Martin Luther King (Branch, 1998; King, 1998; King & Washington, 1968).

Martin Luther King led the movement for equality for African Americans to heights never achieved previously. King succeeded because his approach was different than that of the people who preceded him. The essence of King's message was not legal, but spiritual and the solution that he propounded was based on a person's character rather than on the rule of the law (Branch, 1998; King, 1998).

WHY CHARACTER EDUCATION EASES RACISM

Character education's eases racism because it emphasizes the state of the heart rather than the color of one's skin. At the core of moral education is an awareness that to assess people on the basis of the color of one's skin is exceedingly superficial. Scientifically speaking, biologically humans are about 98 percent similar to one another. What a pity it is therefore that human beings tend to highlight differences. And yet too many individuals focus on the differences, even though they are extremely superficial in nature. Where moral instruction is emphasized, the state of the heart is emphasized much more than the color of one's skin (Jeynes, 1999, 2007a).

With all of this in mind, it is not surprising that in schools where moral instruction is taught racial harmony tends to be higher than in schools where such training is not practiced. For example, a study using the National Educational Longitudinal Study (NELS) indicated that religious schools, on average, experience higher level of racial harmony than public schools as measured by the likelihood of racial fights and the extent racial harmony as perceived by the students (Jeynes, 1999, 2008a, 2008b).

To whatever extent that race relations have improved over the last few decades, the character instruction and emphasis provided by Martin Luther King and his followers is one of the primary reasons why. To the degree that race relations still need to improve, character training will once again emerge as a major pillar in the strategy to improve race relations.

CHARACTER EDUCATION WILL FOSTER ECONOMIC GROWTH

Character education that is taught in the public schools will foster economic growth. The reason why there is this causal relationship is because myriad qualities that are associated with lives of morality and integrity are also some of the most important prerequisites for a society to maintain high rates of economic growth (Jeynes, 2003a, 2006).

For many generations, many writers have noted that certain moral developments in a nation's citizenry are predictive of future economic growth. That is, where there is the rise of moral behavior either as a result of religious revival or adhering to an honored philosophy, consistent economic growth has often followed. For example, around 1400 BC and later in the period of 1000 BC after the people of Israel faithfully followed the leadership of Moses and David, respectively, economic prosperity followed. Shortly after the life of Moses, Joshua led the Israelites into the Promised Land and ushered in a period of prosperity for the Israelites. The next great religious revival in Israel's history was during the reign of King David. In fact, many theologians regard this period as the most meritorious revival of the Old Testament period. What followed, during the reigns of King Solomon, was the most prosperous time in the history of Old Testament Israel. After Israel split into two kingdoms Judah (in the South) and Samaria (in the North), Judah experienced two moral and religious revivals. One of these surges was under King Hezekiah and the other was guided by Josiah. In both cases material prosperity followed shortly thereafter (Henry, 1979; Smith, 1937; Washington, 1969).

A revival of Buddhist secret sects helped usher in the end of Mongolian dominance which had defined much of the Yuan Dynasty (AD 1279–1368) and haunted the latter part of the Song Dynasty (AD 960–1279) in an effort to pacify the Mongols so that they would not invade China. The Buddhist revival helped usher in the Ming Dynasty, which is a rich cultural period in China's history (Durant, 1931; Reagan, 2005; Renard, 2002).

After Christianity became the central religion in Europe and personal morality was emphasized, Europe became the foremost center for economic prosperity and navigation. New England and the Mid-Atlantic states such as New York, Pennsylvania, New Jersey, and Maryland became the Bible Belt of the early colonies in North America. New England, which was the center of the Bible Belt of that period, developed a literacy rate that grew to be what was likely the highest in the world. The Puritans and other groups who inhabited New England placed such an emphasis on maintaining high levels of literacy because they placed such an emphasis on reading the Bible. Although they did not believe that reading the Bible was a prerequisite for experiencing salvation, they certainly believed that it helped. The three primary cities of the stretch of land from New England through the Mid-Atlantic states, Boston, New York, and Philadelphia, were the most prosperous cities in the early North American colonies and in the first few decades after the founding of the United States (Cornog, 1998; Durant, 1975; Gutek, 1997; Hiner, 1988; Jeynes, 2007a).

Various historians and writers noted the rise of the United States and predicted its future state as a world power largely as a result of its moral character and devout religious orientation. The nation's emphasis on character building and religious commitment continued into the early 1960s until the U.S. Supreme Court decisions regarding prayer and Bible reading in the schools. By most measures, it was shortly after this time that the economic power of the United States peaked relative to that of other nations. There is a considerable amount of economic evidence that indicates that the United States began her economic decline in 1973 with the advent of the Arab oil embargo. One should not be surprised at the relationship between the presence of moral instruction and economic prosperity. Many of the qualities that manifest themselves as a result of this instruction are also of immense value for the promotion of economic growth (Buchanon, 1994). A number of these qualities include self-discipline, a development of the work ethic, honesty, integrity, and responsibility (Berman, 2000; Jeynes, 2007a; Organization for Economic Cooperation & Development, 2008).

A Work Ethic

One of the most observed and demonstrated effects of character education is that it produces a work ethic in its participants. Max Weber, probably more than any other social scientist, popularized this relationship in his sentinel work, the *Protestant Work Ethic.* In his treatise, Weber highlighted how an emphasis on character and God's blessing of the diligent yielded willingness among many to work hard, even if it required substantial sacrifice. In Max Weber's treatise, he specifically focuses on Protestantism. He points to the biblical and Calvinistic orientation of the Pilgrims and Puritans as the origin of this orientation in the United States. He then argues that those who responded to this Protestant-bound orientation were numerous enough to spawn its adoption in both the United States and previously throughout much of Europe (Weber, 1930).

Max Weber helped propound the notion that much of the prosperity of the Western world could be explained by this relationship between Protestant character instruction which lionized a work ethic and economic prosperity. Since the time of Weber's sentinel work and the present day, subsequent studies have shown that the linkage between the work ethic and various productive outcomes is not limited to Protestants. Rather, what the current research suggests is that character education, most notably religion-based instruction, often yields a determination to work hard. Studies indicate that there is often a religious component to work ethic in that people develop a determination to both glorify God and a belief that if one succeeds in this endeavor, one will ultimately be blessed by God. Nevertheless, social scientists are generally quite convinced that character instruction fosters the growth of the work ethic (Mentzer, 1988; Weber, 1930).

Self-Discipline

One of the principal teachings of moral education is self-discipline. A disciplined lifestyle encompasses a vast number of dimensions, many of which are connected to economic well-being. One of the most patent of these dimensions is diligence, which is a vital component of the work ethic which was just examined. It is important to recognize, however, that there are other facets to self-discipline that also generally contribute to the economic well-being (Mentzer, 1988).

Moral Self-Discipline is vitally important to economic prosperity. Moral self-discipline refers to living a lifestyle that avoids many of the pitfalls that often serve to undermine the overall well-being of humanity, often including oneself, and are often in contradiction to at least some of the values of truth, appropriateness, justice, and sensitivity, among others. For example, those who live a self-disciplined lifestyle are less likely to take illegal drugs, become drunk, have self-destructive habits such as cigarette smoking, and engage in premarital or extramarital sexual intercourse (Jeynes, 2002b, 2003b, 2006).

There are a plethora of academic studies indicating that substance abuse and premarital and extramarital sexual intercourse are associated with lower academic achievement and reduced job proficiency. It is simply logical, for example, that if a worker is high on drugs or alcohol he or she is not going to perform as well on the job or at school. Even if one is not high while at work, but rather has a hangover or is experiencing withdrawal, these can have a detrimental impact on one's performance both in the workplace and at school. If, as a general rule, the members of society are sober with regard to illegal drugs and alcohol, that nation will nearly always have a higher production per worker than if a large percentage of a society's workers are under the influence of alcohol and illegal drugs. This, in turn, will affect the Gross Domestic Product (GDP) of that country (Buchanon, 1994; Inciardi & McElrath, 2008; Jeynes, 2002b, 2003b, 2006; Nakaya, 2008).

If a person is a chain smoker, is an alcoholic, is a frequent consumer of illegal drugs, or engages in types of sexual behavior that are linked to disease, this tends to reduce the life span of these individuals and also makes it more likely that they will need more frequent medical care than would be the case if they did not engage in these behaviors. To the extent that workers have shorter life spans and are more likely to have critical or chronic health problems, both the GDP and the standard of living of that nation will be reduced (Berman, 2000; Buchanon, 1994; Inciardi & McElrath, 2008; Nakaya, 2008).

A lack of moral self-discipline can also cause a person to experience problems that place burdens upon one's time. For example, many immoral acts cause people to be incarcerated, have legal problems, have complex relationship problems, possess ongoing psychological problems, or encounter increased undesired responsibilities. All of these time distractions usually affect the quality and quantity of one's work. Consequently, to whatever extent members of society practice a self-disciplined lifestyle, at the macro level of the economy, it will virtually always produce a net positive impact on GDP and a nation's standard of living (Berman, 2000; Buchanon, 1994; Inciardi & McElrath, 2008; Nakaya, 2008).

Cooperation: Another quality emphasized in character education is cooperation. Cooperation is a trait that also has major economic ramifications. Research studies have consistently demonstrated that people cooperating yield more impressive overall results than these same people competing against one another. These results are particularly intriguing when one looks at the nature of the studies more closely. In a number of investigations, what these studies have divulged is that many Americans are convinced that competition yields greater results than does cooperation. Research indicates that even when it is clear in the context of the study that cooperation yields greater benefit than does competition, American subjects nevertheless choose to compete against one another rather than cooperate. On the surface, these actions appear counterintuitive. But there appears to be something in the American psyche what causes the nation's citizens to prefer competition over cooperation. This tendency is so poignant that even when it is clear that cooperation benefits both the two subjects participating in the study and that they derive more benefit from that cooperation than any of the other subjects who are competing against one another, American subjects never respond by preferring competition over cooperation (Berman, 2000; Buchanon, 1994; Tisch & Weber, 2004).

A character curriculum will possess tremendous value because it will train youth to appreciate and practice the benefits of cooperation. This is particularly important because a cooperative workforce is in high demand among the nation's major businesses. The reality is that America's major corporations fathom the indispensable role that cooperation plays in everyday business practices. The sincerity of corporate America's desire to see the nation's workers instilled with a spirit of cooperation is reflected in the fact that businesses are increasingly having an effect on the elementary and secondary school curriculum. Today's businesses want the school curriculum to help cultivate some of the qualities they believe are necessary to function well in the business world (Berman, 2000; Buchanon, 1994; Kearns, 1988; Tisch & Weber, 2004).

It is true that there are some people who resent the influence that the business world has on the American elementary and secondary school curriculum. These opponents argue that the business world should not have that much effect on the school curriculum, because it will promote a mechanized system of education in which students do not receive the benefits of a generalized curriculum bur rather a specialized program that is focused on occupational preparation. However, other people argue that businesses have as much right as anyone else to contribute input into the instructional process. Moreover, in order to survive in this society one should have the qualities necessary to flourish in the business world. In addition, there is a considerable overlap between the qualities one needs to thrive in the business world and the traits one needs to be fulfilled in life (Berman, 2000; Buchanon, 1994; Kearns, 1988).

To the extent that people cooperate with one another, the economy will flourish. The economy will flower not only to the degree that people cooperate in the business realm, but when people live in a cooperative society in a general sense the United States will benefit in many ways, including economically.

REFERENCES

Agnew, R., Matthews, S. K., & Bucher, J. (2008). Socioeconomic status, economic problems & delinquency. *Youth & Society, 40* (2), 159–181.

Andreani, G. (2006). Europe and the transatlantic relationship after the Iraq crisis. In N. Kotzias & P. Liacouras (Eds.), *EU-US relations: Repairing the transatlantic rift* (pp. 41–42). New York: Palgrave Macmillan.

Andryszewski, T. (1997). *School prayer: History of the debate*. Springfield, NJ: Enslow.

Ashcroft, J. D. (2006). *Never again*. New York: Center Street.

Bacevich, A. J. (2007). The new American militarism. *Paradoxes of power: U.S. foreign policy in a changing world* (pp. 75–83). Boulder, CO: Paradigm.

Beard, C. A., & Beard, M. R. (1944). *A basic history of the United States*. New York: Doubleday, Doran, & Company.

Beecher, L. (1835). *A plea for the West*. n.p.

Bennett, W. J. (2002). *Why we fight*. New York: Doubleday, Doran, & Company.

Berman, M. (2000). *The twilight of American culture*. New York: Norton.

Bertram, C. (2006). The EU and the future of transatlantic relations. In N. Kotzias & P. Liacouras (Eds.), *EU-US relations: Repairing the transatlantic rift* (pp. 41–42). New York: Palgrave Macmillan.

Blakeman, J. C. (2005). *The Bible in the park: Religious expression, public forums, and federal district courts*. Akron, OH: University of Akron Press.

Blanshard, P. (1963). *Religion and the schools*. Boston, MA: Beacon Press.

Branch, T. (1998). *Pillar of fire: America in the King years 1963–65*. New York: Simon & Schuster.

Buchanon, M. (1994). *Ethics and economic progress*. Norman, OK: University of Oklahoma.

Chad, J., & York, J. (1969). *Urban crisis & opportunity*. Belmont, CA: Dickenson.

Cornog, E. (1998). *The birth of empire: DeWitt Clinton & the American experience, 1769–1828*. New York: Oxford University Press.

Cubberley, E. (1920). *The history of education*. Boston, MA: Houghton Mifflin.

———, ed. (1934). *Readings in public education in the United States: A collection of sources and readings to illustrate the history of educational practice and progress in the United States*. Cambridge, MA: Riverside Press.

Davis, N. (1996). Neighborhood crime rates among drug abusing and non-drug abusing families. *Journal of Child & Adolescent Substance Abuse, 5* (4), 1–14.

Dombrink, J., & Hillyard, D. (2007). *Sin no more*. New York: New York University.

Duke, B. (1986). *The Japanese School*. New York: Praeger.

———. (1991). *Education and leadership for the twenty-first century*. New York: Praeger.

Durant, W. (1931). *Great men of literature*. Garden City, NY: Garden City Publishers.

———. (1975). *The story of civilization*. New York: Simon & Schuster.

Essig, J. D. (1999). The Lord's free man. In J. R. McKivigan (Ed.), *History of the American abolitionist movement* (pp. 319–339). New York: Garland.

Felsenheimer, J., & Gisdakis, P. (2008). *Credit crises*. Weinheim, Germany: Wiley.

Ford, M. (2002). *Father Mychal Judge: An authentic American hero*. New York: Paulist Press.

Fraser, J. W. (2001). *The school in the United States*. Boston, MA: McGraw-Hill.

Giunta, R., & Stephenson, L. R. (2002). *God at Ground Zero: How good overcame evil—one heart at a time*. Nashville, TN: Integrity.

Gutek, G. L. (1997). *Historical and philosophical foundations of education*. Upper Saddle River, NJ: Prentice Hall.

Hardman, K. (1987). *Charles Grandison Finney, 1792–1875: Revivalist and reformer*. Syracuse, NY: Syracuse University Press.

Henry, M. (1979). *Matthew Henry's Commentary*. McLean, VA: MacDonald Publishing.

Hills, S. L. (1971). *Crime, power & morality*. Scranton: Chandler.

Hiner, N. R. (1988). The cry of Sodom enquired into: Educational analysis in seventeenth century New England. *The social history of American education.* Urbana, IL: University of Illinois Press.

Holmes, R. L. (1989). *On war and morality.* Princeton, NJ: Princeton University Press.

Howard, M. (1971). *Studies in war and peace.* New York: Viking.

Ikenberry, G. J. (2008). *The crisis of American foreign policy.* Princeton: Princeton University Press.

Inciardi, J., & McElrath, K. (2008). *The American drug scene: An anthology.* New York: Oxford University Press.

Jeynes, W. (1999). The effects of religious commitment on the academic achievement of black and Hispanic children. *Urban Education, 34* (4), 458–479.

———. (2002a). *Divorce, family structure, and the academic success of children.* Binghamton, NY: Haworth Press.

———. (2002b). Educational policy and the effects of attending a religious school on the academic achievement of children. *Educational Policy, 16* (3), 406–424.

———. (2002c). The challenge of controlling for SES in social science and education research. *Educational Psychology Review, 14* (2), 205–221.

———. (2003a). The effects of religious commitment on the attitudes and behavior of teens regarding premarital childbirth. *Journal of Health & Social Policy, 17* (1), 1–18.

———. (2003b). The effects of black and Hispanic twelfth graders living in intact families and being religious on their academic achievement. *Urban Education, 38* (1), 35–57.

———. (2006). Adolescent religious commitment and their consumption of marijuana, cocaine & alcohol. *Journal of Health & Social Policy, 21* (4), 1–20.

———. (2007a). *American educational history: School, society, and the common good.* Thousand Oaks, CA: Sage Publications.

———. (2007b). Religion, intact families, and the achievement gap. *Interdisciplinary Journal of Research on Religion, 3* (3), 1–24.

———. (2008a). *The White House Conference on inner city children and faith-based schools.* Paper presented for the White House in Washington, D.C.

———. (2008b). White House Summit on inner-city children and faith-based schools. *Preserving a critical national asset.* Washington, D.C.: The White House.

———. (2009). The Bible in the public schools. *The handbook of religion and education* (pp. 91–102). New York: Praeger.

Johnson, B. R., Jang, S. J., Larson, D. B., & Li, S. D. (2001). Does adolescent religious commitment matter? *Journal of Research in Crime & Delinquency, 38* (1), 22–44.

Johnson, B. R., Jang, S. J., & Li, S. D. (2000). The invisible institution and black youth crime: The church as an agency of local social control. *Journal of Youth and Adolescence, 29* (4), 479–498.

Johnson, P. (1997). *A history of the American people.* New York: Harper Collins.

Kearns, D. (1988). *Winning the brain race.* San Francisco, CA: ICS press.

King, M. L. (1998). In C. Carson (Ed.), *The autobiography of Martin Luther King.* New York: Warner.

King, M. L., Jr., & Washington, J. M. (1968). *A testament of hope: The essential writings of Martin Luther King, Jr.* San Francisco, CA: Harper & Row.

Kliebard, H. M. (1969). *Religion and education in America.* Scranton, PA: International Textbook Company.

Kotzias, N., & Liacouras, P. (2006). Introduction: Rupture and continuity in transatlantic relations. In N. Kotzias & P. Liacouras (Eds.), *EU-US relations: Repairing the transatlantic rift* (pp. 3–33). New York: Palgrave Macmillan.

Lal, S. R., Lal, D., & Achilles, C. M. (1993). *Handbook on gangs in schools: Strategies to reduce gang-related activities.* Thousand Oaks, CA: Corwin Press.

Leary, D. (2008). *Why we suck: A feel good guide to staying fat, loud, lazy, and stupid.* New York: Viking.

Lee, W. O. (1991). *Social change and educational problems in Japan, Singapore, and Hong Kong.* New York: St. Matthew's Press.

Levine, R. A., & White, M. (1986). Human conditions: The cultural basis of educational development. New York: Routledge.

Lewis, C. C. (1995). *Educating hearts and minds.* Cambridge, MA: Cambridge University Press.

Lewy, G. (1996). *Why America needs religion.* Grand Rapids, MI: Eerdmans.

Likona, T. (1976). *Moral development.* New York: Holt, Rinehart & Winston.

Love, J. (2008). Contested morality in U.S. foreign policy. In D. K. Lennard (Ed.), *Enemy combatants, terrorism, and armed conflict* (pp. 51–63). Westport, CT: Praeger.

Marsden, G. M. (1994). *The soul of the American university.* New York: Oxford University Press.

McKivigan, J. R. (1999). *Abolitionism and American religion.* New York: Garland.

McLanahan, S., & Sandefur, G. (1994). *Growing up with a single parent: What hurts, what helps.* Cambridge, MA: Harvard University Press.

McLean, B., & Elkind, P. (2003). *The smartest guys in the room*. New York: Portfolio.

Mentzer, M. S. (1988). Religion and achievement motivation in the United States: A structural analysis. *Sociological Focus, 21*, 307–316.

Michaelsen, R. (1970). *Piety in the public school*. London: Macmillan.

Nakaya, A. C. (2008). *Alcohol*. Farmington Hills, MI: Greenhaven Press.

Nye, J. S., Jr. (2007). *Paradoxes of power: U.S. foreign policy in a changing world* (pp. 27–32). Boulder, CO: Paradigm.

Organization for Economic Cooperation & Development. (2008). *OECD factbook*. Paris: Organization for Economic Cooperation & Development.

Orr, J. E. (1989). *The event of the century*. Wheaton, IL: International Awakening Press.

Pfaff, W. (2006). Present and future of tensed EU-US relations. In N. Kotzias & P. Liacouras (Eds.), *EU-US relations: Repairing the transatlantic rift* (pp. 37–46). New York: Palgrave Macmillan.

Reagan, T. (2005). *Non-western educational traditions*. Mahwah, NJ: Erlbaum.

Renard, J. (2002). *101 questions and answers on Confucianism, Daoism, and Shinto*. New York: Paulist Press.

Richardson, J. M. (1986). *Christian reconstruction: The American Missionary Association and southern blacks, 1861–1890*. Athens, GA: University of Georgia.

Sechser, T. S. (2007). The effects of September 11: A rift between Europe and America. In D. Skidmore (Eds.), *Paradoxes of power: U.S. foreign policy in a changing world* (pp. 27–32). Boulder, CO: Paradigm.

Sikorski, R. (1993). *Controversies in constitutional law*. New York: Garland.

Smith, A. (1937). *An inquiry into the nature and causes of the wealth of nations*. New York: Modern Library.

Teichman, J. (1986). *Pacifism and just war*. Oxford: Blackwell.

Tisch, J. M., & Weber, K. (2004). *The power of we*. Hoboken, NJ: Wiley.

Tuttle, R. G. (2006). *The story of evangelism*. Nashville, TN: Abingdon Press.

United Nations. (2005). *The ninth United Nations survey on crime trends and the operations of the criminal justice system*. New York: United Nations.

U.S. Census Bureau. (2001). *Census 2000*. Washington, D.C.: U.S. Census Bureau.

VanDeMark, B. (1991). *Into the quagmire: Lyndon Johnson and the escalation of the Vietnam War*. New York: Oxford University Press.

Wallerstein, J., & Blakeslee, S. (1989). *Second chances: Men, women, and children a decade after divorce*. New York: Tichnor & Fields.

Washington, B. T. (1969). *A new Negro for a new century*. Miami, FL: Mnemosyne.

Weber, M. (1930). *The Protestant ethic and the spirit of capitalism*. Translated by T. Parsons. New York: Scribner.

Williams, M. E. (2003). *The terrorist attack on America*. San Diego, CA: Greenhaven Press.

Winn, M. (2002). *Television, computers and family life*. New York: Penguin.

Woodward, B. (2004). *Plan of attack*. New York: Simon & Schuster.

11

———•◦•———

WHAT WE CAN DO TO RESTORE CHARACTER EDUCATION AND RESURRECT RELIGIOUS FREEDOM IN AMERICA

From virtually every angle that one examines the topic of character education, this country appears in great need of reacquainting itself with this practice. From a historical standpoint, the fact that the United States generally does not practice defined character education instruction is clearly an anomaly. From the days that Plato first proposed the idea of an extensive school system until about 1962 or 1963, American educators recognized the salience of moral instruction. For various reasons that are sometimes puzzling, American educators have drifted away from this emphasis. From an international standpoint, the overwhelming percentage of the major peoples of the world have practiced character education for centuries. These programs had different levels of organization, partially dependent on a nation's state of economic development. Nevertheless, character education initiatives were consistently practiced. Equally significant is the fact that virtually every major international system of schooling practices moral instruction today (Blanshard, 1963; Bunge, 1983; Chen, 1994; Cooper, 2003; Cubberley, 1920, 1934; Cui, 2001; Davies & Evans, 2001; Dupuis, 1966; Fedwick, 1989; Hiner, 1988; Khan, 1997; Kliebard, 1969; Kwiran, 2001; Marrou, 1956; Michaelsen, 1970; Murray, 1982;

Palmer, 2001; Ray, 1976; Reagan, 2005; Renard, 2002; Reynolds, 2001; Schmidt, 2007; Sharma, 1994; Sikorski, 1993).

In addition, the moral state of the country appears to demand the reestablishment of character education. School shootings, broken families, declining achievement test scores, and adolescent crime and immorality all point to the need for character education. Beyond the realm of the youth, American society suffers from many moral ills that have been fostered or multiplied by the dearth of character instruction. American society has debased life through abortion and ill-conceived wars, dismissed a plethora of absolute values, and produced an economic quagmire that is almost entirely rooted in extensive corruption, selfishness, and greed. What is most disconcerting is that the corruption, selfishness, and greed extend to myriad levels of American society. This includes the upper class, particularly among business leaders and politicians who were on the take from Fannie Mae, AIG, and other corporate giants; the middle class, including those who lived well beyond their means and members of some industrial unions; and the lower class, especially those taking advantage of the generosity of the welfare system and those buying houses that they could not afford (Coleman, 2004; Felsenheimer & Gisdakis, 2008; Fox, 2003; Hudson, 2009; Jeynes, 2007a; Lieberman, 2006, 2008; McLean & Elkind, 2003; Morris & McGann, 2004; Muolo & Padilla, 2008; Ryan & Bohlin, 1998).

THE CASE FOR CHARACTER EDUCATION

The arguments for character education are so broad, penetrating, and patent that it is hard to imagine how one could possibly oppose this type of instruction. Indeed, it is a wonder how the United States ever convinced itself that it could stand as about the only major country in the world without an organized widespread program of character education in the classrooms. This is particularly an enigma because in past centuries, the 1600s through 1962, the United States practiced character instruction in the schools to a degree that was perhaps unmatched in the world. It is also a puzzle why a nation that for centuries treasured freedom of religious expression has become, particularly in the minds of Europeans, so intolerant of people of faith. European multiculturalism is founded on the idea of freedom of religious expression and they often find it difficult to comprehend why the United States limits its definition of acceptance and tolerance of culture to race and ethnicity and does not include religion (Chamberlin, 1961; Gangel & Benson, 1983; Levey & Modood, 2009; Morgan, 1986).

There is little question that the present aversion that some Americans have toward character education has its roots in more pervasive insular attitudes toward religion that many Americans in the media, education, Hollywood, and other institutions possess. There are a plethora of examples of this, but a representative example of this media bias is Ted Turner stating that Christianity is "for losers" and calling CNN employees who attended Bernard Shaw's retirement party after celebrating Ash Wednesday "a bunch of Jesus freaks" (Associated Press, 2008, p. 1). The fact that before 1962 and 1963, American moral instruction was deeply rooted in the Judeo-Christian tradition has caused many to resist character training in the schools because they personally resist religion or at least are concerned about the fact that many of the character traits that Americans value the most have their rudiments in religious teaching (Feder, 1999; Marsden, 1994; Olasky, 1988).

One, however, does not have to have character instruction based on religious teaching. Advocates of character training, including many of the founders, asserted that the two were inextricably connected and worked best when presented in conjunction with one another. Indeed, there are many Americans who maintain these beliefs today. There is little question that this is a major reason why so few public schools practice moral instruction today. On the one hand, there are some Americans who oppose character schooling because they believe that in order to be efficacious, it necessitates a central religious element and it is this that makes it unacceptable to them. On the other hand, there are some who believe that moral tutelage can yield an ameliorating impact only if it is rooted in religion. There are a variety of reasons for people maintaining this belief, but more often than not it emerges from a conviction that there are some personal goals that are formidable enough that they can only be reached with the help of God or a higher power. Some of the most renowned examples of this worldview include Alcoholics Anonymous and various and sundry drug addiction programs led by Teen Challenge. Many researchers have conducted studies that indicate that faith-based programs designed to help people overcome addiction are considerably more effective than those that lack the faith component. On this and related bases, numerous social scientists and other leaders believe that character education works best in a religious atmosphere (Adams, 1854; Bennett, 1995; Blanshard, 1963; Feder, 1999; Jeynes, 2007b; Johnson, Jang, & Li, 2000; Johnson, Jang, Larson, & Li, 2001; Kliebard, 1969; Michaelsen, 1970; Ryan & Bohlin, 1998).

It may well be that America's founders and many social scientists are correct in their belief that moral training works best in a religious context and using a faith-based rubric. However, the reality is that in today's society the two cannot be combined to produce moral instruction. That should not, however, lead one to exclude character education from the classroom. There is considerable research that indicates that character instruction yields great benefits even when a religious element is not present. It is not logical to deny public school students the pervasive benefits of character instruction simply on the basis of a concern that the teaching will not yield the same benefits as youth in past generations when the Judeo-Christian ethic abided in the core of the curriculum. It cannot be gainsaid that there are numerous character qualities that members of virtually every culture would agree schools should teach students to practice. One would find it nearly impossible to fabricate a reasonable argument against schooling children in honesty, sincerity, responsibility, courage, kindness, love, acceptance, and loyalty. Simply to contend that one is opposed to such instruction because it would not take place in an atmosphere that would maximize its effectiveness is to do a disservice to America's youth (Adams, 1854; Johnson, Jang, & Li, 2000; Johnson, Jang, Larson, & Li, 2001; Likona, 1976; Reiman, 2004; Ryan & Bohlin, 1998; Washington, 1796; Watson, 2006).

It is equally implausible to argue against character education simply because one does not like religion, especially when those who advocate character instruction desire that the curriculum be nonreligious in nature. One should not deny children the opportunity to grow in virtue simply because of one's personal preferences. In other words, Americans need to be tolerant of the degree of that there are different perspectives on this issue and unite to create a curriculum that is of benefit to the United States as a whole. It is not wise to use differing perspectives as an excuse for inaction and gridlock that produce no resolutions. Americans are disillusioned with the failure of America's leaders to agree and reach consensus on issues that are absolutely essential to resolve for the health of the country. Character education is one of those practices that are virtually universally beneficial to Americans. It strengthens not only students who receive this tutelage but also the people who interact with them and are exposed to people who are now more likely to be trustworthy, truthful, responsible, patient, level-headed, and compassionate (Bennett, 1995; Felsenheimer & Gisdakis, 2008; Jeynes, 2007b).

THE CASE FOR PERMITTING VOLUNTARY PRAYER IN THE SCHOOLS

Freedom of religious expression is one of the cornerstones of the American Constitution. Many of the nation's leaders and, according to Gallup Polls, the overwhelming majority of nation's people believe that the refusal of schools to allow for a moment of silence or voluntary prayer is inconsistent with the nation's constitution. Although the United States is a nation that promotes racial tolerance, the same cannot be said about religious tolerance. The United States has increasingly restricted the places where individual students can enjoy religious liberty (Blanshard, 1963; Kliebard, 1969; Levey & Modood, 2009; Marsden, 1994; Michaelsen, 1970).

Americans would likely allow for more religious liberty if in fact there was a greater cognizance and acknowledgment of the myriad ways in which religious faith has benefited this country over the years and is a source of strength even today. Although to once again bind together character education and religious teaching would be imprudent given the realities of the demographics of the United States as it exists today, this should not be used as an excuse for intolerance toward people of faith. Even if a person is not religious, it is important for that person to be objective enough to appreciate the contributions of religion to character education specifically and to society at large. Just as the appreciation of the contributions of people from other nations intensifies one's appreciation of people from other racial and ethnic backgrounds, the appreciation of the contributions of people of faith increases one's appreciation and acceptance of people of faith. This, in turn, will reduce the feelings of "religiophobia," "Christophobia," and "Judaphobia" that many Americans possess. Just as it is not healthy for a society to encourage a person to feel self-conscious about being of a certain ethnicity and race, it is not healthy for a society to encourage a person to feel self-conscious about religion. Yet, ironically although American public schools encourage students to share about their cultural beliefs, as has been pointed out in this book, it is often only nonreligious cultural expressions that are welcome. Teaching on, first, the historical contributions of religious people and, second, the contemporary contributions of religion will likely increase the tolerance that educators and students have toward religious people (Barton, 1995; Decter, 1995).

Religious Contributions in American History

There is no question that religion played a vital role in the burgeoning and maturation of education in the United States. It is patent that without America's religious foundation the United States would not have developed an education system that became the envy of the world. While some Americans were most concerned about growing cash crops and increasing their financial wealth, Christian Americans developed religious priorities that led them to put a prodigious emphasis on education. Whether one wants to admit it or not, many of the values that Americans cherish today find their roots in the Judeo-Christian traditions of this nation. The Pilgrims and Puritans greatly esteemed literacy, education, self-discipline, and the work ethic. They influenced American education more than any of the settling groups. Americans today value schooling, literacy, self-discipline, and the work ethic largely because of the heritage established by the Pilgrims and Puritans. Americans today value democracy, tolerance, and the respect of people because of the value that the nation's founders placed on character education (Cubberley, 1934; Pulliam & Van Patten, 1991).

As an artifact of the removal of prayer and Bible reading from the schools, it appears that many individuals at various levels of education want to dissociate America's educational traditions from her religious traditions. This has even led to America's religious heritage being ignored, disparaged, and even erased. Concurrently, this emphasis is the current tendency to overlook the positive impact that religion plays in America today (Lewy, 1996; Senior, 1978; Seligman, 2000).

Contemporary Contributions of Religion

There is an expanding body of research that indicates that religious commitment has an ameliorative impact on a wide array of student outcomes. For the majority of America's history, religious commitment was regarded as a positive attribute. Nevertheless, in the last few decades, some members of the media, and in society at large, have directed an increasing number of disparaging remarks toward people of faith. A number of psychologists even view faith as a negative quality. This attitude especially spawned during the hippie and sexual revolution period, when religious views were regarded as restraints against personal and sexual freedom, rather than a means of preserving civilized behavior (Decter, 1995; Jeynes, 1999, 2003a, 2003b, 2008, 2009; Olasky, 1988).

Americans now live in a world in which a prodigious number of restraints have been cast aside as limiting and there are an increasing number of people who are astonished by the result. School shootings are common, 65 percent of African American and 30 percent of American babies are born out of wedlock, and there is no question that corporate corruption companies such as Enron, AIG, Fannie Mae, Lehman Brothers, and Merrill Lynch have caused the collapse of the world economy. Consequently, increasingly people view self-discipline, personal responsibility, personal convictions, abstinence, and other terms often associated with religion in more of a positive way than they did five or ten years ago. From this combination of tragedy, economic crisis, and moral deterioration, Americans are becoming more aware of the advantages of religious commitment (Bryce, 2002; Craig et al., 2008; Dart, 2001; Felsenheimer & Gisdakis, 2008; Fox, 2003; Hudson, 2009; Kim, 2001; McLean & Elkind, 2003; Morris & McGann, 2004; Muolo & Padilla, 2008).

A number of studies indicate that religiously committed teens are less likely to become involved in drug and alcohol abuse. Other studies indicate that religiously committed teens are less likely to engage in sexual behavior or become pregnant while they are still teenagers. Cochran (1993) and Cochran, Beeghley, and Bock (1992) found that adolescent religious commitment tended to be associated with lower drug and alcohol use. Sharon Lock and Murray Vincent (1995) found that among 564 predominantly black adolescent girls, religious commitment played a strong role in predicting low levels of premarital sex. Velma Murry-McBride (1996) addressed this same issue, focusing on 109 middle-income African American females and found similar results. Scott Beck (1991) and his colleagues examined the National Longitudinal Survey of Youth and concluded that Evangelical and Pentecostal Christians were the least likely to engage in premarital sex. Using the National Educational Longitudinal Study (NELS) data set, Jeynes (1999, 2003a, 2003b) found that religiously committed African American and Hispanic students outperformed their less religious counterparts. Furthermore, Jeynes (2003a, 2003b, 2008, 2009) also found that African American and Hispanic students who were religiously committed and from intact families did as well academically as white students. Using the NELS of over 18,000 twelfth-grade students, Jeynes found that on four of five standardized tests, black and Hispanic students who were religious and from intact families did as well as the average white student. In addition, these same black and Hispanic students were less likely to be left back a grade and were more likely to have taken college preparation courses than the white students (Bahr, Hawks, & Wang, 1993; Beck, Cole, & Hammond, 1991; Brownfield & Sorenson, 1991; Miller & Olson, 1988).

In spite of the major quandaries confronting adolescents today, few social scientists envision religion as contributing a major solution to the problem. William Kilpatrick (1993) states the danger inherent in overlooking religious commitment as a potential solution. He writes, "Americans have been led to believe that their children will be able to fight their personal moral struggles with weapons that, upon examination, turn out to be very flimsy" (p. 25). Kilpatrick asserts that simply trying to increase a child's self-esteem or clarifying what values they already possess, as opposed to teaching them values of virtue, will not yield a nation of moral and civil human beings (pp. 25–26).

It is regrettable that in America's rush to question almost every traditional value in the 1960s, religious people got overwrought by the waves of discontent. The United States cannot afford to view religious commitment in such a negative way. Studies indicate that religious commitment has a positive impact on a number of academic and behavioral includes, both for Americans as a whole and minority children as well. The positive effects of religious commitment were ostensible across all academic achievement subject tests, including the test for math, reading, science, and social studies. Students of faith also had a higher GPA than less religious students. Religious commitment especially had an impact on various kinds of school-related behavior, including school-specific behavior and the use of alcohol, marijuana, and cocaine. In the 1960s and early 1970s, myriad teenagers viewed the use of drugs such as marijuana, LSD, and cocaine as "cool." In today's society, when such activities are no longer regarded as "cool," Americans should acknowledge and act on the fact that religious commitment can discourage many of these undesirable behaviors (Beck, Cole, & Hammond, 1991; Dupre, Miller, Gold, & Rispenda, 1995; Jeynes, 1999, 2003a, 2003b, 2008, 2009; Miller & Olson, 1988).

In past years, people of faith were received warmly and esteemed highly. Many parents wanted each of their children to marry an all-American religious spouse. Religious people were regarded as loving, kind, righteous, honest, loyal, and sincere. However, with the onset of the hippie movement, the sexual revolution, and legalized abortion, Christian people were often stereotypically characterized as being narrow-minded, stupid, anti-gay, legalistic, and dishonest. As suddenly as the hippie movement, the antiwar movement, and the sexual revolution took America by storm, so too was the traditional view of religious people turned upside down in a short period of time (Decter, 1995; Olasky, 1988).

THOSE WHO OPPOSE CHARACTER EDUCATION HAVE A VERY WEAK ARGUMENT

Based on centuries of historical practices, international practices, and contemporary moral crises, the argument for character education is very persuasive. Adding to the poignancy of the argument is the feebleness of the declaration that public schools should not have character education. The first and primary claim that opponents of moral instruction make is that the United States is too diverse to make feasible any character instruction program. This issue of diversity arises frequently in American education and does, in fact, relate to a number of issues. On the subject of moral education, however, some claim that America's diversity makes character instruction impossible is vacuous. Do diversity issues mean that the United States should construct a curriculum of moral instruction that is sensitive? Of course it does. Do diversity arguments mean that the nation should not have character education at all? Such an assertion is not tenable. A second claim among opponents is that the present situation in schools is such that there is no time for character education. Instead, due to the emphasis on standards, schools must focus on testing and multicultural education. One can argue, however, that if American schools are testing so much that there is no time to teach morality, then the nation is testing too much. Similarly, one can also question whether the acceptance of other cultures can really take hold if students are not also taught the moral qualities of love, kindness, and compassion. These two objections to character instruction will now be examined (Feder, 1999; Jeynes, 2006; Likona, 1976; Ryan & Bohlin, 1998).

(1) *The United States is too diverse to make feasible any character instruction program*: This argument is untenable for two reasons. First, research indicates that Americans almost unanimously are in favor of schools teaching a variety of personal character traits, including sincerity, honesty, loyalty, courage, responsibility, kindness, just, and integrity. The desire of American parents is that certain character qualities be taught in the public schools and as a number of leaders have stated unless one is criminal it would be hard to object to the teaching of these virtues (Likona, 1976; Ryan & Bohlin, 1998).

Second, although the United States is more religiously diverse than it used to be, American leaders must be careful not to confuse religious diversity with racial and ethnic diversity. This country is one of the most racially and ethnically diverse countries in the world. Nevertheless, the United States is one of the least religiously diverse countries in the world. In his book, *The Next Christendom*, published by Oxford University Press, Phillip Jenkins (2007, p. 104) states,

> The number of adherents of non-Christian religions in the United States is strikingly small. If we combine the plausible estimates for the numbers of American Jews, Buddhists, Muslims, and Hindus, then we are speaking about 4 or 5 percent of the total population . . . The degree of religious diversity in the United States is very limited compared to what we find in many African and Asian nations . . . Ironically, in terms of American perceptions, some of the most diverse lands are to be found in the Middle East, which Westerners often imagine in terms of Muslim homogeneity. In fact, countries like Egypt and Syria are more diverse than the United States. So, of course, is Israel, which is avowedly a Jewish state.

That being the case, the argument that some use that America is too religiously diverse to have any program of character education is a non sequitur (Banks & Banks, 1995; Jenkins, 2007; Likona, 1976; Ryan & Bohlin, 1998).

(2) *There is no time for character education*: A number of educators aver that there is presently no time to teach American students in virtue because schools need to focus on standards and testing, as well as multicultural instruction. Although this is a weak argument, it is a very intriguing one. This is because America's fascination with testing arose immediately following the Supreme Court's removal of prayer and Bible reading from the public schools in 1962 and 1963. For example, the process of removing moral teaching from the schools created a significant hole in the kindergarten curriculum and caused the United States to depart from Friedrich

Froebel's, the founder of the kindergarten, curriculum. Prior to the 1962–1963 period, schools that used the Froebel model included Scripture readings, the singing of hymns, and teaching about virtuous qualities. Since 1962–1963, American educators have filled a part of this void with academically oriented subject matter and their related assessments (Blanshard, 1963; Fleege, Charlesworth, & Burts, 1992; Hamilton, 1969; James & Tanner, 1993; Jeynes, 2006; Kliebard, 1969; Michaelsen, 1970; Sikorski, 1993; Slight, 1961).

Perrone (1990) observes that beginning in the early 1960s, American schools became obsessed with giving young students standardized tests. Since that time, the use of standardized tests in American schools has grown by 20 percent per year. From Froebel's perspective, this orientation fails to produce a moral foundation in children and instead focuses on test performance, which ultimately will only undermine student virtue (Downs, 1978; Hamilton, 1969; Lilley, 1967; Slight, 1961; Ulich, 1957).

WHAT THE CHARACTER EDUCATION RUBRIC AND CURRICULUM LOOK LIKE?

There is no question that the character education rubric and curriculum will look considerably different as it is applied in contemporary times versus how it appeared prior to 1963. After all, the nation has changed considerably since that time. Moreover, the religious orientation that was present prior to 1962 and 1963, which was appropriate for that time period and reflected the people's values of that era, would not be as well accepted today. However, this does not mean that this justifies a policy that forbids basic religious freedoms such as being at liberty to have a moment of silence or to pray voluntarily (Barton, 1995). Moreover, a debilitating double standard emerges when teachers allow students to express the secular components of their culture, but are not permitted to express the religious components. Such a practice is not merely unjust, it also discriminates against people of faith (Hyers & Hyers, 2008; Jeynes, 1999, 2003a, 2003b, 2007b; Marsden, 1994; Ryan & Bohlin, 1998).

The Curriculum Should Value the Presence of Religion Rather Than Disparage Its Existence

If a society's inhabitants and institutions value faith and its principles, people generally will be encouraged to practice religion. In contrast, if a society tends to think disparagingly about religious commitment, people, especially in the impressionable young years, will be discouraged from pursuing God. To the extent that a nation values religious commitment and principles, these principles will likely increase in that nation. Conversely, to the degree to which a nation devalues religious commitment and principles, those principles will probably decline in that nation. In reality, a country's attitude toward religion is like a self-fulfilling prophecy. Ultimately, the values that a nation cherishes are most likely those that will be established. If our nation is really interested in encouraging students who are high in acumen and obedience, moderate in their consumption of alcohol, and abstaining from the use of illegal drugs, then it would be in her own best interests to encourage rather than discourage religious faith (Decter, 1995; Jeynes, 1998; Lewy, 1996; Olasky, 1988; Senior, 1978).

A Character Education Curriculum Should Adapt to Present Day Realities in Content but Also Learn from Successful Implementations from Both the Past and the Present

Adjusting to Present Day Realities

There is little question that American students badly need moral instruction. The events of the last 45 or 50 years are a grim reminder that there is a very good reason why educators have lauded the practice of character education for so many centuries. Moreover, in the eyes of the nation's founders, it would have been inconceivable to found a school system without a central place for character instruction. Realistically, such a program of character instruction cannot be religiously based as it was before 1962 and 1963. That was likely appropriate when the U.S. Supreme Court declared that the country was a "Christian country"; however, the court has declared that such an orientation is no longer fitting. It is undeniable that some will argue that character instruction will no longer be as effective without the presence of religious motivation and that may be true, but realistically that debate should be left to those advocating broader programs of school choice (Adams, 1854; Eavey, 1964; Mann, 1849; Rush, 1798; Washington, 1797).

Learning from Successful Implementations from Both the Past and the Present

Currently, moral instruction represents the number one area in which social scientists suggest that public schools can learn from the faith-based school rubric. Faced with an immense number of behavior problems that ultimately influence school outcomes, many public school districts want to reintroduce moral education into the public schools. There is no question that there are elements of faith-based school moral education that public schools will be unable to replicate, but it is equally true that there are virtues that serve as goals for both public and private religious schools (Bryk, Lee, & Holland, 1993; Halstead & Lewicka, 1998; Jeynes, 2000; LePore & Warren, 1997; McEwen, Knipe, & Gallagher, 1997).

Years ago moral education was a major pillar of public school education. In spite of this fact, after state-sanctioned prayer and Bible reading were removed from the public schools in 1962–1963, the vast majority of public schools no longer focused on moral instruction. As has been addressed in Chapter 7, when this happened virtually every measure of adolescent crime surged to heights several times higher than in 1962 and to levels that past generations would have deemed unimaginable (Haynes, 1999; Jeynes, 2001; Miller, 1998; U.S. Department of Education, 2000; U.S. Department of Health and Human Services, 1998; U.S. Department of Justice, 1999).

Numerous social scientists believe these challenges provide many reasons why educators should seriously examine moral instruction in religious schools. Although, teachers cannot teach virtue in public schools in the same way that they do in Christian and Jewish schools, many educators aver that there are enough moral values common to almost every culture that many of the virtues teachers address in these private religious schools (Ryan & Bohlin, 1998; Smagorinsky & Taxel, 2005).

Research indicates that religious schools are less likely to have gangs, problems with illegal drugs, and racial tension. One cannot credit all of these realities to the existence of character instruction in these schools, but it is likely that it serves as a supplement to the moral training that these students receive at home. Both public and private education will benefit if both types of schools are willing to learn from each other. Public schools excel in such areas as accommodating students with special needs, and although part of this advantage is due to higher funding levels, there are approaches to these students from which private school educators can learn. Equally true, however, is the fact that public schools can learn from how private religious schools practice character instruction. This is particularly true, because generally speaking public schools have not given tutelage in building character for over 45 years. What this means is that virtually none of the public school teachers practicing today have experience teaching moral instruction in the public schools (Jeynes, 2008, 2009).

WHAT WE CAN DO TO RESTORE CHARACTER EDUCATION AND RESURRECT RELIGIOUS FREEDOM IN AMERICA

Encourage a Moment of Silence in the Schools

In Bill Clinton's speech of 1995, referred to in Chapter 7, Clinton asserted that public schools had become too restrictive regarding religious expression. At one point, Bill Clinton agreed with Newt Gingrich about proposing an amendment to allow a moment of silence in the schools. This is an important example indicating that there is a growing cognizance that the present restrictive practices toward a moment of silence inhibit the freedom of religious expression, which is a First Amendment right. Although any public school character education paradigm would not include a religious component, it is crucial that schools not send an antireligious message that would neutralize any positive effects that moral instruction would have. If the public schools prohibit religious expression, the institution would do precisely this. In fact, one could argue that if schools continue to prohibit a moment of silence and/or voluntary prayer and yet concurrently have character education, this prohibition of religious expression would more than cancel any beneficial effects of character education. This would especially be true, because for most American citizens their sense of right and wrong, as well as their character, is built on their faith in God (Jehl, 1994; Jeynes, 1999; Purdum, 1995).

Stop Expressions of Antireligious Bigotry

Chapter 7 presented many examples of antireligious bigotry, whether they were intended or unintended. Although it is primarily the instances of religious bigotry that emerge in the schools that this book is most focused on, it is patent that examples of antireligious bigotry are frequent in this country. The media represents one of the primary sources of religious bigotry and this is likely a major contribution to their loss of credibility among the general public. Increasingly, polls indicate that the American public perceives that the media is biased and unobjective. Although the United States and its schools deserve credit for inculcating vital truths about accepting and loving those of different skin hues as equally valuable, there has been little attempt to address the antireligious bigotry that is common in so many facets of American society today. Schools need to encourage acceptance of Christians, Jews, Muslims, and other groups, not simply people of color. Principals need to remember that Stalin, Mao Tse Tung, and Hitler killed more people because of their religious faith than because the color of their skin was different (Associated Press, 2008; Bear & Carper, 1998; Jeynes, 1998; McCauley, 2000).

Teach Morality as Essential to a Successful Classroom

A large percentage of the America's most severe problems reflect the moral fabric of students graduating from the nation's schools rather than their scholarly prowess. The country's dilemmas regarding corporate scandals, political corruption, and the nation's moral crises deal more with citizens' ethical qualities rather than cognitive abilities. "Teaching morality," however, does not require teaching religious doctrine. Rather, it would involve subscribing to a slate of core values, such as honesty, sincerity, responsibility, and courage. It would also acknowledge the utility of religious faith as a contributing factor to people's morality (Cintora, 1999; Haynes, 1999; Ryan & Bohlin, 1998; U.S. Department of Justice, 1999).

Our Society Should Make It Easier for Parents to Spend Time with Their Children at Home

Although schools are an important source of moral instruction, parents are even more vital. Due to soaring dates of divorce, unwed adolescent births, and the economic pressures of the day that frequently force both parents to work, children often do not have the degree of exposure to their parents that was common in past generations. American society needs to treasure the time that parents and children have together so that they can facilitate the positive moral influence that parents often have on their children (Jeynes, 1999, 2002, 2003a, 2003b, 2005a, 2005b, 2007b).

Our Society, Communities, and Schools Should Be More Supportive of Parents

In those nations in which character education is most emphasized and crime rates are especially low, such as in Japan, Singapore, and some European countries, schools and society at large believe that any character education initiative needs to be supportive of parental values (Jeynes, 2005b). From 1607 until the early 1900s, this was the belief of American public schools and society as well. However, over time teachers became increasingly convinced that they should encourage children to question and even challenge their parents' system of values. Books such as George Counts's *Dare the School Build a New Social Order* (1932) encouraged teachers to think along these lines. And indeed, when one remembers that the values of adults are sometimes far from perfect, the idealist is tempted to think in ethereal terms. Nevertheless, most parents have values that aid in their children's moral development.

CONCLUDING THOUGHTS

The contents of this book have special meaning in twenty-first-century America. Character education represents one of those reforms that the overwhelming number of Americans realize that the nation needs, but somehow does not get widely implemented. However, whether one examines the Columbine massacre, the terrorist attacks of September 11, 2001, or the moral crisis among adolescents, the need for moral instruction is axiomatic. The more recent examples of Wall Street greed, Capitol Hill corruption, and middle- and lower-class material selfishness that caused the world economy to collapse only confirm the need for a citizenry of character. In the immediate post-1963 period, the United States may have been able, at some level, to "get by" without the presence of character education. After all, the nation's adult population and leadership had been trained in character education. It was only the youth that suffered from this lack. Now, however, decades have transpired and the youth that went without school moral instruction are now the leaders of American society, in their 30s, 40s, and 50s. There are others in their early 60s who went at least part of their upbringing without moral education. The United States can afford to delay no longer. The country's future is at stake. Most of the nation's greatest problems have not been economic ones, but moral crises that had economic or violent consequences. The good news is that if the United States returns to its desire to return to emphasis on character, which was a source of national strength for so many years, many of the problems that were caused by a lack of character can be reversed. Clearly, there are a copious number of reasons why the United States is facing the problems addressed in this book. Although character issues may not be the only factor causing these challenges, it represents an important part of the matrix. Beyond this, there can be little doubt that the factors that concurrently cause America's problems are intricately connected, sometimes inextricably so. If one chooses to learn from history, however, it does not take long to conclude that to the extent that this nation was built on character and democracy, as George Washington and other founders assert, it can be built up again. Washington claimed that for democracy to thrive, it must be built on morality and religion. The events of recent decades appear to be reminding Americans of the verity of Washington's claims and the need to rebuild this democracy on the principles of character and religion.

REFERENCES

Adams, J. (1854). In C. Adams (Ed.), *The works of John Adams, second president of the United States* (Vol. IX). Boston, MA: Little Brown. Original statement, October 11, 1798.

Associated Press. (2008). Ted Turner comments on religion. April 1. *Boston Globe* Web site (www.boston.com/news/nation/articles/2008/04/01/ted_turner _comments_on_religion/, retrieved March 16, 2009).

Bahr, S., Hawks, R. D., & Wang, G. (1993). Family and religious influences on adolescent substance abuse. *Youth and Society, 24* (4), 443–465.

Banks, J. A., & Banks, C. A. (1995). *Handbook of research on multicultural education.* New York: Macmillan.

Barton, D. (1995). *The myth of separation.* Aledo, TX: Wallbuilders.

Bear, R., & Carper, J. (1998). Spirituality and the public schools: An evangelical perspective. *Educational Leadership, 56* (4), 33–37.

Beck, S. H., Cole, B. S., & Hammond, J. A. (1991). Religious heritage and premarital sex: Evidence from a national sample of adults. *Journal for the Scientific Study of Religion, 30* (2), 173–180.

Bennett, W. (1995). *The children's book of virtues.* New York: Simon & Schuster.

Blanshard, P. (1963). *Religion and the schools.* Boston, MA: Beacon Press.

Brownfield, D., & Sorenson, A. (1991). Religion and drug use among adolescents: A social support conceptualization and interpretation. *Deviant Behavior, 12* (3), 259–276.

Bryce, R. (2002). *Pipe dreams.* New York: Public Affairs.

Bryk, A., Lee, V., & Holland, P. (1993). *Catholic schools and the common good.* Cambridge, MA: Harvard University Press.

Bunge, F. M. (1983). *Japan: A country study.* Washington, D.C.: U.S. Government Printing Office.

Chamberlin, G. J. (1961). *Parents and religion.* Philadelphia, PA: Westminster Press.

Chen, J. (1994). *Confucius as a teacher.* Beijing: Foreign Language Press.

Cintora, A. (1999). Civil society and attitudes: The virtues of character. *Annals of the American Academy of Political and Social Science, 565,* 142–147.

Cochran, J. K. (1993). The variable effects of religiosity and denomination on adolescent self-reported alcohol use by beverage type. *Journal of Drug Issues, 23* (3), 479–491.

Cochran, J. K., Beeghley, L., & Bock, E. W. (1992). The influence of religious stability and homogamy on the relationship between religiosity and alcohol use among Protestants. *Journal for the Scientific Study of Religion, 31* (4), 441–456.

Coleman, L. (2004). *The copycat effect.* New York: Paraview.

Cooper, D. E. (2003). *World philosophies: An historical introduction.* Malden, MA: Blackwell.

Counts, G. S. (1932). *Dare the school build a new social order.* New York: John Day.

Craig, S., McCracken, J., Hilsenrath, J., Solomon, D., Karnitschnig, M., Lattman, P., Gullipalli, D., Ng, S., Lauricella, T., Rappaport, L., & McKay, P. A. (2008, September 16). AIG, Lehman shock hits world markets. *Wall Street Journal, 252* (65), A1–A2.

Cubberley, E. (1920). *The history of education.* Boston, MA: Houghton Mifflin.

———, ed. (1934). *Readings in public education in the United States: A collection of sources and readings to illustrate the history of educational practice and progress in the United States.* Cambridge, MA: Riverside Press.

Cui, D. (2001). British Protestant educational activities and nationalism of Chinese education in the 1920s. In G. Peterson, R. Hayhoe, & L. Yongling (Eds.), *Education, culture, and identity in twentieth century China* (pp. 137–160). Ann Arbor, MI: University of Michigan.

Dart, J. (2001). Religion influence soars. *Christian Century, 118* (35), 10–18.

Davies, B., & Evans, J. (2001). In J. Cairns, D. Lawton, & R. Gardner (Eds.), *Values, culture, and education* (pp. 190–205). London: Kogan Page.

Decter, M. (1995). A Jew in anti-Christian America. *First Things*, 56, 25–31.

Downs, R. B. (1978). *Friedrich Froebel*. Boston, MA: Twayne.

Dupre, D., Miller, N., Gold, M., & Rispenda, K. (1995). Initiation and progression of alcohol, marijuana, and cocaine use among adolescent abusers. *American Journal on Addictions, 4* (1), 43–48.

Dupuis, A. M. (1966). *Philosophy of education in historical perspective*. Chicago, IL: Rand McNally.

Eavey, C. B. (1964). *History of Christian education*. Chicago: Moody Press.

Feder, D. (1999). Public schools will muck up character ed. *Human Events, 55* (23), 1–9.

Fedwick, L. B. (1989). *Should the children pray?* Waco, TX: Markham Press Fund.

Felsenheimer, J., & Gisdakis, P. (2008). *Credit crises*. Weinheim, Germany: Wiley.

Fleege, P. O., Charlesworth, R., & Burts, D. C. (1992). Stress begins in kindergarten: A look at behavior during standardized testing. *Journal of Research in Childhood Education, 7* (1), 20–26.

Fox, L. (2003). *Enron: The rise and fall*. Hoboken, NJ: Wiley.

Gangel, K. O., & Benson, W. S. (1983). *Christian education: Its history and philosophy*. Chicago, IL: Moody.

Halstead, J. M., & Lewicka, K. (1998). Should homosexuality be taught as an acceptable alternative lifestyle? A Muslim perspective. *Cambridge Journal of Education, 28* (1), 49–64.

Hamilton, H. A. (1969). The religious roots of Froebel's philosophy. In E. Lawrence (Ed.), *Friedrich Froebel and English education* (pp. 156–168). New York: Schocken Books.

Haynes, C. (1999). Religion in the public schools. *School Administrator, 56* (1), 6–10.

Hiner, N. R. (1988). The cry of Sodom enquired into: Educational analysis in seventeenth century New England. *The social history of American education*. Urbana, IL: University of Illinois Press.

Hudson, K. (2009). Loan deadline passes for general growth. *Wall Street Journal, 253* (28), C13.

Hyers, L. L., & Hyers, C. (2008). Everyday discrimination experienced by conservative Christians at the secular university. *Analysis of Social Issues and Public Policy, 8* (1), 113–137.

James, J. C., & Tanner, C. K. (1993). Standardized testing of young children. *Journal of Research and Development in Education, 26* (3), 143–152.

Jehl, D. (1994). The new Congress: The president; Clinton reaches out to G.O.P. on school prayer amendment. *New York Times*, November 16, p. A1.

Jenkins, P. (2007). *The next Christendom*. Oxford: Oxford University Press.

Jeynes, W. (1998). Are America's public educational institutions anti-religious? *Education, 119* (1), 172–175.

————. (1999). The effects of religious commitment on the academic achievement of black and Hispanic children. *Urban Education, 34* (4), 458–479.

————. (2000). School choice: A balanced perspective. *Cambridge Journal of Education, 30* (2), 223–241.

————. (2001). Religious commitment and adolescent behavior. *Journal of Interdisciplinary Studies, 23* (1/2), 1–20.

————. (2002). *Divorce, family structure, & the academic success of children.* Binghamton, New York: Haworth Press.

————. (2003a). A meta-analysis: The effects of parental involvement on minority children's academic achievement. *Education & Urban Society, 35* (2), 202–218.

————. (2003b). The effects of black and Hispanic twelfth graders living in intact families and being religious on their academic achievement. *Urban Education, 38* (1), 35–57.

————. (2005a). A meta-analysis of the relation of parental involvement to urban elementary school academic achievement. *Urban Education, 40* (3), 237–239.

————. (2005b). Parental involvement in East Asian schools. In D. B. Hiatt-Michael (Ed.), *Promising practices for family involvement in schooling across the continents* (pp. 153–179). Greenwich, CT: Information Age Press.

————. (2006). Standardized tests and Froebel's original kindergarten model. *Teachers College Record, 108* (10), 1937–1959.

————. (2007a). *American educational history: School, society & the common good.* Thousand Oaks, CA: Sage Press.

————. (2007b). The relationship between parental involvement and urban secondary school student achievement: A meta analysis. *Urban Education, 42* (1), 82–110.

————. (2008). What faith-based schools are contributing. Paper presentation given for the White House on April 24, 2008 in Washington, D.C.

————. (2009). *Preserving a critical national asset* (pp. 78–81, 84–85, 154). Washington, D.C: The White House Domestic Policy Council.

Johnson, B. R., Jang, S. J., Larson, D. B., & Li, S. D. (2001). Does adolescent religious commitment matter? *Journal of Research in Crime & Delinquency, 38* (1), 22–44.

Johnson, B. R., Jang, S. J., & Li, S. D. (2000). The invisible institution and black youth crime: The church as an agency of local social control. *Journal of Youth and Adolescence, 29* (4), 479–498.

Khan, Y. (1997). *Japanese moral education: Past and present.* Madison, NJ: Fairleigh Dickinson University Press.

Kilpatrick, W. (1993). *Why Johnny can't tell right from wrong*. New York: Simon & Schuster.

Kim, C. (2001). In crises religion moves to the front page. *Quill, 89* (9), 21.

Kliebard, H. M. (1969). *Religion and education in America*. Scranton, PA: International Textbook Company.

Kwiran, M. (2001). In J. Cairns, D. Lawton, & R. Gardner (Eds.), *Values, culture, and education* (pp. 219–232). London: Kogan Page.

LePore, P. C., & Warren, J. R. (1997). A comparison of single-sex and coeducational Catholic secondary schooling: Evidence from the National Educational Longitudinal Study of 1988. *American Educational Research Journal, 34* (3), 485–511.

Levey, G. B., & Modood, T. (2009). *Secularism, religion, and multicultural citizenship*. Cambridge, MA: Cambridge University Press.

Lewy, G. (1996). *Why America needs religion*. Grand Rapids, MI: Eerdmans.

Lieberman, J. (2006). *The shooting game: The making of school shooters*. Santa Ana, CA: Seven Locks Press.

Lieberman, J. (2008). *School shootings: What every parent and educator needs to know to protect our children*. New York: Citadel Press.

Likona, T. (1976). *Moral development*. New York: Holt, Rinehart & Winston.

Lilley, I., ed. (1967). *Friedrich Froebel*. Cambridge, MA: Cambridge University Press.

Lock, S. E., & Vincent, M. (1995). Sexual decision-making among rural adolescent females. *Health and Values, 19* (1), 47–58.

Mann, H. (1849). *Twelfth annual report*. Boston, MA: Dutton & Wentworth.

Marrou, H. I. (1956). *A history of education in antiquity*. New York: Sheed & Ward.

Marsden, G. M. (1994). *The soul of the American university*. New York: Oxford University Press.

McCauley, C. (2000). Teaching about violence: Government is the big killer. *Harry Frank Guggenheim Foundation Review, 4* (1), 1–3.

McEwen, A., Knipe, D., & Gallagher, T. (1997). The impact of single-sex and coeducational schooling on participation and achievement in science: A 10-year perspective. *Research in Science and Technological Education, 15* (2), 223–233.

McLean, B., & Elkind, P. (2003). *The smartest guys in the room*. New York: Portfolio.

Michaelsen, R. (1970). *Piety in the public school*. London: Macmillan.

Miller, B. C., & Olson, T. D. (1988). Sexual attitudes and behavior of high school students relation to background and contextual factors. *Journal of Sex Research, 24* (1), 194–200.

Miller, W. R. (1998). Researching the spiritual dimensions of alcohol and other drug problems. *Addiction, 93* (7), 979–990.

Morgan, J. (1986). *Godly learning: Puritan attitudes towards religion, learning, and education.* New York: Cambridge University Press.

Morris, D., & McGann, E. (2004). *Rewriting history.* New York: ReganBooks.

Muolo, P., & Padilla, M. (2008). *Chain of blame: How Wall Street caused the mortgage and credit crisis.* Hoboken, NJ: Wiley & Sons.

Murray, W. (1982). *My life without God.* Nashville, TN: Thomas Nelson.

Murry-McBride, V. (1996). An ecological analysis of coital timing among middle-class African American adolescent females. *Journal of Adolescent Research, 11* (2), 261–279.

Olasky, M. N. (1988). *Prodigal press: The anti-Christian bias of the American news media.* Westchester, IL: Crossway Books.

Palmer, J. A. (2001). *Fifty major thinkers.* London: Routledge.

Perrone, V. (1990). How did we get here? Testing in the early grades: The games grown-ups play. In C. Kamii (Ed.), *Testing in the early grades* (pp. 1–13). Washington, D.C.: National Association for the Education of Young Children.

Pulliam, J. D., & Van Patten, J. J. (1991). *History of Education in America.* Upper Saddle River, NJ: Merrill/Prentice Hall.

Purdum, T. S. (1995). President defends a place for religion in the schools. *New York Times, 144* (50121), 1.

Ray, B. (1976). *African religions.* Inglewood Cliffs, NJ: Prentice Hall.

Reagan, T. (2005). *Non-western educational traditions.* Mahwah, NJ: Erlbaum.

Reiman, A. J. (2004). Longitudinal studies of teacher education candidates' moral reasoning and related promising interventions. *Journal of Research in Character Education, 2* (2), 141–150.

Renard, J. (2002). *101 questions and answers on Confucianism, Daoism, and Shinto.* New York: Paulist Press.

Reynolds, D. R. (2001). Christian mission schools and Japan's to-a-dobun shoin: Comparisons and legacies. In G. Peterson, R. Hayhoe, & Y. Lu (Eds.), *Education, culture, and identity in twentieth century China* (pp. 82–108). Ann Arbor, MI: University of Michigan, New York: Cambridge University Press.

Rush, B. (1798). *Essays, literacy, morals, and the philosophical.* Philadelphia, PA: Bradford.

Ryan, K., & Bohlin, K. E. (1998). *Building character in schools: Practical ways to bring moral instruction to life.* San Francisco, CA: Jossey-Bass.

Schmidt, A. (2007). *The world religions cookbook.* Westport, CT: Greenwood.

Seligman, A. B. (2000). *Modernity's wager.* Princeton, NJ: Princeton University Press.

Senior, J. (1978). *The death of Christian culture*. Harrison, NY: RC Books.

Sharma, S. N. (1994). *Buddhist social and moral education*. Delhi: Parimal.

Sikorski, R. (1993). *Controversies in constitutional law*. New York: Garland.

Slight, J. P. (1961). Froebel and the English primary school of today. In E. Lawrence (Ed.), *Friedrich Froebel and English Education* (pp. 95–124). London: Routledge.

Smagorinsky, P., & Taxel, J. (2005). *The discourse of character education culture wars in the classroom*. Mahwah, NJ: Erlbaum.

Ulich, R. (1957). *Three thousand years of educational wisdom*. Cambridge, MA: Harvard University Press.

U.S. Department of Education. (2000). *Digest of education statistics, 1999*. Washington, D.C.: U.S. Department of Education.

U.S. Department of Health and Human Services. (1998). *Statistical Abstracts of the United States*. Washington, D.C.: Department of Health and Human Services.

U.S. Department of Justice. (1999). *Age-specific arrest rate and race-specific arrest rates for selected offenses, 1965–1992*. Washington, D.C.: U.S. Department of Justice.

Washington, G. (1796). *Farewell address*, September 19.

Watson, M. (2006). Long-term effects of moral/character education in elementary school. *Journal of Research in Character Education, 4* (1/2), 47–64.

INDEX

About the Author

WILLIAM H. JEYNES, Ph.D., is professor of education at California State University in Long Beach and a nonresident scholar at Baylor University. He is a graduate of Harvard University and the University of Chicago. He has written approximately 70 academic articles and 8 books. His articles have appeared in journals by Columbia University, Harvard University (two Harvard journals), the University of Chicago, Cambridge University, Notre Dame University, and other prestigious university journals. He is a well-known public speaker, having spoken in nearly every state in the country and in every inhabited continent. He has spoken for the White House, the U.S. Department of Justice, the U.S. Department of Education, the U.S. Department of Health and Human Services, the National Press Club, UN delegates, members of Congress, the Acting President of South Korea, Harvard University, Duke University, Notre Dame University, the Harvard Family Research Project, the University of North Carolina at Chapel Hill, and many other well-known universities and churches. He has served as a consultant both for the U.S. and South Korean governments. Dr. Jeynes has been interviewed or quoted by the *Washington Post*, the *Los Angeles Times*, the *New York Times*, the *Wall Street Journal*, the *London Times*, and many other major newspapers. His work has been cited and quoted numerous times by the U.S. Congress, the British Parliament, the European Union, and many State Supreme Courts across the United States. A number of Dr. Jeynes's articles for *Urban Education*, *Education and Urban Society*, and *Marriage and Family Review*, according to these journals' Web sites, are in the top 5–10 of the most cited and read articles published in these journals' history. He has also gained admission into Who's Who in the World.